P9-DTV-165

WITHDRAWN
UTSA LIBRARIES

COUNSELING
WOMEN

THE BROOKS/COLE SERIES IN COUNSELING
PSYCHOLOGY
John M. Whiteley, University of California at Irvine
Arthur Resnikoff, Washington University
Series Editors

LIBRARY
The University of Texas
At San Antonio

COUNSELING ADULTS
Editors: Nancy K. Schlossberg, University of Maryland
       Alan D. Entine, State University of New York at Stony Brook

CAREER COUNSELING
Editors: John M. Whiteley, University of California at Irvine
       Arthur Resnikoff, Washington University

APPROACHES TO ASSERTION TRAINING
Editors: John M. Whiteley, University of California at Irvine
       John V. Flowers, University of California at Irvine

COUNSELING WOMEN
Editors: Lenore W. Harmon, University of Wisconsin—Milwaukee
       Janice M. Birk, University of Maryland
       Laurine E. Fitzgerald, University of Wisconsin—Oshkosh
       Mary Faith Tanney, University of Maryland

COUNSELING WOMEN

EDITED BY

LENORE W. HARMON
UNIVERSITY OF WISCONSIN—MILWAUKEE

JANICE M. BIRK
UNIVERSITY OF MARYLAND

LAURINE E. FITZGERALD
UNIVERSITY OF WISCONSIN—OSHKOSH

MARY FAITH TANNEY
UNIVERSITY OF MARYLAND

BROOKS/COLE PUBLISHING COMPANY
Monterey, California

A Division of Wadsworth Publishing Company, Inc.

Production Editor: *Fiorella Ljunggren*
Interior Design: *Laurie Cook*
Cover Design: *Sharon Marie Bird*

© 1978 by Wadsworth Publishing Company, Inc., Belmont, California 94002.
All rights reserved. No part of this book may be reproduced, stored in a
retrieval system, or transcribed, in any form or by any means—electronic,
mechanical, photocopying, recording, or otherwise—without the prior
written permission of the publisher: Brooks/Cole Publishing Company,
Monterey, California 93940, a division of Wadsworth Publishing Company,
Inc.
Printed in the United States of America
10 9 8 7 6 5 4 3 2 1

Much of the material in this book originally appeared in the *Counseling
Psychologist*.

Library of Congress Cataloging in Publication Data

Main entry under title:

Counseling women.

(Brooks/Cole series in counseling psychology)
Bibliography: p. 293
Includes index.
1. Women—Mental health. 2. Psychotherapist and patient. 3.
Counseling. 4. Sex discrimination against women. I. Harmon, Lenore W.
RC451.4.W6C68   362.2   77-22343
ISBN 0-8185-0240-1

Dedicated to
Women Clients,
whose chances for growth, development,
and fulfillment we meant to
promote by addressing their counselors.

SERIES FOREWORD

The books in the Brooks/Cole Series in Counseling Psychology reflect the significant developments that have occurred in the counseling field over the past several decades. No longer is it possible for a single author to cover the complexity and scope of counseling as it is practiced today. Our approach has been to incorporate within the Brooks/Cole Series the viewpoints of different authors having quite diverse training and perspectives.

Over the past decades, too, the counseling field has expanded its theoretical basis, the problems of human living to which it addresses itself, the methods it uses to advance scientifically, and the range of persons who practice it successfully—from competent and skillful paraprofessionals to doctoral-level practitioners in counseling, psychology, education, social work, and psychiatry.

The books in the Brooks/Cole Series are intended for instructors and both graduate and undergraduate students alike who want the most stimulating in current thinking. Each volume may be used independently as a text to focus in detail on an individual topic, or the books may be used in combination to highlight the growth and breadth of the profession. However they are used, the books explore the many new skills that are available to counselors as they struggle to help people learn to change their behavior and gain self-understanding. Single volumes also lend themselves as background reading for workshops or in-service training, as well as in regular semester or quarter classes.

The intent of all the books in the Brooks/Cole Series is to stimulate the reader's thinking about the field, about the assumptions made regarding the basic nature of people, about the normal course of human development and the progressive growth tasks that everyone faces, about how behavior is acquired, and about what different approaches to counseling postulate concerning how human beings can help one another.

John M. Whiteley
Arthur Resnikoff

PREFACE

This book contains the major portion of two issues of *The Counseling Psychologist*, a publication of the Division of Counseling Psychology of the American Psychological Association. The two issues are "Counseling Women," published in 1973, and "Counseling Women II," published in mid-1976.

As editors of the first issue, Laurine E. Fitzgerald and I felt a keen responsibility to set a tone that would help our readers appreciate the need for a new approach to counseling women—an approach unbiased by preconceived notions of what women are or should be. The contributing authors were no less committed. They shared the attitude that "whatever will help the readers see the problem most clearly is what we should do" and granted us unheard-of liberties with their manuscripts so that we might achieve that goal.

We were also very aware that, in order to gain a maximum audience, we had to strike the right balance between innovation and tradition. It seemed prudent at that time to lean slightly toward the traditional end of the spectrum, for we knew that we were attempting to help create massive social changes. The Epilogue to "Counseling Women" said "This single issue of *The Counseling Psychologist* is but one step on the long trek . . . [toward] the sensitization of men and women counseling psychologists to the changing needs of girls and women. Now is the time—who and where are the next step's initiators?" That step was taken three years later, when the editorial board of *The Counseling Psychologist* commissioned the issue "Counseling Women II." I was convinced that the time was right for a much harder-hitting approach to the problems of counseling women than we had taken in the first issue. I was therefore delighted when Janice M. Birk and Mary Faith Tanney accepted the invitation to develop "Counseling Women II," with the understanding that they would "go further."

This commitment was carried out in several ways. One was the inclusion of a "reaction section." In the first issue we had been unwilling to invite reactions—something that is usually done in topical issues of *The Counseling Psychologist*. Being quite unsure of the kind of reaction that would greet our issue, we did not want to provide a forum for arguments against a new approach to counseling women. The excellent reaction articles that conclude "Counseling Women II" show beyond any doubt that the counseling of women is indeed a topic of scholarly as well as practical concern.

The first issue of "Counseling Women"—which represents Section 1 of this book—was designed to highlight the deficiencies in our counseling theories and practices as applied to women. The second issue dared to "go further" in another sense by talking about counseling women with very specific problems in their lives—the single-again woman, the rape victim, the mastectomy patient, and the "perfect mother," just to cite a few. Discussions of these and other crisis situations, together with articles dealing with other dimensions and aspects of counseling interventions for women, make up Section 2 of the book and provide an especially useful tool for members of the counseling profession. The book is intended for them and for graduate students. It will also be useful for some undergraduates.

One often-asked but as-yet-unanswered question is "What about counseling men?" We view this as a legitimate question and one that deserves concern. We understand that the changes that are taking place in our society create confusion and uncertainty in both sexes, but as counselors we know that confusion and uncertainty often precede growth. Women are changing in their self-perceptions and life-styles—and, consequently, in their relationships with men. Obviously, men must change their lives in response, and counseling men in transition is an important task for counselors. Indeed, if societal changes offer problems for both sexes, one might ask why changes in our approach to counseling were first prompted by the demand for change from women. In answer to that question, it seems to me that social change is always initiated by the group that will experience the greatest immediate reward as a result of the change. Thus, my answer to those who ask "What about counseling men?" is "Counseling women comes first—not in importance but in time." And those who are interested in counseling men in transition will find this book helpful in understanding some of the elements that necessitate the transition.

The individual articles are presented here as they appeared in the original publication, with two exceptions. Helen S. Farmer has added material to her article on "What Inhibits Achievement and Career Motivation in Women?" and Beverly A. Belson has completely redone the bibliography that appeared in the first issue. This up-to-date, comprehensive bibliography represents the final chapter of this book. But the final chapter of the changes undergone by the counseling profession as a result of the women's movement that began in the mid-1960s has yet to be written. The changes we have seen so far are exciting, and the potential changes in the future increase my zest for the practice of counseling psychology.

Lenore W. Harmon

CONTENTS

1 COUNSELING WOMEN: I   1

A Tide in the Affairs of Women: The Psychological Impact of Feminism on Educated Women
     Esther Manning Westervelt   1
Women in Groups
     Rita M. Whiteley   34
Perspectives on Counseling Bias: Implications for Counselor Education
     Nancy K. Schlossberg and John J. Pietrofesa   59
Career Counseling for Women
     Louise Vetter   75
Sexual Bias in Personality Theory
     Mary Austin Doherty   94
Facilitating the Growth of Women through Assertive Training
     Patricia Jakubowski   106
. . . and Soma
     Lenore W. Harmon   123
Women's Changing Expectations . . . New Insights, New Demands
     Laurine E. Fitzgerald   128

2 COUNSELING WOMEN: II   135

Male Is Greater than Female: The Socialization of Status Inequality
Rhoda K. Unger   135
Physical Sex Differences: A Matter of Degree
Dorothy V. Harris   153
What Inhibits Achievement and Career Motivation in Women?
Helen S. Farmer   159
Cognitive-Developmental Theory: A Guide to Counseling Women
L. Lee Knefelkamp, Carole C. Widick, and Barbara Stroad   173
Counseling for the Strengths of the Black Woman
Doris Jefferies Ford   186
Psychotherapy and Women's Liberation
Jean Holroyd   193
Women Counselors for Women Clients? A Review of the Research
Mary Faith Tanney and Janice M. Birk   208
Supermoms Shift Gears: Re-entry Women
Linda Brooks   218
Counseling "Single-Again" (Divorced and Widowed) Women
Alice L. Aslin   230
The Myth of the Perfect Mother
Bobbie L. Wilborn   241
Psychosocial Issues in Counseling Mastectomy Patients
Wendy S. Schain   250
An Intervention Model for Rape and Unwanted Pregnancy
Patricia Freiberg and Margaret W. Bridwell   261
A Research Perspective on Counseling Women
Clara E. Hill   270
Seeking the Holy Grail, or The Status of Women in Counseling
Annette M. Brodsky   277

Emerging Truths on the Psychology of Women, as through a Glass Darkly
    Dorothy A. Evans   284
A Bibliography
    Beverly A. Belson   293

Index   307

COUNSELING WOMEN: I

1

A Tide in the
Affairs of Women:
The Psychological Impact of
Feminism on Educated Women

ESTHER MANNING WESTERVELT

The only thing one really knows about human nature is that it changes.
Oscar Wilde

THE FEMINIST REVOLUTION: TIDAL WAVE OR
HARMLESS RIPPLE?

"Let me assure you, there is no more exciting revolution today than the women's revolution." Liz Carpenter was not indulging in political bombast when, as a prime mover among women in politics, she made this statement to a group of women delegates and observers at the Democratic National Convention (Sherr, 1972). The women's revolution, the disparagement of cynics and conservatives notwithstanding, is a social convulsion of a magnitude hitherto unknown in human history. It both reflects and portends cataclysmic changes in basic structures and processes of society and in the psyches of individual men and women. It has been long in the making. Its current phase energizes and focuses forces that were temporarily directed into other channels by the ravages of World War II and the search for an elusive "security" following it. Although the revolution's pace has been uneven and remains unpredictable and all of its outcomes are not yet foreshadowed, its present direction is clear and (unless a nuclear holocaust sends humanity back to the caves) its advance inexorable. For some men and women the movement is a promise; to others, a threat. None can be wholly indifferent to it, for it can, and someday will, touch every life.

Many groups have a vested interest in assessing the psychological impact on women of the movement's ideology and of the light it casts on the changes which have occurred in women's lives. Among these are politicians seeking the women's vote; employers pondering how much women will demand of affirmative action plans; educators attempting to appraise the extent to which educational policies and practices must be modified to meet the demands of women; advertisers, manufacturers, retailers seeking to appeal to female consumers. Counselors, whose commitment is to fostering human development and who are often partners in the decision-making processes of young and mature women, have a self-evident interest in this question, one which is both more sophisticated and more altruistic than that of many other "movement-watchers." Counselors know that changed or changing perceptions of self and society generate new sources of conflict and ambivalence and of guilt and shame, as well as new sources of motivation and new patterns of aspiration. The current phase of the women's revolution emerged during a period of turbulent social and political activism, especially among the young (it is sometimes regarded as merely one facet of this activism, but this view places the movement in far too narrow a perspective). Counselors who have been seeking an ordered understanding of the nature and the psychological repercussions of new systems of values and mores in the realms of political action, educational relevance, sexual behavior, and so on, now encounter in feminism a force that has the potential to infiltrate the wellsprings of personality and behavior at a deeper level than any of the other "movements" which have generated the turmoil of the decade just past.

We need look no further than the popular press to know that the question we raise is worth asking. Feature stories and filler items paint the revolution as swirling through some lives like a tornado, drifting into others like an insidious breeze, and touching still others as no more than a faint echo of distant thunder. Wives who leave husbands *and* children, proclaiming themselves liberated; women, some young, some older, who eagerly share with a larger public the insights gained from consciousness-raising groups; women demanding, and sometimes getting, more status and pay in employment and/or expanded opportunities in education; mothers going back to school; women working as telephone linesmen or atomic scientists; women's rights organizations meeting and marching—all get press coverage in everything from the *Wall Street Journal* to the *Ladies Home Journal*. Of course, the press, especially the traditional women's magazines and the women's pages of newspapers, does not overlook the housewife who rejoices in such domestic achievements as casserole cookery and do-it-yourself decorating, the executive's wife who claims to find the roles of companion to husband and children, hostess, and arbiter of fashion a full and satisfying career, or the peripatetic ladies of the international set merrily at play in various romantic spots. Only the woman who works for economic necessities gets minimal coverage; her presence in our midst is most apt to be remarked in sober reports of Labor Department statistics.

We do not have to read the popular press to know that the feminist ideology is making waves. We can hear affluent chatelaines of gracious homes complain of the emptiness of their lot, and we can hear the edge of defensiveness in the voices of those who insist that being a wife is a career in itself. "But don't you envy me?" asked one of the latter whom I met in a Caribbean inn. "My husband has given me an open ticket. I can spend the whole winter here if I want, but *you* have to go back to work." We hear young women express the determination not to repress selfhood for a mere man: "I don't want to marry until I know what I want to do with myself." We hear young married women discussing motherhood as an option, not a certainty: "Perhaps I will have children some day. I'm not ready yet; maybe I never will be unless we just happen to be living in the right kind of place at a time when having a baby won't interfere too much with whatever both of us are doing." We hear frank objections to sexist behaviors: "That professor treats women as if they were children. He calls us 'my dear' and never listens to what we say." Or, "The management talks about affirmative action but you can see they don't mean a word they say. A woman who can't type doesn't stand much chance of getting a job here."

At the same time women of all ages still study bridal dresses in shop windows with lively interest; weddings still take most of the space on society pages; cosmetic counters, wig salons, and baby shops still do a thriving business; and building homes for families is a top industry in America. Nevertheless, the proportion of women between the ages of 20 and 24 who are single is increasing dramatically, along with the average age of marriage. In 1971 the U.S. birth rate fell to its lowest level since birth figures were first recorded in 1820, while the fertility rate for women between 15 and 44 years of age fell to its lowest level since 1940 (81.9 births per 1,000) (Bureau of the Census, 1972b). The proportion of women in the labor force continues to grow; however, this growth has been occurring for two decades; thus any association with feminist ideology would appear to be as cause rather than effect. Recent data on the life planning and career aspirations of young women reveal a shift toward greater emphasis on career and higher career aspirations. It has been estimated that the number of women over 30 who are students in higher education has doubled over the past decade (Elsner, 1972) and that most of these seek education with a view to future employment (Women's Bureau, 1971a). Trends like these may represent, however, responses to social rather than ideological pressures and, in any case, tell us much less than we need to know about the psychological impact of the latter.

Feminists themselves assert that the impact of feminism is both sociologically broad and psychologically deep. They point to statistics like those just cited as evidence for sociological impact and document psychological impact with personal accounts from movement leaders, members of consciousness-raising groups, participants in women's studies courses, and various other highly verbal women, of new insights about womanhood in our society that have irrevocably altered their self-concepts, life goals, and life styles. Unquestionably, feminist ideology has profoundly affected the psyches and behaviors of women like these but we cannot therefore assume that its effects on other women are comparable. If we wish to make some educated guesses about the latter possibility we must examine available empirical evidence in the light of relevant theories of personality and development. We may then make some deductions about the impression of feminist ideology on the self-concepts, the motivations, the sources of anxiety, and the behaviors of at least a limited population of women. Educated women have, as a general rule, more exposure to this ideology than others (although, thanks to television, all women have had some). Also, due to our patterns of social mobility and systems of communication, educated women tend to set trends for other women: what they value today, other women value tomorrow. It therefore seems reasonable, and it is certainly more feasible, to limit our examination to this population. Since I shall define "educated" as some higher education or equivalent experience, the population we will consider comprises almost a third of the total population of women 18 years of age or older. The scope of the definition does not permit a more accurate estimate of the size of the group, but its capacity to set trends has been demonstrated many times (witness the flight to the suburbs, which began with the affluent and educated).

LIMITATIONS ON GENERALIZATIONS ABOUT POPULATIONS

Logical inferences about the psychic experiences of any population, much less one as large as that under discussion, are subject to certain limitations as regards their applicability to individuals. After all, the word "individual" means exactly what the dictionary says it does: "single; particular; separate." Each individual is a unique combination of genes and the product of exposure to a unique combination of social experiences. Furthermore, even apparently identical family environments do not exert identical sets of influences on the development of children growing up within them. For example, Lipman-Blumen, in a study of sex-role ideology among wives of graduate students in the Boston area (age range, 18 to 54; median age, 23.4), found that differences in sex-role ideology were not a function of such factors as family income, education, or occupation; childhood religion; urban versus rural background; mother's employment; family composition; sibling position; or family disruption by divorce, separation, or death. The sources of influence on the women in this 1968 study, 73 percent of whom subscribed to what the study's measures defined as "contemporary sex-role ideology," appeared to be rather more subtle factors, such as the relationship between parents (especially on the dominance-submissiveness continuum), a mother's satisfaction with her life (daughters of dissatisfied mothers were more likely to hold a contemporary view), and the daughter's level of attachment to and admiration of her parents (Lipman-Blumen, 1972). We know from our own experience that young women of comparable intellectual capacities and comparable family backgrounds who live in the same community, have attended the same schools, belonged to the same circle of friends, and now attend the same college may have quite different perceptions of women's roles, sex-appropriate behaviors, and career salience. We still know relatively little about the subtleties of the interactions which influence development, but we have ample evidence of their operation.

Secondly, America encompasses a wide variety of social and cultural environments. Today's educated women are not all white and middle-class. While gross differences in social background did not, in the Lipman-Blumen study, appear to influence sex-role ideology as defined there, the definition, since it concerned *role,* was a function of attitudes toward education, marriage, career, and associated values. There are cultural differences in conceptions of the nature of femininity that entail more than roles and that influence personality development at a deeper level through differential emphasis on such qualities as practicality, assertiveness, ambition, vitality, nurturance, and so on (Block). To some extent culturally different groups— Southern Blacks, Northern Blacks, Orientals, Puerto Ricans, Mexican-Americans, American Indians, Eskimos—foster ideals of femininity, as well as definitions of women's roles, which reflect both the experiences of their pasts and the exigencies of their presents. A case in point is the middle-class Black family, where girls as well as boys plan for high-status employment and mothers as well as fathers are professionals, not merely for the sake of income and status but also because, in that sub-culture, a nurturing woman is a capable, productive woman.

Some of today's educated women have known extreme poverty in childhood and youth; some are still caught in its grip. Poverty places limits on options, limits which tend to reduce ambivalence about achievement. For the poor or socially marginal woman who gains access to higher education the question is not whether to achieve; it is how to achieve. Affluent women have freedom to exercise options; their perception of this freedom is expressed in such remarks as, "I want to lead an interesting life," or "I'm not going to be put on the shelf when I'm forty."

A markedly significant demographic factor is age. Many of today's educated women and many of those still pursuing an education are no longer young. Many leaders in the women's movement also are no longer young, although the new feminism has been regarded as primarily the province of young, highly educated women. Ideological differences within the movement appear to be partly a function of age differences. Older leaders seem to place more emphasis on equal rights for women and to minimize sex differences, while younger leaders place more emphasis on demands for individual freedoms which will produce revolutionary innovations in our social structures and processes (for example, the abolition of career compulsions for both men and women) and allow women to develop and express all aspects of selfhood, including a proud affirmation of biological femaleness. Young feminists appear to object more than do older ones to attempts to squeeze women into a social mold created by men for men, a mold which, in their view, currently constricts and distorts male personalities.

Marked age differences in values, rather than merely in status and role, are inevitable in any society characterized, as ours is, by rapid change. To the extent that value systems differentiate cultures, different generations may be said to exist within different cultures. Since for individuals the "real" world is a psychological construct, different generations inhabit different "real" worlds. The environments from which we come always partially shape our perceptions of and responses to the environments in which we find ourselves. Today's mature woman was young in a world her daughter can never know; her daughter is young in a world which her mother never knew when she was young (Mead, 1970). Furthermore, the pace of change in this country has tended to make the span of time we call a "generation" something less than the age difference between parents and children. Not long ago a generation's span was considered to be approximately twenty years; today "generations" are more usually separated by a decade. We speak of "the generation now in its twenties," "the generation now in its thirties," etc. We can, therefore, assume that the impact of feminism on the self-concepts, motivations, attitudes, and behaviors of older women will be different from (although not necessarily less than) the impact on younger women.

Age is also closely associated, for the average woman more so than for the average man, with changes in self-concept and role. The aging process poses a far greater threat to the self-esteem of American women than to that of American men, for not only has sexual attractiveness long been a key element in our stereotype of the ideal woman but also has our society, far more than most, associated sexual attractiveness in women with youth. American women struggle to maintain the appearance of youth because to lose it is to become that most repellent of creatures—an "old bag." Since we tend to regard physical allure as an invaluable asset for even the achieving woman (though not for the achieving man), achievement does not excuse a woman from the rigors of the losing battle against the physical ravages of time. Time also brings a rapid succession of role changes to most women. Between the ages of 18 and 25 many educated women are relatively free of family responsibilities; between the ages of 25 and 35 most are mothers of young children; between the ages of 35 and 45 most have children in school or college who do not demand incessant care; after the age of 45 most find the load of family responsibilities suddenly lightened. These role changes are accompanied by changes in perceptions of the self as a "needed" individual in the family.

The diminution of the sense of being needed changes the self-concept and lowers the level of self-esteem. As one woman put it, "There I was, 45, my children on their own, my husband a success, and all I'd been doing for twenty years was making like a wife, mother, and hostess. Nothing I'd been doing was important to anyone anymore. Everyone seemed to be telling me, 'Go away, don't bother us. You're finished—die.'" The undergraduate also has problems associated with age, but they are of a different order. One describes hers thus: "I am a woman. I have been socialized to want to be desirable to men, to be 'feminine.' Yet to be successful in my chosen field and in school, I must exhibit 'masculine' traits. It is confusing and disrupting to me" (Tesch, 1972).

Although differences in developmental experiences, in social and cultural backgrounds, and in age produce variations in some elements of the problems associated with femininity and feminine roles with which women must cope, there is one experience common to all educated women (and most others, also) alive in America today that cannot fail to generate some degree of conflict or, at the very least, confusion in all women. That is the experience of being exposed to clashing ideologies about the nature of femininity and the roles of women. All women have been exposed through at least some socializing agents (if not parents, then the school and the media) to traditional conceptions of "woman's nature" and "woman's place." Since the mid-1960's feminism has become an aggressively marketed ideology. We might imagine that the impact of the latter on older women would be less, since exposure came at a later, less malleable age. We must remember, however, that younger women have had a more intense exposure to *traditional* concepts, since during the two decades following World War II there was a sharp rise in emphasis on the centrality, in a woman's life, of domestic roles, especially the child-rearing role. Authorities on child development, such as Spock, urged mothers to believe that any mother could rear a human masterpiece if she brought adequate skill and devotion to the task. As Slater remarks, in our product-oriented society the mother was "given the opportunity to turn out a really outstanding product" (Slater, 1972). Sociologists like Talcott Parsons lent credence to this notion by stressing the critical importance of role differentiation in the home to socialization, with the mother taking the "expressive" (emotional) role and the father the "instrumental" (doing) role (Parsons and Bales, 1955). A recent study of prize-winning picture books for pre-school children reports that during the past five years the ratio of male to female central characters, which has long favored the male, has increased (Weitzmann, Eifler, Hokada, and Ross, 1972). Thus the degree to which a woman has been exposed to one or the other of the conflicting ideologies cannot be assessed on the basis of age alone or solely on the basis of any other demographic and sociological factors.

Social and cultural differences are possibly more apt to exert some influence on the overt behaviors with which different women respond to the persistent, passionate debate over what a woman should be and become than on the patterns of psychological response which underly the behaviors. That is, to estimate the strength of the psychological impact of feminism on women we must look below the level of patterns of behavior.

HOW IDEOLOGIES INFLUENCE FEMALE DEVELOPMENT

Ideologies exert both indirect and direct influences on female development, although most theories of development take little account of the covert influence and its effects are not always easy to identify. Covert influence is exercised when ideologies are elements of theories and assumptions about females that affect the attitudes and behaviors toward them of parents, educators, counselors, employers, and so on. Direct influence is exercised when they are acknowledged elements of the communications and expectations of socializing agents.

Ideological (i.e., doctrinaire) notions about women usually provide the foundation for mechanistic theories of female development. Vitalistic theories (e.g., "Nature intended women for . . .") also derive from ideological bases. Organismic theories count ideologies as operant factors in the developmental process. Vitalistic theories are held in low repute today, but both mechanistic and organismic theories of female development have many adherents. Both types of theories lend support to the assumption that there will be some similarities in psychological response patterns that cut across both sociological differences and differences in overt responses. But these theories differ in their premises and their conclusions. Organismic theories, while accepting the existence of sex differences, hold that men and women are subject to identical laws of development which postulate constant interaction among social, physical, and psychological characteristics and forces, as well as interaction among elements within each set; no single characteristic or constellation of characteristics, such as sex, can predetermine the outcomes of the developmental process. Many mechanistic theories, on the other hand, are built on the premise that women, for biological and/or social reasons, are so different from men that their development is governed by special laws. By postulating relatively simple cause-and-effect relationships, mechanistic theories enable their proponents to ascend to dizzying heights of generalization. Before turning to organismic theories, let us briefly consider illustrations of this approach. Biologically derived explanations of the psychology of women are a fertile source of examples. Tiger and Fox offer one:

> With the females, the old primate program is quite reliable; they will first come to maturity, and perhaps indulge in some premarital sex play with what appears to be a "programmed" adolescent sterility that protects them against having infants when they are themselves too inexperienced as persons. Then they will marry, or take part in whatever organization of breeding their community has. Once they have an infant, they will assume full adult status and be rewarded accordingly. . . . Working from the general primate base, nature has produced a creature whose learning patterns, over its lifetime, have been mapped as carefully as the instincts of

lower animals. . . . If our analysis of male-female differences is at all correct, then the greater participation of women in national life will not come about within the framework of the system as it stands. The realities of male-female interaction will simply get in the way. It may need something much more drastic like laws [i.e., *laws made by men*] that compel boards of directors to have female members, or female quotas in legislatures, before the greater participation . . . could be effected (Tiger and Fox, 1971).* (Interpolation mine)

In other words, women are impervious to the psychological impact of ideologies; they are not "programmed" to respond. We should note in passing, however, that even the actualities of life among the primates, as reported by primate ethnologists, are distorted in the sweeping statement above; families, genera, and species vary widely in sex-typed behaviors and in division of roles by sex; within a single species both of these may be modified by differences in the physical environment. Comparative studies of different species and of the same species in different habitats have suggested to ethnologists that it is the female who determines the relation of the male to the group, rather than vice versa (DeVore, 1972).

Some mechanistic explanations of female characteristics, and of female roles ordained by these, derive more from history and/or sociological conditions at a given point in time and space than from biology; although such explanations often include inferences about biological characteristics which have been drawn from social circumstances. Freud's conclusion that "Anatomy is destiny" is an oft-cited example of this type of inference. [The *lacunae* in Freud's theories of the psychology of women are discussed elsewhere in this book and in other publications (Bardwick, 1971; Horney, 1967; Thompson, 1971).] Another example is Parsons' theory of role division in the nuclear family, already mentioned; Parsons does not venture into the realm of biology, however. We daily encounter lay versions of such theories; for example: "Most women won't seek much responsibility outside the home; home and family have to come first for them." "Fellowships are wasted on most women; most of them will marry, and after that they won't contribute much to their fields." "Women should put homemaking first in their lives, because men and children need a relaxed, loving home where they can retreat from the pressures of work and school." And, most common of all, "Women's biological roles will always keep them from being equal to men outside the home."

Such arguments ignore the effects of changes in social and economic circumstances on the relationship between women's biological roles and their other activities and on the preeminence of those roles in women's lives. In agrarian societies women made their economic contributions within or near the home; in our society this is no longer possible for most women. In societies

*From *The Imperial Animal,* by Lionel Tiger and Robin Fox. Copyright © 1971 by Lionel Tiger and Robin Fox. Reprinted by permission of Holt, Rinehart and Winston, Publishers.

which depended heavily on manual labor and in which the mortality rate was high, the number of children a woman could produce was an important measure of her contribution to society; in our society population growth is a major problem and we are striving to keep the birth rate down. These arguments in addition reflect myths distilled from selected aspects of past experience and outmoded ideologies. [The assumptions underlying many "logical" generalizations about women are often derived from myth; we cannot pursue this fascinating topic here, but it has been the subject of several thoughtful works (Janeway, 1971; Beard, 1962; de Beauvoir, 1953).]

Mechanistic explanations, despite their shortcomings, are tempting because they are tidy. Organismic explanations are not tidy; they deal with a variety of factors and with many patterns of interaction among factors. They have loose ends because our knowledge of the human animal and the human condition is not yet complete. They have the advantage, however, of providing a rationale, incomplete though it may still be, for variations in "human nature" and for changes in the human condition which are obvious to all diligent observers.

Even a cursory glance at the physiological factors that function in the development of sex differences shows how limited an influence these have over the development of a woman's total personality. Of all genetic sex differences the most fundamental are the difference in sex chromosomes (xx in females and xy in males) and the difference in hormonal systems. The sex chromosome difference causes the male to be more variable than the female; his death rate is higher both before and after birth, and he is more often born defective. The sex chromosomes determine whether sex organs will be male or female and what the hormone system will be. The hormone system influences growth processes through interaction both with the entire endocrine system, of which it is a part, and with all other parts of the organism. As Darlington remarks, this means that "Not only the sex chromosomes, and the hormone system set in action by them, but all the other chromosomes, also varying, play their part in governing the whole character of a man or a woman" (Darlington, 1964). The sex chromosomes are only one of a total of 23 pairs; since genetic variation in the other pairs is independent of sex, there is a wide genetic variation within each sex even in such secondary sex characteristics as distribution of body fat and body hair, vocal range, height, and so forth, despite the influence of the hormone systems over these. Variation in the genetic components of such psychological characteristics as intelligence and temperament will obviously be much greater.

Nevertheless we sometimes encounter the contention that the hormone systems are responsible for sex differences in patterns of emotional response and of intellectual functioning. It is true that the hormone system, as a part of the endocrine system, has, through the hypothalamus and the limbic system as a whole, both afferent and efferent connections with the cerebral cortex. However, emotional responses arising from the interactions within this total system are, as we all know, basically a component of the survival mechanisms of organisms. They are not species-specific but also, in humans, very largely the result of socialization. When, through our sensory and cognitive processes, we perceive a feared object, the endocrine system responds; but we have *learned* what objects to fear. We also learn to find certain characteristics and behaviors sexually attractive and others not; what we learn varies from culture to culture as well as among individuals. In addition, as implied above, there is a wide variation in patterns of hormonal functioning even among "normal" members of each sex because the hormonal system develops in interaction with other genetic characteristics of the organism. Perhaps for this reason, the effect of the administration of androgens (male sex hormones) or estrogens (female sex hormones) upon behavior in experiments with lower mammals is not always predictable; estrogens administered to males may produce either masculine or feminine sexual behavior; the behavior induced by the administration of the hormone may be either specific to the sex of the host animal or to the hormone (Altman, 1966). Estrogens and androgens are produced by both sexes, the level of the former being higher in the female and the level of the latter higher in the male; individual levels vary.

In other words, the hormone system is not a governor which "programs" one sex for one pattern of responses and the other for another, nor is it an entity fixed by an individual's sex and impervious to modification by the other genetic characteristics of individuals and by their learning experiences. Genetic sex differences serve the purposes of sexual reproduction; they are *not* the mechanisms responsible for the evolution of complex, far-reaching systems of differentiation of roles and behaviors by sex. Genetically speaking, sex is only one of many components of the individuality of a woman or a man.

This being the case, why do we find, within any given society or culture, certain average differences between the sexes in behavior and temperament? The answer lies in the interaction between developing human beings and their external environments. Sex is a key element in this interaction for two reasons: sex is the primary category for the classification of human beings (and many other sexually reproducing organisms), and division of roles by sex occurs to a greater or lesser extent in all social organizations, animal as well as human (division may be limited to the purely biological roles of reproduction or, as among humans, encompass a wide variety of activities which are wholly independent of the reproductive process).

Because sex is the primary category for the classification of self and others, gender identity is a fundamental component of personality. Gender is a function of sex; but sex is a constellation of physical characteristics, while gender is a psychological and cultural concept. As Stoller points out, the sexes are denoted by the terms "male" and "female," and gender is denoted by the terms "masculine" and "feminine." Gender is an element in the self-concept and a dimension of status and role. In Stoller's words, "Gender identity starts with the knowledge and awareness, whether conscious or unconscious, that one belongs to one sex and not the other, though as one develops, gender identity becomes much more complicated" (Stoller, 1968). Even in the very young child gender is a direct reflection neither of cultural concepts of gender nor of biological sex characteristics. According to Kohlberg and others of the cognitive-developmental school, when, at about the age of 2, a child begins to think of itself as a member of its sex, it is then predisposed to seek and value activities appropriate to its gender identity. Perceptions of what is gender-appropriate will be influenced both by the social characteristics of the child's family and by the dynamics of interpersonal relationships within it. Thus, while the physical characteristics of sex develop in interaction with other genetic components of the organism, gender identity develops in interaction both with these and with the external environment and is therefore much more readily subject to modification over time.

Gender identity emerges with the recognition of gender categories; then comes awareness of genital sex differences; then awareness of masculine-feminine stereotypes, which are the products of ideologies. Gender identity is a basic source of valuing, since individuals value that which is like themselves and see themselves as being or able to be like that which they value; otherwise the level of cognitive dissonance would be intolerable.

The acquisition of gender identity opens the way for the perception of gender roles; gender identity continues to develop in interaction with gender roles and with other roles. Gender roles is an extremely complex construct; it subsumes both roles and sex-appropriate behaviors which may or may not be directly associated with the performance of one or another role. Cultural concepts of gender roles are essentially ideological in origin. Stoller defines gender roles as "the overt behavior one displays in society, the role which he plays, especially with other people, to establish his position with them insofar as his and their evaluation of his gender is concerned" (Stoller, 1968). There is, however, no invariant association between strength of gender identity and adoption of the gender roles most generally accepted in a given culture. Gender-role preferences are acquired through interaction with the social environment, including the ideology or ideologies pertinent to gender roles extant in that environment. Cognitive-developmental theories of the development of gender identity and the acquisition of gender roles postulate interaction, beginning in early childhood, with a wider and more varied environment than do theories of identification and imitation (which emphasize the child's identification with and imitation of the same-sex parent and, later, significant others of the same sex) or social-learning theories (which regard the child's acquisition of gender-typed attitudes and behaviors as primarily a function of rewards for such behaviors from parents and others). Cognitive-developmental psychologists regard gender identity as an element of cognitive organization which influences perceptions and valuings in an ever-widening sphere of experience. Therefore, both gender identity as an aspect of self-concept and perceptions of gender roles continue to develop in interaction with other qualities of the self (e.g., age, physique, intelligence) as well as with the social environment. For example, high general intelligence appears to predispose *young* children toward high same-sex-typing on standard measures of sex-typed interests, while it predisposes *adolescents* toward low same-sex-typing on such interest measures (Kohlberg, 1966).

Theories of the development of gender identity and the acquisition of gender roles explain why ideologies about women have the power to modify, during the course of a lifetime, the constellation of attitudes and behaviors which, at some point in time and space, are regarded as the core of femininity. They also show why individual women never become mirror images of some ideological model of Woman. A critically important premise is that biological sex membership has a positive value because it is a mark of gender identity. A woman *likes* being a woman. She does not wish to exchange her femaleness or her feminine gender identity for maleness or a masculine gender identity even when she desires or actively seeks greater access to the gender roles assigned to males. Therefore she will reject those elements of any ideology which denigrate femaleness or femininity. But the femininity which she cherishes is not a predestined fruit of biological femaleness; it is a configuration of attitudes toward self and others and of behavior styles that have been and continue to be learned and that are interwoven with all aspects of her total personality and life style.

This learning begins in early childhood when she first thinks of herself as female. At this point some very elementary behaviors begin to take on the impress of "femininity" as it is expressed in her culture and within her family. For example, little girls and little boys begin to manifest differences in posture and movement in the second year of life, but what these differences will be depends both on cultural styles in such sex differences and on the strength of the child's attachment to father, mother, or an older sibling (Birdwhistell, 1970). A little girl whose attachment to her father causes her to adopt some of his mannerisms and, later, some of his interests is not opting for a masculine gender identity; she is affirming a feminine gender identity in ways which are attractive to her, and she will adapt these ways to the dimensions of her developing selfhood, including her femaleness. For gender identity, once acquired, is irreversible in normal individuals. As a component of the self-concept, it continues to develop in interaction with all of life's activities, not only with those required by gender-typed roles but also with all other components of self and social experience.

But, in our society and most others, *cultural* conceptions of the affirmation of gender identity are tied to gender-typed roles and gender-typed behaviors. Feminist ideology and traditionalist ideology differ sharply in their conceptions of gender roles and gender-appropriate behaviors. Differences in conceptions of gender roles are reflected in differences among women in gender role perceptions and preferences and, for individual women, changes in these perceptions and preferences—changes which are usually preceded by a period of confusion and conflict, since they entail changes in the self-concept. Differences in conceptions of gender-appropriate behaviors, especially those acquired early in life, such as physical mannerisms and external modes of interpersonal interaction (for example, most little girls early learn that they get more from their fathers by coaxing than by demanding), are less apt to be reflected in differences among women within any given cultural group and, for individual women, in changes from one set of behavior styles to another. But the fact that these behaviors are much more resistant to change than are gender role perceptions and preferences does not mean that they are forever immutable or that they may not be sources of guilt, shame, and conflict for individual women who have accepted an ideology which does not endorse them.

GENDER ROLES AND GENDER BEHAVIORS: POINTS OF CONFLICT BETWEEN FEMINISTS AND TRADITIONALISTS

Gender Roles

In simple societies some pattern (there were many) of division of roles by sex served the social and economic function of efficient division of labor; it also served the psychological function of enabling women or men to affirm their femininity or masculinity, as well as other individual qualities, through obviously meaningful participation in the society. Modern America is not a simple society. Division of labor by sex is not merely inefficient—it is impossible: the talents and skills upon which our system depends are not sex-typed. The relatively few gender roles available in our society are apt to be obstacles rather than avenues to personally meaningful social roles. The woman encapsulated in a suburban development and the man trapped in a dissatisfying but remunerative job may both feel that the performance of their gender roles of wife and breadwinner is destroying individuality and denying them the opportunity to make a more worthy contribution to the community, or sector of the society, with which they identify. Therefore, the most obvious points of conflict between feminists and traditionalists—those which focus on gender roles—are probably the least controversial for the educated woman. Feminists would abolish all gender-typed roles except for the biologically fixed aspects of parental roles, and these, some feminists hope, will soon be assumed by laboratory technicians. Traditionalists regard gender identity as most fully affirmed through a limited set of gender-typed roles: sex object, housewife, mother, hostess, and such "womanly occupations" as teacher, nurse, social worker, secretary, and so on down the all-too-familiar line. Although the major socializing agents in our society still tend to reinforce traditionalist stereotypes, so that, for instance, quite young children will sex-type occupations (Schlossberg and Goodman, 1972), both first-hand and second-hand, feminist interpretations of some of this experience appear to be moving educated women toward the feminist position on gender roles.

Currently available data certainly suggest that this is the case. The career aspirations of college women seem to be rising; more than half of those recently surveyed probably aspire to some eminence in a chosen field, and a much larger majority than that expect that work outside the home will occupy a significant proportion of their adult years; at the same time, the proportion anticipating or desiring large families is sharply declining (Wilson, 1971). Women who may not have anticipated extended participation in the labor force when they were undergraduates are now, in their middle years, so engaged. The chances are two out of five that a married woman with one to three years of college education who is living with her husband will be in the labor force. Those chances are better than one in two if she has had four or more years of college education; if she has a doctorate or comparable degree, the chances are better than eight in ten (Women's Bureau, 1971a). If a woman is divorced, the chances are two out of three that she will be employed (Women's Bureau, 1971b). Women are also increasing as a proportion of "multiple-job holders" or "moonlighters" (Women's Division, Institute of Life Insurance, 1972).

These changes have been accompanied by increasingly insistent demands for equality of opportunity in undergraduate and graduate education and for expanded opportunities for continuing education in a wide variety of fields for women of all ages. Mounting pressure for equal opportunities in all levels and almost all fields of employment has produced legislation and executive orders at state and federal levels that some women are learning to use to their advantage. Although employers and educators can hardly be said to have responded to these demands with alacrity, they are moving in the desired direction and the movement seems certain to continue. Neither the demands nor the responses can be ascribed solely to feminist protest, however; some of the activity (e.g., the Equal Pay Act) preceded the surge of protest. But feminism undoubtedly accelerated the pace of a trend which was generated by patterns of change in women's roles, and it certainly gave women who might otherwise have continued to endure discrimination silently, if not serenely, the courage to speak out. The rebellion against sex discrimination is now widespread; its ranks include factory operatives and service workers as well as women in professional and managerial occupations.

The drop in the birthrate and the rise in the average age of marriage for women, mentioned earlier, are undoubtedly related to changes in career aspirations, changes in patterns of labor force participation, and expansion of opportunities for education and employment. And all of these are indications of the combined impact of personal experience and feminist ideology upon women's perceptions of possible life styles. For the younger woman some of the most influential personal experiences may be second-hand—her observations of her mother's life and the lives of her mother's peers. For the older woman at least some of the significant experiences have usually been first-hand.

In the economic realm many younger women have observed, and many older women have been forced to recognize, that marriage does not invariably or even usually relieve women of any social class of the need to earn. In families where both parents are employed, ability to maintain a given standard of living is, generally speaking, partially a function of the mother's income, although the father (partly because of sex discrimination in employment) usually makes the larger contribution. When divorce occurs, the mother's economic burdens frequently mount astronomically; the limited data available indicate that only slightly more than half of divorced fathers make payments under support orders even during the first year after divorce and that over two-thirds make no payments at all by the end of four years (Citizens Advisory Council on the Status of Women, 1972). The divorce rate is climbing steadily; during the 1960's and the 1970's the annual number of divorces rose by 80 percent while the number of remarriages increased by 40 percent (Bureau of the Census, 1972a). But for many women the ability to earn represents far more than a means to cope with financial needs; it empowers a woman to exercise greater control over her life style than she can if she is economically dependent.

Even without feminist agitation most educated women today would probably perceive economic activity as at least potentially salient in their lives. But it seems safe to say that feminists have done much to sharpen women's perceptions of the limits sex discrimination places on such activity. The undergraduate is not flattered by the professor who waggishly urges her not to sit in the front row because her lovely legs will distract him; she perceives him as a dark cloud on her career horizon. Employed women and those seeking employment resent the implication, spoken or unspoken, that for them employment is optional or temporary, second in importance to domestic responsibilities, present or future, and apt to be abandoned by them at any time. Women who are clearly not subordinating careers to domestic responsibilities take exception to the all-too-frequently encountered assumption that they have relegated to second place all affectional and practical commitments to husband, children, and friends. Yet these and innumerable other comparable expressions of cultural stereotypes of "woman's place" are part of the experience of almost every woman and have been for a long time. The feminist revolution has made only a slight dent in the closely held lines of sex discrimination in employment and its port of entry, education, despite the pressure also exerted by the changed economic roles of women. But it has made women consciously and constantly aware of the existence and the manifestations of such discrimination and, in so doing, has reduced the incidence of conflict associated with employment roles which sometimes was agonizing and always was aggravated by the attitudes upon which discrimination is based.

In the political realm women of all ages have ample opportunity to observe and experience the powerlessness of women. When a women's college becomes coeducational, men, even while they are still a relatively small minority of the student body, move into key positions of political leadership and of political influence over the choice and resolution of issues. In political arenas outside the campus the participation of women has been even more insignificant. The proportion of women in appointive offices has slightly increased (although not in those of major importance), and much of this increase can be attributed to feminist pressure; the proportion of women in elective offices, from the local to the national level, does not yet appear to be changing. Issues of critical importance to women (e.g., abortion) are resolved by men. Only the most courageous political leaders dare stand with women against special-interest groups even when, as in the case of abortion, there is evidence that a majority of women favor a given resolution. A volume could be written on the hazards encountered by women who venture to run for public office. Here we will limit ourselves to a single illustration: two women candidates for judgeships in New York State were found not qualified by the same State Bar Association which found men of comparable qualifications to be qualified.

In 1972 there were clear changes in women's political behavior; the most marked was a sharp upswing in the number of women candidates and convention delegates. Statements by women who were not themselves candidates for office, news stories, a 1972 women's opinion poll (Harris, 1972), and informal conversations—all suggest that the women's movement has also made women more conscious of their political impotence. The pressures on women to participate in political activity, however, are not as direct as are those to participate in economic activity, as a general rule; for most women active political participation is motivated less by personal need than by public morality. It seems unlikely that women will soon storm the political bastions *en masse,* despite feminist pleas that they seize the seats of power.

The apparent effects of feminism on the political psychology of women are less dramatic but nonetheless notable. The poll cited above and workers in the 1972 campaigns both found that many women no longer follow their husbands' lead in voting decisions, that they ask their own questions and place their own interpretations on the answers. (Even television noted this phenomenon—Archie Bunker's wife made it clear that Archie's conscience would not be her guide in the privacy of the voting booth.) Politicians manifest awareness of this emerging independence by promises addressed to the "women's vote"; keeping the promises is, of course, another matter— witness the ambivalence and inaction on issues like child care, abortion, prosecution for rape, et al. Feminism seems to have decreased the amount of conflict experienced by women over opposing their husbands or other significant males on voting decisions and to have possibly increased their motivation to influence the votes of such males. For some women, feminism has probably also raised the level of guilt associated with political inactivity (Harris, 1972), but it has probably not yet moved educated women to accord the same salience to political roles that they do to economic roles.

In the social realm, most especially the realm of the family, the division between feminist and traditionalist positions is greater than in the economic and political realms. Today's traditionalists can accept a woman's need and right to engage in economic and political activities *provided* these do not interfere with the family responsibilities to which traditionalists assign primacy. They acknowledge that economic and political participation can be personally rewarding and socially valuable. But their conception of the personal rewards and social values of domestic roles contrasts vividly with that of the feminists. The traditionalist says:

> It seems quite safe . . . to say that the adult feminine role has not ceased to be anchored primarily in the internal affairs of the family, as wife, mother, and manager of the household (Parsons and Bales, 1955).

The feminist says:

> There is something horribly repugnant in the picture of women performing the same menial chores all day, having almost interchangeable conversations with their children . . . each agonizing over what is considered her personal lot (Jones, 1970).

While the debate goes on, younger women are observing and older women are discovering that a woman's family roles today are both constricted and constricting. Although the old English Common Law tenet that "husband and wife are one person and that person is the husband" has been legislated out of juridical existence, many wives find that it still pretty well describes the wife's marital condition. The pattern of his day determines the pattern of hers. His employment decides where they live and how often they move. Even if she is herself employed, more frequently than not she cannot get credit in her own name, whether at a department store or a lending institution. If she wants to establish a business of her own, she will have at least as much trouble securing funding as would a black ghetto male. She is an economic non-person in a more fundamental sense, for the work of the housewife and mother is accorded no economic value in calculations of the gross national product and the gross national income (Kreps, 1971). She is rarely allowed to serve public decision-making bodies, including those, such as urban and regional planning councils, whose deliberations will have a direct impact upon her and her family.

Both the content and the variety of domestic roles has been seriously eroded. In our technological, consumer economy the components of the housewife's role which are *essential* are extremely limited in number. For example, cooking and sewing, except the most rudimentary, are now optional recreations rather than necessary occupations for the homemaker. Perhaps the most striking outcome of the availability of our many technological aids to housekeeping is a rise (to which advertisers have given much impetus) in standards of cleanliness and order to a level which chains housewives to a monotonous, meaningless pursuit of inconsequential dirt and disorder. Since a marked portion of today's nuclear families live in a succession of houses, the planning and furbishing of a home does not demand of a woman investment of self in the creation of a center that will express the individuality and serve the needs of a growing family over a long period of time. Few women today can plant a garden on what someone I know calls the "fifty-year plan." As a community volunteer the housewife finds her scope of action severely delimited by the authority of professionals and their attitudes toward volunteers. But the most painful constrictions are those on the family role which we most glorify—the role of mother. During her children's earliest years, today's mother spends most of her waking hours in the company of small children, and most of her accustomed adult activities and associations must be set aside; after the children enter school, however, a large share of the mother's functions as teacher and mentor is preempted by school teachers, recreation leaders, group activity leaders, and so on. In most types of communities, this transfer of responsibility does not free the mother for other activities, however; she now becomes handmaiden to her children's commitments, serving as co-ordinator, chauffeur, facilitator. Children are caught up in an educational process that usually widens the gulf between the interests of children and of parents, and it is the mother who is expected to put aside her personal interests for the sake of an effort to keep in touch through participation in P.T.A., community activities for children, and so forth, and by being available to her children in their relatively small amounts of free time.

Depletion of the content of domestic roles and segregation of housewives from other sectors of society are results not only of curtailed economic and social functions of the home in our era but also of the horizontal mobility of families and the types of residential patterns which have sprung up all over the country since World War II. The residential developments that now characterize all our major metropolitan areas and penetrate deep into areas only recently rural are, for the most part, colonies of transients. "Arcadia Hills," "Brookside," "Pleasant Meadows," and like appellations are tinsel bows on hastily assembled packages of houses of a size and type intended to sell within a limited price range. Each development's population tends to be socio-economically homogeneous and to be similar in age and family composition. Development houses (invariably advertised as "homes") serve primarily as physical shelters for families. They are mass-produced and lack both individuality and permanence; they are as disposable as last year's raincoat. Many suburban and most ex-urban developments lack community centers and shopping facilities; they offer no ready routes to casual neighborhood interaction or to civic and political participation.

The involvement of the housewife, or her family, in the life of such non-communities is not only temporary but, of necessity, superficial. Community action, when it does occur, tends to be generated by discontent with public services and/or taxes and consists of demands for improvements to be provided by others (developers or municipalities) with no increase in taxes—in other words, it expresses the passive attitude of the consumer rather than the active engagement of the foresighted citizen. Mature women describe life in such locations as "living in a vacuum" (Westervelt, 1973). Rootlessness and passivity deprive children and young people of the experience of being "someone" in a community. The turning away of some of our abler young adults from the career-ladder climb and the suburban transience and/or urban impersonality that it demands probably is a reaction, in part, to too many years of life in a non-community.

Although many educated women, young and mature, suspect or have discovered that family roles assigned to women are unsatisfying and dead-ended, marriage continues to be a highly significant factor in women's life planning. Few women are ready to accept the feminist dictum that

> The family has fallen apart. . . . The family unit is a decadent, energy-absorbing, destructive, wasteful institution. . . . The new sense of collective action among women is fast destroying the decadent family ideology along with its ugly individualism and competitiveness and complacency (Dunbar, 1970).

Informal observations and research both indicate that the average junior and senior high school girl, as well as the average college woman, expects to combine a career interest with marriage *but* she also expects marriage and motherhood to interfere in some way with career continuity and thinks a mother's employment may be bad for children (Rand and Miller, 1972). While today's young woman may perceive herself as having more options regarding sexual behavior than did her mother (her sexual mores appear to depend more on those of her peer reference group than on those of her parents [Teevan, 1972]), available evidence suggests that exercise of her options for sexual freedom may be, in her view, a necessary means toward establishing a long-term stable sexual and, possibly, parental partnership. The female partner in an extramarital liaison appears to be more apt than the male to hope and believe that the relationship will become permanent (Eslinger, Clarke, and Dynes, 1972; Lyness, Lipetz, and Davie, 1972). Data also indicate that educated, mature married women rank the roles of "wife" and "mother" as most important in their lives (Westervelt, 1973). Counselors of mature women find that loss of a husband through divorce, or even a husband's inability to provide full financial support for his family, is associated with loss of self-esteem for the women.

Evidence of the continuing salience of marriage and maternity in women's lives should not be interpreted as indicating that the marriage-career role conflict is still the central conflict in the lives of educated women, however. Data on career aspirations, already cited, imply that this conflict is rapidly diminishing in importance. Its persistence as an issue for discussion is more a function of the assumptions of educators and counselors than of the perceptions of women themselves, especially of young women. Those of us who teach and/or counsel have ample opportunity to observe that stresses and crises in sexual relationships, in or out of marriage, do not, as a rule, interfere with a woman's ability to work and achieve either in a career or in another area of current interest. Years of research have shown that there is no direct association between career success and marital status (Aregger, 1966; Astin, 1971). Zinberg points out that the need to acquire a feeling of accomplishment is a developmental need associated with ego strength and is independent of sex (Zinberg, 1972). Since relatively few educated women today perceive domestic roles as a *long-term* source of a sense of achievement, it is inevitable that they perceive the pursuit of personal achievement as psychologically separate from sexual relationships.

This does not mean that young women are unaware of what older women have learned through experience: that the burden of adjusting personal goals to marital responsibilities falls more heavily on women than on men. Many men still expect a sexual partner, in marriage or outside it, to be a major source of support and assistance in their pursuit of self-development. For this very reason, women are far less apt to expect such support and assistance, but many young women, now more than formerly, seek to assure themselves of it before making a commitment to marriage. Furthermore, their awareness of the growing instability of marriage—the knowledge that divorce may leave them alone with small children before they are 30 or leave them alone at 50 with all children grown when a husband to whose achievement they have devoted their prime years leaves to marry a woman in her 20s—forces them to establish goals for self-development which are independent of the vicissitudes of marriage. While young women still marry with the hope that the partnership will be mutually rewarding and permanent and still expect to adjust career plans or other avenues to self-development to the needs of family, relatively few intend to totally abandon these for marriage or see them as incompatible with it. For them marriage is a fundamental element in life planning but it is *not*, as it was for many of their mothers, a life plan in itself.

Not only do young women no longer regard personal achievement and marital satisfaction as mutually exclusive goals; they also regard these as essential, complementary aspects of life's experiences. Given the social and legal supports with which our society buttresses the institution of marriage, this is a realistic perception. It is not evidence that, in this realm, women have remained untouched by feminist ideology. The search for a stable sexual partnership is rooted in physiological drives for sex and maternity and spurred by psycho-social forces. In our culture, and probably in others which are comparable, the sex drive in women appears to emerge as a significant influence on behavior at a later stage of adolescence than it does for men (although sex differences in this may be rather small among the college-educated population) and to attain maximum strength at a later age than in men (Kinsey, Pomeroy, Martin, and Gebhard, 1953). The strength of the sex drive and its capacity for satisfaction may still be, for most educated women in our society, partly a function of perceived stability and/or acceptability of a sexual relationship. Masters and Johnson (1966) remark that "sexual response to orgasm is the physiologic prerogative of most women, but its achievement in our culture may be more dependent upon psychosocial acceptance of sexuality than overtly aggressive behavior." The undergraduate woman experiences a sharp increase in her sex drive just at the time when cultural and social restraints upon her sexual activities have been relaxed; research indicates that she is more apt than her counterpart of even ten years ago to exercise her new-found freedom (Lyness et al., 1972). Nevertheless, both the cultural values attached to stable sexual relationships for women and biological and psychological compulsions toward child-bearing experienced by at least some women enhance the purely sexual value of a permanent partnership. The older woman whose sexual experiences have been satisfying and whose sex drive has attained maximum strength will find that this drive persists at a high level well into her later years; Masters and Johnson (1966) state that "there is no time limit drawn by the advancing years to female sexuality." But she knows that she will also find extra-marital sexual partners ever less available as she grows older. Therefore she also has a physiological and psychological, as well as a social, stake in establishing or maintaining a durable relationship with a male.

As long as our culture and our society continue to place social and legal obstacles in the way of extra-marital sex and parenthood, we must regard the female's search for a satisfying marriage as the expression of normal physiological and psychological developmental needs rather than a testimony that she is ready to commit her total self to the demands of marriage as traditionalists would have her do. Marriage satisfies (or may satisfy) *one* set of primary needs; it does not thereby gain primacy as an avenue or a goal for development. When the present trend to wider acceptance of extra-marital relationships and non-traditional types of family organization (e.g., communal living) becomes institutionalized through appropriate legislation pertaining to marital responsibilities, legitimacy of children, and so on, feminist ideas about freedom in sexual relationships and the abolition of the nuclear family in favor of "families" organized around communal associations will be more frequently reflected in social arrangements and individual life plans. It is important to note that feminist ideals for family organization represent, in one sense, a revival of the once prevalent extended family. The organization they espouse would include individuals of all ages not all of whom would be members of heterosexual or homosexual "couples"; in contrast to the traditional extended family, however, the ties which bind individuals together are those of common interests rather than those of blood, sex, and legal contract.

There is a higher-level need that also operates to attract most women and undoubtedly most men to marriage: the need to share life's experiences in a context of intimacy and trust with a person or persons who also share some of one's interests. This need is intensified by the impersonality and individualistic competitiveness which characterize most activities at school, at work, and even at play in our society. Despite the obviously decreasing likelihood that marriage will provide enduring satisfaction of this need, it maintains first position as a possible source of such satisfaction. This is in part because an extensive mythology purveyed by a host of institutions ranging from organized religion to the advertising industry portrays marriage as the prime route to the affirmation of gender identity and the performance of gender roles in our society and in part because other types of close personal relationships, especially for women, are not yet highly visible or widely accepted. It is, of course, unlikely that any dyadic relationship could ever realize the expectations which most couples appear to bring to marriage. Evidence already cited suggests that women are aware of this. Marriage is chosen for lack of other options for intimacy.

At least some women are conscious of a need to expand their sphere of intimacy. Such women respond positively to the feminist emphasis on "sisterhood." "Sisterhood" stands for bonds among women and for active valuing of qualities which have been denigrated as "feminine" in societies dominated by males. Its goals differ sharply from, for example, those of most college sororities. (Wallace [1966], in a 1959-60 study of a small liberal arts campus, found sororities to be organized systems of competition for dates that served to reduce the social distance between women caused by such competition. He concluded that the pursuit of male attention as a female priority interfered with the development of same-sex friendships among women and with women's social integration both during and after college.) "Sisterhood" repudiates the traditionalist emphasis on the primacy of the male as a source of female status and roles. Through sisterhood women can band together to help each other resist male domination and to actively oppose male objectives for society. And through sisterhood, say feminists, "we share with each other the exhilaration of growth and self-discovery. ...We share experiences ... that mean nothing to men but *women understand*" (Steinem, 1972). Sisterhood turns a critical eye on men; "female hardheadedness rejects the misguided masculine notion that men are rational animals" (Greer, 1971).

"Sisterhood" is a central component in the feminist ideology; it is also the one for which there is least social support. Most social functions are still planned for couples. Although it is now common for young as well as older women to enjoy a holiday together, one would never guess it from looking at the coquettish couples pictured in resort advertisements. In many cities women alone cannot safely venture out at night (although a knowledge of karate helps). Most important of all, male domination of the political and economic hierarchy makes male support appear to be the *sine qua non* of advancement for the ambitious woman. Sisterhood, like the Brotherhood of Man, works best on paper, since competition for limited opportunities tends to pit members of subjugated groups against each other.

Although the role of "sister" in the feminist sense is not facilitated by many contemporary social circumstances, the increasing inability of heterosexual relationships, in and out of marriage, to meet needs for intimacy and trust, an inability which may become more prevalent as more women are pitted against men in the rapidly mounting resistance of women to sex discrimination, will probably enhance the moral and social values of the ideal "sister" as a gender role for women. We can certainly observe, especially among younger women, rising suspicion and hostility toward achieving women who make no great effort to help other women (this type of woman has been dubbed the "Queen Bee") but who not long ago commanded admiration and emulation. Sisterhood also offers ego support to women because it affirms the importance and the value of gender identity; it urges women to know and respect themselves and other women both as women and as individuals with many non-sex-typed qualities. It may well become a steadily stronger influence on women's perceptions of gender roles.

On the whole, it would appear that feminist ideology, as well as forces of social and economic change, is modifying women's role perceptions and expectations. The greatest impact appears to be on perceptions and expectations of economic and achievement roles; the attractiveness and significance of these roles is clearly growing. Feminist influence on perceptions and expectations of family roles is necessarily of a different order, since these roles are inextricably intertwined with fundamental aspects of biological and psychological development. The effect has been to heighten women's perceptions of the unsatisfying elements of these roles and the narrow limits accorded to them by our society but not, so far, to stimulate many women to reject these roles altogether or sharply to modify them through new systems of role relationships. They retain salience for most women but appear to be losing their capacity to totally dominate life plans. Women's perceptions of their role relationships to other women are also doubtless changing but perhaps only for a considerably smaller proportion of women than the other changes we have discussed.

Gender Behaviors

Many gender-typed behaviors are learned very early in life before conscious perceptions of gender roles are formulated. Gender-typed behaviors are therefore deep-seated elements of the self-concept and, as noted earlier, not easily unlearned. There appears to be no direct association, however, between overt gender-typed behaviors and role performance in individual women. Nor is a change in gender role perceptions or in role preferences necessarily accompanied by a change in styles of behavior. The popular image of the achieving woman as brash, noisy, and rudely assertive has been belied thousands of times by the success of women who appeared to be the embodiment of feminine gentleness, modesty, and grace.

Feminist ideology nevertheless launches a strong attack on traditionalist conceptions of gender-appropriate behavior styles, especially in the areas of aggression, competition, nurturance, and independence. Traditionalist ideology does not actually discourage aggression in women; instead it encourages aggression through covert manipulation, especially of the male. Feminist literature, on the other hand, is replete with exhortations to women to "oppose," "destroy," "assert," "demand," "insist." "If," says the feminist, "assertiveness is a virtue in man, it is a virtue also in woman" (Tanner, 1970).

Behavior styles like those of Bernadette Devlin or Betty Friedan are admired. Conventionally feminine modes of aggression are deplored:

> Women must refuse to be meek and guileful, for truth cannot be served by dissimulation. Women who fancy that they manipulate the world by pussy power and gentle cajolery are fools. It is slavery to adopt such tactics (Greer, 1971).

Obviously, the *need* to aggress in the pursuit of individual goals is not a sex-typed characteristic, but *modes* of aggression are learned in a society that differentiates modes by sex. Thus modes of aggression are sex-typed both as manifestations of the self-concept (especially gender identity) and as expectations held by others. If a woman learns in childhood to be overtly aggressive, she will not suffer anxiety over such behavior, since it accords with her self-concept; as a result, others will tend to accept her behavior, whatever their sex-typed expectations. But most women in our society are not socialized to be overtly aggressive; when such women attempt to change their modes of aggression, they are trying by conscious means to revise a part of the self-concept that lies partly below the level of consciousness. In part for this reason, they are very apt to be sensitive to the negative responses of others and to revert to more habitual modes. Until major changes have occurred in our socialization practices, it is highly unlikely that our campuses will be populated with youthful Bella Abzugs. It is even more unlikely that many women in middle age will suddenly discard the velvet glove for the mailed fist. An increasing proportion of young and older women appear willing to assert themselves through group activities such as demonstrations and student strikes, however. Others may be weighing the merits of open aggression versus subtle manipulation as a means to ends.

Competitive behaviors are usually regarded as aggressive behaviors. Feminists, however, deride cut-throat competition for *recognition* for individual achievement, although they by no means deride the psychological satisfactions of individual achievement for women. Traditionalists expect that women who do achieve will do so under old rules and for the conventional rewards of acceptance by the establishment (male-dominated), a stable career, and public acknowledgment of success. Feminists urge women to compete, not against each other, but together for greater political and economic power through which they can attain not only equal opportunity for women but new opportunities for both men and women through revolutionary changes in society. In this respect feminism is closely allied with neo-Marxist youth movements. As we all know, the issues involve not only economic and political structures and processes but also public morality. It is far too soon to estimate the long-range impact on the public and private lives of men and women of the social ideals represented by these movements; only when a new generation takes over the reins of political power will we know how deep and lasting the effects have been. Meanwhile there is much to suggest that more young women are motivated to seek equal opportunity within the existing system than to create a new one.

The most frequently idealized of all feminine qualities is a woman's capacity to nurture. We do not know whether or not women's nurturing tendencies have biological roots; we do know that almost all cultures teach women, both by precept and expectation, to perform nurturing functions. Feminists neither reject nor denigrate woman's capacity to nurture, but they do not consider it an innately sex-typed characteristic nor one which should determine the roles which women are permitted to perform. In our society we equate nurture with service roles, in the home and outside it. It represents, we believe, a constellation of attitudes and behaviors which makes good teachers, social workers, secretaries, and so on, but poor scientists, academicians, executives, and public administrators. Women who aspire to the latter roles must substitute dominance for nurturance. Feminists strenuously oppose this notion. "It is not a sign of revolution," says Greer (1971), "when the oppressed adopt the manners of the oppressors and practice oppression in their own behalf." This is not a revival of the old canard that women, as the "gentler" sex, will inevitably create a better society if given a chance. Rather, it is an exhortation to women not to deny or repress whatever may be their inclinations, whether innate or learned, to concern themselves with the quality of interpersonal relationships and the welfare of others in *any* roles to which they gain access (and they are to seek access to all roles, especially positions of power). It is also an urgent plea to women to affirm proudly these dimensions of personality and behavior, not to the exclusion or detriment of other qualities but as a complement to them.

External evidence of how great a response this feminist principle has so far generated in women is lacking, as we might reasonably expect it to be, since women's access to "masculine" roles is still severely limited and men still decree the patterns of interpersonal relationships in those roles. For example, if it is the case, as Bernard (1964) suggests, that academic women are more willing than academic men to devote a major share of time and energy to teaching, women thereby deprive themselves of opportunities to rise to positions of influence in the academic establishment, which gives its highest rewards to research, not teaching. Therefore, especially in our larger and more prestigious institutions, women are not in a position to modify standards of behavior. The recent rise in the career aspirations of women may even be associated, for many women, with a devaluing of nurturing tendencies, especially in public life, since these are associated with lower-status employment. If these tendencies have been acquired through a long process of enculturation, the need to devalue them could be a source of conflict; on the other hand, there is some question whether a society as impersonal, individualistic, and fragmented as ours now is can socialize young people of either sex to *strong* inclinations toward nurture. It is possible that this feminist ideal for female behavior runs counter both to the male value system as conceived by feminists and to recent influences on the socialization of females.

On the issue of independence-dependence, feminists and traditionalists are at opposite poles. Traditionalists have long taught women that an outward show of dependence on significant males (fathers, husbands, professors, employers) is an essential component of feminine behavior even when the male is in one or more ways (economically, emotionally, intellectually, or socially) the dependent member of the pair. We have already noted that the ability to depend on a male for economic and social support is an important element in the self-esteem of many women. As is abundantly clear from the feminist positions that we have already reviewed, feminists regard independent behavior as absolutely essential to the advancement of women. Women must not ape men, and they must not docilely adopt styles of behavior that traditionalist sources define as "feminine." They must not accept masculine logic, and they must actively engage in formulating and verbalizing their own systems of reasoning. If men complain that women are illogical ("Men with their heads reflect on this and that—But women with their hearts on heaven knows what!" [Byron, 1823]), women must remember that

> Male logic can only deal with simple issues: women . . . are more aware of complexity. Men have been forced to suppress their receptivity, in the interests of domination (Greer, 1971).

As an oppressed population, women must use what they have learned in that position to think and act on their own initiative in a society which is no longer comfortable for either men or women. They must be ready to accept the consequences of independence: opposition and rejection. At first glance, there would appear to be little evidence that feminine behavior is moving rapidly in this direction. But a more thoughtful consideration of the condition of women today gives credence to the conjecture that independence is being thrust upon women by social forces as well as urged upon them by feminists. Pressures toward independence include those associated with women's freedom of choice in sexual matters, the instability of marriages, and women's increased economic responsibilities. Some women may cling to an outward show of dependence on males, in part through habit, in part to gain social acceptance, and in part as a prop for self-esteem, but most women will have often to act independently to foster their own development and fulfill their responsibilities to others. Changes in women's role choices certainly suggest that among educated women much seemingly dependent behavior is more apparent than real. If increased experience with independence makes women more ready to display it openly, it is highly probable that other feminist ideals for female behavior will be more commonly accepted as "feminine" or, at least, as acceptable for females as well as males.

THE SIGNIFICANCE TO COUNSELORS OF THE PSYCHOLOGICAL IMPACT OF FEMINISM

The educated American woman finds herself within a maelstrom of pressures and counterpressures, ideological and situational. The more intelligent she is, the more conscious she will be of the confusion out of which she is striving to mold a life. The social and political apathy which appears to be spreading in the nation among young and old at the moment will not soften the impact of the pressures and counterpressures with which she contends or dispel her confusion. The realities of her situation are not figments of the feminist imagination, although feminist protest may have made her more keenly aware of them. The voices of the movement may become less shrill, but its impetus will not subside, because it derives from the urgent need of women to break the bonds which now hamper their development and their meaningful participation in society. Today's woman has been socialized to live in a world that no longer exists, to give primacy to roles that have become psychologically and socially constricting and whose duration is highly uncertain, to acquire behavior styles that ill fit the responsibilities she is likely to have to carry. During the past few years vocal feminists have enabled her to realize that many women share her plight; there is little wonder that she has listened to them thoughtfully even when she could not fully accept their propositions.

At present many educated women question whether the realities they perceive and experience fit either the feminist or the traditionalist model. As a result, many are dealing with a different set of psychological problems than were their predecessors of only a few years ago. Most no longer see themselves as forced to choose between marriage and career; thus the necessity for such a choice is no longer a source of conflict. A number, especially among undergraduates, resist and resent efforts to stress the importance of career in a woman's life. As they are already aware that career is important but are very possibly uncertain how to achieve it, such efforts can heighten their anxieties and distract them from more immediate goals, such as the acquisition of confidence in personal competency. They know that the pursuit of a career involves struggles against sex discrimination, difficulties in integrating public and private roles because of lack of child care and housekeeping services, and, all too possibly, strains in relationships with husbands who have been taught to believe that masculine gender identity is most powerfully affirmed through performance of the masculine gender role of breadwinner.

These perceptions have led to some changes in the educated woman's self-concept and in the sources of her self-esteem. Although she is very likely to have been socialized to need to see herself as sexually attractive and to derive self-esteem from the attentions of males, her needs to succeed in other than sexual realms of activity are increasing. In her efforts to understand herself and to set directions for her future she will strive to assess all the facets of her individuality. Her level of self-esteem will be in part a function of her capacity to identify and express these facets. The task of achieving a sense of uniqueness of personality and purpose is never an easy one; for women it entails certain special problems.

The undergraduate carries on this task at a time when the combined pressures of biological drives for sexual satisfactions and cultural support of traditional gender roles for both men and women who are reaching marriageable age offer a ready alternative to the painful process of enhancing and affirming her individuality. Feelings of shame over her inability to achieve a sense of well-rounded identity and feeling of guilt not only over her inability to meet whatever standards of achievement she has set for herself but possibly also over her resistance to traditional gender roles may sharply lower her self-esteem. She may seek to raise it by a flight to conventional roles.

The older woman who has found the gender roles for which she opted in youth unsatisfactory or untenable embarks upon a search for identity at a time in life when, so it seems to her, most of her male peers and some of her female peers have long since surmounted this developmental hurdle. She feels shame at what she sees as a failure to attain an appropriate level of maturity and, at the same time, guilt because she cannot find selfhood and satisfaction in the roles society has prescribed for her. If she does not deal with her shame and guilt, persistent anxiety will cause decision-making to be impulsive, difficult or impossible.

The undergraduate may also deal with problems of behavioral styles as well as future life styles. Are the "feminine" behaviors she has learned dishonest? Is she a coward or worse because she cannot comfortably display aggression or independence? Or will she gain her ends most readily by gender styles which are expected of her by male peers and mentors? Does she wish to be regarded as a radical (i.e., a deviant)? Is she abandoning not only her femininity but also her selfhood if she changes her personal style? In any case, *can* she change no matter how much she desires to do so?

In other words, sources of guilt and shame in today's educated woman are far more likely to be perceived inadequacies in areas of individual non-sex-typed qualities and achievements than inadequacies in sexual qualities and activities, although the latter have, of course, not lost their capacity to stimulate guilt and shame, especially when a sexual relationship fails. Counselors need to understand, however, that many educated women now deal with problems of personal accomplishment and achievement independently of problems of sexual experience; the two areas are separate sources of self-esteem. Love is no longer woman's whole existence (not that it ever was, but more women know this now). If women suspect that they are receiving sex-typed guidance, and they are very ready to be suspicious, they will break off communication with a counselor; they resent a counselor's assumption that the condition of being female automatically establishes certain priorities.

Conflicts are apt to center on alternate routes to self-fulfillment, especially self-fulfillment integrated with marriage, and on the degree of pressure with which the individual can cope in order to achieve, if achievement seems essential to self-fulfillment. Although both feminism and various youth movements eschew conventional career patterns as routes to achievement, perceptions of the sources of power and security in our society plus the recent attrition in job opportunities for college graduates appear to incline young people of both sexes to seek a foothold in the "Establishment" rather than to withdraw from it into retreat or revolution. This has strengthened young women's motivation to seek equal opportunities, and they will resist being implicitly or explicitly counselled to accept the *status quo* in career opportunities for their sex. They may expect the counselor to serve as an advocate for what they perceive as their educational and employment rights.

Although educated women, far more now than formerly, seek to combine career or comparable activities outside the home with marriage (or at least a stable sexual partnership) and, in many cases, with child-rearing, this does not mean that some single new pattern of integration of these various roles is emerging. At present there seem to be four major means of resolving the issues involved. In the first, husbands and wives work out all aspects of career and domestic responsibilities together: an on-going process of planning and decision-making which entails careful consideration of what is best for both partners and for children, if any, at any given point in time. In such a partnership the wife can usually expect to maintain career continuity and to interrupt her career only if she prefers to do so and if family circumstances permit (among highly educated couples such interruptions are becoming less common than they once were). The second mode of integration of roles generally occurs only with couples who have children. It depends upon the wife's willingness to interrupt or defer her career development in order to devote the major share of her time to children when they are very young. It is also likely to depend on her willingness to lower her career aspirations and/or to adjust these to the demands of her husband's career. This mode has been very prevalent among women now in their 30's and early 40's. The third means involves a rejection of conventional career patterns, and often of conventional marriage, in favor of non-traditional living styles. (Some of these styles, especially those which accentuate the values of simple, rural life, require a reversion to much earlier patterns of sex roles, with women assigned to household chores and men to heavy outdoor work.) Fourth, there are still young women who manage to repress motivations for individual achievement, or retreat from them for fear of failure, or wholly invest themselves in the achievement goals of a husband and turn hopefully to marriage as an outlet for all their developmental needs. Observations of women in continuing education and women returning to the labor force suggest that this last solution will be temporary for most women; that is, these young women have merely postponed the time at which they must deal with the needs of their individuality.

I call these four means to role integration the cooperative, the compromising, the cop-out, and the conventional and predict that during the next decade the cooperative will become the most prevalent.

SUMMARY

Feminist ideology has had an impact on the psychology of educated women. Its effects to date have been to change sources of guilt and shame and to modify both the content of conflicts over plans and decisions and the relative strength of various sources of motivation. The impact is only beginning to be noticeable but will become increasingly visible as the ideology itself loses the appearance of novelty (which is, in any case, an illusion) and becomes a more accepted part of the culture of educated women. The roots of the movement lie deep in history; in the Western world the changes that brought it into being began centuries ago and have now reached into the lives of every sector of the population. Acceptance of an ideology appropriate to these changes has been and will continue to be accelerated by feminist eloquence, women's studies, active measures to eliminate sexism from socialization practices, economic pressures on women, legislation for sex equality, the growing inability of marriage in a society like ours to satisfy the expectations that men and women bring to it, and new styles in family living.

Our concern has been to identify the most salient aspects of the psychological impact of feminism on educated women at this point in time. We do not venture to predict what will be the eventual effects on the psyches of both men and women of evolving changes in cultural conceptions of femininity, changes which will inevitably modify conceptions of masculinity and alter the content of gender identity for both sexes. We rest content to close with Byron's (1823) lines:

> There is a tide in the affairs of women,
> Which, taken at the flood, leads—God knows where:
> Those navigators must be able seamen
> Whose charts lay down its current to a hair.

REFERENCES

Altman, J. *Organic foundations of animal behavior.* New York: Holt, Rinehart and Winston, 1966.

Aregger, C.E. (Ed.). *Graduate women at work.* London: Oriel Press, 1966.

Astin, H.S. *The woman doctorate in America.* New York: Russell Sage Foundation, 1971.

Bardwick, J.M. *Psychology of women.* New York: Harper & Row, 1971.

Beard, M.R. *Woman as a force in history.* New York: Collier Books, 1962.

Bernard, J. *Academic women.* University Park, Pennsylvania: Pennsylvania State University Press, 1964.

Birdwhistell, R.L. *Kinesics and context.* Philadelphia: University of Pennsylvania Press, 1970. Chapters 6 & 7.

Block, J.H. *Conceptions of sex role: Some cross-cultural and longitudinal perspectives.* Institute of Human Development, University of California, Berkeley. Mimeographed.

Bureau of the Census, Social and Economic Statistics Administration, U.S. Department of Commerce. *Perspectives of the recent upturn in divorce and remarriage.* Washington, D.C.: U.S. Government Printing Office, 1972a.

Bureau of the Census, U.S. Department of Commerce. *Current population reports,* Series P-20. Washington, D.C.: U.S. Government Printing Office, 1972b.

Byron, G.G. *Don Juan.* Canto VI, Verse 11, 1823.

Citizen's Advisory Council on the Status of Women. *Memorandum: The equal rights amendment and alimony and child support laws.* Washington, D.C.: U.S. Government Printing Office, 1972.

Darlington, C.D. *Genetics and man.* New York: Schocken Books, 1964.

de Beauvoir, S. *The second sex.* New York: Alfred A. Knopf, 1953.

DeVore, B.I. Sex differences and natural selection. Paper delivered at a conference on *Women: Resource for a changing world,* Radcliffe Institute and Radcliffe College, April 1972. Tape cassette.

Dunbar, R. Female liberation as the basis for social revolution. In R. Morgan (Ed.), *Sisterhood is powerful.* New York: Vintage Books, 1970, 477-492.

Elsner, D.M. Mrs. Suzy Coed. *Wall Street Journal,* 1972, *180*(50), September 12, 1.

Eslinger, K.N., Clarke, A.C., & Dynes, R. The principle of least interest, dating behavior, and family integration settings. *Journal of Marriage and the Family,* 1972, *34,* 269-272.

Greer, G. *The female eunuch.* New York: McGraw-Hill, 1971.

Harris, L. & Associates. *The 1972 Virginia Slims American women's opinion poll: Women in politics and the economy.*

Horney, K. *Feminine psychology* (H. Kelman, Ed.). New York: W.W. Norton, 1967.

Janeway, E. *Man's world, woman's place: A study in social mythology.* New York: William Morrow, 1971.

Jones, B. The dynamics of marriage and motherhood. In R. Morgan (Ed.), *Sisterhood is powerful.* New York: Vintage Books, 1970, 46-61.

Kinsey, A.C., Pomeroy, W.B., Martin, C.E., & Gebhard, P.J. *Sexual behavior in the human female.* Philadelphia: W.B. Saunders, 1953.

Kohlberg, L. A cognitive-developmental analysis of children's sex-role concepts and attitudes. In E. Maccoby (Ed.), *The development of sex differences.* Stanford: Stanford University Press, 1966.

Kreps, J. *Sex in the marketplace.* Baltimore: Johns Hopkins Press, 1971.

Lipman-Blumen, J. How ideology shapes women's lives. *Scientific American,* 1972, *226*(1), 34-42.

Lyness, J.L., Lipetz, M.E., & Davie, K.E. Living together: An alternative to marriage. *Journal of Marriage and the Family,* 1972, *34,* 305-311.

Masters, W.H. & Johnson, V.E. *Human sexual response.* Boston: Little, Brown, 1966.

Mead, M. *Culture and commitment.* Garden City, New York: Doubleday, 1970.

Parsons, T. & Bales, R.F. *Family, socialization and interaction process.* Glencoe, Illinois: The Free Press, 1955.

Rand, L.M. & Miller, A.L. A developmental cross-sectioning of women's careers and marriage attitudes and life plans. *Journal of Vocational Behavior,* 1972, *2,* 317-331.

Schlossberg, N. & Goodman, J. A woman's place: Children's sex typing of occupations. *Vocational Guidance Quarterly,* 1972, *20,* 266-270.

Sherr, L. Democratic women. *Saturday Review: Science,* 1972, *55*(32), 6-8.

Slater, P.E. *The pursuit of loneliness: American culture at the breaking point.* Boston: Beacon Press, 1972.

Steinem, G. Sisterhood. *MS,* 1972, *1*(2), 46-59.

Stoller, R.J. *Sex and gender.* New York: Science House, 1968.

Tanner, L.B. (Ed.). Lilith's Manifesto. Women: A journal of liberation, Fall, 1970. *Voices from women's liberation.* New York: New American Library, 1970.

Teevan, J.J., Jr. Reference groups and premarital sexual behavior. *Journal of Marriage and the Family,* 1972, *34,* 283-291.

Tesch, P.A. The phantom image. Paper delivered at a conference on *Women in higher education: Some unanswered questions,* Johnson Foundation, Wingspread, Racine, Wisconsin, March, 1972. University of Wisconsin-Milwaukee. Mimeographed.

Thompson, C.M. *On women.* (M.R. Green, Ed.) New York: New American Library, 1971.

Tiger, L. & Fox, R. *The imperial animal.* New York: Holt, Rinehart & Winston, 1971.

Wallace, W.L. *Student culture.* Chicago: Aldine, 1966.

Weitzman, L.J., Eifler, D., Hokada, E., & Ross, C. Sex-role socialization in picture books for pre-school children. *American Journal of Sociology,* 1972, *77,* 1125-1150.

Westervelt, E.M. New feminists and suburban housewives: Allies or opponents? In J. Katz (Ed.), *The quest for autonomy in adult women.* New York: Van Nostrand, 1973.

Wilson, K. Report to member colleges—college research center. Princeton: Educational Testing Service, 1971. Mimeographed.

Women's Bureau, Employment Standards Administration, U.S. Department of Labor. *Continuing education programs and services for women.* Washington, D.C.: U.S. Government Printing Office, 1971a.

Women's Bureau, Employment Standards Administration, U.S. Department of Labor. *Women workers today.* Washington, D.C.: U.S. Government Printing Office, 1971b.

Women's Division, Institute of Life Insurance. *Family news and features,* May 30, 1972.

Zinberg, D. *College: When the future becomes the present.* Paper delivered to the New York Academy of Sciences, Conference on *Successful women in the sciences,* May, 1972.

Women in Groups

RITA M. WHITELEY
University of California—Irvine

All history attests that man has subjugated woman to his will, used her as a means to promote his selfish gratification, to minister to his sensual pleasures, to be instrumental in promoting his comfort; but never has he desired to elevate her to that rank she was created to fill. He has done all he could to debase and enslave her mind; and now looks triumphantly on the ruin he has wrought, and says the being he has thus deeply injured is his inferior. . . . But I ask no favors for my sex . . . all I ask of our brethren is that they will take their feet from off our necks and permit us to stand upright on that ground which God designed us to occupy (Grimke, 1838, pp. 10 ff.).

A few minor changes in idiom to up-date the language would make this statement by the 19th century feminist Sarah M. Grimke quite contemporary, as any woman who has had her 20th century consciousness raised will attest.

This article is for the men who still don't know what women are doing in those "groups," (isn't it just Bridge Club without the Bridge?) and for anyone else who would like a better understanding of the issues that women are working on with each other and with themselves in their efforts to bring to their own lives the liberation demanded by Sarah Grimke and others so long ago. (The Feminist Movement has a much longer and more interesting history than most of us realize. For an excellent account see *The Rebirth of Feminism*, by Judith Hole and Ellen Levine, 1971.)

A major innovation of 20th century feminists—and one which may contribute greatly to a better outcome for the contemporary movement—is the "group." The earliest and most familiar in name is the consciousness-raising group, which focuses on making women aware of their condition *as women* and on breaking down the barriers that exist between women as a result of their social conditioning. The emphasis is on making women aware that their relationship with men is a *class* relationship. This challenges the traditional view of male-female relationships as individual interactions between two unique, "equal" persons. Consciousness-raising is to overcome the psychological isolation of women produced by the culture's treatment of

With: Patricia F. Becker, Joan Z. Cohen, Mira Craig, Beverly Hotchner, Patricia Jakubowski, Ann G. Montgomery, and Linda Sobota.

male-female relationships. The isolation could be broken down if women could get together, begin identifying with one another, stop competing with one another and step outside the self-rejection that precludes intimacy with other women.

A feminist writer remarks:

> Women see each other all the time, open their mouths, and make noises but communicate on only the most superficial level. We don't talk to each other about what we consider to be our real problems because we are afraid to look insecure, because we don't trust or respect each other, and because we are afraid to look or be disloyal to our husbands or benefactors (Jones, 1970, p. 60).

The earlier consciousness-raising groups had a distinctive anti-therapy orientation, and indeed, "therapy" of any sort is still greatly suspect in the movement. The reasons for the initial anti-therapy bias of consciousness-raising groups still exist, for the most part. Basically, therapy suggests individual personal problems—that it is the individual, in this case the woman, who must work out her own neurotic problem or her own particular difficulties in her "personal adjustment." What consciousness-raising was all about was making women aware that their "problems" were not the result of individual failures in relationships but a common and shared result of the experience of being a woman in a sexist society. Thus, it is the male-dominated social structure that is the patient, not the woman.

Another reason for the continuing distrust of therapy in the women's movement is the recognition on the part of feminists that traditional psychotherapy is a male-dominated profession employing male-defined criteria of mental health derived from male-developed theories of personality. Although psychoanalysis with Freud's view of "anatomy as destiny" is the arch-villain, most theories of personality, with the possible exception of the behaviorist school, while rejecting particular formulations of Freud, accept the implications of his theory and treat the behavior of women as biologically inherent rather than the product of social conditioning. Here we are concerned with psychotherapy particularly, but feminist analysis regards the data of all fields of behavioral inquiry as contaminated by the social judgments which society imposes on the "nature" of women.

Hole and Levine in *Rebirth of Feminism* (1971) present an exerpt from Ruth Herschberger's *Adam's Rib* (1948) to illustrate this kind of feminist analysis.

> The problem of preconceptions marring the validity of "scientific" observation is thrown into sharp relief by Ruth Herschberger when she writes a fictional account (based on an actual study) of an interview with a female chimpanzee whose behavior patterns, vis-a-vis a male chimpanzee, had been duly observed and recorded by a scientist. The lady chimpanzee exclaims at one point:

> When Jack takes over the food chute, the report calls it his
> "natural dominance." When *I* do, it's "privilege"—conferred
> by him . . . while I'm up there lording it over the food chute,
> the investigator writes down "the male temporarily defers to
> her and allows her to act as if dominant over him." Can't I get
> any satisfaction out of life that isn't *allowed* me by some male
> chimp? Damn it! (Herschberger, 1948, cited in Hole and
> Levine, 1971, pp. 173-174)

It is a small step from the top of the food chute to the therapist's couch.

Recently there is a new interest in therapy as an extension of consciousness-raising. The result is therapy groups for women only, which are either led by female therapists or are leaderless. For an excellent discussion of this type of group, see "Encounter Groups for Women Only" by Betty Meador, Evelyn Solomon and Maria Bowen (1972).

As Meador et al. state,

> We do not intend to explore here the dividing line between culturally
> imposed restrictions and personal human limitations to growth and
> actualization. If such a line exists, and many people, particularly in the
> women's movement, say it does not, it is unclear at best (p. 336).

The move toward therapy as an extension of consciousness-raising is a move from definition and analysis of the problem in class terms to action by individual women in the context of that definition. Thus, the purpose of therapy is no longer helping the woman understand, accept and properly adjust to her "femininity," which is traditionally viewed as rooted in her biology and defined in terms of passivity, serving, submissiveness and dependence. Instead such groups are helping women to examine the consequences for them personally of the conditioning of the culture, to discover their own individuality rather than depending on their relationships with a man and children for their identity, to experience and nurture their own power and potency as a person rather than denying and suppressing these parts of themselves to please men and feed male egos, and, finally, to support women in whatever efforts they wish to make in redefining the sex roles they have in their relationships with others.

Although the movement from consciousness-raising to therapy is a current trend, it should be noted that many of the groups being formed at the present time involve women who are not politically conscious and who are not especially knowledgeable about issues in the evolution of the movement and the role of women's groups. Many of the groups are loosely structured around a particular interest or problem or "cause" that brings a specific group of women together. The content and process of the groups often move loosely back and forth from external problem-solving to social analysis to therapy for individual members.

The fact that such groups *are* being formed, however, in larger and larger numbers in many different places and among women of diverse socioeconomic backgrounds, attests to the validity of the movement's position that there is something radically wrong with the lives of women in our culture as they have been programmed to live them. While many women are still unaware of or hostile to women's groups, it is not unusual to encounter women who indicate some identification with the women's movement but at the same time reject the idea of a group experience as something they could benefit from.

Some of these women view joining a group as exchanging one kind of dependency for another. Others express a disrespect for other women as intimates and thus display their internalization of the culture's view of valuable time being that which is spent in the company of men. Possibly, many are not ready for a commitment to some kind of personal action or change which joining a group may represent.

Carol Hanisch and Elizabeth Sutherland in their treatise "Women of the World Unite—We Have Nothing to Lose But Our Men," cited in Hole and Levine, 1971, make this comment on resistance to the women's movement itself:

> A lot of women who may say they just want to play the traditional roles are simply fearful—or are unable to imagine other ways of being. Old roles can seem to offer a certain security. Freedom can seem frightening—especially if one has learned how to achieve a certain degree of power inside the prison. Maybe they are just afraid of choices. We don't seek to impose anything on women but merely to open up all possible alternatives; we do seek choice, as one of the functions which makes people human beings. We want to be full people, crippled neither by law or custom or our own chained minds. If there is no room for that in nature, then nature must be changed (p. 228).

The group from which the excerpts in the latter section of this article came is a loosely structured, leaderless one which began with a "cause" of sorts and moved into other areas. Most of the women in the group (which includes the author) either are Ph.D.'s or are in the process of completing a Ph.D. or graduate work at a lower level. Most are in the counseling profession and are employed by a university or secondary school and chose to use pseudonyms in the excerpts. The "cause" that served as the initial organizing impetus for the group was the dissatisfaction some of the women in the group felt about a confrontation of sorts they had with male colleagues where they worked. The group quickly moved beyond the original concern that brought them together.

The following excerpts were chosen to illustrate the kinds of issues women work on in groups. Regardless of the nature of the group, moderate to radical in membership, themes tend to emerge in the process of examining their situation as women. Although nearly a year has passed between publication and the meetings from which these excerpts were made, the issues remain timely.

The idea of a group of women getting together and taking themselves and each other very seriously without the permission, guidance and approval of men is very threatening to men. If you don't believe it, try it and watch the reaction. Jones (1970) analyzed the phenomenon as follows:

> The true objective nature of men must never become common knowledge lest it undermine in the minds of some males but most particularly in the minds of women the male right to rule. And so we participate in the process of our own domination.

In the following excerpt the group responds to one husband's complaint and gets into the issues of "playing by men's rules" and "checking it out with the man." "Checking it out with the man" is what we do with our decisions, ideas, plans and values in order to see if they are "okay," "reasonable," "intelligent," "rational" and approved of by a higher authority, since we are not capable generally of determining this for ourselves, due to our intrinsically emotional nature.

The women were refusing to "play by men's rules" in that they refused to define the value of what they were doing in terms of its relationship to men and they were beginning to question men's systems of defining "good behavior" for women.

Diane: Jack said that he thought this group was all right, but to really be good at all it ought to be meeting with men. I said that, well, the whole point of it was that we didn't feel we were being very successful in dealing with men about these issues and that we're regrouping to work out the issues with ourselves before we again try to work it out with men. He said that he didn't understand that. And he said, "if you're just going to talk Women's Lib in the abstract and how men persecute women, etc., then I don't think that's going to do any good. But if you're interested in working out individual kinds of relationships with men, then men would respond to that." What he was saying was that this would be more valuable if this were a male-female encounter group where we worked on our relationships with each other (between men and women), rather than an all-female group where we just sat around and talked about women in general.

Alice: Divide and conquer!

Carol: I can see the value of both, but I don't like the either/or quality of what he is saying. I really agree that the encounter group with men might be a growing experience for us and for them, but I wouldn't want to eliminate this experience.

Diane: Well, I think what he objects to is women confronting him with "this is the way men are and this is the way women are and women are persecuted, etc.," because he says "if *you've* got an axe to grind with *me,* that's fine. But I resent your talking about men or women in general and applying it to our relationship."

Alice: A lot of men I've talked with, including Ted, especially those who consider themselves liberal on most issues, get very hurt over being generalized about as having sexist attitudes. They protest that they are "different," that we are laying something on them that they don't feel, as if only construction workers and truck drivers are sexists. It seems to be similar to the reaction of white liberals to having their unconscious racism exposed.

Diane: Yeah, that's the feeling.

Alice: I had a really frustrating exchange with Ted and his brother, which ended up in them feeling very hurt and defensive. They were talking about a couple they know professionally. They were commenting on the dominance and superiority of the woman, professionally and personally, and they were really putting her down, making cracks about how she castrates men. I pointed out the implications of their finding that relationship so remarkable and their strong feelings about it.

Diane: If it had been the other way around, no one would ever have commented about it.

Alice: Right. And they got so defensive, so uptight, and they really couldn't even deal with that one point from my point of view, my perspective of what was going on between us. They just couldn't stand it. They would bring in all this extraneous stuff rather than deal with my point. And I wasn't saying "you male chauvinist pig, you evil person"; I was just saying, "you are reflecting the societal attitudes you've been brought up with, and yes, even *you* carry around sexist attitudes." But it really upset them. It's similar to a white liberal reaction in that they are people who have a big investment in feeling that they are ethical and loving persons, and these kinds of issues threaten them with the prospect of losing that image of themselves—like confrontation about their attitudes is saying, "well, maybe you're not the good person you think you are."

Gloria: Sounds like the men on our staff!!

Diane: Sure! Because a lot of men on our staff think they're a lot farther ahead than the general run of men, and I'm sure they are.

Gloria: And they feel that they *should* be.

Diane: And they *certainly* feel they *should* be; and so when we accuse them of not measuring up, or being one of these men that we're labeling in a certain way, they get much more uptight than an ordinary person off the street who'd say, "yeah, yeah, yeah" or "that's probably true" or "forget it." They get that hurt, kind of, "You don't *realize,* I'm much more liberated than that." I don't know what you do about it.

Alice: Ted said after that, "I really have thought about this a lot, and I came to the conclusion that your interest in Women's Lib is broader than just our relationship." He meant *that*—as opposed to "You're in Women's Lib because of the inadequacy of our relationship," or "Your interest in Women's Lib is a symptom of something wrong with how I am."

Eve: That must have been helpful for him to see that, really.

Alice: But I didn't realize he had been thinking the other—how much he had been personalizing it.

Helen: Yeah, like Alice wouldn't need that if everything were okay.

Diane: I don't know what that says about the possibilities of having male-female groups. I just wanted to throw in that comment of Jack's about our group.

Alice: I guess one of my reactions to Jack's comment is that it smacks of that same old garbage—"What could women be doing with each other that is really constructive?"

Betty: I guess that was partially what I was responding to earlier, but couldn't put it very well—something of a feeling of a put-down, not a constructive comment.

Diane: Yeah, that's what he was saying.

Eve: I don't feel that the purpose of what I'm doing here is just learning to deal better with men, although that's part of it. Another part is learning to feel better about ourselves and about each other.

Gloria: And about our role. I think the kinds of things we talk about here, feel strongly about here, are different than the way we usually present ourselves. Maybe some of the things we can help each other with have to do with awareness of how we come across, awareness of how we present ourselves sometimes in a way that gets us the most benefits—a calculated female way to get certain returns in a relationship. Everyone of us has relationships in which we play various roles, and one of the things this group has me thinking about is the times when women play roles that lead to men seeing them in the very ways we're complaining about.

Diane: Like sexual plaything.

Eve: It comes in handy sometimes.

Gloria: Very handy.

Diane: Especially with men who won't respond to anything else.

Eve: They get very annoyed with that, because they say you can't have it both ways. "If you want to be liberated, then you can't lapse back into that old junk—because then you're getting the best of both worlds."

Alice: What's wrong with that?

Helen: And only *men* can do *that.*

Eve: Well, that's how they feel, though. I've heard that from a lot of men.

Gloria: And they don't object so much to you coming on the other way; what they object to is when you come on liberated. Yet I don't think there's anything wrong with coming on all kinds of different ways, because you relate to different people different ways.

Diane: Except that I think it's unfair to men in a way—to come on both ways, because then they don't know which end is up. And that also reinforces in them that kind of hideous, game-playing behavior that just drives me crazy—convention behavior. And I hate that!

Alice: I really disagree that it's an either/or thing. Because *men* get to do either/or. Because *they* can really control it. They can control how they come on. They can play sexy or . . .

Helen: And *we're* supposed to be able to figure it out.

Alice: Yeah, and they can play intellectual or then can play friend. And nobody demands that they rigidly express only a certain part of themselves to make it easier on everyone. I don't think we're asking for some special thing.

Diane: But I don't really *like* that.

Gloria: I think I just want to be able to have the same freedom without being typecast. But given where people are right now, that's only going to reinforce their old image of you.

Betty: If the only reason for me to change my behavior is so that I don't reinforce an old, worn-out point of view, then that's not a good enough reason to change.

Diane: Well, it's a reason for *me* to alter my behavior, 'cause I can't *stand* to be involved in one of those rapo games—the kind of thing that goes on at conventions all the time. Like men cozing up to you and . . .

Helen: You're playing along.

Diane: And you're playing along.

Helen: And then you yell "rape."

Diane: And then you yell "Rape! Help! Get away from me." If a man wants to proposition me, I'd much rather him come up and say "How about it?" And then me be able to give him a "yes," "no," or "maybe." I really *hate* those kinds of things.

Betty: Well then, you don't have to act that way.

Diane: No, I don't.

Helen: Well I guess the only problem is in deciphering the message from the man. I guess *my* problem is in understanding what the message is. Well, *men* are playing games these days, too. There's this big business about let's be open and free with each other and honest and all that kind of stuff. So while *you're* being open and honest, that means one thing to you and something else to a man.

Betty: I'm thinking about an experience I had at a convention in Atlantic City. I was walking back to my hotel room when I passed this guy I had seen in some group meetings. He said, "Oh, I always wanted to talk to you; I've been noticing you." So we sat down on the steps and started talking, and he went into this big, open and honest thing, and I started freezing. He started coming closer and I started backing off. Then he said how cold I was.

Diane: Like "what's the matter with you?"

Betty: And I just started cutting the conversation off, not very well, but very abruptly; ended it off very rapidly and walked away. I came back to my room and I was very upset. I thought, "Gee, he sees me as a cold bitch. Why did I start that interaction; why didn't I just cut if off right away!" And, really, what the whole thing boiled down to was that I had all these irrational beliefs, and it was stupid for me to be so concerned about what his reactions were.

Diane: Okay, now that's exactly the kind of thing that would happen to me.

Betty: I think we need to work through our own irrational beliefs; it's not that we have to learn to present ourselves better to men.

Diane: I really get shook when somebody says, "oh, you cold fish!"

Betty: As I talk more in this group, I get more feelings of self-confidence and I'm more sure that, when I'm turning that guy off, it's not because I'm a cold, hostile bitch or because I am seductive but because maybe I was sucked in for some flattery and I was interested in flattery but I wasn't interested in anything else. So I didn't handle it very well, but that doesn't make me a bad person.

Gloria: When I brought this up, I was referring to a woman coming on in pretty obviously sensual ways to attain certain ends in a relationship in the most expedient manner. If I'm going to come on that way with a man a lot, then I shouldn't get mad at him for treating me that way.

Betty: That's a different situation.

Gloria: I think a lot of women do that and then, when some man comes back and treats them like a plaything, they get on their Women's Lib soapbox. I guess I'm talking about being more aware of how you come across.

Diane: I agree.

Alice: Maybe we're talking about several different things—like I agree that *anybody* who uses flattery and the promise of a good screw to achieve ends that more honestly and ethically should be achieved by some other means—like knowledge, work, etc.—deserves what he or she gets. But I'm objecting to what seems to me to be a demand for a one-dimensional woman if you want to be respected as a person. If you think of a man who comes to a party—or even a professional meeting—he can play sexy, come out with double-meaning jokes, do the bedroom stare, and all sorts of things, and then when he wants to, when he's ready, can switch over and have a serious discussion about something with you. And nobody cries "foul."

Betty: They accept the switch.

Alice: Right. They accept him in a variety of roles and behavior without saying "if you do that, then I'm justified in not taking you seriously in some other way." From my point of view, I'm just asking for the same kind of flexibility to be perceived when I want to move from certain kinds of behaviors to others or to present myself in different ways, with the same flexibility to be accepted as having the right and the capacity to be those different things. And a lot of times what you're being denied is not only the right but the *capacity.* Men want to cry "foul" when we express various parts of ourselves, but we've always accepted it in them—and so have they.

Eve: That's like allowing them to define the rules again.

Carol: That's one of the biggest problems. We're always playing by their rules.

Helen: And, you know, to me some of what Jack was saying is trying to get into the rules games again—like "You guys aren't playing it my way, and I've got a better way for you to play it."

Gloria: And if you don't play it my way, there's something the matter with you.

The psychological core of sexism has to do with personal power, and the culture conspires against the woman at all stages of her life to deny her personal power. The denial pervades the legal structure, the economic structure, her religious life, family life, and, probably most destructive of all, the psyche of the woman herself.

From the moment of birth the culture carefully feeds back to her its view of her nature, its expectations, which she must adopt for herself, and systematically rewards passive, deferential, dependent behavior. She learns to fear her strength as a barrier to love, social approval and "fulfillment."

Anyone who still doubts the reality of that socialization process need only look at Matina Horner's study "Fail: Bright Women" (1969) or Philip Goldberg's (1968) results when he asked a group of college women to evaluate a series of scholarly essays in one study and contemporary paintings in the second; each study presented the same works twice—once with a male author and once with a female author. "In both studies the women subjects judged the work of men to be significantly better than the *identical* work of women" (Goldberg, 1968). That women devalue one another's performance reflects their image of their own capacities.

The messages about achievement are just as insidious. A woman may be taught to value achievement by her family, but her own implementation of those values is expected to be a marriage to a man who actually can and will achieve. Even the item construction of a well-known vocational-interest test takes account of this message to women when it asks women to choose between being married to a rancher or to a corporation president and asks men to choose between *being* a rancher or a corporation president.

The 1968 Miss America protest documents (Morgan, 1970) succinctly pinpoint the societal expectations of achievement for females:

> In this reputedly democratic society, where every little boy supposedly can grow up to be President, what can every little girl hope to grow to be? Miss America. That's where it's at. Real power to control our own lives is restricted to men, while women get patronizing pseudo-power, an ermine cloak and a bunch of flowers; men are judged by their actions, women by their appearance (pp. 523-524).

In the following excerpt the group members begin to examine their beliefs about their abilities and expectations of achievement. The excerpt begins during a discussion of a talk by a feminist speaker who had recently visited a local campus.

Betty: She said one thing that touched me a great deal. I didn't realize how much it affected me until she said it. She talked about how women from different campuses were fighting to get administrative and higher level positions opened up for women. She had recently been at a meeting where fifteen women had been successfully working together to open these positions, and many of these women approached her and individually told her that they didn't feel they were the ones who should be put in that position, that someone else could do it better.

Diane: They were scared?

Fran: They didn't think they could do it!

Betty: She found this amazing that these women were that afraid—that they didn't have enough confidence in themselves to do the job—they were very afraid of success.

Eve: I'm surprised she found that so amazing.

Diane: And some of them were very well-known women, too. She said, "If I told you their names you'd know some of them."

Betty: It hit me when she said that and about two days later I had a personal experience that confirmed it.

Diane: Did you say, "Yes, I'll do it?"

Betty: No!

Diane: Oh no! (laughing) You said, "I can't!"

Betty: It's really amazing. I couldn't believe that I got that upset. Bill had run into this guy who worked for a certain organization, and Bill mentioned that I had given a speech on a certain topic, and one thing led to another, and this guy apparently had a decent-sized grant, and he became interested in me doing some staff training at a very large salary. Bill told me this. So I procrastinated about three days before I called the guy back. Meanwhile some staff changes took place and he booked me up with another person, a woman, and I procrastinated another three days before I called her. So finally I called her, and it was getting a little late . . . but I finally called and spoke to her about setting up a meeting. I finally went down to see her . . . today is Wednesday? . . . I guess it was this morning. (Laughter and exclamation from group member . . . "I guess it was this morning!?")

Betty: Well, it's faded from memory. (More laughter)

Betty: Last night I got depressed and I said to myself, "I'm *never* going to let Bill talk me into doing this kind of thing again."

Diane: Oh no! It's Bill's fault!

Betty: Right! Because I don't want to do it, I never wanted to do it, and I *can't* do it. And I felt shaken. And I said, "you know, I *can't* do this, and I don't know how to do this, I *can't* do it, and I don't even want to do it, and don't even want to go. I don't even want to go through the process—"

Diane: Of saying, "I can't do it"?

Betty: Yeah. And of feeling that I'm a fake and all my weaknesses are going to be out in the open and I can't possibly carry it out. And I would much rather not even be presented with the opportunity. And the feelings were very strong—and it took Bill a while before he was finally able to talk me into seeing that there was no guarantee that they were going to offer me anything—and that made me feel a lot better. (Laughter from the group)

Fran: Well, what happened?

Betty: I saw her and she *was* interested and I was incredibly tense, very, very, tense, and my mind kept wandering off. I couldn't think of things to say and my face felt all frozen and I talked very quietly and I couldn't smile very much. All I could think of was, "God, here I am talking about leadership training!!" (Laughter)

Eve: Well, I think that sometimes there are things that we really aren't able to do and we have to know what our limitations are and not try to do anything and everything because it's offered.

Diane: Sometimes it's hard to differentiate, though. Like I err on the side of "Gee, I don't think I can do it," when I know that sometimes men take on jobs in which they don't know what the hell they're doing. Now why can't *I* do that!

Betty: But they figure it out.

Diane: Yeah, they figure it out, and they do a reasonably good job. So I have real trouble making that kind of decision. I guess I'm always afraid someone will come along who does have experience or knowledge in the area and then say, "My God, they put *you* in that position? You don't know what the hell you're doing!"

Betty: But realistically there's not that much involved and the emotional reaction is out of proportion, so there must be something else going on—not just an ordinary fear of "oh, maybe I'll fail, or maybe I won't do so good, or I'm not sure what to do."

Alice: I wonder if one of the things that goes on about this is that being a woman is like having a wooden leg psychologically. I mean, you think of yourself as a handicapped person. It's like anything you achieve you can feel good about it, and there's not quite the risk about it, because if you don't make it you can say "because I'm a woman I didn't quite expect myself to anyway. And if I *do* do something very well, then I'm all the better off." If we do operate that way, then when we get in situations where that "out" isn't there, then I think *I* would get very anxious at times where my "out"—meaning my lower expectations—is taken away from me and I have to perform.

Diane: Perform like everybody else.

Alice: Right.

Diane: They have the same expectations of you that they have of everybody else.

Alice: Yeah.

Diane: It's like everything we achieve is gravy and we're so much the better for it. But nobody expects us to do that, necessarily, but if they *did* then you don't have any "out" at all. You have to put up or shut up.

Eve: It can keep a lot of women from doing anything but being a housewife.

Betty, Diane, and Alice, although achievement-oriented women by most standards, reveal their self-doubt and personal limit-setting—Betty and Diane through avoiding opportunities and Alice through establishing special circumstances in which her low expectations serve to minimize risk. The socialization of a female in our society robs her of confidence in her creative and productive energy and produces a psychological substratum of intellectual inertia that dogs her efforts to reject the adulthood for which she has been prepared. Vivian Gornick described her own such struggle (1971):

> And there are moments, and perhaps there always will be, when I fall back upon the old cop-out. Why should I trouble to win a chess game or a political argument when it is so much easier to lose charmingly? Why should I work when my husband can support me; why should I be a human being when I can get away with being a child? Women's liberation is finally only personal. It is hard to fight an enemy who has outposts in your head (p. 55).

In another interaction, Carol talks about her resentment of her husband's "parenting" of her while she acknowledges her own participation. Carol and Bob both seem to be struggling with the role expectations they brought to the marriage. A woman is expected to grow up and marry a man older, stronger, physically larger, more educated, more sophisticated sexually—and more experienced—who will take care of her and make all of her important decisions for her. A strong, high-achieving woman is pressed to choose in marriage, if she marries, an even stronger, higher-achieving husband in order to appropriately relate to him from an inferior position or else suffer either the pity or the censure of society. The parent-child implications in these role stereotypes are obvious.

Bob appears to be encouraging Carol to move toward equal responsibility in the marriage, without recognizing her equality as an adult person. Carol sees herself participating in the relationship they have but ambivalent about changing it.

Preceding this excerpt, group members were discussing playing bridge and tennis with men and receiving criticism and ridicule from them for their performance.

Alice: But it's *my* stupid thing! Why does the other person have to get all bent out of shape?

Carol: I don't know! I don't know what to think about this! That's been my verbal, intellectual argument to myself and Bob. We've hassled about this on numerous fronts, from bridge on up to life! "Baby, it's *my* life. Why are *you* so involved with *my* contract, or why do you get so upset about *my* grade?" But he's also saying to me, "here's why I'm involved with you; how much money you make next year really makes a difference to me, and if you don't get a job, if you screw around here and don't go out and interview and get a shitty job for next year—that's why I'm mad that you haven't done anything and that's why I'm involved and that's how come I'm having something to do with it. It's not just *your* life, we happen to be married." Well, I say the same thing as you, Alice, "I'm over here and you're over there and you're that person and I'm this person and how come you're so involved with me?" Then he proves it to me.

Betty: If you weren't married, what would you do about the job?

Carol: I'd do essentially the same things I'm doing now—the only difference would be that he wouldn't be sitting there worrying about it, reminding me, "Have you had an interview? Have you called so-and-so? I'm scared that you're not going to get a job." The only difference is *that* wouldn't be there. I would've done it anyway, the way that I did it.

Betty: So would you still *want* to get a job?

Carol: Oh, yeah! I would still *get* a job.

Diane: Just the anxiety would be missing.

Helen: That must do something to your confidence.

Alice: Sounds like the parent-child struggle we were mentioning earlier.

Carol: Yeah, all over. And I do that to him. I was engaged to one guy before I met Bob and went with another for two years before that one. And I rejected them both and went out searching for the perfect parent figure to marry! (Laughter) Yeah, these other two guys were different from Bob, and the way in which they were different was that I was as big as they were. I don't mean physically, I mean in psychological forcefulness.

Helen: You are psychologically as big as Bob!

Diane: You are!

Helen: Probably bigger!

Carol: I realize that. I've got a lot over him in a lot of different ways, but I'm *still* throwing that parent to him. And, oh, I'm still being his child.

Helen: Why don't you just *stop?* Say to yourself, stop it!

Carol: It's so hard.

Discussion of softball game at picnic where Carol and Bob were interacting:

Alice: He was telling you how to bat and so forth. I joined in and said "hit it between so and so." And he turned to me and shouted, "She can't do that! Don't tell her that! She'll just make an out. Maybe *you* could do it, but Carol can't do that!"

Diane: Oh! Just like a Daddy!

Carol: (Laughing) Should I have been embarrassed about that?

Alice: You should have turned around and said . . .

Helen: "Shut up!"

Fran: "Climb off!"

Alice: "Stick it in your ear!"

Carol: Instead I turn around and say, "Yes, Daddy."

Diane: "Oh, right! I *can't* do that, I forgot."

Eve: Well, I don't know how it is with Bob, but in many cases the man is worried that other people will think how could he marry such an incompetent boob who can't get a job, who can't do all these things that other wives can do who are married to successful enterprising men.

Helen: I get a different feeling about him. I think Carol has got to be superwoman. She's got to out-do all these women.

Eve: That's what I'm saying—indirectly that's where it ends up, because "Wow! that makes me superman, because I've got her."

Carol: Don't forget that Carol is in there wanting to be superwoman too. Bob didn't just lay that on me, it's me anyway.

Diane: And what's great about it then for him is that not only is she superwoman, but "I made her that because *I told* her how she ought to bat and how she ought to do it!"

Carol: Okay, yeah. That really hurts me! (Laughing) That's one thing that is my final blow. In an argument—I tell myself a thousand times that I would be where I am without him. I'd be doing what I am doing right now without him anyway. I guess he affected the "when," because the summer I met him I wasn't applying to graduate programs and two months after we met I was.

Betty: Sounds like your confidence is really getting undermined, because you're always wondering if you're doing it because he made this possible or his influence is there.

Carol: But the thing I really want to keep clear in my own head, and, incidentally, in yours, is that *I'm* doing this to Bob. Now, true, maybe he was out looking for the perfect child for a wife . . .

Diane: You both agree and participate in how you interact.

Carol: I'm treating him exactly as I treated my father. I *let* him do all of this to me. And, intellectually, we talk about it and say "look at what we do." But we're not getting out of it.

Alice: Do you feel scared about playing some other thing with him?

Carol: I think so.

Alice: What would happen if you say, "I don't need you for my parent"? What would that do to your relationship?

Carol: I don't know. We've been over a lot of this intellectually, and he says, "I'm wanting that to happen, I'm waiting for that to happen within you, to stop playing child, and I could stop playing parent. I'd really *like* it if we weren't into this parent-child bit. That'd be okay with me!" He's giving me good feelings about that future.

Alice: Sounds like what he's saying, though, is *you* stop first.

Carol: Yes.

The reasons for Carol's ambivalence about changing the relationship may lie in the uncertainty she expresses regarding her achievement—"Could I have done it without him?" It reflects a distrust of her own power, her own drive. She also expresses fear of the change; what she is afraid of is not clear. Perhaps it is a loss of the "certain degree of power inside the prison." Possibly she doesn't really believe she can be loved as a female who is also an adult. The issues are unclear, but it *is* clear that Carol is left with the initiative, as Bob says in true parent form, "I will treat you like an adult when you begin to act like one" (i.e., prove it, on *my* terms).

The socialization of women as domestic servants and vocational camp-followers of men has critical consequences for women who try to build some sense of identity for themselves apart from their relationship with men. The group considers some aspects of this dilemma and again confronts members with their own prejudice.

Gloria is mentioning a woman she had worked with:

Gloria: What she really is looking for is an identity for herself, something to say when people ask her, "What do *you* do?" Right now she thinks if she could say, "I'm a mother," that would be quite "acceptable." The emphasis seems to be on the image of herself she wants to project in answering that question, not on what she really feels. I suspect a lot of women opt for motherhood because that gives them an identity.

Eve: Well, what it amounts to is they don't have many other choices.

Alice: What is it they are trying to answer is in response to the question, "What do you do?"

Gloria: Or, "Who are you?" I think a lot of women want to answer that without saying "I'm married to so and so." They want to be able to say, "I'm Sally and I'm a sociologist." This woman I was talking about found her attempts at a career too upsetting and risky, but now she finds *not* having one—being viewed as only her husband's wife—pretty upsetting too. And I think she sees being able to say, "I'm a mother" as a legitimate excuse for not doing anything else. Yet I have many friends who *are* mothers who want to be able to say, "I'm a mother and I'm also a sociologist, etc." They feel that "Oh, I'm at home with the children" isn't an adequate answer to that question.

Diane: The question seems to be "What do you do that's worthwhile?"

Alice: "And worthy of respect and interest." But the criteria for that are all based on careerism and the kinds of activities men more traditionally can do. No wonder they feel bad about their answers.

Gloria: I have a friend who lives in New York and she belongs to a women's group there. She's the only one in the group who doesn't have a "career." I know her well enough to know she's pretty happy with what she's doing—her two children, her potting, her Planned Parenthood activities, and all the things she does—she's very happy with all that. But she's very self-conscious about having to say . . .

Eve: To justify it.

Gloria: The minute you say, "What do you do?" she gets terribly defensive and goes into an elaborate rationale for *why* she's not "doing something." And *when* she's going to do something else.

Helen: That's a terrible question to have put to you.

Diane: Yes, but a lot of people ask "Are you working?" . . . just as part of cocktail party conversation when you don't know anything about a person; that's what you are likely to say.

Alice: It seems like the question is then, "Is there anything interesting about you?" I know, myself, I am guilty of reacting with a "no" answer to myself when I encounter a woman who says something like "I'm at home with the children." And I usually write off that person without exploring what other things she may be into.

Eve: Sexist.

Alice: Yeah.

Helen: But I think we all do it to some extent.

Alice: But it shows how much we identify with those attitudes.

In the following session the women discuss their own difficulties as professional persons who also try to fulfill the traditional wife-mother sex roles. Gloria and Alice are typical of women who want to move out of culture-bound role definitions but find themselves too firmly entrenched in the value system they hope to modify if not escape.

After mentioning that she long had hopes of going to law school and how difficult it was to spend her time that way with two pre-school children to care for, Gloria despairs of ever being able to realize her goal. The group questions her discouragement about the future.

Gloria: But maybe by then I'd be less motivated to spend the time in law school and studying or be unable to go for some reason.

Eve: You might not be. You might be that much freer to do it then.

Gloria: But I *could* do it now, if I were willing to arrange my priorities that way.

Diane: But what about the sacrifices—to your marriage, to your kids?

Gloria: There'd be plenty—and I feel so responsible. I *am* responsible, let's not kid ourselves, for so much of that—the maintenance of the marriage, the kids and what happens in their day-to-day lives. When you're married to a doctor, it's hard to argue that your career obligations are as important as his. Right now part of me feels that somebody has to put some career things aside and it's obviously me. But since nobody, least of all George, is telling me I can't go to law school, maybe that says something about my own set of priorities.

Diane: A lot of it has to do with others and how willing they are to bend and help you out and take on the responsibilities you take on now. In fact, that's about 90% of it.

Alice: I was thinking about that today, and I find I'm still having a lot of problems in that area. Ted's rhetoric is great about accepting the changes I'm pushing for. He agrees with me all the time about everything. But he doesn't *do* that much that's different. Like we have a large wicker basket in the bedroom for laundry, and all you have to do is pull up the top and drop it in, but he drops it in piles on the floor around it. And he'll say, "umm . . . I *should* do that, you're right! It's my male chauvinism, oh, this is terrible. Yes, my mother, etc., it was my upbringing, uh huh." And it still piles up. The rhetoric is just fine. I couldn't ask for better rhetoric.

Helen: Maybe you need to get it across better that you really mean for him to do it.

Eve: Or you're just not going to.

Alice: Yeah, but then I have trouble with the consequence of that. I've tried being funny about it.

Helen (sarcastically): Have you tried being hysterical?

Alice: Well, subtle versions of nagging.

Diane: What about if you just didn't say anything about it one way or another and just let it pile up? And just didn't do the laundry?

Alice: Well, I do that, but I have a person who comes in two days a week and I'm really embarrassed on those days when she comes, because things look so bad.

Eve: Well, let *him* be embarrassed. Why are you embarrassed?

Diane: Because that means you're not a good wife and mother?

Alice: Yes. And I'm sure her values are such that she goes around mumbling to herself and saying . . .

Diane: You're asking yourself to fit all expectations.

Gloria: To be all things to all people! Work full time in a professional career, be a total professional and play companion to Ted, a supermother to Mark . . .

Diane: And the cleaning woman's got to be impressed with your housekeeping too. Really, Alice, what difference does it make what the cleaning woman thinks! I say that, but I realize that I run around and pick up things in a frenzy when the babysitter comes.

Alice: I don't clean up their stuff. I clean up mine. But I feel terrible about it. I just . . . feel bad. I don't do it anymore. I just feel bad about it. My choices seem to be to feel bad or be a nag, and that feels bad too.

Gloria: Leave it there, don't clean it up, and tell her not to pick it up either.

Eve: Yeah, stop being responsible for it.

Alice: Oh sure; do *you* want to try to deal with Mrs. Martin about it? "Just leave that, Mrs. Martin." "No, I'll do it, I'll do it. I don't mind!" That takes up more energy to deal with her about it than to just pick it up myself. (Laughter)

Diane: And it becomes a contest over who's the best housekeeper . . .

Alice: Who's the best woman. No, they can leave it, and she'll pick it up. In fact, Mark said yesterday, "I think we're going to have to have Mrs. Martin come tomorrow instead of Friday." And Ted asked "Why?" And Mark said, "Well, all the glasses are dirty and all the silverware's dirty and there isn't anything to eat off of or drink out of. . ." (Laughter) And I wanted to scream, "Well, why in the hell don't you wash them!!!" (Laughter) "Why does somebody with a vagina have to wash them!!!!"

In the next group meeting where redefining housework responsibilities is discussed, Alice has some progress to report:

Alice: Well, I think we've gone through some stages—like at first Ted was agreeable to being helpful and "sharing" responsibilities, but it wasn't "sharing" in the real sense. It was rather that he was helping me do *my* work. He still saw it as *my* job, *my* work.

Diane: Yeah, and that attitude doesn't change.

Alice: No, it hasn't much. But I guess there are some signs of moving beyond that.

Betty: Like what?

Alice: I got really excited the other day when Ted was in the kitchen doing the dishes and I had been reading something that I wanted to share with him. So I walked in the kitchen and, before I could say a word, he turned and held up a dirty soup bowl and said, "Look at this! It takes a lot of work to get these clean when they have dried soup on them! From now on I want you to rinse out your soup bowls instead of just leaving them in the sink like this!" He said it in a kind of nasty way, too.

Gloria: That's wonderful!

Diane: He's beginning to take it seriously!

Alice: Yes! That's what I thought! I also had this funny, evil feeling of pleasure—a sort of satisfaction and relief because I stood there and looked at him behaving in a sort of nagging, petty, concerned-with-trivia way, when I had come in to him all prepared to share something important to me. It was such a role reversal!

Diane: You usually play the other role—the housewifey woman . . .

Gloria: Who's too concerned with the dishes or the dirty floor or the mundane child-rearing responsibilities to respond to her husband's intellectual interests.

Alice: Right! Right!

Eve: How do you mean "relief"?

Alice: That it wasn't just something about *me*. Washing dishes could do that to *him*, too. It wasn't *me* who was just sort of innately petty and witchy. It's the role!!!

Betty: That's a really good discovery!

The group did not stay with Gloria's ambivalence toward pursuing a law degree. What response was made appeared to support her reluctance and sense of futility, perhaps because the other women share both her perspective on her role and her doubts about her capacity to accomplish her goal in such circumstances. Usually there is little reward and support to be gleaned from family and friends for such a goal. A woman making such efforts is likely to be bombarded with messages to the effect that her importance and, indeed, worth for others lie in what she does for them, not in what she might dream to do for herself.

Alice's experience speaks for itself and indicates the value of the group's support for individual members to continue working on issues outside the group.

When the women in the group found the boundaries of their own liberation from social role conditioning on particular issues, the group "blocked" and movement halted. A difficult issue which obviously frustrated group members was the situation of Helen, who was considering the potential problems of living together with her male friend and her young daughter.

Helen: I've been thinking about in my case, since I have a daughter, what effect would that have on Pam? The social stigma of going to school, etc.

Carol: I think right now if you're talking about living together instead of getting married, for 98% of the women, you're talking about a one-up, one-down position, no matter what. No matter how subtle it is, the woman, probably in her head, in the guy's head and in all of society's head, is one-down.

Helen: I think it's society's.

Diane: I think it's society's, but I don't think it necessarily has to be true in any one relationship.

Carol: But it's very hard, and I think there are very few people now who can buck their learning and society's inputs to not have some of that one-down feeling for the woman.

Gloria: I think it's a one-down feeling only if you have a child. If you are just *you,* an independent person, you're not one-down.

Alice: Except that a woman doesn't feel that independence like a man does, especially if she's programmed from birth to grow up and get a man to marry her. The equality of independence is only theoretical, and most of us aren't liberated enough to really experience that in that kind of relationship.

Carol: It seems to me that the business of "trying harder," putting more effort into pleasing the other person, etc. you do when you live together—as Gloria was mentioning—is like saying I've really got to struggle to keep him because I'll be worse off without him.

Alice: I would think it would be difficult for you, Helen, in that what meanings or interpretations or perceptions that Pam would make of the situation aren't within only your control.

Diane: Or what her friends would say.

Alice: Right, that there are other kinds of inputs into her about that kind of situation. If it could be within the control of you and Pete, and be a threesome thing, then it could be managed very well, with understanding and communication. But when she starts getting inputs from other people who may perceive it in other terms, in a way like, "what's wrong with your mother that the guy won't marry her?" or "what's wrong with the two of you? Doesn't he really want you?" Really ugly things like that would be very hard for her.

Diane: On the other hand, I think Helen is in a real bind; because I wouldn't marry *anybody* now without living with him first. And we're almost saying, "Helen, *you* can't do that." This is just really hard for you. I don't know how you handle that.

Gloria: There are all sorts of ruses or facades you could use to deal with the perceptions of others, but they wouldn't fool Pam, of course. She's too old for that.

Diane: She would run right after a playmate and say, "That's not my father. That's my mother's boyfriend."

Eve: "And they're living together!" (Laughter)

Alice: Maybe you can talk with Pam and get her to understand that this is what you're doing and why.

Eve: Well, you may get *her* to understand, but what about her friends?

Alice: OK, and explain to her that different people have very different ideas about these things, and she may find that other people don't like this sort of thing.

Carol: Why not get married and save all the hassle?

Helen: I'm not ready and neither is he. Neither of us are certain enough of the relationship. The natural thing to do, if it weren't for Pam, would be to live together. His leaving [due to a company transfer] makes it so much harder, too. If I don't go with him, I don't know what two years' separation would do to the relationship. And I know that I don't want to marry someone I haven't lived with and know very well.

Diane: Well, what if you don't pretend and just do it.

Helen: Well, I could handle it. But I just don't think I should do it with Pam.

Eve: Well, maybe you're thinking too much of Pam. We do that, you know. There's so much pressure on us to put anything that might be in the child's interest totally before our own interests as persons.

Diane: Yeah. Does he have any ideas about how you could solve this thing?

Helen: We've talked about it a lot. And I think it finally hit him a few days ago how much more I really have to lose—not lose, deal with, I guess, in trying to work out a way for us to be together. I just don't know if there's an answer to this.

Quite evident here is the conflict between Helen's private sense of what would be an arrangement most enhancing of her "self," i.e., one in which she would have an opportunity to experience more intimately the relationship before making a deeper commitment to it, and the public sanctions against such a relationship (for females only; a male parent in the same situation is often admired either secretly or openly as a consummate exploiter or as a sympathetic figure looking for a mother for his children).

Especially striking in this vignette is the symbolic position of Pam, the child female vulnerable to society's definitions of her worth and desirability. Helen's seeking to maintain her own growth through an equal and choosing relationship may not survive her identification with the vulnerability of the daughter. The group's sense of defeat perhaps belies such an identification for all of them.

After the group disbanded through attrition to new jobs in new places, some of the members wrote about the meaning the group experience had for them. Most of the women saw the experience as one which changed their feelings about other women and ultimately themselves.

Fran: For me the group was an opportunity to relate to the women I know in a totally different way; to experience an honesty and intimacy with other women that I have never felt before.

Alice: I think we all found a genuine enjoyment of each other, a stimulation and excitement in each other's ideas and observations of our experience, which shattered some of our assumptions about ourselves and other women as intellectually competent beings. I used to think that if I wanted to have a really good discussion with someone about ideas, I had to go to a man. And I now realize I turned that belief back on myself unconsciously and felt insecure about myself intellectually. In the process of coming to respect other women's minds, I came to have more respect for my own.

Betty: I feel more respect for myself as a woman. Before our group, I didn't realize that, in some insidious way, I thought less of myself because I was a woman. I had always wanted to have all the strength and drive I attributed to man and all the sensitivity and warmth I attributed to woman. To be very strong, to be very soft. To be the former was to be "castrating." To be the latter was to be professionally passive. I could be both but usually not at the same time. In the group I learned greater acceptance of myself and trust in my own reactions and wants, whether or not they fit stereotyped feminine behavior. When I learned that many of my feelings were not a "sickness" but shared by other women, I felt stronger and less disappointed in myself. I am learning in a new way how to be a strong, professionally committed woman and how to use my abilities, for when this group started I was just becoming aware of my conflicted feelings about professional productivity, of my incompletely understood fears about career success and failure, of my feelings of having risen too fast, when my self-concept hadn't caught up with what was happening to me professionally, and when I had almost decided to be soft rather than strong, and still thought that I had to be "either/or."

Gloria: The group has really been a good experience for me on several levels. It's been a chance to try to work through some issues of great interest and concern to me; I've had an opportunity to explore feelings and test out ideas without having to deal with indignation, derision or outright hostility so often encountered elsewhere when women's issues are even mentioned. Before this, I usually avoided doing things with groups of women—I guess I really bought the notion that things done with "just women" were somehow less worthwhile, less important and enjoyable than things done by or with men. That simply hasn't been true of this experience. It's been interesting and fun, as well as a time to share some personal concerns and feelings that I found I really *needed* to share, in a group of women I enjoyed more and more as I got to know them better outside of the professional setting in which most of us work.

Eve had a different experience of the group:

Eve: My modus operandi in the group was mostly to sit back and listen; I didn't want to appear a leader who was more knowledgeable as a result of my prior experience—at least that is what I told myself until I began writing this appraisal. What was really happening to me was a classic case of "I'm not OK, you're OK."—a feeling that has plagued me in my relationships with women as far back as I can remember. I did feel "ahead" in the sense that the problems they discussed vis a vis men and role expectations were experiences I had worked through. But I felt my colleagues to be much more verbal, clever, creative, and attractive than I. Now I realize that I am faced with the competitiveness phenomenon again in a different guise. I am upset to recognize that my former groups had not helped me to deal with this problem and that I am far from liberated!

This epiphany makes me feel that our group is only in its first stage of evolution—the stage of dealing with issues in the world at large. It is far easier for women to deal with issues with husbands or male relationships and professional hang-ups as women, because those ideas and interchanges are all out there somewhere. It is neither so safe nor so comfortable to deal with each other here and now and to look at how we are interacting with and feeling about each other. Once, early in the group, I brought up some of those feelings, and the group attempted to deal with those personal, potent feelings. But people left feeling uncomfortable, and we never got back to that level of interchange again. I now realize that if we are to be a successful group, we must do that. In a large sense, this gives us a *raison d'être* for continuance.

Eve's goals for relating to the other women appear to be more personal, when most of the others were content to share feelings about themselves and their relationships outside the group. In this initial stage of coming together with other women, most of the group seemed to value the process of developing a new perspective on themselves and their individual human condition through the sharing and support of others.

Eve's observation on the group's avoidance of personal confrontation raises the question of how deeply felt and permanent were the women's changed attitudes toward other women. As Eve remarked later, "Perhaps this sense of caring or community is the last stage of development that follows on the heels of having struggled through the other stages."

The process of "consciousness-raising" has been likened to the practice of revolutionary groups, particularly the Chinese peasants, of "speaking bitterness." Juliet Mitchell (1971) labels it a "reinterpretation made by middle-class women . . . in a country riddled by psychotherapeutic practices" (p. 62). She relates the process as follows:

These peasants, subdued by violent coercion and abject poverty, took a step out of thinking their fate was natural by articulating it. The first symptom of oppression is repression of words; the state of suffering is so total and so assumed that it is not known to be there. "Speaking bitterness" is the bringing to consciousness of the virtually unconscious oppression. . . . In having been given for so long their own sphere, their "other" world, women's oppression is hidden far from consciousness (this dilemma is expressed as "women don't want liberating"); it is this acceptance of a situation as "natural" or a misery as "personal" that first has to be overcome. "Consciousness-raising" is speaking the unspoken (p. 62).

The consequence of the process reported by the women in this group varied from more self-acceptance to an awareness of anger:

Helen: I feel better about myself—or at least have a better sense of the legitimacy of my feelings and concerns.

Gloria reported . . .

a heightened awareness of the assumptions of the relative value and competence of men and women instilled in me as I grew up; what women *ought* to want and how they *ought* to go about getting it in order to be "good women." To some extent the experience has helped to free me from the "oughts" and allowed me to at least start looking at what *I want.*

For Diane,

the group became . . . a catalyst for growth and self-discovery and the impact has extended far beyond the issues that first brought us together.

Alice: A common complaint about women's groups is that they make women angry. My own experience is that the group didn't "make" me angry. It just helped me discover that I was. I had told myself I felt depressed. Now I have some sense of being angry and can begin to ask myself what I'm angry about and work on the problem. I think for a woman the most difficult consequence of experiencing her anger is facing up to the decision that inevitably comes—what are you going to *do* about it? One answer, "nothing," forces her to experience *choosing* the state she is dissatisfied with, and SHE knows that "choice" is made out of discouragement that has seeped into her since birth. The other possibility is uncharted territory, but there are plenty of signs around that say "danger" and "travel at your own risk," and "the management will not be responsible for lost or misplaced . . ." and there are little voices in her that say "girls can't do that" (you'll fail) and "we don't like little girls who . . ." (nobody will love you if . . .).

While the women in the group report mostly positive feelings and experiences from the group, the excerpts make it clear that change and growth aren't so easy and even thinking about it comes hard. *Doing* something, as Alice observes, is even more difficult. The last part of her statement is also instructive of where this process might take a person:

After finally securing not only Ted's agreement but actual participation in doing housework and then finding myself having anxiety attacks when the time came for him to do his share, I began to learn something about myself. I began to realize that what I learned in growing up female was that to be loved and to have worth and value as a person I was supposed to serve others, "do for" others, take care of others. When I stepped out of those role behaviors, I feared the loss of the rewards that went with them. The realization of what I was feeling and why just made me more angry at first. I felt trapped by my intellectual rejection of a belief system that I couldn't disengage from emotionally. Through sharing and struggling together with these feelings, what is happening now is that I have stopped doing many of the old things and I continue to receive caring and respect from Ted; and I am feeling it.

REFERENCES

Goldberg, P.A. Are women prejudiced against women? *Trans-Action,* April, 1968, 28-30.

Gornick, Vivian. Woman as outsider. In Gornick, V. & Moran, B.K. (Eds.), *Women in a sexist society.* New York: Basic Books, 1971.

Grimke, Sarah. *Letters on equality of the sexes and the conditions of women.* New York: Burt Franklin, 1838.

Herschberger, Ruth. *Adam's rib.* New York: Pellegrini and Cudohay, 1948.

Hole, Judith & Levine, Ellen. *The rebirth of feminism.* New York: Quadrangle Books, 1971.

Horner, Matina. Fail: Bright women. *Psychology Today,* 1969, *3,* 36-41.

Jones, Beverly. The dynamics of marriage and motherhood. In Morgan, R. (Ed.), *Sisterhood is powerful.* New York: Vintage Books, 1970.

Meador, Betty, Solomon, Evelyn, & Bowen, Maria. Encounter groups for women only. In Solomon, N.A. & Berzon, B. (Eds.), *New perspectives on encounter groups.* New York: Jossey-Bass, 1972.

Mitchell, Juliet. *Woman's estate.* New York: Pantheon Books, 1971.

Morgan, Robin (Ed.). *Sisterhood is powerful.* New York: Vintage Books, 1970.

Perspectives
on Counseling Bias:
Implications
for Counselor Education

NANCY K. SCHLOSSBERG
University of Maryland

JOHN J. PIETROFESA
Wayne State University

We are concerned about the ease with which educators, and counselors in particular, adopt as "God-given" certain notions about appropriate behavior. For example, when counseling a 55-year-old widow about entering college, a black man about becoming a banker, or a single adult male about adopting a female child, the counselor's "God-given" notions about appropriate behavior can play an unconscious part in counseling. Counselors defend themselves as being conveyors of reality and not decision-makers for their clients. Yet client self-reports contain many references about the negative impact counselors have had on career development. For some counselors, dispensing discouragement rather than encouragement has been the order of the day. Many minority group members and women have been limited by inappropriate counseling and testing.

Counselor bias is here defined as an opinion, either unfavorable or favorable, which is formed without adequate reasons and is based upon what the bias holder assumes to be appropriate for the group in question. Bias is evident whenever it is assumed that someone can or cannot take a certain course of action because of her or his age, social class, sex, or race. The difference between bias and prejudice is the ease with which bias can be discarded when a new reality is made evident. Bias becomes prejudice when the role ascription serves a deep-seated need of its holder. Prejudice is resistant to information which might lead to a changed belief. Some people need scapegoats, and re-education is often impossible in instances like this. Allport (1958, p. 12) states, "In most cases prejudice seems to have some 'functional significance' for the bearer." A great deal has been written about prejudice and its relationship to personality disorder; but little has been written about bias and its effects in the helping relationship.

We are assuming that counselors are like people in general—no better, no worse. We all share one thing: we make judgments about appropriate behaviors for different groups of people. Such prejudgments may be important in influencing the behavior of others.

Rosenthal and Jacobson's studies (1968) illustrate the degree to which attitudes about particular children's competency do, in fact, affect performance. As expectancy rises, so does performance. One person's expectations of another's behavior come to act as a self-fulfilling prophecy. Thus, if a counselor assumes that: 65-year-olds should not enter doctoral work; 45-year-olds should not begin to produce and raise children; 25-year-olds should not be college presidents; women should not be corporate executives; men should not do laundry, bed cleaning, diaper changing, or combing of little girls' hair; lower-class blacks should not live side by side with millionaires—then this will probably be reflected in the counseling interview.

Even though a large percentage of women work, and a large percentage of workers are women, their position has startingly declined in recent years. The facts are alarming; women work at lower-level, lower-paying jobs than men. While more women are working than ever before, they are under-represented in the professional technical categories. Women also receive proportionately fewer advanced degrees than in the 1920's (Millett, 1968; Manpower Report of the President, 1967).

Complicating the picture is the fact that each sex occupies different levels on the status hierarchy and the sexes are unevenly distributed as to field of endeavor. It has been substantiated that

> American education is blighted by a sex-split in its curriculum. At present the whole field of knowledge is divided along tacit but well understood sex lines. Those subjects given the highest status in American life are "masculine"; those given the lowest are "feminine" . . . thus math, the sciences . . . business administration . . . are men's subjects . . . and the humanities are relegated . . . "suitable to women" (Millett, 1968, p. 14).

> Discrimination in the world of work can be easily seen when one examines the number of women in certain high-status fields. For example, only 208 women are listed among the 6,597 members of the American Institute of Physics. One half of the women are employed as physics teachers. Of the 600,000 people classified as in engineering and related technical fields, only 6,000 are women. About 7 percent of chemists, 3 percent of all dentists, and 4 percent of the doctors are women (Cassara, 1963, p. 77).

This unbalanced occupational distribution of the sexes needs to be critically examined from the vantage point of counselors.

This article offers no incontrovertible data but merely tries to bring perspective to a topic which we need to acknowledge and act upon. We are educable. We can help ourselves with new perspectives. We can free ourselves from ideas which restrict our thinking and which, in turn, may restrict our client's behavior. As one counselor said to a class, "men may marry women who are willing to be kept barefoot, pregnant, and behind the plow; it's quite another thing for counselors to impose these views on counselees."

COUNSELOR BIAS AND SEX-ROLE ASCRIPTION

Sex bias appears to be an important component of some individuals' emotional makeup. Traditionally, women have been viewed as biologically inferior human beings. Because of this discrimination, women have maintained a position secondary to men in family life, education, and work. Ginzberg (1971) stated,

> The increasing acceptance of women as workers represents a clear challenge to guidance. The field has paid inadequate attention to women at every stage of the career process: in curriculum and course selections, in career planning, and in assisting those who seek to return to the labor force after a period of homemaking and childbearing (p. 318).

Since people in general hold strong beliefs about sex-appropriate behavior, we can assume that counselors also hold these notions. Since these notions are currently being challenged as biased, counselors need to be aware of the degree to which they try to push counselees into certain directions because of their own sex biases. Gardner (1971) states,

> Right now, in our excessively sexist society, it is unlikely that anyone without special training in feminism can create conditions which would encourage females to "exercise their right to select goals of the counselor." The goals of counselors trained in traditional programs can hardly be expected to do other than reflect the sexist values (p. 173).

Counseling Interview

While it can be assumed that counselors "support" equality for both sexes, several works have dealt with sex-stereotyping attitudes of clinicians. These works will be described in some detail to examine the generally untested notion that counselors do in fact counsel from a stereotyped framework.

In a landmark study, Broverman *et al.,* (1970), utilizing a sex-role-stereotype questionnaire, studied actively functioning clinicians. They hypothesized that "clinical judgments about characteristics of healthy individuals would differ as a function of sex of person judged and, furthermore, that these differences in clinical judgments would parallel stereotypic sex-role differences." They also felt that behaviors and characteristics considered to be healthy for a sex-unspecified adult will resemble behaviors judged healthy for males and differ from behaviors judged healthy for their female counterparts. The subjects were 79 clinically trained psychologists, psychiatrists, or social workers (46 males, 33 females)—all working in clinical settings. Ages ranged from 23 to 55 years, while experience covered the spectrum from internship to extensive professional work. The authors utilized the Stereotype Questionnaire composed of 122 bipolar items—each pole characterized as typically masculine or feminine. The results indicated that high agreement existed among clinicians—both male and female—about the attributes characterizing healthy adult men, healthy adult women, and healthy adults with sex unspecified.

It appears that a "double standard of health" exists among clinicians. The researchers note that

> More likely, the double standard of health for men and women stems from clinicians' acceptance of an "adjustment" notion of health; for example, health consists of a good adjustment to one's environment. In our society, men and women are systematically trained, practically from birth on, to fulfill different social roles. An adjustment notion of health, plus the existence of differential norms of male and female behavior in our society, automatically leads to a double standard of health. Thus, for a woman to be healthy, from an adjustment viewpoint, she must adjust to and accept the behavioral norms for her sex, even though these behaviors are generally less socially desirable and considered to be less healthy for the generalized competent, mature adult (p. 6).

Clinicians are significantly less likely to attribute traits which characterize healthy adults to a woman than they are to attribute these same traits to a healthy man. The clinicians appear to reflect stereotypes no different from the general population. This tends to support our earlier contention that counselors are no better or worse than other societal members in terms of sex bias. Obviously, clinicians need to examine critically their attitudes and position with respect to the adjustment notion of health.

Thomas and Stewart (1971) tried to "determine whether secondary school counselors respond more positively to female clients with traditionally feminine (conforming) goals than those with traditionally masculine (deviate) goals." Information concerning the home, school, self-description, and personal values of high school girls were presented on audiotape to 64 practicing counselors, and their responses were analyzed by sex and experience. The findings are as follows: "(a) Female counselors gave higher Acceptance scores to both deviate and conforming clients than did male counselors; (b) counselors, regardless of sex, rated conforming goals as more appropriate than deviate; (c) counselors, regardless of sex, rated female clients with deviate career goals to be more in need of counseling than those with conforming goals" (p. 352).

Hawley (1972) found that the feminine model held by 52 female counselors-in-training allowed a wider range of educational and career choices than the feminine model held by 45 female teachers-in-training. She suggested that counselors such as those represented in the study can help female clients become aware of a variety of life styles and career choices, without implying that any one choice is superior to any other.

Naffziger (1972) studied attitudes towards women's roles among counselors, counselor educators and teachers of both sexes. He found that women described their ideal woman as one who is more extrafamily-oriented than the ideal projected by men. Although both men and women rejected the intrafamily-oriented ideal woman, women more strongly rejected her. Women were more accepting of working mothers. Women projected the ideal woman as being more responsible for the success of the marriage. Men suggested that career women are less attractive to men. On the other hand, men supported ideal women who would argue against authority. Naffziger found no significant differences by age (under 35, over 35) in the definitions of their ideal woman.

In another noteworthy study, Friedersdorf (1969) explored the relationship between male and female secondary school counselor attitudes toward the career planning of high school female students. The subjects were 106 counselors in Indiana schools. Twenty-seven male and 29 female counselors role-played a college-bound high school girl, while 23 male and 27 female counselors role-played a non-college-bound high school girl. The Strong Vocational Interest Blank for women was completed. The following conclusions were drawn:

1. Male and female counselors responded differently when role-playing as a college-bound high school girl versus role-playing as a non-college-bound high school girl.
2. Counselors perceived college-bound high school girls as identifying with cultural activities and skills involving verbal ability.
3. Items which reflected differences between college-bound versus non-college-bound girls were not the same for male and female counselors.
4. Both male and female counselors have at least some relatively distinctive attitudes toward which levels and types of occupations are realistic and appropriate for both college-bound and non-college-bound girls.
5. Male counselors associated college-bound girls with traditionally feminine occupations at the semi-skilled level; female counselors perceived the college-bound girl as interested in occupations requiring a college education.
6. Male counselors tended to think of women in feminine roles characterized by feminine personality traits.
7. Female counselors tended to expand the traditional image of female work roles and projected women's roles into careers presently occupied.
8. Male counselors perceived the college-bound girl as having positive attitudes toward traditionally feminine occupations regardless of the classification level of the occupations. Occupations traditionally

engaged in by men were not considered by male counselors as occupations that college-bound girls would like as careers.*

The implication, obviously, is that some of the counselor attitudes reflected might have great impact on the goals of the female clients as expressed in counseling sessions.

In order to test the hypothesis that counselors were biased against women entering a "masculine" occupation, Pietrofesa and Schlossberg (1970) arranged interviews between counselor trainees and a coached female counselee in the counseling practicum at an urban university. During the counseling session the counselee informed the counselor that she was a transfer student to the university, that she was entering her junior year of college and could not decide whether to enter the field of engineering, a "masculine" occupation, or enter the field of education, a "feminine" occupation.

Each interview was tape-recorded. At the end of the interview, the counselor was informed that the counselee had been coached and that the sessions and tapes were to be used for a research study. Counselors were requested not to mention their interviews to other counselors. After all counselors had conducted interviews, a brief discussion was held among the counselor group concerning their feelings about the counseling sessions. No other information was given the counselors. The subjects (counselors) in the study were students in a practicum during fall and winter quarters, 1968-69. The counselor group, then, consisted of 29—i.e., 16 males and 13 females. Tapes were reviewed and tabulated as to their bias by a male graduate student in guidance and counseling, a male counselor educator experienced in supervision of the counseling practicum, and a female college professor who was a former school psychologist with a research specialty. Frequencies and percentages were calculated, and chi square was then used in a variety of configurations. The final stage of the project involved a content analysis of all biased statements.

The raters designated a counselor's statement as biased or prejudiced against the female counselee when she expressed interest in the "masculine" field and the counselor rejected this interest in favor of the "feminine" vocation. Statements of rejection then included disapproval of the female counselee's desire to enter the "masculine" field—comments that implied disadvantages in entering that field, etc. A counselor's statement was considered biased for the female counselee when she expressed interest in the masculine occupation and the counselor supported or reinforced this expressed interest. Statements of positive bias toward females ranged from direct approval to statements that subtly implied advantages in entering the masculine field.

*From *A Comparative Study of Counselor Attitudes toward the Further Educational and Vocational Plans of High School Girls,* 1969 unpublished study by Nancy W. Friedersdorf. Reprinted by permission of Purdue Research Foundation. All rights reserved.

The results of this study indicated that counselor bias exists against women entering a masculine occupation. Female counselors, interestingly enough, displayed as much bias as did their male counterparts. Percentage results strongly reinforce the conclusion that counselors are biased against women entering masculine fields. Of the total bias statements, 81.3 percent are against women, whereas only 18.7 percent are biased for women. A content analysis of the 70 biased statements made by the counselors in this study reveals that most negatively biased statements emphasized the masculinity of the field; working conditions and promotional opportunity were mentioned, but with less frequency. Thus, the pressures against women working in a field stereotyped as masculine were prevalent among this group.

In order to tabulate the statements, ten categories were devised so that negative bias (NB) and positive bias (PB) statements could be classified as to content. The following examples of bias statements will give the flavor of the kinds of pressure counselors imposed.

Salary—Amount of monetary return
(NB) Money isn't everything.
(PB) You could make much more money as an engineer.
Status—Perception of self in vocation
(NB) The status of a woman is higher in the field of teaching.
(PB) There is more prestige in becoming an engineer.
Marriage and Family—Family attachment
(NB) Would your husband resent your being an engineer?
(NB) You would only be gone from home during school hours if you taught school.
(PB) Being an engineer would not interfere with your becoming married.
Parents—Parental support
(NB) How do your parents feel about your entering engineering instead of education?
(PB) I am glad your parents want you to become an engineer.
Educational Time—Amount of time necessary for preparation to enter the vocational field
(NB) Engineering would take five years, and elementary education would be four years. . . . These are things you might want to consider.
(PB) It may take longer to become an engineer, but it is well worth it.
Educational Preparation—Classes one must take to enter the field and the kinds of classes already taken
(NB) The course work in engineering would be very difficult.
(PB) Your classwork up to now shows that you would do well as an engineer.
Promotional Opportunities—Advancement in position
(NB) There might be a holding of you back because you are a woman.
(PB) Your chances of promotion would be good in engineering.

Hiring—Opportunity to enter field
    (NB) They are not supposed to discriminate against women, but
    they still get around it.
    (PB) The opportunities for a woman in engineering are good.
Working Conditions—Where, with whom, what kinds of work, and/or
under what conditions work is done
    (NB) Engineering . . . it is very, you know, technical and very, I
    could use the term "unpeopled."
    (PB) You could work at a relaxed pace as an engineer.
Masculine Occupation—Identification of occupation as masculine
    (NB) You normally think of this as a man's field.
    (PB) There is no such thing as a man's world anymore.

Pietrofesa and Schlossberg drew the following conclusions:

1. Counselors display more bias against females entering a so-called
   "masculine" occupation than for females entering a so-called
   "feminine" occupation.
2. Female counselors display as much bias against females as their male
   counterparts.
3. Content analysis of bias statements indicate that major stress is placed
   upon the "masculinity" of the occupation.*

Several other studies have looked at in-counseling behaviors of
counselors and their impact on women clients. Parker (1967) noted a
relationship between directive and non-directive responses of male therapists
and the sex of the counselee. Therapists made significantly more non-directive
responses than directive responses to female clients than to their male
counterparts. Heilbrun (1970) developed this thesis one step further when he
tested the hypothesis that female clients' dependency needs were frustrated by
the non-directive approach of male therapists and, as a result, they left
therapy prematurely. The results of the study supported this contention. The
Parker and Heilbrun research involved male counselors, and yet the sex of the
counselor may be a most important ingredient. Pringle (1972), in an
incomplete study analyzing the interaction effects of (1) the sex of the high
school client, (2) the sex of the high school counselor, and (3) the client
behavior presented in the initial stages of the counseling interview, has
preliminary findings which suggest there are significant differences occurring
as a function of the match between counselor sex, client sex and client
behavior.

From the studies cited, it appears that counselors do ascribe roles to men
and to women and that counselor interview behavior reflects these biases.

Counseling Materials

When discussing counselor bias, it is essential to examine materials which
are commonly used and relied upon in the counseling interview. Counselors

*From *Counselor Bias and the Female Occupational Role,* by J.J. Pietrofesa and N.K.
Schlossberg. Copyright 1970 by Reproduction Service. Reprinted by permission.

need to evaluate critically every tool they use—whether it is description of fields in the *Occupational Outlook Handbook*, an interest inventory, a career brochure, or a college catalog. Does the information being presented or the test content reflect stereotyped roles for men and women? Do the materials contain biased statements which could lead a counselee in one direction rather than another? Do the materials reflect the past rather than the future? Are the materials reinforcing outmoded views of "women's place"?

Since interest inventories play a crucial role in career counseling, stemming partly from clients' continual insistence for specific feedback and answers, we must certainly assess the inventories to determine whether they are a freeing or restricting influence. Cole (1972), in a scientific description of present interest inventories, sees them as restricting: "The use of traditional women's occupational scales may have a severely limiting effect on the careers women consider" (p. 8). Harmon (1973), in a paper delivered at the American Personnel and Guidance Association Convention, listed and discussed the major interest inventories which contained "characteristics which may contribute to sexual bias."

Despite the growing awareness among leaders in the area of tests and measurements, practitioners—both men and women—are often unaware of the sexual bias inherent in the major inventories as presently constructed. In a recent meeting, the authors asked if the trained counselors present felt that the two most widely used inventories, the Strong Vocational Interest Blank and the Kuder, were biased. A minority felt the inventories were biased. The counselors, generally considering the inventories as unbiased, seemed amazed by the presentation of a detailed description of the bias inherent in each test.

The extent of bias has been documented for one of the best inventories available, the Strong Vocational Interest Blanks, by Schlossberg and Goodman (1972b). They point out four major limitations of the Strong Vocational Interest Blanks.

> *First*, the Strong includes thirty-three occupations for men which are not listed for women—such as psychiatrist, author, journalist, physicist; it also includes thirty-seven occupations listed for women but not available for men, including elementary teacher, art teacher and medical technologist. Since four hundred members of an occupation are an appropriate norm group for a SVIB scale, and census data indicate that in most instances at least four hundred persons of the opposite sex are employed in an occupation reserved for one sex on the SVIB, no justification exists for differential norm groups of each sex.
>
> The *second* major limitation stems from the fact that when the same person takes both forms of the SVIB, the profiles turn out differently. For example, in a pilot study in which twenty-eight men and women took both forms of the SVIB, one woman scored high (A or B+ standard score) as a dental assistant, physical therapist, occupational therapist on the women's profile, and physician, psychiatrist, psychologist on the men's form. One man scored high on personnel director, rehabilitation counselor, social worker, physical therapist, and community recreation administrator on the men's form, and guidance counselor, medical technologist, engineer, dietician, occupational therapist, physical

therapist, registered nurse, licensed practical nurse, radiologic technologist, and dental assistant on the women's form.

The *third* major limitation stems from the current manual and handbook which offers guidelines to counselors which, if followed, could be harmful. For example, the current manual states, "Many young women do not appear to have strong occupational interests, and they may score high only in certain 'premarital' occupations: elementary school teacher, office worker, stenographer-secretary." "Such a finding is disappointing to many college women, since they are likely to consider themselves career-oriented. In such cases, the selection of an area of training or an occupation should probably be based upon practical considerations—fields that can be pursued part-time, are easily resumed after periods of non-employment, and are readily available in different locales."

Fourth, the use of the Strong Vocational Interest Blanks may also be attacked on legal grounds—that the SVIB deprives women of their right to the Equal Protection of the Law and that the use of the SVIB is in violation of Title VII of the Civil Rights Act of 1964 (Schlossberg and Goodman, 1972b).*

This detailed analysis is merely illustrative of one instrument. However, an equally biased picture becomes apparent no matter what guidance material one examines. For example, the opening paragraph in American College Testing Program's brochure describing their Career Planning Program reads:

> We all make career decisions—decisions affecting our educational and job futures. Sometimes we make these decisions by default because of what we didn't know or didn't do. Sometimes we are able to take charge, to discover our possibilities and weigh our choices. This report is designed to help YOU take charge.

However, at the bottom of the profile, there is a special note addressed to counselors:

> Counselors Notes: When a student is unlike other students entering an educational program, predictions for that program should be used with caution. For example, care should be used in interpreting predictions for a student of one sex in a program in which the other sex predominates (American College Testing, 1971).

A forthcoming revision of the Strong Vocational Interest Blanks is an attempt to eliminate sexual bias. Clearly, we need further studies and revision of all guidance tests, materials, and occupational information. Analysis of these materials should be in terms of bias—not just against women but against all groups.

---

*From *Revision of the Strong Vocational Interest Blanks. Resolution to the American Personnel and Guidance Association,* by N.K. Schlossberg and J. Goodman. Wayne State University, 1972. Reprinted by permission.

IMPLICATIONS FOR TRAINING

Counselors, both male and female, have biases about female counselees. Counselor education programs must accept counselor bias as a fact and attempt to bring biased feelings into the open, so that counselors are able to control them or, better yet, remove them from their counseling and human encounters. Westervelt (1963) writes:

> Counselors who express the conviction that women's primary and socially essential roles are domestic and maternal and take place in the home may be reflecting a covert need to keep them there.
>
> Girls and women in the lower socio-economic brackets who particularly need counseling help to recognize and plan for paid employment will get little assistance from such counselors. Nor, of course, will these counselors help intellectually and educationally privileged girls to use their gifts and training to best advantage.
>
> ... No formal, university-sponsored, graduate-level, degree-awarding program in counselor education requires even a one-semester course in social and psychological sex differences which affect development or provides focus on sex differences in a practicum or internship in counseling. . . .
>
> Trends toward the integration into counselor education, at basic levels, of more subject matter from social psychology, anthropology, sociology, and economics would also provide more exposure to materials on psycho-social sex differences and changing sex roles. Again, however, the effect of such exposure will depend on the student's initial sympathetic interest, since the material will be only a small part of a much larger whole (pp. 21-22).

Westervelt (1963) makes references to the role and, more so, the importance of the practicum in the training of counselors:

> Counselors, guidance workers, and student personnel workers . . . should have as many opportunities as possible to counsel with females—and, ideally, with females of all ages, in order that no matter what the age level with which they eventually work, they get an opportunity to observe first hand the patterns of continuity and discontinuity in feminine development. Counseling experience should not, however, be limited to working with females; opportunity to counsel with boys and men is most important, both because it will provide insights into psycho-social sex differences and because it will provide a chance to explore useful variations in approaches to counseling the two sexes. All counselors-in-training should be helped to identify, understand and work with sex differences in their counseling practicum or internship (pp. 26-28).

Before one can implement these notions spelled out by Westervelt, the first task is to convince counselor educators that they, too, probably hold biases about age, sex, social class, and color. Each person might not hold biases in all four areas, but it is unquestionably true that each one of us holds certain beliefs about what is appropriate behavior for these groups. It is difficult to face these beliefs in ourselves; once recognized, it is difficult to control them in our counseling and programming.

The second task is for counselor educators to build this into training counselors. In which classes do we discuss these notions? How do we make explicit aspects of counselor behavior about which we know so little? While cognitive dimensions of age and sex bias can be integrated throughout a counselor education program, the practicum experience might afford the best opportunity to effectively deal with the more basic feelings of counselors. It also provides a vehicle where counselors come face to face with girls and women of all ages.

The third task is to begin developing materials for use in training counselors. One possibility would be the development of a self-administered instrument which might yield several bias scores. A more fruitful one, however, would be the use of situational vignettes where counselors are more likely to express what they truly feel. Paper-and-pencil inventories seem to allow for a more superficial, simply verbalized, egalitarian point of view than do situational experiential tasks.

A TRAINING MODEL

We suggest and have implemented a four-pronged training model. The goal is simple—to enable counselors and teachers to participate with their constituency in an unbiased fashion. The following components are simply suggestive and obviously have to be adapted to specific settings in order to be operational.

1. Expanding the cognitive understanding of participants regarding the role of women through lectures and readings.
2. Raising the consciousness of participants regarding sexual bias through group techniques.
3. Promoting the acquisition of non-biased helping skills among participants through audio-video taping and role playing.
4. Fostering skill development in program planning and implementation among participants through tutorial projects.

Each of these components will be briefly summarized so that the nature of training can be envisioned. This approach is based on fifty-six hours of training. We have found the most effective approach to be an intensive period of one week followed by sixteen hours of follow-up sessions during the year.

Expansion of Cognitive Understanding

The intellectual dimension provides a convenient initial component. The approach must be interdisciplinary in nature. For example, experts in the fields of medicine, law, education, psychology, sociology, etc. have much to contribute to an understanding of women in our world. Lectures, panels, reading, and discussion provide the beginning steps of our training model.

Consciousness Raising

After intellectual awakening, and before skill acquisition, counselors need to personalize their learnings. It is not enough to know intellectually that dentistry is a female occupation in Greece and could become a reality in our culture. Counselors must begin to look at their consciousness and deal with their values, attitudes, beliefs, and biases about sex roles.

A starting point might be to read "Woman Which Includes Man, Of Course" (Wells, 1970), which is a description of sex-role reversal. This becomes the basis for self-exploration in group discussion. One technique we have found effective during this stage is the inner-circle/outer-circle, or "fishbowl," technique. In a recent workshop, seven members volunteered to sit in the inner circle with two co-leaders. In addition, the inner circle contained an empty chair. Each outer-circle participant observed one member of the inner circle; the focus, in this case, was a discussion of Wells' book. The observer's reactions to the inner-circle participants' behaviors were to be fed back to that circle member at a later time. In addition, outer-circle participants could move freely into the empty chair when impelled to speak. After consciousness-raising experiences, including the "fishbowl" exercise, one male participant decided he could best attack sexual bias by applying for a job as a first-grade teacher in his school district.

Acquisition of Helping Skills

Once a cognitive and effective base has been established, attention can be directed to specific skill acquisitions. Educational experiences are incomplete unless the participants can do something more effectively than when they began. Role playing and supervised practice provide the vehicle from which specific skills can emerge.

Step One: Participants role-play situations which may elicit sex-biased behaviors. The trainers develop a paragraph which describes a specific situation involving two or more people. For example, one situation might involve a mother pressuring her daughter to become a teacher, while the daughter would like to become a doctor. The mother and daughter seek the help of a counselor to resolve the conflict. The scenario is role-played through to resolution and then discussed.

Step Two: Participants pair-off as "helper" and "helpee." The helpees present situations in their lives in which sex role is an issue, while the helpers attempt a facilitative intervention. For example, one male helpee might discuss his relationship to his children while his wife works, or even his feelings about his wife's working. Another helpee might discuss the pressure she feels at work or a conflict with her children. The helper responds using attending, responding, and initiating skills according to the Carkhuff model (1972a, 1972b). Discussion follows each exercise, starting with the feelings of the helpee, helper, the other participants, and the supervisor. Evaluations, in terms of helper effectiveness, are made immediately using the five-point Carkhuff Scale.

Step Three: Counselors participate in video and audio taping of actual counseling sessions. The tapes are shared and immediately critiqued in terms of implementation and acquisition of counseling skills. Special attention is paid to situations where counselor biases might effect the counseling interaction and counselee decision making.

Program Development

In addition to understanding intellectually the role of women, raising one's consciousness, and developing more effective human-relationship skills, counselors must foster change in their own work settings. Consequently, participants are asked to release their creative potentials to foster innovative programs resulting in better situations for women.

Step One: Supervisors work with participants in outlining systematic steps of program development.

Step Two: Participants work in groups with the task of zeroing in on a specific measurable, observable program which will improve conditions for women and which can be implemented in their own work settings.

Step Three: Participants return four months later with an outline of their goals, activities, and evaluation to share with their counterparts.

In summary, participant experiences then would range from reading to actual supervised practice. Training would move from the usual cognitive vehicles—i.e., reading and listening—to learning through modeling, observation, and discussion. Actual participation in role playing and supervised practice would be included in the formal program. Training would be followed with continuous evaluation of field practice and program development.

Evaluation would involve (1) participant self-evaluation and (2) program evaluation. Participant evaluation could include paper-and-pencil tests, observation of self and others, and peer and supervisor feedback. The typical pre-post testing and participant critiques would be part of the evaluation of program development. All individual evaluation of participants would be confidential. Group data would be available for research.

SUMMARY

Sexual bias, whether displayed knowingly or not, affects counselor performance. Several studies have supported this fact. Counselors reflect such bias through in-counseling behaviors and through some of the materials they use.

This article discusses the relevant research surrounding this problem and proposes a model of training to help counselors reduce sex bias.

REFERENCES

Allport, G. *The nature of prejudice.* New York: Doubleday and Company, Inc., 1958.

American College Testing. Career planning program. 1971.

Broverman, I.K., Broverman, D.M., Clarkson, F.E., Rosenkrantz, P.S. & Vogel, S.R. Sex-role stereotypes and clinical judgments of mental health. *Journal of Consulting and Clinical Psychology,* 1970, *34,* 1-7.

Carkhuff, R.R. *The art of helping.* Amherst, Massachusetts: Human Resource Development Press, 1972. (a)

Carkhuff, R.R. The development of systematic human resource development models. *The Counseling Psychologist,* 1972, *3*(3), 4-11. (b)

Cassara, B. *American women: The changing image.* Boston: Houghton-Mifflin, 1963.

Cole, N.S. On measuring the vocational interest of women. No. 49, March 1972. *The American College Testing Program,* P.O. Box 168, Iowa City, Iowa 52240.

Friedersdorf, N.W. A comparative study of counselor attitudes toward the further educational and vocational plans of high school girls. Unpublished study. Lafayette: Purdue University, 1969.

Gardner, J. Sexist counseling must stop. *Personnel and Guidance Journal,* 1971, *49,* 705-714.

Ginzberg, E. *Career guidance: Who needs it, who provides it, who can improve it?* New York: McGraw-Hill, 1971.

Harmon, L.W. Sexual bias in interest testing. *Measurement and Evaluation in Guidance,* 1973, *5,* 496-501.

Hawley, P. Perceptions of male models of femininity related to career choice. *Journal of Counseling Psychology,* 1972, *19,* 308-313.

Heilbrun, A.B. Toward resolution of the dependency-premature termination paradox for females in psychotherapy. *Journal of Consulting and Clinical Psychology,* 1970, *34,* 382-386.

Manpower Report of the President. Washington, D.C.: Department of Labor, 1967.

Millett, K. *Token learning: A study of women's higher education in America.* National Organization for Women, New York, 1968.

Naffziger, K.G. *A survey of counselor-educators' and other selected professionals' attitudes toward women's roles.* (Doctoral dissertation, University of Oregon) Ann Arbor, Michigan: University Microfilms, 1972, No. 72-956.

Parker, G.V.C. Some concomitants of therapist dominance in the psychotherapy interview. *Journal of Consulting Psychology,* 1967, *31,* 313-318.

Pietrofesa, J.J., & Schlossberg, N.K. Counselor bias and the female occupational role. Detroit: Wayne State University, 1970. (ERIC Document Reproduction Service No. CG 006 056)

Pringle, M. The responses of high school counselors to behaviors associated with independence and achievement in male and female clients: An interaction analysis. Ann Arbor: University of Michigan, unpublished dissertation, 1972.

Rosenthal, R., & Jacobson, L. *Pygmalion in the classroom.* New York: Holt, Rinehart and Winston, Inc., 1968.

Schlossberg, N.K., & Goodman, J. Imperative for change: Counselor use of the Strong Vocational Interest Blanks. *Impact,* 1972, *2,* 26-29. (a)

Schlossberg, N.K., & Goodman, J. Revision of the Strong Vocational Interest Blanks. Resolution to the American Personnel and Guidance Association, March 29, 1972. Mimeographed, College of Education, Wayne State University, 1972. (b)

Stewart, N.R., & Hinds, W.C. Behavioral objectives to direct simulated experiences in counselor education. Videotape presentation at APGA, New Orleans, March, 1970.

Thomas, H., & Stewart, N.R. Counselor response to female clients with deviate and conforming career goals. *Journal of Counseling Psychology,* 1971, *18,* 352-357.

Wells, T. Woman which includes man, of course. *Newsletter Association for Humanistic Psychology,* 1970, *7.*

Westervelt, E. The recruitment and training of educational/vocational counselors for girls and women. Background paper for Sub-Committe on Counseling, President's Commission on the Status of Women, 1963.

Career Counseling
for Women ;

LOUISE VETTER
Ohio State University

The occupational behavior of women has not been treated comprehensively in the counseling literature, largely because women as workers have been perceived as individually transient and collectively insignificant due to the type and level of jobs available to them in our society. Oppenheimer (1968) documented the sex-labeling of jobs. She found that "female jobs" are those which depend on skilled but cheap labor, those where most of the training is acquired before employment, and those where career continuity is not essential. Female jobs are jobs which exist all over the country, hence mobility or the lack of it is not usually a serious handicap. In view of these facts, it is necessary to document the need for career counseling with women, before discussing the application of career development theories to women and before discussing factors which affect vocational behavior in women.

NEED FOR CAREER COUNSELING

If we define "career" as the sequence of occupations in the life of an individual, then we need to look at the following facts (Women's Bureau, 1972b):

About 32 million women are currently employed. These women constitute about 38% of the labor force. Ninety percent of women will be employed at some time in their lives. The median wage paid to women is less than 60% of that paid to men and the differential is increasing.

The following evidence suggests that women *do* take their jobs seriously (Women's Bureau, 1972a). Of the 32 million women in the labor force in March, 1971, nearly half were working because of pressing economic need. They were either single, widowed, divorced, or separated or had husbands whose incomes were less than $3,000 a year. Another 5.4 million had husbands with incomes between $3,000 and $7,000. When absentee rates due to illness and injury are examined, little difference between men and women is found; they average 5.2 days a year for women and 5.1 days a year for men. Studies on labor turnover indicate that net differences for men and women are generally small. In manufacturing industries the 1968 rates of accessions per 100 employees were 4.4 for men and 5.3 for women; the respective separation rates were 4.4 and 5.2.

Recent federal legislation, executive orders and the pending Twenty-Seventh Amendment to the Constitution (the Equal Rights Amendment) will undoubtedly have major impact on women's career patterning. For example, Executive Order 11246, as amended, requires that most federal contractors (producing both goods and services) have an affirmative action plan for hiring and promoting women in jobs where they are currently under-utilized.

The foregoing information is typically not included in the educational programs for preparing counselors. However, if vocational counseling should occupy a central place in counseling psychology, as suggested by Samler (1964) at the Greyston Conference, these facts, as well as the following theoretical and empirical findings, deserve coverage in pre-service and in-service counseling programs.

THEORIES OF CAREER DEVELOPMENT

Although Osipow (1968) indicated that "few special explanations or concepts have been devised to deal with the special problems of the career development of women" and that "most of the masculine-based tests and theories fail to really provide a useful vehicle for the understanding of the career development of women" (p. 247), four theoretical approaches which have relevance to women will be considered, along with two tentative sets of postulates proposed specifically for looking at women's careers. The interested reader is referred to reviews of career development by Tennyson (1968) and by Holland and Whitney (1969); Kievit's (1972) review and synthesis of the literature on women in the world of work; Astin, Suniewick and Dweck's (1971) annotated bibliography on women's education and careers; and to extended critiques of the theories of career development by Osipow (1968) and Crites (1969). The four general approaches to be considered are those of Super, Roe, Holland, and Blau, Gustad, Jessor, Parnes, and Wilcock. Psathas (1968) and Zytowski (1969) have presented approaches based exclusively on women's experience.

Super's Developmental Self-Concept Theory

Super suggested that persons strive to implement their self-concepts by choosing to enter the occupation they see as most likely to permit them self-expression. He further suggested that the particular behaviors people engage in to implement their self-concepts vocationally are a function of the individual's stage of life development. Vocational behaviors can be better understood by viewing them within the context of the changing demands of the life cycle.

According to Super (1963a), self-concept formation requires people to recognize themselves as distinctive individuals, yet at the same time be aware of the similarities between themselves and others. A person's self-concept is continually developing. Vocational maturity (Super, 1963b), defined in terms of the congruence between an individual's vocational behavior and the expected vocational behavior at that age, allows the observer to assess the rate and level of an individual's development with respect to career matters.

Super (1957) identified four types of career patterns which men follow: stable, conventional, unstable, and multiple-trial. He also provided a possible classification of women's career patterns. These are: stable homemaking (no significant work experience), conventional (work after education but not after marriage), stable working (single women who work continuously), interrupted (married women who work, then are fulltime homemakers, then return to work), unstable (in and out of the labor force at irregular intervals), and multiple-trial (a succession of unrelated jobs).

Research. Crites (1965) reported that his research indicated only a few differences between boys and girls in their self-reports of vocational attitudes, thus leading him to conclude that sex may not be an important factor in the maturation of vocational attitudes. However, a later study by Smith and Herr (1972), using Crites' Vocational Development Inventory-Attitude Scale with 534 girls and 489 boys in the eighth grade and 495 girls and 502 boys in the tenth grade, found "females possessed more maturity in terms of their attitudes toward work and career planning than did males in the eighth and tenth grades" (p. 181). Putnam and Hansen (1972) in a study of 375 eleventh-grade girls found that self-concept and own feminine role concept were useful in predicting vocational maturity (measured by Crites' scale). They found that the more the girl viewed her role as being liberal or contemporary, the higher was her level of vocational maturity.

Mulvey (1963) studied the career patterns of 475 women who had graduated 20 to 27 years previously from the public high school of Providence, Rhode Island. She found that one-third of her sample accepted homemaking and child-rearing exclusively as a career but suggested that the work role is more central to a woman's existence and more internalized than many writers would contend. Level of education and level of aspiration were the most important determinants of career pattern. The career patterns were closely related to the life developmental cycle.

In a current study (Vetter, in process), a national cross-sectional sample of 4,807 women was categorized into career patterns. Of the total group, 22% fell into the stable homemaking group, 27%—conventional, 3%—stable working, 14%—double track, 16%—interrupted and 18%—unstable. The multiple-trial category was not used because of overlap with other categories. Marital and family status, educational and attitudinal variables are being studied in relationship to the career patterns.

Roe's Personality Theory of Career Choice

Roe was concerned with the effects of early childhood experiences on the development of personality. In particular, she contended that early experiences influence peoples' orientation to the interpersonal world around them in a way that leads them to move toward or away from people. She also developed an occupational classification system which allows predictions about the nature of the occupations that people would prefer if they were person oriented, as opposed to those they would approach if they were not oriented toward people (Roe, 1957).

Research. Osipow (1972) indicates that, while a considerable body of research exists testing Roe's theory, most of it has yielded data that do not support the theory in its general outline. He feels that, if the theory were redefined and the links between early childhood experiences and personality were more clearly delineated, it might be shown to have greater validity than is at first apparent.

Kriger (1972) has proposed one such redefinition of Roe's original scheme to account for women's career development. She used this formulation to study the careers of 66 women (22 homemakers, 22 career women in female-dominated occupations, and 22 career women in male-dominated occupations) who were married, living with their husbands, mothers of at least one child, middle-class, and graduates from college. She interpreted her results as supporting the contention that the primary vocational decision for women is the decision between "working" and "not working," with the choice of a specific occupational area a secondary choice. The decision to have a career was seen as a function of the child-rearing mode of the parents, whereas the particular field of occupation and the level within it that a woman chooses to pursue were seen as a function of her level of achievement motivation.

Holland's Career Typology Theory

Holland (1966) postulated six types of individuals and six corresponding work environments. The six types are:

Realistic: aggressive, physically oriented, "masculine" person who prefers the concrete rather than the abstract;

Intellectual (later called Investigative): the person who is primarily concerned with thinking rather than acting and who tends to avoid close, interpersonal contact;

Social: the person who seeks close, interpersonal relations through such vocational activities as are found in teaching or therapy;

Conventional: the person who exhibits great concern for order, rules, regulations and self-control;

Enterprising: the person who uses verbal skills to manipulate and dominate other people;

Artistic: the person who seeks self-expression through artistic means.

Holland (1966) states that "in our culture, most persons can be categorized as one of six types" (p. 9) but then goes on to say:

> Unfortunately most of our empirical knowledge about personality and vocational behavior has been obtained in studies of men. Consequently, it is difficult to construct a theory of personality that applies equally to men and women. The present theory is no exception: it is based chiefly on studies of men and is probably less useful for understanding the behavior of women. A special but closely related theory for women is desirable, but at this point I have none to offer (p. 13).

However, he did develop a classification for female student vocational choices, which included seven categories: Intellectual, Social-Intellectual, Social-Conventional, Social-Enterprising, Social-Artistic, Conventional and Artistic (Holland and Whitney, 1968).

Research. Holland and Whitney (1968) used the classification scheme cited above to study the stability of vocational choices of 1,571 college women freshmen over a period of 8 or 12 months. They found that about 60% of the women selected the same occupation on both occasions, 14% selected an occupation in the same subgroup, 5% selected an occupation in a closely related subgroup, and 5% selected a remotely related occupation in the same major class; thus 84% of the women's successive occupational choices were in the same major occupational class. Another 9% selected "closely related" or "related" occupations in a related major group. Only 1% indicated clearly unrelated second choices, with an additional 5% of the responses unclassifiable or undecided.

A group of 1,576 college men were studied at the same time, with 69% of the successive occupational choices being in the same major class. Ten percent were in a "closely related" or "related" subgroup in a related major class, with 11% making an unrelated second choice, and 10% unclassifiable or undecided.

A possible interpretation of these results is that women are more vocationally mature at the college freshman level. Another possible interpretation is that the women perceive fewer options open to them and so make fewer changes among the limited number of choices available.

Harvey (1972) found correlational evidence which supported the validity of Holland's Vocational Preference Inventory for adult women. However, the *Social* scale and the *Artistic* scales of the VPI remained in doubt.

A Conceptual Framework for Occupational Choice—Blau, Gustad, Jessor, Parnes, and Wilcock

Blau *et al.* (1956) presented a conceptual scheme for use in systematic research which could be the basis for a theory of occupational choice. The interdisciplinary collaborators (from sociology, psychology and economics) identified two analytically distinct aspects within the social structure which affect occupational choice: (1) the matrix of social experiences which channel the personality development of potential workers and (2) the conditions of occupational opportunity which limit the realization of their choices. Occupational choice was conceived as a continually modified compromise between preferences for and expectations of being able to enter various occupations.

In addition, Blau and his colleagues stated that it is an over-simplification to conceive of occupational choice and selection as occurring at one point in time, even if this is defined as a limited time interval rather than as an instant, and even if the effects of earlier developments are taken into consideration. They suggest that a series of successive choice periods must be systematically analyzed to show how earlier decisions limit or extend the range of future choices.

Parnes, one of the collaborators, appears to be partially implementing the conceptual scheme in a longitudinal study of women aged 30-44 (Shea, Spitz and Zeller, 1970).

Toward a Theory of Occupational Choice for Women—Psathas

Building on the approach of Blau *et al.* (1956), Psathas (1968) described a number of factors which appear to operate in special ways for women on their way to occupational choices. He indicated that an understanding of the factors which influence entry of women into occupational roles must begin with the relationship between sex role and occupational role. He cited as first-order relationships the intention to marry, time of marriage, reasons for marriage and husband's economic situation and attitude toward his wife's working.

Additional factors to be considered include family finances, social class, education and occupation of parents and values. He reiterates the idea that the setting in which the occupational choice is made must be considered, along with the developmental process by which it is made.

Apparently this approach has not generated any research.

Toward a Theory of Career Development for Women—Zytowski

Zytowski (1969), working independently of Blau *et al.* and of Psathas, presented nine postulates in an attempt to characterize the distinctive differences in the work life of men and women, the developmental stages unique to women, their patterns of vocational participation, and the determinants of the patterns. The postulates are:

1. The model life role for women is described as that of the homemaker.

2. The nature of the women's role is not static; it will ultimately bear no distinction from that of men.

3. The life role of women is orderly and developmental and may be divided into sequences according to the preeminent task in each.

4. Vocational and homemaker participations are largely mutually exclusive. Vocational participation constitutes departure from the homemaker role.

5. Three aspects of vocational participation are sufficient to distinguish patterns of vocational participation: age or ages of entry, span of participation, degree of participation.

6. The degree of vocational participation represented by a given occupation is defined as the proportion of men to the total workers employed in the performance of that job.

7. Women's vocational patterns may be distinguished in terms of three levels, derived from the combination of entry age(s), span and degree of participation, forming an ordinal scale.

8. Women's preference for a pattern of vocational participation is an internal event and is accounted for by motivational factors.

9. The pattern of vocational participation is determined jointly by preference (representing motivation) and by external (e.g., situational and environmental) and internal (such as ability) factors.

Research. Wolfson (1972) studied postulate seven and postulate nine by defining five career patterns and studying the relationships between the patterns and 29 motivational, external, and internal factors. She used the three patterns defined by Zytowski (Mild—very early or late entry, a brief span and a low degree of participation; Moderate—early entry, a lengthy span, and a low degree of participation; and Unusual—early entry, a lengthy or uninterrupted span, and a high degree of participation) and two additional groups: a group which had never worked since leaving college and High Moderate group, composed of women from the Moderate group who had worked eighteen years or more.

The sample consisted of 306 women who had participated in a 25-year follow-up study of counseled versus non-counseled students. Career patterns were not predictable from information known about a student when she was a college freshman but were predictable from data collected five years later. Variables related to education and marriage were the most powerful predictors of vocational patterns. The number of years spent in college and the percentage of graduates increased progressively from the "Never Worked" group to the "Unusual" group, with the implication that career commitment is closely correlated with the amount of education obtained. Marital status was a highly discriminating factor. Husband's income, number of children, age of youngest child, and satisfaction with marriage also discriminated among vocational pattern groups. The findings were interpreted as suggesting that the High Moderate and Unusual groups probably represent a vocationally oriented population, and the other three a homemaking-oriented population.

Postulate four is refuted on the basis of evidence from the Women's Bureau (1971) in so far as 40% of women who are married and living with their husbands are employed. In addition, unless by definition a man must be present to constitute a home, a high percentage of widows and divorced women are employed in addition to maintaining households and many single women workers are responsible for maintaining their own homes.

FACTORS AFFECTING CAREER CHOICES AMONG WOMEN

Occupational sex stereotyping occurs early in the socialization of children. Schlossberg and Goodman (1972) studied children's sex stereotyping of occupations. They found that kindergarteners and sixth graders felt that a woman's place was clearly *not* fixing cars or television sets or designing buildings. The children did say that a woman could work as a waitress, nurse or librarian. In contrast, they did not feel that men had to be similarly limited.

Meyer (1970) studied the views of 132 boys and girls in grades three, seven and eleven toward the sex-linking of occupations. She found that boys and girls have strong stereotypic ways of behaving toward traditionally sex-linked occupations.

Harmon (1971) found that college women had considered a very restricted range of occupations during adolescence. This may have resulted from the kind of stereotyping noted above.

Horner (1969) has documented a motive to avoid success in college women. Anticipation of success over a male can provoke anxieties in women such as fear of loss of femininity and self-esteem. Thus, fear of success can inhibit positive achievement and directed motivation and behavior.

Goldberg (1968) reported that 140 college women evaluated a professional article more negatively if they thought it was authored by a woman, even in traditionally female professions. When the author was presented as a man, the women consistently rated the article as more valuable and the author as more competent.

Gray-Shellberg, Villareal and Stone (1972) studied the resolution of career conflicts by 57 male and 57 female college students and 72 male and 63 female noncollege adults. A significant number of women in the two samples studied were motivated to subordinate their interests to those of a fiancé or husband, and the men, too, perceived this as the accepted state of affairs. The stereotypes revealed in the subjects' responses reflected strong societal expectations that a woman shall be supportive of a man and not seek self-expression through a career. The authors indicated that the removal of economic, political and legal barriers to women's achievement, while important, will probably not significantly affect the occupational status of women unless it is accompanied by a fundamental change in both external and internalized expectations of the "proper" female role.

Women have been led to believe that maternal employment is related to potential juvenile delinquency in their children. Actually, studies show that whether or not a mother is employed does not appear to be a determining factor in causing juvenile delinquency. It is the quality of a mother's care rather than the time consumed in such care which is of major significance (Women's Bureau, 1972b).

The implication that married women take jobs away from men has probably deterred some women from seeking employment. In fact, there were 18.5 million married women (husband present) in the labor force in March 1971, while the number of unemployed men was 3 million. If all the married women stayed home and unemployed men were placed in their jobs, there would be 15.5 million unfilled jobs. Moreover, most unemployed men do not have the education or the skill to qualify for many of the jobs held by women, such as secretaries, teachers, and nurses (Women's Bureau, 1972b).

Home—Career Dimension

Watley and Kaplan (1971) did a follow-up study in 1965 of 883 women who had won National Merit Scholarships during the years 1956-60. They found that 85% of the women said that they definitely planned on having a career. Those seeking an immediate career scored higher on scholastic ability tests than those who either planned no career or planned to delay entering them. Many more women, regardless of their plans, expressed problems relating to their gender than expressed problems that interfered with making and implementing their plans. The problem of discrimination was cited most frequently.

Harmon (1970) studied the career commitment of 169 women 10 to 14 years after college entrance. Differences between the "career committed" and "noncommitted" groups were found, but none of them offered a basis for predicting career commitment before women begin programs of higher education. These results are consistent with those of Astin and Myint (1971). They found that post-high school experiences were the best determinants of career outcomes. Educational attainment and marital-family status best predicted whether women would choose to pursue careers in the sciences, professions and teaching, or to be housewives and office workers.

Tangri (1970) studied the occupational choices of 200 college women. She found that Role-Innovators (those whose choices are of occupations now dominated by men) aspire to a higher level of accomplishment in their field than Traditional choosers. They also expressed greater commitment to their vocations. She found that Traditionals tend more than Role-Innovators to displace their achievement concerns onto future husband, whereas Role-Innovators are more likely to generalize from their own generally high level of expectations for self to expectations for future husbands. Role-Innovators reported as many romantic relationships and significantly more non-romantic friendships with the opposite sex than did Traditionals.

Almquist (1969) studied the occupational choices and career salience of one class in a women's college of a medium-sized university over the four years of their college experience. Career salience was defined as the extent to which the women planned to be employed in addition to being married and having a family. "Atypical choosers" were those women who want to enter jobs in which over 70% of the workers are now male. She found no support for the hypothesis of deviance which would suggest rejection of the traditional obligations of the female role; rather, there was support for an enrichment hypothesis, with broader learning experiences which lead to a less stereotyped version of the female role in which work in a high level career is a significant part. Career salient, atypical choosers had more work experience and more varied work experience related to their ultimate career choices than did noncareer salient, typical choosers. Their mothers more often had a consistent history of working, and they had been influenced by college professors and people in the occupation who influenced and persuaded them to pursue an important career themselves.

Levine (1969) studied the marital and occupational plans of single women in four professional schools. Almost all women in law and medicine did not plan any withdrawal from the labor force, while the majority of those in nursing and teaching planned to withdraw from the labor force when they have young children to care for. Descriptions of experiences in graduate professional schools suggested that women in law and medicine were learning that they could maintain feminine identity and sex role without leaving the profession. In addition, they were treated as members of a high status professional school. In contrast, the women in nursing and teaching were discovering that there is a separation between important aspects of sex-role and work-role. Moreover, women in the nursing and teaching tended to feel that they are treated as members of low status groups within the university and reacted by planning to devote time and energy in the future to the marital position.

Turner (1972) studied socialization and career orientation among black (N=28) and white (N=45) college freshmen women. She found that blacks were far likelier than whites to expect full-time paid employment. Fifty-four percent of blacks, but only 16% of whites, expected full-time paid employment, while 53% of whites and 21% of blacks expected to be homemakers, working for pay, if at all, only before children were born or after they were grown. Socio-economic status did not lead to differentiation of these expectations. There was no overlap of demographic, developmental and attitudinal variables that differentiate high and low career expectation among blacks and whites. High career expectation among whites was related to: parental behavior which stressed competitiveness as opposed to obedient and "good" behavior; equalitarian, self-striving attitudes toward women's roles; less paternal disappointment should the student drop out of college, as well as a tendency toward lower parental aspirations for the student's highest academic degree. Among blacks, full-time career expectations were related to perceptions of the preferences and expectations of significant others regarding their career involvement, as well as to appreciation of parental strictness. They also stressed the importance of holding a good job in order to find a high-status husband.

Since blacks expect so much more career involvement than whites and since black mothers were far more likely to have worked, and worked earlier during the students' childhoods, it might seem plausible that the students' career expectations would be related to maternal work history among both races. Instead, the extent of maternal employment during the students' childhoods in the study did not differentiate high and low career expectations among either race. The findings suggested that these young black women may be especially responsive to the expectations of significant others that they carry the responsibility implied by full-time employment. They expect to work full-time while preferring less work involvement and reporting negative attitudes toward their mothers' employment. For black women, full-time career expectation may imply a deep sense of responsibility more than an anticipation of personal fulfillment.

Tucker (1971) studied the self- and inter-group perceptions of homemakers, elementary teachers and research scientists as related to feminine sex-role and occupational choice. Homemakers saw themselves as having feminine characteristics and viewed teachers and scientists as masculine, but they saw teachers as feminine when compared to scientists. Teachers attributed to scientists the same masculine traits that homemakers did, but they saw homemakers as similar to themselves. Scientists attributed some feminine characteristics to themselves and some masculine traits to the other two groups. Homemakers were not work oriented, nor did they overtly express dissatisfaction with their concept of themselves in the culturally accepted feminine sex-role. Homemakers and teachers viewed scientists as having masculine characteristics, having excellent social skills and as being independent, creative problem solvers—characteristics which the scientists did not perceive themselves as having.

This attribution to scientists of characteristics incongruent with the scientists' self-concepts might well be a discouraging factor in the choice of science as an occupation by many women, even if they have the initial interests and aptitudes necessary for successful pursuit of this field.

Nagely (1971) studied 40 college-educated working mothers, 20 employed in traditional female occupations and 20 who had careers in male-dominated occupations. Pioneers were found to be more career-committed than Traditionals and to have more successfully integrated the roles of homemaker and worker. Pioneers' fathers were more highly educated, and their husbands were employed at higher occupational levels. Pioneers more frequently reported that their fathers approved of women working outside the home. Pioneers were also more likely to refuse to give up their careers if requested by their husbands, more reluctant to move to another city for their husbands' professional advancement, and feel that their professional activities were as important as their husbands. They also indicated that they had a greater voice in determining how the family income was spent, took more responsibility for disciplining their children, and were more likely to feel that their husbands should help with household tasks. They were also more likely to report that being a woman was a disadvantage in their fields. The woman who makes the strongest recommendation for combining career, marriage, and family is the one who reports that her career allows her to make full use of her talents.

Rossi (1965) reported that, of 3,500 women college graduates of the class of 1961, one-fifth had no career goals other than homemaking; not quite half reported long-range career goals in traditional fields in which women predominate; only 7% were pioneers with long-range career goals in predominantly masculine fields.

Astin (1969) studied 1,657 women who earned their doctorates in the United States during 1957 and 1958 (86% of the total group). She found that 91% of them were in the labor force and 81% were working full time. Women who interrupted their careers did so because of child bearing and child rearing; the median length of time for such interruptions was 14 months. Over half the women had been or were still married at the time of the survey; the married women had smaller families than women in general. Astin's findings suggested needed changes: encouragement of young women to achieve advanced training and establishment of scholarships in career fields that women usually do not enter. She also suggested that opportunities for part-time study and employment need to be increased, that day-care centers are needed, that tax laws should be changed to permit deductions for household workers, and that discriminatory practices against women in higher education roles and the world of work need to be eliminated.

Farmer and Bohn (1970) studied the level of career interest in women and the relationship to home-career conflict reduction. They designated six scales of the Strong Vocational Interest Blank for women as Career scales and eight as Home scales. They found that scores on Career scales were increased and scores on Home scales were decreased when 50 working women (25 married, 25 single) were instructed to respond as though men liked intelligent women, men and women were promoted equally in business and the professions, and raising a family well were very possible for a career woman. Whether the responding woman was married or single did not affect the responses. The authors concluded that the level of vocational interest in women, irrespective of their marital status, would be raised if home-career conflict were reduced.

As pointed out by Kievit (1972), it is evident that college students, college graduates, and women in the professions have been the subjects of much of the research effort to date. She says:

> If indeed the concern with women workers is based on the valuing of work as a source of life satisfaction for all citizens, as well as manpower resources to meet requirements of a changing technology and economy, surely more intensive study of clerical, skilled, semi-skilled, and less prestigious service occupations is needed (p. 67).

All too often in career counseling with men the only role considered is that of the occupational role. Bailyn (1970) points out that the husband's approach to integrating family and work in his life is as important to marital satisfaction as his wife's attempt to integrate career and family. In this study, marriages tended to be happier when the husband found satisfaction in both career and family than when the husband was either just career- or family-oriented.

Male Attitudes

Male attitudes about the vocational roles which adult women should pursue are an important factor in determining what adult women will do (or will be permitted to do).

Entwisle and Greenberger (1970) studied the responses of 270 boys and 305 girls, ninth graders in seven schools of various socioeconomic and ethnic composition in Baltimore, to questions on women's role. Girls expressed more liberal views than boys on whether women should work, hold the same jobs as men and derive satisfaction from problem solving. However, both groups responded negatively when questioned about women holding men's jobs. The greatest disparity existed on the question of whether women should work at all, with girls responding positively and boys negatively. Among the boys, blacks were more liberal than whites and middle-class whites were more liberal than blue-collar whites. A greater discrepancy was found between middle-class girls and boys than between blue-collar girls and boys, with the middle-class sex difference especially marked among the high IQ group. This suggests that girls with the greatest work potential will face strong opposition from their future mates.

Nelson and Goldman (1969), in studying the attitudes of high school students and young adults toward the gainful employment of married women, found general acceptance by men of the dual role for women except in the case of their own wives.

McMillan (1972) studied the attitudes of college men (1,085 unmarried male dormitory residents in a midwestern university) toward career involvement of married women. The attitudes of the total sample regarding career involvement for their future wives were categorized as follows:

12.0%: no further work career after marriage;
37.8%: work in profession after marriage until the time of children, and then no further work unless absolutely necessary;
39.6%: work in profession after marriage until the time of children, devoting full time to family during the children's early years, and then returning to the profession as the children grow older;
3.8%: work in the profession rather continuously after marriage, taking off only short periods of time as required for family matters;
6.8%: none of the above options, since I do not plan to get married.

Thus, nearly half of this sample did not consider the possibility of a lifetime career for their spouses, even with an interruption for childraising. Among the different majors being pursued by the male students, the most notable differences seemed to be that business majors and science and mathematics majors preferred less career involvement for their future wives than did education majors and humanities and social science majors.

Meier's (1972) study of college youth's attitudes toward social equality for women found female undergraduates (N=99) scoring higher on feminine social equality than male undergraduates (N=120). She also found that, where the mother predominates in the attitudinal socialization of the child and when the mother exhibits involvement in occupational roles outside the home, the males were more positive about female social equality. If this finding is generalizable, then, as more women are taking their place in the occupational world, the attitudes of their children will become more accepting of the mother's right to be there.

Kaley (1971), in studying the attitudes toward the dual role of the married professional woman, found that married professional women have positive attitudes toward their dual role of career and marriage while married professional men have negative attitudes toward the dual role. She indicated that a review of research on the attitudes of professionally employed men and women toward women's dual role supports the hypothesis that negative attitudes held by both men and women inhibit qualified women from seeking higher education and professional careers.

Simpson (1969), in studying employing agents from six fields of humanities and social sciences in six institutions of higher education, found that employing agents discriminate against academic women when they choose between equally qualified candidates for faculty posts. However, they select a statistically significant number of superior women in preference to less well qualified men. Simpson found no significant difference among deans, departmental chairmen or faculty in their discriminatory behavior toward equally qualified male and female candidates or in their selection of superior candidates over less qualified males. He also found that, generally, those who discriminate against academic women also exhibit negative attitudes toward women in general.

The myth that men do not like to work for women supervisors probably discourages women from considering administrative careers. Actually most men who complain about women supervisors have never worked for a woman. In one study where at least three-fourths of both the male and female respondents (all executives) had worked with women managers, their evaluation of women in management was favorable. On the other hand, the study showed a traditional/cultural bias among those who reacted unfavorably to women as managers (Women's Bureau, 1972b).

CONCLUSIONS FOR COUNSELORS

Suniewick (1971) pointed up a conflict which is reflected in the data currently available. On one hand, statistics show that women are discriminated against in their pursuit of education and in their attempts to find careers. On the other hand, conflicts they face as they attempt to enter worlds formerly the province of men and as they endeavor to change their image and status are pointed out. She asserted that obvious implications of research findings are seldom mentioned—implications that changes need to occur in the institutions that educate women, in the world of work, and in women themselves as they deal with the conflict between career and marriage. She stated that "the obvious finding is that women are not being helped to resolve the conflict; rather they are being asked to accept their roles as wives and mothers and to make their career goals secondary to the other 'natural' functions of women in society" (p. 21). She asked how it is possible for a woman to endeavor to live as an individual as she sees fit when underutilization of woman-power, sex-labeling of jobs, woman's responsibility for children and family, prejudice against women in the world of work, and other cultural limitations continue to hinder woman's equal access to work. She sees little evidence of change occurring in educational institutions to assist women is gaining access to fields of study normally open only to men, although the need for the professions and vocations to accept qualified women on an equal basis with men has been clearly shown.

If "women" are "people," it will naturally be assumed that, as adults, they will combine a number of roles, such as worker, parent, household member, community participant. The counselor will work with these people to enable them to maximize their individual development.

However, we have not yet reached this stage in American culture. In many instances, women are viewed as a separate class rather than as individuals with individual abilities, interests and aspirations. Administrators, employers, teachers and counselors make decisions about women's education and women's employment on the basis of their sex rather than on their individual interests, abilities and capacities.

Counselors must not continue to perpetuate such a situation. (Neither should anyone else, but this article is intended for an audience of counseling psychologists.) It seems time for counseling psychology to pick up the challenge, rather hesitantly offered by Samler (1964), to become involved in social action—to make it a definite part of our professional task to set out to affect the status quo.

A number of sources are available to the counselor who is working in career counseling with girls and women. These include publications of the Women's Bureau (1966, 1970), Berry, Kern, Meleney, and Vetter (1966), Westervelt (1966), Bruemmer (1969, 1970), Mathews (1969), Murphy (1966), Eyde (1970), and the National Vocational Guidance Association's monograph (1972) on counseling girls and women over the life span.

REFERENCES

Almquist, E.M. Occupational choice and career salience among college women. (Doctoral dissertation, University of Kansas) Ann Arbor, Michigan: University Microfilms, 1969. No. 69-21, 484.

Astin, H.S. *The woman doctorate in America.* New York: Russell Sage Foundation, 1969.

Astin, H.S. & Myint, T. Career development of young women during the post-high school years. *Journal of Counseling Psychology,* 1971, *18,* 369-393.

Astin, H.S., Suniewick, N., & Dweck, S. *Women: A bibliography on their education and careers.* Washington, D.C.: Human Service Press, 1971.

Bailyn, L. Career and family orientations of husbands and wives in relation to marital happiness. *Human Relations,* 1970, *23*(2), 97-113.

Berry, J., Kern, K.K., Meleney, E., & Vetter, L. *Counseling girls and women— Awareness, analysis, action.* Kansas City, Missouri: University of Missouri and Missouri Department of Labor and Industrial Relations, March, 1966.

Blau, P.M., Gustad, J.W., Jessor, R., Parnes, H.S., & Wilcock, R.C. Occupational choice: A conceptual framework. *Industrial and Labor Relations Review,* 1956, *9,* 531-543.

Bruemmer, L. The condition of women in society today: A review—Part 1. *Journal of the National Association of Women Deans and Counselors,* 1969, *33,* 19-22.

Bruemmer, L. The condition of women in society today: An annotated bibliography— Part 2. *Journal of the National Association of Women Deans and Counselors,* 1970, *33,* 89-95.

Crites, J.O. Measurement of vocational maturity in adolescence. *Psychological Monographs,* American Psychological Association, 1965.

Crites, J.O. *Vocational psychology.* New York: McGraw-Hill, 1969.

Entwisle, D.R. & Greenberger, E. *A survey of cognitive styles in Maryland ninth graders. IV: Views of women's roles.* Baltimore: Center for the Study of Social Organization of Schools, Johns Hopkins University, November, 1970.

Eyde, L.D. Eliminating barriers to career development of women. *Personnel and Guidance Journal,* 1970, *49,* 24-27.

Farmer, H.S. & Bohn, M.J., Jr. Home-career conflict reduction and the level of career interest in women. *Journal of Counseling Psychology,* 1970, *17,* 228-232.

Goldberg, P. Are women prejudiced against women? *Trans-Action,* 1968, April, 28-30.

Gray-Shellberg, L., Villareal, S., & Stone, S. Resolution of career conflicts: The double standard in action. Paper presented at 80th Annual Convention of the American Psychological Association, Honolulu, Hawaii, September, 1972. (mimeo)

Harmon, L.W. Anatomy of career commitment in women. *Journal of Counseling Psychology,* 1970, *17,* 77-80.

Harmon, L.W. The childhood and adolescent career plans of college women. *Journal of Vocational Behavior,* 1971, *1,* 45-46.

Harvey, D.W.H. The validity of Holland's Vocational Preference Inventory for adult women. (Doctoral dissertation, The University of Connecticut) Ann Arbor, Michigan: University Microfilms, 1972. No. 72-14, 234.

Holland, J.L. *The psychology of vocational choice.* Waltham, Mass.: Blaisdell Publishing Company, 1966.

Holland, J.L. & Whitney, D.R. *Changes in the vocational plans of college students: Orderly or random?* Iowa City: Research and Development Division, American College Testing Program, April, 1968. (ACT Research Report No. 25)

Holland, J.L. & Whitney, D.R. Career development. *Review of Educational Research,* 1969, *39,* 227-235.

Horner, M.S. Fail: Bright women. *Psychology Today,* 1969, *3*(6), 36-41.

Kaley, M.M. Attitudes toward the dual role of the married professional woman. *American Psychologist,* 1971, *26,* 301-306.

Kievit, M.B. *Review and synthesis of research on women in the world of work.* Columbus, Ohio: ERIC Clearinghouse on Vocational and Technical Education, The Center for Vocational and Technical Education, The Ohio State University, March, 1972. (Information Series No. 56)

Kriger, S.F. Need achievement and perceived parental child-rearing attitudes of career women and homemakers. *Journal of Vocational Behavior,* 1972, *2,* 419-432.

Levine, A.G. Marital and occupational plans of women in professional schools: Law, medicine, nursing, teaching. (Doctoral dissertation, Yale University) Ann Arbor, Michigan: University Microfilms, 1969. No. 69-13, 353.

Mathews, E.E. The counselor and the adult woman. *Jouranl of the National Association of Women Deans and Counselors,* 1969, *32,* 115-122.

McMillan, M.R. Attitudes of college men toward involvement of married women. *Vocational Guidance Quarterly,* 1972, *21,* 8-11.

Meier, H.C. Mother-centeredness and college youths' attitudes toward social equality for women: Some empirical findings. *Journal of Marriage and the Family,* 1972, *34,* 115-121.

Meyer, M.M. Patterns of perceptions and attitudes toward traditionally masculine and feminine occupations through childhood and adolescence. (Doctoral dissertation, Michigan State University) Ann Arbor, Michigan: University Microfilms, 1970. No. 70-15, 084.

Mulvey, M.C. Psychological and sociological factors in prediction of career patterns of women. *Genetic Psychology Monographs,* 1963, *68,* 309-386.

Murphy, G. *New approaches to counseling girls in the 1960's.* Washington, D.C.: Women's Bureau, U.S. Department of Labor, 1966.

Nagely, D.L. Traditional and pioneer working mothers. *Journal of Vocational Behavior,* 1971, *1,* 331-341.

National Vocational Guidance Association. *Counseling girls and women over the life span.* Washington, D.C.: National Vocational Guidance Association, Division of the American Personnel and Guidance Association, 1972.

Nelson, H.Y. & Goldman, P.R. Attitudes of high school students and young adults toward the gainful employment of married women. *The Family Coordinator,* 1969, *18,* 251-255.

Oppenheimer, V.K. The sex-labeling of jobs. *Industrial Relations,* 1968, *7,* 219-234.

Osipow, S.H. *Theories of career development.* New York: Appleton-Century-Crofts, 1968.

Osipow, S.H. Implications for career education of research and theory on career development. Paper presented at National Conference on Career Education for Deans of Colleges of Education, Columbus, Ohio, April, 1972.

Psathas, G. Toward a theory of occupational choice for women. *Sociology and Social Research,* 1968, *52,* 253-268.

Putman, B.A. & Hansen, J.C. Relationship of self-concept and feminine role concept to vocational maturity in young women. *Journal of Counseling Psychology,* 1972, *19,* 436-440.

Roe, A. Early determinants of vocational choice. *Journal of Counseling Psychology,* 1957, *4,* 212-217.

Rossi, A.S. Who wants women scientists? In Mattfeld, J.A. & Van Aken, C.G. (Eds.), *Women and the scientific professions.* Cambridge, Mass.: The M.I.T. Press, 1965.

Samler, J. Where do counseling psychologists work? What do they do? What should they do? In Thompson, A.S. & Super, D.E., *The professional preparation of counseling psychologists: Report of the 1964 Greyston Conference.* New York:

Bureau of Publications, Teachers College, Columbia University, 1964, 43-68.

Schlossberg, N.K. & Goodman, J. A woman's place: Children's sex stereotyping of occupations. *Vocational Guidance Quarterly,* 1972, *20,* 266-270.

Shea, J.R., Spitz, R.S. & Zeller, F.A. *Dual careers: A longitudinal study of labor market experience of women.* Columbus, Ohio: Center for Human Resource Research, The Ohio State University, May, 1970. (Volume I)

Simpson, L.A. A study of employing agents' attitudes toward academic women in higher education. (Doctoral dissertation, Pennsylvania State University) Ann Arbor, Michigan: University Microfilms, 1969. No. 69-9810.

Smith, E.D. & Herr, E.L. Sex differences in the maturation of vocational attitudes among adolescents. *Vocational Guidance Quarterly,* 1972, *20,* 177-182.

Suniweick, N. Beyond the findings: Some interpretations and implications for the future. In Astin, H.S., Suniewick, N. & Dweck, S. *Women: A bibliography on their education and careers.* Washington, D.C.: Human Service Press, 1971, 11-26.

Super, D.E. *The psychology of careers.* New York: Harper and Row, 1957.

Super, D.E. Self-concepts in vocational development. In Super, D.E., *et al. Career development: Self concept theory.* New York: CEEB Research Monograph No. 4, 1963. (a)

Super, D.E. Vocational development in adolescence and early adulthood: Tasks and behaviors. In Super, D.E., *et al. Career development: Self-concept theory.* New York: CEEB Research Monograph No. 4, 1963. (b)

Tangri, S.F.S. Role-innovation in occupational choice among college women. (Doctoral dissertation, The University of Michigan) Ann Arbor, Michigan: University Microfilms, 1970. No. 70-4207.

Tennyson, W.W., Career development. *Review of Educational Research,* 1968, *38,* 346-361.

Tucker, B.Z. Feminine sex-role and occupational choice: A study of self and intergroup perceptions of three groups of women. (Doctoral dissertation, Temple University) Ann Arbor, Michigan: University Microfilms, 1971. No. 71-10, 837.

Turner, B.F. Socialization and career orientation among black and white college women. Paper presented at 80th Annual Convention of the American Psychological Association, Honolulu, Hawaii, September, 1972.

Vetter, L. *Career patterns of a national sample of women.* Columbus, Ohio: The Center for Vocational and Technical Education, The Ohio State University, in process.

Watley, D.J. & Kaplan, R. Career or marriage?: Aspirations and achievements of able young women. *Journal of Vocational Behavior,* 1971, *1,* 29-43.

Westervelt, E.M. Woman as a complete human being. *Journal of the National Association of Women Deans and Counselors,* 1966, *29,* 150-156.

Wolfson, K.T.P. Career development of college women. (Doctoral dissertation, University of Minnesota) Ann Arbor, Michigan: University Microfilms, 1972. No. 72-20, 160.

Women's Bureau, U.S. Department of Labor. *Counseling girls toward new perspectives.* Washington, D.C.: Women's Bureau, 1966.

Women's Bureau, U.S. Department of Labor. *Expanding opportunities for girls: Their special counseling needs.* Washington, D.C.: Women's Bureau, 1970.

Women's Bureau, U.S. Department of Labor. *Women workers today.* Washington, D.C.: Women's Bureau, 1971.

Women's Bureau, U.S. Department of Labor. *The myth and the reality.* Washington, D.C.: Women's Bureau, March, 1972. (a)

Women's Bureau, U.S. Department of Labor. *Twenty facts on women workers.* Washington, D.C.: Women's Bureau, 1972. (b)

Zytowski, D.G. Toward a theory of career development for women. *Personnel and Guidance Journal,* 1969, *47,* 660-664.

Sexual Bias in Personality Theory

MARY AUSTIN DOHERTY
Alverno College

Understanding human behavior is the goal of psychology. Yet dissatisfaction with the one-hundred-year yield from psychological theories and methods continues to mount. In a recent issue of *The Counseling Psychologist,* for example, (Franklin, 1971) readers were urged to lay aside theoretical formulations of personality development learned in graduate school as irrelevant to work in counseling clients of minority groups. The present article is a reinforcement of that suggestion as it relates to another group—women. That women as clients constitute a minority group requiring adequately trained counselors is a basic assumption of this article and of this entire section.

The purpose of this article is to raise questions regarding personality theories that constitute the rationale upon which the counseling psychologist bases his or her principles and methods for assisting clients. If personality theories and methods of gathering data on selected psychological variables can be seriously questioned regarding their relevance and appropriateness for women, then it will also be necessary to question counseling methods and approaches based upon these theories.

It will be difficult for both the reader and the author to engage in this critique. Theories explaining or describing human development and behavior have been advanced for half a century, and, although some consider the attempts premature, we have reached the point where syntheses of existing theories have begun to appear (Maddi, 1971). Also, studies of sex differences and their development as well as lengthy works on the psychology of women have been accumulating at an accelerating rate (Maccoby, 1966; Garai and Scheinfeld, 1968; Bardwick, 1971; Sherman, 1971). At this point in time it is not popular to stand back and ask whether our assumptions about "man" have been valid or indeed whether we have examined our assumptions about "man" at all. Although psychologists have become increasingly sensitive to the generalization bias as it affects social classes and cultures, they have failed to detect the "generic bias" which seeks to explain the behavior of humans, both men and women, in terms of "man."

Since theorists are a product of their own time and culture and develop theories out of their own experience and work with a unique population, it is the task of the counselor to examine these theories to ascertain whether the principles derived from them are compatible with contemporary culture and life styles of clients. It is the purpose of this article not to discuss selected theories of personality in detail but to raise questions regarding their relevancy for women.

The first psychological theory, though not a theory in the strict sense, is important to review because it may enable us to examine some of the assumptions underlying contemporary theories. It is essentially an "historical" theory. As psychologists have become more confident of their discipline during the past few decades, they have been willing to readmit to their ranks the philosophers of earlier centuries. It is the theory of these Western philosophical psychologists which I shall summarize briefly.

From writings of ancient Greek, medieval and early modern thinkers, two main themes regarding human personality and the relationship of the sexes emerge. First, the male is the prototype of humanity; the female is understood in relationship to him. What is observed in the man is characterized as human; the same traits observed in the woman to a greater or lesser degree (e.g., more emotional, less intelligent) are characterized as feminine. Hence there is a preoccupation with discovering the "essence" of femininity but not the "essence" of masculinity.

The second theme is the dichotomy established between the cognitive and affective aspects of human functioning and the assignation of them to the man and woman, respectively. The positive valuation of cognitive or rational behavior and the less positive or negative valuation of affective or sensual behavior paralleled the positive valuation of man over woman. It is instructive for the student of language to consider that phrases used in the past to describe the relationship of reason to the emotions—"give them direction because they are fickle and inconstant," "control them so they will not lead one astray"— are similar to those used to describe man's relationship to woman.

The significance of this second theme for our discussion of contemporary personality theories is twofold: Western civilization's exaltation of the rational and its strong anti-sensual bias, and the virtual identification of woman with her sensuality, her body. So pervasive are these ideas that to question the primacy of the rational or to suggest that man is as closely identified with his body as woman is is to court not only ridicule but professional oblivion.

To clarify this point, let us consider psychoanalytic theory. Although seriously questioned by many psychologists, Freudian and neo-Freudian theories continue to exert enormous influence in our understanding of personality dynamics. Since there are several critical analyses of the Freudian position on the psychology of women (Horney, 1967; Thompson, 1971; Sherman, 1971), my point here is simply to emphasize that Freudian theory reflects aspects of the two themes or basic assumptions described above.

Regarding the first assumption, both Freudian theory and vocabulary assume man as the prototype of the human person. Concepts of the Oedipal complex and penis envy reflect this assumption. The following selection from his writings illustrates not only Freud's (1965) conviction regarding woman's incompleteness but also the psychic consequence—a weakened superego.

> [In the girl] the castration complex prepares for the Oedipus complex instead of destroying it; the girl is driven out of her attachment to her mother through the influence of her envy for the penis, and she enters the Oedipus situation as though into a haven of refuge. In the absence of fear of castration the chief motive is lacking which leads boys to surmount the Oedipus complex. Girls remain in it for an indeterminate length of time; they demolish it late and, even so, incompletely. In these circumstances the formation of the super-ego must suffer; it cannot attain the strength and independence which give it its cultural significance, and feminists are not pleased when we point out to them the effects of this factor upon the average feminine character (p. 129).

Only by considering the male the complete human could Freud assert that something is missing in the female and proceed to construct a theory of femininity on that premise.

Regarding the second assumption, while admitting Freud's contribution to psychology in his recognition of the importance and significance of the irrational in human development, I believe his well-known assertion that for women, but not for men, anatomy is destiny illustrates his position regarding the identification of the woman with her body. Had Freud not been influenced by the assumptions of the man as prototype of humanity and the woman as identified with her body, it is difficult to see how he could not have been impressed by a similar identification of man with his body in his concern with his sexual organ and physical strength. There is no assertion on Freud's part that man's anatomy is his destiny, and yet such a conclusion follows quite naturally from Freud's premises.

Basic education for a prospective counselor of woman should include a careful reading of Freud's original writings on the topic of feminine psychology (they are not extensive) and critical discussions with groups of men and women regarding his assumptions and conclusions. Such an analysis of Freud's writings on women may be considered by many to be unnecessary because his ideas in this area have been so effectively challenged that they are no longer influential. But one need only scan some recent works on the psychology of women (Bardwick, 1971) to recognize that the Freudian theory regarding women has its adherents. Our need, therefore, is to illuminate for ourselves our own attitudes and ideas so that we may begin to recognize the assumptions upon which our working theory of personality is based.

A currently popular theory employed by many counselors in developing principles of therapy and counseling is Erik Erikson's (1963a) psychosocial theory. Since he is one of the few theorists who have explored adult development and since his central theme of identity has provided a conceptual tool for analysis of some basic sociological and political questions, it is important to assess the adequacy of his eight-stage theory of development for understanding contemporary women.

While it may appear during the course of the ensuing discussion that the assessment of Erikson's theory is predominantly negative, I wish to emphasize that it is only because Erikson is willing to grapple at all with the question of the identity of women that we can discuss the theory. In an earlier draft of this article, I attempted to analyze the fulfillment or actualization theories for their contribution to our understanding of women. But as is well known, not only do these theories not deal with this question but empirical investigations of their propositions are based predominantly on samples of men. What it means for a woman to be self-actualized or to realize her potentialities in contemporary America is largely unexplored.

Therefore, the major questions to be asked of current personality theory will be directed to Erikson's theory but on the assumption that the questions can be applied to other theories and empirical investigations, with the hope that they may assist us in the formulation of more sophisticated theories of human development.

The assessment of Erikson's theory is threefold. First, an analysis of his theory within the framework used in this article requires the question of whether Erikson's model is essentially a male model and, therefore, inappropriate to an understanding of women. Secondly, since Erikson's theory is based on polarities—trust-mistrust, autonomy-shame-doubt, initiative-guilt, industry-inferiority, identity-role confusion, intimacy-isolation, generativity-stagnation, integrity-despair—it is within the framework of this article to question the validity and psychological soundness of this approach as currently used in personality theory. Treating polarities, notably the masculine-feminine polarity, as bipolar ends of a unidimensional scale has retarded sophisticated conceptualizations of their dynamic interaction and, in the case of our understanding of the sexes, fostered a view of human development constricting to both sexes. And, lastly, since in the area of the psychology of women Erikson is most widely known for his theory relating feminine identity and inner space, I shall discuss this area briefly.

An exhaustive analysis of Erikson's theory making explicit its assumptions of the male as model of humanity is beyond the scope of this article. By citing a few examples from Erikson's works, I hope to encourage the reader to develop a critical stance regarding the relevance of the theory for understanding women.

It seems legitimate to raise the question of how valid for understanding women is a theory which deals with its central theme of identity as it is observed in men and seeks to explain identity in women through some accommodation of the theory. That the development of the man is for Erikson prototypical of the human is evident in his attempts to explain "differences" in development. "Different" from what? Except, perhaps, the norm established by the theorist himself. Erikson virtually admitted this in the preface to

Youth: Change and Challenge (1963b), when he pointed out that theorists have failed to develop fully the problem of identity formation of female youth. Erikson (1968) maintains that the young woman achieves her identity not prior to the stage of intimacy, as does the male, but during this stage as she "relinquishes the care received from the parental family in order to commit herself to the love of a stranger and to the care to be given to his and her offspring" (p. 265).

The following excerpts indicate that for Erikson (1968) there exists a model of development of identity with which the development of identity in the young woman must be compared. "For example, woman's life *too* [emphasis added] contains an adolescent stage which I have come to call a psychosocial moratorium, a sanctioned period of delay of adult functioning" (p. 282). He continues:

> Young women often ask whether they can "have an identity" before they know whom they will marry and for whom they will make a home. Granted that something in the young woman's identity must keep itself open for the peculiarities of the man to be joined and of the children to be brought up, I think that much of a young woman's identity is already defined in her kind of attractiveness and in the selective nature of her search for the man (or men) by whom she wishes to be sought. This, of course, is only the psychosexual aspect of her identity, and she may go far in postponing its closure while training herself as a worker and a citizen and while developing as a person within the role possibilities of her time (p. 283).*

Contrast this with Erikson's (1963a) description of the "young adult" from his summary of the sixth stage, "Intimacy vs. Isolation."

> The young adult, emerging from the search for and the insistence on identity, is eager and willing to fuse his identity with that of others. He is ready for intimacy, that is, the capacity to commit himself to concrete affiliations and partnerships and to develop the ethical strength to abide by such commitments, even though they may call for significant sacrifices and compromises. Body and ego must now be masters of the organ modes and of the nuclear conflicts, in order to be able to face the fear of ego loss in situations which call for self-abandon: in the solidarity of close affiliations, in orgasms and sexual unions, in close friendships and *in physical combat* [emphasis added], in experiences of inspiration by teachers and of intuition from the recesses of the self. The avoidance of such experiences because of fear of ego loss may lead to a deep sense of isolation and consequent self-absorption (pp. 263-64).†

*From *Identity: Youth and Crisis,* by E. Erikson. Copyright © 1968 by W.W. Norton & Co., Inc. This and all other quotations from this source are reprinted by permission.

†From *Childhood and Society* (2nd Ed.), by E. Erikson. Copyright © 1963 by W.W. Norton & Co., Inc. This and all other quotations from this source are reprinted by permission.

Although I assume the above description is meant to serve as a general theoretical statement of the development of the young person, it is clear from a careful reading of the statement itself and, particularly, by contrasting it with the preceding quotation that Erikson has the male adult as his model.

That Erikson is ambivalent about the identity of women as including roles of "worker" and "citizen," as suggested in the excerpt about young women above, can be demonstrated by contrasting the following two statements.

From his general description of identity:

> The integration now taking place in the form of ego identity is more than the sum of the childhood identifications. It is the accrued experience of the ego's ability to integrate all identifications with the vicissitudes of the libido, with the aptitudes developed out of endowment, and with the opportunities offered in social roles. The sense of ego identity, then, is the accrued confidence that the inner sameness and continuity prepared in the past are matched by the sameness and continuity of one's meaning for others, as evidenced in the tangible promise of a career (Erikson, 1963a, p. 261).

From his description of woman's "identity":

> The singular loveliness and brilliance which young women display in an array of activities obviously removed from the future function of childbearing is one of those esthetic phenomena which almost seem to transcend all goals and purposes and therefore come to symbolize the self-containment of pure being—wherefore young women, in the arts of the ages, have served as the visible representation of ideals and ideas and as the creative man's muse, anima, and enigma. One is somewhat reluctant, therefore, to assign an ulterior meaning to what seems so meaningful in itself, and to suggest that the inner space is tacitly present in it all. A true moratorium must have a term and a conclusion: womanhood arrives when attractiveness and experience have succeeded in selecting what is to be admitted to the welcome of the inner space "for keeps" (Erikson, 1963b, p. 283).

It is not my purpose here to discuss the validity of Erikson's search for identity. When the lives of women are studied with the same seriousness as the lives of men, the data will illuminate what is presently virtually an unexplored area. As I have stated before, my purpose in questioning Erikson's attempt to describe the differences in women's personality development is a far more serious critique than questioning the accuracy of his observations. That Erikson "observes" the "differences" in women is precisely the point. That a theory of personality should be based upon the development of the man and that the development of the woman must be contrasted with it cannot be considered a theory of personality. Not only is it a theory not appropriate for women—it is not appropriate for men. What is the alternative? A personality theory describing the development of the human person, both man and woman, and the differential biological and social influences affecting both of them. To illustrate my point using Erikson's theory as a framework: what might it do for our understanding of the human person if we, and Erikson, wrestled with the myriad and differential aspects of the achievement of identity by women *as well as* men, in and through emotional distance from human persons, *as well as* in and through intimate personal relationships? Such a theoretical formulation has not even received serious attention. That Erikson, who has continually emphasized the importance of the social milieu in shaping personality, could formulate a theory based on a male model is a measure of the pervasiveness of this view of "humanity."

Consideration of the second aspect of our assessment of Erikson's theory—his use of polarities—presents me with a methodological problem. If I believe what I have written above concerning the inadequacy of a male model of personality development in understanding women, even when it includes supplements describing the development of women, then an analysis of Erikson's polarities seems not only unnecessary but theoretically indefensible. My justification for pursuing this question of polarities is precisely its relationship to the broader question discussed above. Carlson (1972) has suggested that our understanding of personality might benefit enormously from the development of a conceptual framework in which components of polarity were investigated for their vital, continuing contribution to human development. She has presented cogent arguments for the investigation of both components of a polarity as dimensions intrinsically bound together in a complex fashion.

The psychologist's tendency to define human as male reflects the tendency to conceptualize the masculine-feminine polarity in the same unidimensional fashion as other psychological polarities. For this reason I believe there is value in reflecting on the link between the polarities of Erikson's eight stages and the masculine-feminine polarity. In both instances the polarities are viewed as unidimensional with the thrust toward the more "positive" pole. But both human experience and empirical evidence have demonstrated that characteristics defined as ends of a dimension—e.g., passive-aggressive, dependence-independence, feminine-masculine—coexist and interact dynamically within the individual. Let us consider, as an example, the interaction of personality-trait dichotomy with the masculine-feminine dichotomy in Erikson's second stage.

In reflecting on the autonomy-shame-doubt dimension of this stage, it is clear that for Erikson movement toward autonomy is attained through self-control and will power and should be achieved without loss of self-esteem. Although Erikson indicates that the child's sense of autonomy must be continually reworked throughout life, Erikson's discussion of this stage polarizes autonomy and shame rather than explores their dynamic relationship. Although shame enters into the attitudes and beliefs of most people (Lynd, 1961), it is not intrinsic to Erikson's formulation that shame and doubt may be appropriate responses to certain life situations and "loss of face" a valid expression of growth and integrity.

My reason for choosing this stage as an example should be obvious. It serves as a parallel to the masculine-feminine polarity and allows us to raise parallel questions. For example: Has our conceptual dichotomization of autonomy and shame contributed to the general inability of adults (primarily males?) to submit to "loss of face" even for a highly valued goal and/or in the face of clearly recognized misjudgment? Has our conceptual dichotomization of masculine and feminine contributed to the general inability of adults (both male and female?) to submit to being identified by characteristics ordinarily attributed to the other sex?

Although the form of questioning employed above illustrates the central problem in the current use of polarities in psychology, questions specific to the appropriateness of these polarities for an understanding of women also arise. Although this latter consideration is not the major point under discussion here, a few questions will be posed to illustrate the necessity for critical examination of theories for their suitability in understanding women if one is not convinced by the argument presented above regarding their general inappropriateness for men and women. Examples of such questions are: How, for the girl and woman, is the development of autonomy at this stage and throughout her life explained in the light of empirical findings regarding low self-esteem among women? How do we relate growth in autonomy with societal discouragement of autonomy in women and societal approval of experiences which shame women and attempt to break their willpower? Why is the ability to live with some indecisiveness—which is related to shame (Lynd, 1961)—considered a weakness in women at a time in history when certainty in many areas is unattainable?

Questions similar to those raised here can be formulated for each of Erikson's stages. The result of such serious questioning will enable the counselor to examine his or her own assumptions regarding appropriate behavior of women and men.

Related to the discussion above is the final aspect of Erikson's theory which we proposed to discuss: his identification of womanhood and inner space. One reason Erikson's view of women is considered by many to be at best inadequate, at worst a distortion is his virtual identification of woman with mother. His formulations are not unlike Freud's identification of woman with her body. For, although Erikson repudiates Freud's assertion of the girl's preoccupation with her "missing" organ, the penis, he insists that the existence of the productive inner-bodily space is central to her search for identity. The following quotation is illustrative of this position: "Women have found their identities in the care suggested in their bodies and in the needs of their issue and seem to have taken it for granted that the outer world space belongs to the men" (Erikson, 1968, p. 274).

That Erikson (1968) is sensitive to a critique of his position is evident in the following quotation, but his last sentence, nevertheless, reveals the basis for the legitimacy of the criticism.

> In assigning a central place to generative modalities, I, too, seem to repeat the often obsessive emphasis on sexual symbols in psychoanalytic theory and to ignore the fact that women as well as men have all-human organisms fit for, and most of the time enjoyed in, activities far removed from the sexual. But while both sexual repression and sexual monomania isolate sexuality from the total design of human actuality, we must be interested in how sex differences, once taken for granted, are integrated in that design. Sexual differences, however, besides offering a polarization of life styles and the maximization of mutual enjoyment . . . nevertheless retain the morphology of procreation (p. 279).

Providing an illuminating summary of Erikson's position regarding the masculine-feminine polarity and his identification of femininity with motherhood is the following quotation (Erikson, 1968):

> Men, of course, have shared and taken care of some of the concerns for which women stand: each sex can transcend itself to feel and to represent the concerns of the other. For even as real women harbor a legitimate as well as a compensatory masculinity, so real men can partake of motherliness—if permitted to do so by powerful mores (pp. 285-6).

The change in the parallel structure of the last sentence (which in true parallel form would read . . . so real men harbor a legitimate as well as a compensatory femininity) as well as the concluding phrase regarding the necessity of powerful mores reveal Erikson's model of personality as male, his polarity of masculine and feminine, and his definition of women and their role.

Our assessment of psychology's approach to the understanding of women would be incomplete if it failed to reflect the increasing concern of psychologists with questions of sex differences. Recent investigations of differences in behavior between women and men are based on the assumption that such research is free of the biases inherent in the personality theories discussed above and, therefore, more likely to yield "objective" data regarding women. It is important, therefore, to raise, regarding research on sex differences, the question basic to this article: are investigations of sex differences based upon the assumption that man is the prototype of the human species? I will deal briefly with this question by pointing out two major problems inherent in research on sex differences: definitions of constructs and selection of research topics.

Recently the work of Horner (1970) has reopened the question of the motivation of women and subjected it to greater scrutiny. McClelland's (McClelland *et al.*, 1953) theory on achievement motivation was not able to account for nor to predict the behavior of women. Horner's investigations have indicated that the phenomenon "motive to avoid success" is more prevalent in women than in men. Although the publicity accorded this research focused needed attention on the familial and professional conflicts experienced by women, a larger question is involved. An assessment of the current status of research in motivation reveals that motivation has been defined largely as a masculine construct based upon male values of competition. To discover, then, that women are not "motivated," that is, that they are not like men, says nothing about motivation in women. Indeed it is questionable whether current definitions and research in motivation-as-competition yield data appropriate to understanding men today. As long as psychologists continue to generalize to women from definitions or constructs developed in research on men, women will inevitably be described as "not male" and, more important, we will fail to develop a psychology appropriate to understanding either women or men.

Another example of a definitional problem can be drawn from research on emotion and emotionality. The stereotype that women are more emotional than men finds support in psychological research largely because emotional behaviors attributed to men, such as anger, aggression, and hostility, are often not included in classifications of emotionality. These latter consist of behaviors reflecting anxiety, fear, and neuroticism, usually attributed to women (Sherman, 1971).

In stating that manifestations of emotionality, as usually defined, are ordinarily attributed to women is not to suggest that such findings themselves are not open to question. They are. But a more fundamental question is the definition itself which reflects the cultural bias. For example, why do we define as "fear" a one-year-old female child's remaining near the mother for a longer period in a new situation (one minute vs. twenty seconds) (Kagan, 1972) but not define as "fear" the male child's more immediate *active* behavior in the same situation? Do psychologists engage in this selective defining and observing because they "know" that females are more emotional (*more* than whom—the norm?) and, therefore, their behavior must be explained? A classic study supporting this contention that the norm of adult behavior in our society is male adult behavior (Broverman *et al.,* 1970) should be required reading for all counselors of women.

The second problem related to investigations of sex differences is the selection of research topics. For example, for every study of nurturance there are hundreds of studies of aggression. Serious investigations of nurturance, with its biological and environmental components, in both men and women would be of enormous significance in understanding interpersonal relations at all levels of human interaction. What is the explanation for the neglect of this important research area? Is it the undervaluing of characteristics generally attributed to women? Is it because nurturance has become synonymous with mothering and, therefore, concluded to be nonexistent in the general population?

Again, it might be well to reinforce the point made throughout this article that even studies which attempt to present, without obvious bias, data on sex differences resort to an identification of woman with mother. For example, the following statement by Lynn (1972) concludes a discussion of different cognitive styles in women and men.

> In conclusion, I hope that women can add much that is uniquely theirs to our vocational and public life. I join with Erik Erikson in the wish that when women gain full participation they will add maternal concern to the cares of the world governing (p. 257).

For my own conclusion I hope that psychologists will begin to develop theories of personality based on observations and studies of contemporary women and men and that, in the meantime, counselors of women will adopt a critical stance with respect to current personality theories and investigations of sex differences.

REFERENCES

Bardwick, J.M. *Psychology of women: A study of bio-cultural conflicts.* New York: Harper & Row, 1971.

Broverman, I.K., Broverman, D.M., Clarkson, F.E., Rosenkrantz, P.S., & Vogel, S.R. Sex-role stereotypes and clinical judgments of mental health. *Journal of Consulting and Clinical Psychology,* 1970, *34,* 1-7.

Carlson, R. Understanding women: Implications for personality theory and research. *Journal of Social Issues,* 1972, *28,* 17-32.

Erikson, E. *Childhood and society* (2nd ed.). New York: Norton, 1963. (a)

Erikson, E. *Youth: Change and challenge.* New York: Basic Books, 1963. (b)

Erikson, E. *Identity: Youth and crisis.* New York: Norton, 1968.

Franklin, A.J. To be young, gifted and black with inappropriate professional training: A critique of counseling programs. *The Counseling Psychologist,* 1971, *2*(4), 107-112.

Freud, S. *New introductory lectures on psychoanalysis.* New York: Norton, 1965.

Garai, J.F. & Scheinfeld, A. Sex differences in mental and behavioral traits. *Genetic Psychology Monographs,* 1968, *77,* 169-299.

Horner, M. Femininity and successful achievement: A basic inconsistency. In J. Bardwick, E. Douvan, M. Horner, & D. Guttmann, *Feminine personality and conflict.* Monterey, Cal.: Brooks/Cole, 1970.

Horney, K. *Feminine psychology,* London: Routledge & K. Paul, 1967.

Kagan, J. The emergence of sex differences. *School Review,* 1972, *80,* 217-227.

Lynd, H.M. *On shame and the search for identity.* New York: Science Editions, 1961.

Lynn, D.B. Determinants of intellectual growth in women. *School Review,* 1972, *80,* 241-260.

Maccoby, E.E. (Ed.). *The development of sex differences.* Stanford: Stanford Univ. Press, 1966.

Maddi, S. *Perspectives on personality: A comparative approach.* Boston: Little, Brown & Co., 1971.

McClelland, D.C., Atkinson, J.W., Clark, R.A., & Lowell, E.L. *The achievement motive.* New York: Appleton, 1953.

Sherman, J. *On the psychology of women: A survey of empirical studies.* Springfield, Ill.: Charles C Thomas, 1971.

Thompson, C.M. *On women.* Edited by Maurice R. Green. New York: New American Library, 1971.

Facilitating
the Growth of Women
through Assertive Training

PATRICIA JAKUBOWSKI
University of Missouri at St. Louis

Many women find that their anxiety about producing interpersonal conflicts often prevents them from taking stances and expressing their true feelings, beliefs, and opinions. In other words, their anxiety prevents them from being assertive. Three converging trends are largely responsible for a growing awareness and concern about this problem. The first trend is the wide-spread acceptance of the cultural imperative for self-growth which, in addition to giving birth to encounter and sensitivity groups, has also caused an increasing number of women to view self-actualization as their birthright. As women assess their own potentials for growth, they discover that their difficulty in tolerating interpersonal conflict and in standing up for their rights is an obstacle to achieving greater self-fulfillment. The second converging trend is the growing inflexibility of the sex roles. As this develops, women are experimenting with different role behaviors and are stepping outside of the home and being exposed to situations—all of which have revealed many previously unsuspected inadequacies in their interpersonal skills. The third converging trend is the growth of the women's movement and the resulting stimulation of both awareness and self-examination. While in one way it increases women's self-acceptance, in another way it causes many women to raise their personal aspirations to be *strong* and *effective* as well as feminine. A major component of this strength and effectiveness is personal assertiveness. Women keenly feel internal pressures for growth at the same time that they feel unprepared to meet their raised aspirations. Thus, there is an increased awareness and concern about personal limitations and a great desire to overcome these limitations. A major limitation for many women is not being able to be as assertive as they would like. This has led to a growing demand for assertive-skill training.

Before describing the assertive-training procedure, it is important to distinguish among assertive, non-assertive, and aggressive behavior.

This article was originally published under the name Patricia Jakubowski-Spector.

Assertive Behavior

Assertive behavior is that type of interpersonal behavior in which a person stands up for her legitimate rights in such a way that the rights of others are not violated. Assertive behavior is an honest, direct, and appropriate expression of one's feelings, beliefs and opinions. It communicates respect (not deference) for the other person, although not necessarily for that person's behavior. This definition incorporates many of the characteristics suggested by Alberti and Emmons (1970) and Lazarus (1971). There are various levels of quality in assertive responses. For example, when a woman's verbal message clearly conveys an assertion of her rights but her body posture, voice level, facial expression, and breathing tempo all convey undue anxiety and may even contradict her verbal message, her assertive response is of a lower quality than if both her verbal and non-verbal behaviors were consonant.

Although Serber (1971) argues that the term "assertion" should also include such interpersonal skills as being able to give and take tenderness and affection, I agree with Lazarus (1971) that to do this would stretch the term beyond its lexical boundaries. Assertion would become so broad that it would be a relatively meaningless concept.

Non-Assertive Behavior

Non-assertive behavior is that type of interpersonal behavior which enables the person's rights to be violated by another. This can occur in two ways: First, she fails to assert herself when another person deliberately attempts to infringe upon her rights. For example, when a friend, who rarely returns favors, asks her to babysit, *knowing* that she's made other social plans for the evening, her failure to tell the friend her plans enables the other to take advantage of her. Second, the other person does not want to encroach upon her rights, but her failure to express her needs, feelings, etc. results in an inadvertent violation. For example, when a neighbor drops in for coffee, *not knowing* that she is terribly busy, her failure to assert her needs results in her sacrificing or violating her own rights.

A non-assertive person inhibits her honest, spontaneous reactions and typically feels hurt, anxious, and sometimes angry as a result of her behavior. She frequently sends double messages. Verbally she says, "Sure, I'll be glad to babysit," while non-verbally her tight mouth, weak voice, and averted eyes indirectly communicate the opposite message.

Most non-assertive behaviors are situation specific; that is, they characteristically occur only in certain situations. Alberti and Emmons (1970) have called this "situational non-assertiveness." Although most people have some situational non-assertiveness, some people are generally unable to assert themselves under most or nearly all situations. A "generally non-assertive" person is not able to do anything that would disturb anyone.

He is constantly giving in to any request made of him or feels guilty for turning someone down. He has always done what his parents wanted of him. He feels he has no ideas of his own and is cowed by others. Whereas most persons will at least protest a little when their rights are badly abused, the general non-asserter will say nothing at all (Alberti and Emmons, 1970, p. 38).

Their deep feelings of inadequacy, extreme inhibition, and lack of appropriate emotional responsiveness require more extensive and complex therapy than the assertive-training procedure which is discussed in this article.

In some cases non-assertive behavior can be construed as a subtle type of manipulation in which the individual abdicates her rights in order to influence certain kinds of behavior from the other person. Figure 1 illustrates how this takes place. Since these bargains or exchanges are seldom explicitly stated, the other person usually fails to fulfill the terms of the unspoken bargain and generally takes the self-sacrifice for granted. The woman then feels bitter and cheated. It would be better if she were more assertive and directly asked to have her needs met.

Figure 1. The Unspoken Bargain.

I Won't Assert Myself When You:	In Exchange for Your:
Boyfriend...... constantly talk about your girlfriends, socialize only with your friends, ridicule my opinions.	dating only me, changing these objectionable behaviors without my having to ask you to.
Husband....... make me the scapegoat for your business frustrations, give me the "silent" treatment, are abrupt in sex.	staying married to me and maintaining our home.
Employer...... constantly ask me to work on my lunch hour for no extra pay, unfairly criticize me.	giving me a raise without my having to ask for it, never firing me.

Aggressive Behavior

Aggressive behavior is that type of interpersonal behavior in which a person stands up for her own rights in such a way that the rights of others are violated. The purpose of the aggressive behavior is to humiliate, dominate, or put the other person down rather than to simply express one's honest emotions or thoughts. It is an attack on the person rather than on the other person's behavior. Aggressive behavior is quite frequently a hostile overreaction or outburst which results from past pent-up anger. Letting someone else know your angry feelings at the time they occur can be assertive behavior. Making that person responsible for your feeling angry, or degrading the other person because you feel angry is aggressive behavior. Figure 2 compares non-assertive, assertive, and aggressive behavior. Because assertion and aggres-

Figure 2. A Comparison of Non-Assertive, Assertive, and Aggressive Behavior.

	Non-Assertive Behavior	*Assertive Behavior*	*Aggressive Behavior*
Characteristics of the behavior:	Emotionally dishonest, indirect, self-denying, inhibited	(Appropriately) emotionally honest, direct, self-enhancing, expressive	(Inappropriately) emotionally honest, direct, self-enhancing at expense of another, expressive
Your feelings when you engage in this behavior:	Hurt, anxious at the time, and possibly angry later	Confident, self-respecting at the time and later	Righteous, superior, depreciatory at the time, and possibly guilty later
The other person's feelings about herself when you engage in this behavior:	Guilty or superior	Valued, respected	Hurt, humiliated
The other person's feelings about you when you engage in this behavior:	Irritated, pity, disgusted	Generally respect	Angry, vengeful

Adapted from *Your Perfect Right: A Guide to Assertive Behavior (2nd Ed.),* by R.E. Alberti and M.L. Emmons. Copyright 1974 by Impact Publishers, Inc. Reprinted by permission.

sion are frequently confused, a series of brief examples may help to further distinguish the two. In each of the following examples, the first response is aggressive and the second is assertive.

• Complaining about the unsatisfactory nature of love-making:

Bill, you're really inadequate as a lover. If this is how our sex life is going to be, we might as well forget it right now. I could get more satisfaction doing it myself.

Bill, I'd like to talk about how we could act differently in sex so that I could get greater satisfaction. For one thing, I think you really need to slow down a lot so that I could start tuning into my own sensations.

- Refusing a roommate's request to borrow clothes:

    Absolutely not! I've had enough of your leeching clothes off of me.

    I'm sorry, but the last time you borrowed my sweater, you were careless with it and really got it dirty. I don't want to loan you any more of my clothes.

- Refusing to type term papers for a boyfriend:

    Where in the hell do you get off asking me to type your papers? What do you think I am—some sort of slave?

    I think that it's time I told you how I feel when you constantly ask me to type your papers. I'm getting irritated, and I feel like I'm being taken for granted when you assume that I'll type for you. I hate typing, and I think that you're asking too much when you expect me to do that for you. Please don't ask me to type any more.

- Reprimanding one's children:

    You kids are so sloppy . . . sometimes I hate you. You've got to be the worst kids in the whole city! If I had known motherhood was going to be like this, I would never have had any kids at all!

    Listen, I feel as though I'm being taken advantage of when you are this sloppy in cleaning up after yourselves. I can't enjoy myself with you in the evening when I have to spend all that extra time cleaning up after your mess. This is a problem that must be solved. What are your ideas?

- Refusing a request to babysit:

    No, thanks! You couldn't pay me enough to babysit for your kids. Why don't you stay home once in a while?

    Beth, I'm sorry but I feel too tired to babysit after working all day. I hope that you can find someone else.

As therapists become sensitized to deficits in assertive skills, they will frequently find that upon closer examination many psychological problems also involve assertive problems. The following examples will illustrate how the presenting problems were ultimately treated with assertive training:

- *Presenting problem:* Mild depression soon after the wedding in the absence of other marital problems. This may occur particularly among women who have had some fulfillment in their careers before marriage, who have established their own identities, and who do not want to "live vicariously" through their husbands.

    Assertive problem: Fears of becoming too dominated or "totally submerged" by her husband's personality are exacerbated by not knowing how or being afraid to stand up for her legitimate rights. A frequent underlying issue concerns how the woman can be assertive *and* a good wife.

• *Presenting problem:* Consistent inability or great difficulty in "achieving" orgasm in intercourse with a boyfriend.

Assertive problem: Attempts to use Masters and Johnson's (1970) sexual shaping therapy are thwarted when the woman cannot be assertive to tell the man what she finds sexually stimulating, irritating, etc., to refuse sex when she's not sufficiently stimulated, or to ask for tenderness after sex. Common underlying assertive issues concern the woman's right to refuse sex and her fear of hurting the man if she tells him that she is not being sexually satisfied.

• *Presenting problem:* Various somatic complaints—headaches, stomach aches, back aches—which have a psychogenic origin.

Assertive problem: When the situations that arouse the tension and anxiety are ones in which the woman fails to stand up for her rights and where she inhibits her spontaneous reactions, swallowing her hurt, irritation, or humiliation, the woman can benefit from assertive training.

• *Presenting problem:* Impulsively quits attractive jobs and bitterly complains about how she was "treated" by her employer and fellow employees: "The other workers didn't do their job, and I had to do all their work as well as my own. The boss unjustly criticized me for mistakes the others made. I kept having to do extra work and run errands for my boss during my lunch hour" etc.

Assertive problem: Quite commonly in this type of employment problem the woman is failing to assert reasonable small complaints as they occur. Instead she continues pretending that she is not irritated until her anger finally overwhelms her, and she suddenly quits her job.

• *Presenting problem:* Teacher can't establish good classroom control. She either exerts passive leadership and her students run completely wild, or she over-reacts with severe punishment for minor infractions of classroom rules.

Assertive problem: In addition to learning facilitative communication skills and learning how to systematically apply contingent social reinforcement and other teaching techniques, this teacher also needs assertive training in order to learn how to facilitatively confront students with their behavior and to appropriately stand up for her rights as a teacher so that she neither denies her rights—and exerts non-assertive, passive leadership—nor aggressively over-reacts in the defense of her rights.

ASSERTIVE-TRAINING PROCEDURE

In the strict sense of the term, "skill training" involves a defined set of behaviors which are gradually acquired through an instructional program which has clear, behaviorally defined entry and terminal points and clear instructional steps between these two points. The learner gradually acquires and refines her skills as she completes each successive instructional step, finally terminating with a defined set of behaviors which she can execute with some specified degree of proficiency. Unfortunately, at this time assertive-training programs are not yet fully developed as "skill-training" programs according to a strict definition. However, the literature has been expanding in the last two years, and the foundations for a more systematic training approach are being rapidly laid (McFall and Marston, 1970; McFall and Lillesand, 1971).

This article will describe a semistructured assertive-training approach which has three goals: (1) to educate the woman to her interpersonal rights; (2) to overcome whatever blocks exist to acting assertively; and (3) to develop and refine assertive behaviors through active practice methods. Many techniques may be used to achieve these goals; however, only a few will be described here. Modeling is a promising technique in assertive training, but due to space limitations it will not be discussed here. Interested readers are referred to Bandura (1971), Friedman (1971), McFall and Lillesand (1971), and Rathus (1973). Although this assertive-training program will be described as occurring in a series of successive steps, in actual practice these steps may occur in virtually any order.

Awareness and Motivation

When the therapist, using situations which are drawn from the client's life, carefully distinguishes among assertive, aggressive, and non-aggressive behavior, the client usually realizes quickly that she has an assertive problem. It is generally easy to motivate such a client to want to acquire assertive skills, since, by the very fact that she has sought therapy, she has already admitted to herself that she is unhappy. Usually all that is necessary is that the therapist discuss the bad effects that the non-assertive behavior has on the client's life. However, if the therapist has failed to distinguish between assertion and aggression, some women may reject this training because they associate both assertion and aggression with masculinity, and they may greatly fear that assertive training will cause them to lose their femininity. In working with women, it is extremely important that these distinctions be carefully drawn.

The creation of awareness and motivation to acquire assertive skills is quite different in non-therapy situations (i.e., consciousness-raising groups of married suburban women). Here the women may not even admit the existence of an assertive problem of any significant proportion. In many cases their entire life style is so dependent upon their acting non-assertively that to even consider changing is an overwhelming threat. In these cases assertion as a "way of life" will probably not be accepted, but training groups which deal with much more limited behaviors, such as teaching the women to be assertive with service personnel (i.e., garage mechanics), are more likely to be successful. Perhaps after some gain is made in these limited areas, these women may be more ready to change in other more personally relevant areas.

Developing a Belief System

A major goal of assertive training is building a personal belief system which will help the client to support and justify her acting assertively. This is important so that the client: (1) can continue to believe in her right to act assertively even when she is unjustly criticized for her assertive behavior; (2) can counteract her own irrational guilt that later occurs as a result of having asserted herself; (3) can be proud of her assertion even if no one else is pleased with this behavior; and (4) can be more likely to assert herself.

An important part of this belief system concerns the client's acceptance of certain basic interpersonal rights. While most of these interpersonal rights are very simple, and naturally assertive people act on these rights without even considering them as such, this is not the case with non-assertive people, many of whom do not really believe that they have a right to their feelings, beliefs, or opinions. These interpersonal rights are usually identified in the context of discussing several specific situations in which the clients failed to assert themselves. A recently developed stimulus film (Jakubowski, Pearlman, and Coburn, 1975) which succinctly presents a variety of assertive situations could be used to accelerate this discussion process. The scenes in this film are designed to stimulate the viewers to consider such important issues as the nature of one's interpersonal rights, personal obstacles to acting assertively, and the relative merits of alternative assertive responses.

The following example illustrates how several group members helped one woman to identify and accept her right to refuse an acquaintance's request to borrow her records. Although this example illustrates a simple verbal discussion method of assuring a woman her rights, a leader is certainly not limited to this approach and could use other techniques which would achieve the same goal.

Case Example

Susan: Why didn't you tell her that you didn't want to loan that record?

Anne: I was afraid that she'd think I was petty.

Leader: What about your right to say "No"?

Anne: I don't know. . . . I guess deep down I believe I *shouldn't feel* that I don't want to loan my records.

Leader: So what's wrong with your feeling that way?

Anne: Well . . . it's wrong to be selfish. I shouldn't be so possessive about my things.

Ericka: That's sure different from the way I see it!

Anne: What do you mean? (curiously)

Ericka: If you've got bad feelings about loaning records, then you really shouldn't loan them. I mean, like . . . I don't mind loaning some of my things. It's not any big moral issue . . . I'm not doing it to be a better person. It's just that I don't really mind loaning things like my hair dryer and stuff. But—wow—when it comes down to clothes, I do mind. I believe my feelings matter. *They should matter,* if not to other people, at least to myself. I have a right to have my feelings respected. And you've got a right to your feelings, and I don't see anything wrong with that! The other person may not like your feelings, but that doesn't take away from the legitimacy of your feelings.

Leader: Anne, are you still worried about what the other person will think of you?

Anne: Well . . . if I've got a right to my hang-ups—my little idiosyncrasies—I guess that the other person will just have to respect that. If they don't like it, well, I'm sorry. I guess that's just too bad.

In helping the client to build a belief system which will effectively support her assertive behavior, it is important that, in addition to believing that she has certain rights which she is entitled to exercise, she also hold two other convictions.

The first conviction is that *she will be happier if she appropriately exercises her rights.* When a person is learning how to become assertive, she is not merely changing a simple behavior; she's also changing how she interacts with others and consequently how she feels about herself and, to some extent, even what she values! Most importantly, she has to learn to accept her own thoughts and feelings even when they are different from how one "should" supposedly feel. This self-acceptance almost invariably results in a raised self-concept and increased personal happiness. There is, however, one important exception. If the woman's relationship with another person is *dependent* upon her continuing to act non-assertively, then her becoming assertive may very well end the relationship unless the other person can also reciprocally change. When the relationship is with an intimate male and the woman wants to maintain the relationship, it is advisable that the therapist also see the male in an attempt to prepare him for the experience and to help him change. Sometimes the end result of such intervention is a more satisfying and healthy relationship.

The second conviction is that *non-assertion is hurtful in the long run.* It hurts relationships, since it prevents the person from sharing her genuine thoughts and feelings, and this essentially limits the closeness and intimacy that can grow only out of risking authentic encounters with others. As Jourard (1964) has so cogently commented, "Being polite out of fear of being offensive and hiding one's discontent with the situation or the behavior of the other is a sure way of either destroying a relationship or of preventing one from really forming" (p. 38). Furthermore, non-assertion can inadvertently reinforce hurtful behavior on the part of others. For example, when a wife acquiesces to her domineering and critical husband, her non-assertive behavior may serve to strengthen his destructive behavior. In addition, the wife's modeling of self-effacing behavior may bring about ambivalent feelings within the daughter concerning her own femininity, viewing it as a source of weakness rather than strength.

When the client has the needed assertive skills in her repertoire but is inhibited from acting upon them because she lacks an appreciation of her rights, a discussion about rights and the resulting insight alone are frequently sufficient to prompt assertive behavior. However, usually the client also has certain anxieties about assertion which must be overcome before assertion can comfortably occur. These anxieties also need to be reduced if the client does not have the requisite assertive skills in her repertoire.

Anxieties about Assertion

Occasionally the therapist will find that the client's fears about acting assertively function as rationalizations which then allow the client to continue her non-assertive behavior. The client may say, *"If only* I didn't have all these fears, I could be assertive and take care of myself." However, the true situation may be that the client's non-assertive behavior is being heavily reinforced through her being relieved of the responsibility for taking care of herself. In these instances the therapeutic issue becomes one of confronting the person with her commitment to change. The therapist and client will need to work together to develop ways of changing the reinforcement contingencies so that assertion, rather than non-assertion, is reinforced.

When the irrational fears function as genuine obstacles to acting assertively, the therapist can use any one of several techniques for reducing these anxieties. One of the most common techniques is through rational-emotive therapy in which the client's irrational beliefs are attacked. With non-assertive individuals these irrational beliefs are likely to take the following form:

> "Wouldn't it be awful if the other person's feelings got hurt when I asserted myself? I could never forgive myself. The person would never recover from the hurt. He'd be permanently damaged. His life would be ruined forever, and I'd be totally responsible."

> "Wouldn't it be awful if the other person thought I was a castrating bitch when I asserted myself? How horrible if he always thought of me as a bitch. It would be absolutely terrible if in fact I were a bitch."

> "Wouldn't it be awful if I made a fool of myself when I was assertive? I'd be so humiliated that I couldn't stand myself. It's absolutely horrible to make mistakes. It's unforgivable."

Since the rational-emotive techniques have been amply described elsewhere (Ellis, 1962; Ellis and Harper, 1972), they will not be discussed here.

Behavioral Rehearsal

Those clients who do not have the needed assertive skills in their repertoire must acquire these skills *in addition* to their developing a supportive belief system and reducing their anxieties about assertion. Behavioral rehearsal is the most common technique used to teach these skills. This procedure involves a special kind of role-playing experience, in which the client practices or rehearses those specific assertive responses which are to become part of her behavioral repertoire. In contrast, the role-playing experiences in psychodrama (Corsini, 1966; Moreno, 1946) are used for catharsis or insight rather than for skill training. Although behavior rehearsal is thought to be a promising behavior-therapy technique, only recently has it received experimental support. McFall and his colleagues (McFall and Marston, 1970; McFall and Lillesand, 1971) have experimentally tested a standardized semiautomated behavior-rehearsal procedure in which the learners practice refusing various requests which are presented via taperecording. This work represents a major step toward developing specific assertive-skill training packages. Until more of these specific skill programs are developed, therapists will continue to use behavior rehearsal as a series of non-systematic role-playing experiences in which the client practices a wide range of assertive behaviors.

Behavioral rehearsal can be quite useful in reducing a client's anxiety about assertion in two ways: (1) when the client perceives her increased skill in handling successively difficult role-play experiences, her confidence increases, and (2) when the client learns through the course of the role play that nothing catastrophic happens when she enacts the assertive response, her irrational anxiety decreases.

The following steps are most commonly used in arranging the non-systematic role-play experiences for the client:

Step 1: A rationale for the client. The client is given a brief explanation of how behavior rehearsal may help her to acquire assertive skills. The client's hesitations and embarrassment about role playing are discussed.

Step 2: Devising the first role play. The therapist and client discuss situations the client has had difficulty in responding to assertively. They decide to role-play either a significant encounter that has occurred recently or one that is to occur in the near future. This situation is discussed until the therapist understands the other party's behavior well enough to role-play that person. If the therapist cannot play the other party, she may ask the client to demonstrate that person's behavior to her through role-play.

Step 3: The first role play. The client plays herself while the therapist plays the other party. The client is instructed to role-play as though the scene were happening right then and to act as she usually does in that situation. The therapist is careful to play the role in such a way that the client is not overwhelmed with feelings of failure or anxiety. Succeeding role plays portray increasingly difficult encounters.

Post-discussion. The therapist elicits the client's reactions to her performance, including her thoughts regarding possible alternative responses. The therapist reinforces the client for any small approximations of more effective behavior. If additional feedback is needed and no video equipment is available, the therapist imitates the client's performance so that the client can then observe her own behavior.

Step 4a: Role-play reversal. The therapist and client reverse roles. The therapist demonstrates more effective assertive behavior.

Post-discussion. The therapist elicits and selectively reinforces the client's reactions to the role-play experience. The client is encouraged to evaluate the demonstrated behaviors and to determine which of these she could incorporate.

Step 4b: An exception to the reversal. If, during the first role-play discussion, the client clearly indicates that she is now ready to change her performance and says something to the effect of "If I had to do it over again now, I'd do it a lot different," the therapist re-enacts the first role play and skips the role reversal, as it is now unnecessary. This procedure is then identical to the Step-5 role play.

Step 5: The third role play. The first role-play situation is replayed. The client practices the more effective assertive responses which were previously demonstrated and discussed.

Post-discussion. The therapist asks for the client's reactions to her performance. As always, the therapist warmly reinforces the client and provides positive feedback before supplying a limited amount of negative feedback, which is always followed with concrete suggestions for improvement.

Step 6: From this point on, the role plays are increasingly difficult.

Step 7: Transfer. As soon as the client can comfortably and effectively role-play a particular situation, the therapist and client discuss how the client can try out her newly acquired behavior outside the office. It is vital that the client meet with success rather than failure in these first crucial experiences. Therefore, these situations must be carefully screened so as to maximize client success and minimize client failure.

Case Example

In this example a 21-year-old woman is learning how to assert her right to govern her own life. The therapist is concentrating on the content of the client's verbal message to her mother and is gradually shaping more assertive verbal responses through successive role-play experiences. If this client were seriously deficient in her non-verbal messages—extremely quiet voice, speech disfluency, no eye contact, inappropriate smiling, immobile body expression, or standing an inappropriate distance from the other person—these behaviors would also become the focus of behavior rehearsal. Serber (1972) has fully desribed the behavior-rehearsal procedure which would be used in the event that the client's non-verbal behaviors interfered with her being fully assertive.

The dialogue in the following example is condensed so that the sequence of role plays in steps 3 and 6 can be more clearly illustrated. The symbols "Ther/Mom" and "Ther/Clt" refer to the therapist playing the role of the mother and the therapist playing the role of the client, respectively. A likely future encounter between the mother and daughter is being role-played as the dialogue starts.

Step 3: The first role play

> *Ther/Mom:* Honey, I just want to remind you that you have a dentist appointment tomorrow, and don't forget to tell him about that chipped tooth, and remember that there's free parking in the back of the building.
>
> *Client:* Ma, I know that. Listen, I can take care of myself.
>
> *Ther/Mom:* Of course you can, dear. I know that. I just wanted to remind you because I knew you'd feel so bad if you forgot.

Discussion

> *Therapist:* What were your reactions to your performance?
>
> *Client:* Not too good. It's what I always do, and it doesn't seem to make much of an impact on my mother.

Step 4a: Role-play reversal

> *Therapist:* OK, let's reverse roles. I'll play you. When I do, notice both what I say and what effect it has on you as the mother.
>
> *Ther/Clt:* Ma, I think it's time that I told you how I feel. I know that you love me, but, to tell you the truth, when you tell me what to do—like you just did—I feel as though I'm 2 years old and that's awful! I would like you to stop treating me that way.

Discussion

> *Client:* You sounded sure of yourself. I felt like you were telling me something that was very important to you. But if I were really my mother, I'd also feel kind of defensive.
>
> *Therapist:* How was my response different from your typical one?
>
> *Client:* I guess that I usually don't give all that much feedback to my mother. Mostly I say, "Aw, Ma" and assume that she'll get the message. How'd you ever come up with that reply?
>
> *Therapist:* I took stock of my thoughts and feeling and simply reflected back what I felt when she acted that way and specifically how I wanted her behavior to change. I kept calm by remembering that I had a right to tell her how I felt and a right to at least ask her to change. I also reminded myself not to try to put her down. Now, before we do another role play, you mentioned that your mother would get defensive. What did you mean by that?
>
> *Client:* That she wouldn't like that. She might get hurt or angry.
>
> *Therapist:* Yes, she might not like that. After all, you're telling her that she's not perfect and that you'd like her to change a little. Is that so unreasonable?

Client: I hadn't thought of it that way.

Therapist: If she gets a little defensive, that's OK. She has a right to. But remember that you're not saying that she's a bad mother. You're just asking to take responsibility for your own life and not to be 2 years old. OK? Let's try it again.

Step 5: The third role play

Client: Mom, did you know that when you tell me how to go to the dentist like that, I feel just like I am 2 years old again? I know that you don't mean to do that, but that's how I feel. I would like you to stop reminding me how to take care of myself.

Ther/Mom: But, honey, I was *just* trying to help you.

Client: But it's just that which I object to. In the future, please stop reminding me.

Discussion

Therapist: Great . . . I liked the way you modified my statement and really made it your own. That was certainly assertive! You stood up for yourself, but you didn't put her down. How'd you feel?

Client: It was easier than I thought it would be.

Therapist: OK, this time I'm going to make it a little harder.

Step 6: Increasingly difficult role playing

Ther/Mom: My goodness! A mother can't say two words without her daughter jumping down her throat. OK, tell me just what I should do . . . never say anything?

Client: See, I can't carry on a conversation with you without it ending in a fight!

Ther/Mom: So who's arguing now? All I asked you is what I should do!

Discussion

Therapist: OK, do you see what's happened here? Your mom got defensive and you got sucked into fighting. You forgot your assertive message. When you assert yourself, you have to remember what your goals are. Here your goal is to get your mother to stop reminding you. Let's try that again. Would you like me to demonstrate how to do that?

Client: No. I think I can do it.

Step 6

Client: Mom, I don't mean to jump down your throat. I just would be happier if you would simply not remind me to do things.

Ther/Mom: But you have often forgotten to do things in the past. You just haven't remembered.

Client: Yes, I have forgotten in the past. But now I want to take total responsibility for remembering my own appointments and other things. If I forget, then I'll also take the consequences. Deal?

Future role plays would expose the client to a variety of potential maternal reactions ranging from complete indifference to hostility. The client needs to learn assertive responses which are appropriate for *each* of these situations. In addition, role plays which prepare the client for other people's negative reactions to her assertive behavior are needed. For example, when people who have confused assertion with masculinity wrongly reprimand the client for her so-called "unfeminine" assertive behavior, the client will need to know how to defend herself.

An Aggressive Phase

I have noticed that clients often pass through an aggressive phase in the course of assertive training. While outside the therapy office, the client solely relies on her own judgment about when and how to assert herself. She uses her own feelings as a guide in formulating assertive statements which were developed during the therapy session. The key characteristic of this phase is that clients are completely unaware that the responses that they have so devised are aggressive rather than assertive. This trial-and-error process of gradually learning how to use feelings to prompt assertion rather than aggression may be absolutely necessary in order for the client's assertion to be naturally shaped rather than bound by artificial rules about "how to properly assert oneself" (Skinner, 1969). Those clients who are extremely anxious about being aggressive will require some special procedures to desensitize them to their own aggression (Palmer, 1971).

It is important that the therapist not punish the woman for these so-called "aggressive mistakes." Even mild therapist disapproval may reinstate the non-assertive behavior pattern. Male therapists may be particularly vulnerable to this therapeutic error, as some research suggests that male psychologists react more unfavorably to a female's "bitchiness" than do female psychologists (Haan and Livson data as reported by Goodall, 1973). It is more important that the non-assertive client learn to accept her "aggressive mistakes" than it is for that client to learn a "perfect" assertive response or learn a "perfect" distinction between assertion and aggression.

An important correlate of this phase concerns how the client handles her anxiety when she anticipates an assertive encounter with another person. If she reduces her anticipatory anxiety through forcing herself to become angry *at the other person,* she will probably act aggressively during the encounter. Her thoughts are likely to be: "Who in the hell does he think he is anyway! If he doesn't like what I have to say, he can shove it!" etc. In contrast, in the Goldstein et al. (1970) procedure, the clients' anger seems to be directed toward the client's *irrational fears* rather than at the other person. The difference is a small but significant one. In this case, their thoughts are likely to be: "I don't want to be afraid! I refuse to be afraid! It's stupid and unfair, and I won't be dominated by fear!" When this approach is used, the client is more likely to act assertively than aggressively.

The outcome is more uncertain when clients deliberately "cut themselves down" in an attempt to goad themselves into acting assertively. Their behavior may be non-assertive (if they are too self-critical), or aggressive (if in the process they've become unreasonably angry at the other person), or assertive (if their self-criticism acts as a negative reinforcer so that, in order to escape their own self-derogatory thoughts, they finally make an assertive response). When the client is using such self-critical thoughts, they are likely to take the following form: "Oh, you're so weak . . . it's disgusting. You act like a doormat for the whole world to walk on!"

If the client imagines a confidence-building scene just before the encounter, she may be more likely to act assertively. Here any imagery that arouses feelings of confidence, pride, or self-worth and which reciprocally reduces anxiety can be used (Lazarus and Abramovitz, 1962). For example, one female client imagined a scene in which she was being warmly hugged. For her this scene aroused feelings of security, being loved and cared for, etc.—all of which reduced her anxiety.

A FINAL COMMENT

In the course of training, clients usually do a fair amount of "assertion for the sake of assertion." By the end of training, hopefully they have a natural assertiveness which they can choose to exercise if they wish to. When people know that they have the necessary skills to assert themselves, they frequently feel less of a need to do so. When they decide not to assert themselves, it's because they *choose to* and not because they're afraid to, and that makes all the difference in the world!

REFERENCES

Alberti, R.E. & Emmons, M.L. *Your perfect right: A guide to assertive behavior.* San Luis Obispo, Calif: Impact, 1970.

Bandura, A. Analysis of modeling processes. In A. Bandura (Ed.), *Psychological modeling: Conflicting theories.* Chicago: Aldine-Atherton, 1971.

Corsini, R.J. *Role-playing in psychotherapy: A manual.* Chicago: Aldine, 1966.

Ellis, A. *Reason and emotion in psychotherapy.* New York: Lyle Stuart, 1962.

Ellis, A. & Harper, R.A. *A guide to rational living.* North Hollywood, Calif.: Wilshire Book Company, 1972. (Originally published, 1961.)

Friedman, P.H. The effects of modeling and role-playing on assertive behavior. In R. Rubin, H. Fensterheim, A. Lazarus & C. Franks (Eds.), *Advances in behavior therapy.* New York: Academic Press, 1971, 149-169.

Goldstein, A.J., Serber, M., & Piaget, G. Induced anger as a reciprocal inhibitor of fear. *Journal of Behavior Therapy and Experimental Psychiatry,* 1970, *1,* 67-70.

Goodall, K. Garden variety sexism: Rampant among psychologists. *Psychology Today,* 1973, *6*(9), 9.

Jakubowski, P., Pearlman, J., & Coburn, K. *Assertive training for women: A stimulus film.* Washington, D.C.: American Personnel and Guidance Association, 1975.

Jourard, S.M. *The transparent self.* Toronto: Van Nostrand, 1964.

Lazarus, A.A. *Behavior therapy and beyond.* New York: McGraw-Hill, 1971.

Lazarus, A. A. & Abramovitz, A. The use of "emotive imagery" in the treatment of children's phobias. *Journal of Mental Science,* 1962, *108,* 191-195.

Masters, W.H. & Johnson, V.E. *Human sexual inadequacy.* Boston: Little, Brown & Company, 1970.

McFall, R.M. & Lillesand, D.B. Behavior rehearsal with modeling and coaching in asserting training. *Journal of Abnormal Psychology,* 1971, *77,* 313-323.

McFall, R.M. & Marston, A. An experimental investigation of behavior rehearsal in assertive training. *Journal of Abnormal Psychology,* 1970, *76,* 295-303.

Moreno, J.L. *Psychodrama: Volume I.* New York: Wiley, 1946.

Palmer, R.D. Desensitization of the fear of expressing one's own inhibited aggression: Bio-energetic assertive techniques for behavior therapists. Paper presented at Association for the Advancement of Behavior Therapy Conference, Washington, D.C., 1971.

Rathus, S.A. Instigation of assertive behavior through videotape-mediated assertive models and directed practice. *Behaviour Research and Therapy,* 1973, *11,* 57-65.

Serber, M. Book Review. *Behavior Therapy,* 1971, *2,* 253-254.

Serber, M. Teaching the nonverbal components of assertive training. *Journal of Behavior Therapy and Experimental Psychiatry,* 1972, *3,* 179-183.

Skinner, B.F. *Contingencies of reinforcement: A theoretical analysis.* New York: Appleton-Century-Crofts, 1969.

. . . *and Soma*

LENORE W. HARMON
University of Wisconsin—Milwaukee

While the main concern of psychologists is to understand the psyche, the interaction of psyche with soma is especially important in counseling with women at this particular time in history. The purpose of this article is to attempt to help counselors understand how women feel about their bodies and some related current issues.

STANDARDS OF APPEARANCE

Several years ago I asked a class how they thought counseling women was different from counseling men. One young man answered immediately, "First, you have to get yourself together." He was telling the class, very openly, that he had to deal with his own physical attraction for a woman client before he could deal with her problem. Until this year, when people have become more sophisticated about what not to say, the first answer to my question has always been some variation on his theme. Some women today are more likely to be insulted than complimented by the problem he expressed.

Women of all ages have found that they have something in common. Each of them in her youth was presented by her decade, her socio-economic situation and her subculture with some standard of physical beauty which was practically unattainable. Whether her particular standard was communicated to her in the form of a silent film star, Miss America, the Barbie doll, women in TV advertisements, a Botticelli painting or the Venus de Milo, the effect was the same. She could not quite measure up. She was too short, too tall, too fat, too thin; her hair was too curly, too straight, or the wrong color. Some part of her anatomy was unacceptable. I have seen women burst into tears over the implication that their nose was too large or their breasts not large enough. These sensitivities are not funny; they are tragic.

The fact that many women have grown up in our society with no greater goal than to look "good," according to the prevailing standard, indicates a vast collective capacity for personal failure and all the psychological concomitants of failure among American women. It is as though a school created a complete curriculum in only one subject and then programmed the majority of students into repeated failure experiences. The students would fail to learn the one subject offered, but, worse still, they would be hampered in learning all other subjects by the experience.

Today some women are beginning to suspect that the standards of appearance to which they aspired so unsuccessfully (although their lack of success was an internal event not necessarily evident to the beholder) were projections of the needs of someone else: the needs of parents to have attractive children, the needs of men to possess attractive wives and lovers, or the needs of businessmen to create markets for their products. They are rejecting the idea that physical appearance is all they have to offer. They are learning to evaluate themselves in terms of internal qualities and talents. They are finding greater satisfaction in developing their intellectual and creative talents than in fighting a daily battle with wrinkles and dark hair roots or in keeping up with the latest styles, although they have not necessarily given up these activities.

When people react to a woman in a way which suggests that they are attuned only to the physical aspects of her presence, that woman's reaction is a function of her level of awareness of how destructive the physical standard has been for women and of her own anger at having cooperated in promoting that standard. She is likely to feel that the other person is promoting the body standard at her expense by not recognizing her capabilities. If the woman reacts in an overtly negative way, the typical response of the other person is "I meant it as a compliment." Many women don't see it that way. Reactions to their appearance are seen by them as symbolic of society's one-dimensional view of women, and they are angry at not being recognized for all their potential.

The implication for counselors is that they must begin to think of a woman's body as only one part of all that each woman is. If every counselor could imagine what it would be like if all his acquaintances reacted to him only in terms of his physical appearance, without reference to his skills, attainments, and capacity for growth, he might understand the sensitivity women are displaying over references to their appearance. While women's attitudes have been called an overreaction by some, those who say so do not seem to understand the magnitude of what women have lost by way of self-esteem in their attempts to meet unattainable standards of physical beauty.

This author believes that women's sensitivities will subside when (1) they are secure in their own multiple ways of gaining self-esteem and (2) they believe men also accept them as multifaceted human beings. Then, perhaps, comments on a woman's physical appearance or sexual potential may be regarded as compliments. Until then, such comments, as well as casual physical contacts (in which the toucher is perceived as having power over the touched), are likely to meet with negative responses from feminists and from other women who intuitively understand the issues.

BODY CONTROL

The assumption that we each control our own bodies is easier to accept from some frames of reference than it is from others. The terminally ill whose lives are prolonged by artificial means have little control over their own bodies. The ethics and personal values of physicians as well as the prevailing laws exercise almost complete control over the bodies of the terminally ill.

Women have begun to realize that they have controlled their own bodies only if control is viewed from a narrow frame of reference. In a broader sense, it is clear that women have not controlled the legislatures, the courts, the law-enforcement agencies or the medical and legal professions where important decisions are made about women's bodies.

Some of the major issues involved are birth control, abortion and rape. Birth control has been and still is being denied to some women on the basis of moralistic legislation which is (misguidedly) aimed at controlling behavior. Women argue that birth-control measures are to prevent conception but they are withheld in a futile attempt to prevent intercourse. Naturally they are angry at legislative attempts to control their behavior, especially since the results are pregnancies and children which neither society nor the woman involved wants or is prepared to care for.

Some women are also fearful of the effects of birth-control measures on their bodies, and they enter into a program of birth control with some ambivalence, which may affect their relationships with their sexual partners. They question why effective birth-control methods have been primarily developed for women, who must then bear the physical risks of using them. The hypothesis many of them have formed is that, since men do the research and development, their values dictate that contraception is not the male's responsibility nor should he have to take any risks to implement it. This idea implies that women and their needs are of little importance. Obviously, the women who hold these views are angry and insistent that they be consulted in developing birth-control measures.

Abortion is another area where legislatures, often with the advice and consent of physicians, have legislated values. The reasons given against abortion often include the psychological effect on the mother, in terms of guilt and loss. While women are not naive about the ambivalence and confusion which surround an unwanted pregnancy and its termination, they argue that the guilt and ambivalence associated with an abortion are, in most cases, as easily dealt with as the guilt, ambivalence and loss associated with bearing a child and giving it up for adoption. They contend that dealing with an abortion is certainly an easier psychological task than raising an unwanted child.

Women are angry when someone else decides *for them* that it is better *for them* to bear a child than to have an abortion. The recent Supreme Court decision regarding abortion was met with cheers by many women who have never had and never expect to have an abortion, simply because it upheld *their* right to make the decision whether or not to have an abortion.

Rape represents the ultimate in external control of a woman's body. It is a symbol both of her physical weakness and of her status as a physical property to be possessed. Yet laws regarding rape tend to protect the accused by making the attacked woman suspect of having caused the attack. Women resent the insensitivity of the law and law-enforcement agents to the victim's outrage and the victim's rights. They charge that laws regarding rape were written from a masculine point of view and address themselves to male outrage and male rights.

The issue of women's physical weakness is broader than the issue of rape. Women are taught that, because they are weaker (we will not explore the nature-nurture evidence at this point), they must limit themselves; some places, some times, some jobs are not safe for them. These beliefs contribute to a self-fulfilling prophecy regarding women's weakness. Because woman is regarded as weak, she does nothing to preserve her strength or expand her capacity to handle external threat or heavy work. Most men who insist on their right to a daily game of handball or a weekly game of golf would be astonished if their wives or female co-workers insisted on the same privilege. Women, themselves, lack awareness of how they contribute to their own physical weakness and how physical weakness limits their experiences. The increased female enrollment in karate and judo classes is one evidence that women are taking increasing interest in their physical condition as a means to control their bodies. Other forms of exercise, of course, would work toward the same end. However, tennis and swimming are more often seen as a means to a more acceptable physical appearance than as a means to greater strength and control of one's own body. There is little understanding that a woman who can depend on her body can go more places in safety and do more interesting things than one who cannot depend on her body.

Woman's need to control her body has some important implications for counselors. First, counselors need to understand that, at least among feminists, there is a distrust of male professionalism, which appears to have evolved moral, ethical and legal systems that are not responsive to the full range of women's needs. Indeed, these systems are perceived by some women as profound infringements on their rights as individuals. One does not have to be a woman to understand her outrage when she discovers she is pregnant because her "birth control" pills were placebos given in the name of science, or because her gynecologist neglected to tell her to have her diaphragm refitted after childbirth. One does not have to be a woman to understand her fear when she has to go alone through the abortion experience, especially if it is a questionable, illegal procedure without anesthetic, or her indignation when she must feign "mental illness" in order to obtain an abortion. One does not have to be a woman to understand her frustration and anger over being raped and then questioned as though she were the criminal. Such experiences have been widely reported, and they contribute to a distrust of professionals among some women.

Counselors are suspected of the same callousness toward woman's need to control her body as most other professionals. Counselors who cannot accept the feminist viewpoints regarding women's body which are reported here cannot expect to be able to help the women who do hold them with their psychological problems. The interaction between psyche and soma is too great. Counselors who can accept the feminist viewpoints regarding women's body which are reported here often have public-relations problems. In most cases it will be necessary for them to come out from behind the facade of counselor ambiguity to attract women clients to help the counselor can offer. Increasingly, young women who have been exposed to feminist ideology will not consult a psychologist who has not been recommended by a trusted sympathetic person. Without such an endorsement, they expect to find misunderstanding. The tragedy is that accepting and skillful counselors and women who need counseling are not finding each other because of the fears of women and the ambiguous image presented by many counselors. Concerned counselors should make themselves known to women's groups on campuses and in communities.

Finally, counselors shoud be attuned to the positive effects of good physical condition on building a positive self-image. It seems entirely possible that one adjunct to therapy, especially with some women, might be a physical-fitness program.

CONCLUSIONS

Counselors should not believe that either the counselor's attitude toward the client's body or the client's attitude toward her own body is immaterial in psychological counseling. An understanding of both counselor and client attitudes is extremely important, especially in counseling women.

Women's Changing Expectations . . . New Insights, New Demands

LAURINE E. FITZGERALD
University of Wisconsin—Oshkosh

SEX DISCRIMINATION AND FEDERAL LAWS

Recent appointments of Affirmative Action officers, workshops and conferences on implementation of "affirmative action," news and feature articles *re* goals and timetables for action—all would lead the public to believe that industry and educational institutions are *responsive* and, perhaps, proactive to this topic. In too many situations, however, it would appear that *reactivist* measures have been taken, only; women as individuals and in small groups have had to force the issue with their "day in court." The decade of the seventies has seen the institution of revisions, guidelines and amendments to several important Federal policies.

The July 1, 1972, Education Amendments to the Equal Pay Act of 1963 removed the exemption of executive, administrative and professional employees from the original Act; a Federal court has held that women performing work which is "substantially" equal to that of men should receive the same pay. With regard to *admissions,* the antidiscrimination provision applies only to institutions of vocational, professional and graduate higher education and public institutions of undergraduate higher education; any public institution of undergraduate higher education which traditionally has had a policy of admitting only students of one sex is exempt. Private undergraduate schools of higher education are not covered.

Title VII of the Civil Rights Act of 1964 was amended by the Equal Employment Opportunity Act of 1972. This Act is enforced by the Equal Employment Opportunity Commission (EEOC), which issued "Guidelines on Discrimination because of Sex." These guidelines bar hiring based on stereotyped characterization of the sexes . . . superceding state laws of a "protective" or restrictive nature—e.g., weight-lifting, hours limitations, etc. These guidelines extend benefits to both sexes that may have previously existed only for women, such as rest periods or special work equipment. Additional stipulations consider pregnancy, miscarriage and abortion, and childbirth as health and temporary disability situations.

Executive Order 11246, as amended, prohibits employment discrimination based on sex, as well as race, color, religion, or national origin, by Federal contractors or subcontractors and by contractors who perform work under a federally assisted construction contract exceeding $10,000. Revised Order No. 4 requires goals and timetables for women as well as minorities, under the Office of Federal Contract Compliance (OFCC) "Guidelines," and requires incorporation of the requirements for women in the previously mandated affirmative action plan, no later than by April 2, 1972.

LIFE-LONG EDUCATION AND WOMEN'S CENTERS

The Minnesota Plan for the Continuing Education of Women—a coordinated program of special seminars, counseling and advisement, limited scholarship funding, research and placement—was among the first of the "continuing education programs for women," now more popularly termed "continual education," "life-long learning," or "women's centers." The Plan at the University of Minnesota was jointly funded by a grant from the Carnegie Foundation, with additional monies and staff support from the University. The concept of a "center" for counseling and advisement *re* careers, post-secondary education and placement spread quickly, and several hundreds of these programs exist just one decade later. A national organization has been founded, the Continuing Education of Women (CEW), and at least one national women's personnel organization, the National Association of Women Deans and Counselors, has given major divisional status within its executive board structure to continuing education.

A women's center may be a community-based operation or may be located within a higher educational community. Typically, counseling and advisement *re* careers, training and placement are central functions. Rarely are these centers allied with a counseling center, and, although many centers utilize the counseling skills of some of their staff, increasingly counseling psychologists are not involved in the activities, planning, counseling and testing of the women clients. A general conclusion, based upon attendance at CEW meetings and from self-reports of women participants, is that "most counselors and tests aren't really relevant to our needs."

Related to the activities of the centers for women are the "women's studies" courses. Emerging in just three or four years, estimates of more than 1000 courses are offered by more than 300 colleges and universities and even a few high schools. Basically, these courses seek to fill gaps in women's information about themselves, their history, and their culturally assigned roles. The courses are located in various departments of colleges and universities but seem to be found most frequently in the English literature, sociology, history, psychology and law departments. Typical courses deal with women as portrayed in literature, women as writers, women's roles in society, women heroines in history, the feminine personality, and women and the law. Increasingly popular are the para-psychology courses dealing with Freud/women.

THE PROPOSED TWENTY-SEVENTH AMENDMENT TO THE U.S. CONSTITUTION

Since the Nineteenth Amendment (women's suffrage) open hearings, there has been no single unifying topic for women such as the proposed Equal Rights Amendment. The wording of the Amendment is as follows: "Equality of rights *under the law* shall not be denied or abridged by the United States or by any state on account of sex." At the time of this writing, twenty-eight states have ratified the proposal, and it will be considered or reconsidered by the remaining states in the immediate future and during the remaining six-year period, or until thirty-eight states have ratified. Newspaper, magazine, radio and television coverage of the "issues" and discussions of the ramifications of the Amendment have made it a major awareness and educational factor in the women's movement.

Of particular importance to counselors is women's awareness, and for too many women for the first time, of the legal limbo in which a married woman finds herself: of the laws which determine the narrow range of her life-style or employment choices; of the discrimination which is sanctioned, legally, and operant in many states regarding her credit rating, ability to enter into contractual agreements, the purchasing and disposition of property; her domicile rights and the right to retain her name after marriage. In the State of Michigan, for example, there are more than 2000 laws which grant, extend or withhold privileges on account of sex. The majority of the laws are based on assumptions regarding ability based on sex—e.g., weight-lifting—rather than sex-linked characteristics as in the case of a wet-nurse law.

Women seeking vocational, placement, financial or marriage counseling frequently make "decisions" and later are confronted by conflicting legal restrictions. In response to the need for facts before decisions, women's centers offer "counseling" which includes information about legal status . . . particularly related to marriage, divorce or separation planning. The Equal Rights Amendment will enhance the legal equity of men and women but has been of great significance to women who are now becoming informed about their legal status.

STUDENT ORGANIZATIONS AND PROGRAMMING

The oldest college student governing and programming organization, on a national level, is the Intercollegiate Association of Women Students (IAWS), a women's group founded in 1923 in the Midwest. Located on most college and university campuses, local groups affiliate with the national but may use another name to meet local campus needs. Some groups are the "Women's Commission," the women's residence-hall governing group, the "Coed Council," etc. The common bond is national affiliation—which benefits the local campus by linkage with issues, programming ideas, resolutions and resource materials emanating from national conventions and central national offices.

Beginning in 1963, the IAWS initiated programming regarding women's career opportunities and changing economic/employment status, necessary involvement with Federal legislation affecting women, women's colleges and women's studies, and the Equal Rights Amendment, since it includes the drafting of women for military service. Affiliate membership with the American Council on Education (ACE), the American Association of University Women (AAUW) and the National Association of Women Deans and Counselors (NAWDC) has provided for exchange of ideas and inclusion of the awareness and input from college women. Additionally, the IAWS women have had impact on high school women who increasingly demonstrate greater awareness of limitations and opportunities for women in society.

On many campuses the women students have sought assistance from resource centers already provided as a part of the "system"—e.g., counseling centers and health services. When these have been found lacking, the students have diverted funds and energy to community women's centers and supported the formation of "RAP" groups—somewhat akin to consciousness-raising groups but focused upon survival techniques within the male-dominated collegial system. Some organizations have initiated their own career-information resource rooms and attempt to provide academic counseling using their own membership as advisors.

NATIONAL WOMEN'S ORGANIZATIONS

The decade of the 1960's saw the formation of fifteen or twenty national women's organizations, all of which have a definite relationship to the women's movement. The National Women's Party (consistently a supporter of the Equal Rights Amendment since its inception as a suffragist group), the League of Women Voters, the American Association of University Women were well established, with the latter two hardly evidencing a "feminist" orientation. However, in 1968 the AAUW conducted a total membership survey on the attitudes of college-educated women toward working women, toward higher education, toward the changing economic/political-legal status of women. Finding overwhelming support for the renewed focus on women, this Association is currently spearheading a coalition of thirteen guidance, personnel and educational groups which endorse a "Statement on Women in Higher Education." Topics include recruitment and admissions, financial aids, program flexibility, part-time study, curriculum, continuing education, advising and counseling, placement, housing, health services, employment recruitment and hiring, salaries and conditions of employment, in-service training, students, faculty and administration and trustees and regents as women who have a role in decision making.

The National Organization for Women was founded by Betty Friedan in 1966 at the time of the Fiftieth Anniversary of the Women's Bureau, Department of Labor; the Women's Equity Action League (WEAL) was founded by women educators and lawyers in Ohio in 1969 as a result of the default of the Governor of that State to appoint a Women's Commission.

Both of these organizations focus on social, political, legal and economic aspects of women's roles. WEAL has become actively involved in investigations of sex-stereotyped standardized testing and was involved in the Title VII Civil Rights Act hearings, specifically noting the color stereotypes of test forms (pink and blue) and the limited career options on the Strong Vocational Interest Blank (W). NOW has been particularly active in content assessment of vocational and occupational resource publications and of textbooks used in public schools and has completed a study of Caldecott and Newberry Award winning children's books—noting pictures, activities and other role determinants evidenced for girls and women. These two groups, NOW and WEAL, are fairly typical of the feminist organizations and of the activities engaged in by women of all educational and socio-economic classifications who have become involved in the women's movement.

Most professional organizations have appointed—or development has been spontaneous and from within the women's membership—a women's task force or caucus grouping. The phenomenon of the "women's caucus" during national and regional conferences began in the 1960's and quickly became the nucleus for women researchers and strategists within each of the professional disciplines. The Modern Language Society, as an example, has made new contributions to women's understandings of self-concept development, role-model identifications, and aspiration-inspiration cycles among women as a result of the study of sex linkage and meaning of words in the English language. The ascription of "masculine" to those words which might describe an executive or managerial position or to leadership roles may well be a major determinant in dissuading a young woman from pursuing a career requiring those attributes.

Recent studies initiated as a direct result of women's caucus activities within the field of anthropology have shed new light on the culture-restrictive nature of roles ascribed by our civilization to "primitive" cultures . . . this from a sophisticated and supposedly culture-free social scientific group. With few and notable exceptions, cross-cultural anthropological study has been completed by men; new replications by women produce different results due to responses elicited by women researchers from both men and women.

Women who have traditionally been active, organized and "traditional" within formal religious groupings have become proactive. The Presbyterian women have formulated a statement regarding women's new, active and involved roles within that religious group. In March of 1973, by Papal decree, women will be allowed to give Communion if they are selected as "qualified persons" by bishops, to serve areas in which there is a shortage of priests. Major modifications of roles for young women of Jewish faith have been made in the past few years, and equity from the pulpit has been won. Assessment of contemporary responses from each of the religious groupings, in the light of interests expressed by women and directly as a result of women's initiation, is producing change for greater involvement.

POLITICAL AWARENESS

One of the last cultural arenas for women's participation has been governmental and/or political. Perhaps because of the relative recency of ballot power, and possibly because of legal restrictions and practice, women have not been significantly involved in politics. There appears to be general agreement that the words "political" and "politics" are masculine . . . as reported by MLA researchers. Connotations of "power," also masculine, are allied to political activity. At any rate, women are just now indicating awareness and interest and are participating in the "risks" necessary for political leadership activity.

Non-partisan women's political "consciousness-raising," in the form of national, state and regional caucus meetings, began less than twenty months ago. Recently, Houston, Texas, was the site of the National Women's Political Caucus. The meeting received a great deal of national publicity, since consensus was not immediate; it is interesting to reflect upon the conflict-resolution process as being not unlike *men's* political meetings.

Pending Federal legislation, submitted by the Hon. Patsy Mink of Hawaii, would lend massive Federal support to the elimination of sexist educational materials—texts, tests, resource/reference career literature and sports education.

Results of Gallup Poll samples, comparing 1937 with 1971, indicate a change in Americans' attitudes toward women in politics. In 1937, 66% of the sample said they would not vote for a woman for President; by 1971, 66% approved of the idea. These survey results are consistent with changes reported in attitudes evidenced by elementary and high school students toward women in the professions, in politics and in the dual careers of homemaking and employment.

IMPLICATIONS

Throughout the foregoing articles, data are available regarding the psychological impact of feminism on educated and educable women, bias in career and vocational counseling for women and in the professional education afforded counselors. The ways in which women have responded by group consciousness-raising sessions, assertive behaviors and assessment of bodily self have been examined. Less well documented are actions taken on the national level and Federal legislative level and the impact of a proposed Constitutional Amendment.

Industrial and educational institutions are mandated, by Federal legislation and action, to "affirmative action." It is a two-edged sword of progress; more women will be sought for "show-case" positions, as well as positions of genuine importance and influence. Women must be capable of assuming these responsibilities, and career influences to this end have to be significant in the educational and training choices girls and women will make in the immediate future. We have already sensed the reluctance of women to venture in uncharted areas of personal involvement, culturally restricted by many factors, but at the same time there is a rising surge of female consciousness which will need professional support to this end.

The mature woman who returns to employment or views education as a stepping-stone to economic or personal employment security represents a potentially new clientele for many college and employment counselors. These women have faced underestimation, underutilization and underemployment and have a heightened sense of personal worth as a result of the current women's movement. They are particularly responsive to realistic assessment of their potentials and may be unusually sensitive to a counselor's use of tests which are less than appropriate, language usage which connotes sexism, reliance on reference materials which tend to exclude women, or a patronizing or paternalistic approach.

The changing legal status of women and greater understanding by women of legal rights and restrictions will have relatively little initial impact for most counselors/clients. However, a spiraling divorce rate, alternate marriage planning and contract marriages may well be important factors to consider in the light of legal realities. Increasingly, women will plan to work most of the life span and will need assistance in planning; sheer numbers of women in the total population will force a change in work assessment for all persons.

The facts that women non-professionals assume para-professional skills of a helping nature in group settings, the existence of educational programming initiated by women students and the expansion of women's studies courses give some indication of areas needing immediate attention from the field of counseling psychology. Even more, extensively researched information is needed about women's personality development, view of self and of body imagery, women's trust and confidence building and life-style responses which do not conform to the "cultural norm."

In recent months most professional organizations in the social and behavioral sciences have produced or initiated monographs or programs addressing the "problem with women." The body of knowledge is growing, albeit slowly, but committed response does not seem commensurate with the already compiled data/research. The question remains—do we wish to counsel with women *as women,* or will the focus remain as it has been? Will we be concerned primarily with the attrition rate of women counselees, counselor preferences expressed by clients, nature of problems discussed with men or with women—or will we examine causal factors?

Hopefully, the eight articles in this section of the book will be thought-provoking and not merely provoking. Supplemental readings are suggested for further examination. No answers can be proffered, but, if questions, doubts, concerns have been raised, then the mission has been partially accomplished. Women have already learned that uncertainty about a "given," discussion with peers, and search are the paving stones to a changed response and thus to a new status.

COUNSELING WOMEN: II 2

Male Is Greater
than Female:
The Socialization
of Status Inequality

RHODA K. UNGER
Montclair State College

Concurrent with the development of a new focus of study—the psychology of women—the concept that sexual equality is the "norm" in the interpersonal transactions between males and females is increasingly being questioned. A recent review of the literature concluded that adult male-female relationships essentially are similar to relationships between individuals varying in other dimensions of ascribed status, such as social class, race, or age (Unger, Note 1). The current review will focus on the socialization of status inequality in male and female children and the implications of this process for adult behavior.

Sexual equality may actually be an exception. Surveys of interpersonal transactions between males and females indicate that the male is more powerful (Henley & Freeman, 1975; Unger, Note 1). Male dominance is due to the almost uniform and universal ascription of higher status to maleness than to femaleness. Many differences between men and women which are attributed to gender may be viewed more parsimoniously as status differences. Since this status asymmetry is based upon ascribed status, which is a rather permanent characteristic of individuals, it is not easily changed by the performance capabilities of the individuals involved. The effect of status asymmetry upon the power relations of males and females extends throughout the entire behavioral domain, even in areas where relative status does not appear to be relevant. Much of the variance in male-female relationships can be explained by relative status, but, because status is so highly correlated with gender, explanations have tended to be based on sex.

For the purposes of this review, various terms relating to status and power will be defined in a rather general way. *Status* may be defined as an individual's position in a hierarchy of power relations within a social unit as measured by his or her relative effectiveness in control of interpersonal behaviors and in group decision making (Sherif & Sherif, 1969). Sherif and Sherif also suggest that relative status can be measured by the ability of the individual to apply sanctions to other members of the group in cases of non-participation or lack of compliance with the goals and norms of the group. Status is not identical to the ability to influence another's behavior under any condition. Sociologists usually recognize two kinds of status—ascribed and achieved. *Achieved status* is based on performance variables or function, such as the role one performs within an organization or a family. *Ascribed status* is an attribute of an individual based upon who he or she is. Determinants of ascribed status include age, race, social class, and gender. In the case of children, other determinants of ascribed status may be physical size, physical attractiveness, and body build. As we shall see, these characteristics are by no means independent of gender and, in fact, may be some of the base on which status/gender confusion is founded.

If females have a lower ascriptive status than males, sex differences in power must automatically exist. Social power is defined here as the relative effectiveness of attempts to influence others. Social power is only one of several related dimensions along which one may differentiate an individual's position in a social system. Although these terms are conceptually distinct, they are empirically related. As stated previously, social power refers to the ability to influence others, as opposed to status, which represents potential ability to influence others. Social power can be assessed by asking children questions like "Who can get you to do what he (sic) wants you do do?" (Gold, 1958), or by naturalistic observations of groups to analyze the percentage of successful influence attempts by various individuals. Social power may be distinguished from social or emotional acceptance, which is determined by asking "Who likes whom?" or by analyzing group relationships sociometrically. Both terms can be distinguished from social or personal competence. Although objective competence is obviously a basis for the perception of competence by oneself and others, they are not the same thing. The operational definition which is probably the most useful is one used by Lippitt and Gold (1959) in which children were asked "Who is good at doing the things you do at school?" Glidewell and his associates (Glidewell, Kantor, Smith, & Stringer, 1966) analyzed all the various findings on relationships between components of social status in children and estimated that the correlation between emotional acceptance and perceived competence is .40, the correlation between emotional acceptance and perceived social power is .60, and the correlation between perceived competence and perceived social power is .30. Their data indicate that social power is more closely related to emotional acceptance of another child than to his or her competence. There is also some indication that the determinants of social status are different for boys and girls.

THE PERCEPTION OF SOCIAL STATUS AND POWER

Sex-Role Stereotyping as Power Typing

Sex-role stereotyping may more accurately be viewed as power typing. Johnson (Note 2) demonstrated that certain forms of power are regarded as stereotypically male while other forms are regarded by both males and females as stereotypically female. Using French and Raven's (1959) typology of the bases of social power, she found that legitimate power (based upon some authorized or contractual relationship), expert power (based upon possession of some needed skill or competency which is not possessed by another), and informational power (based on possession of some data needed by another) are characterized as male. In contrast, referent power (based on the need to belong to a group and to further its goals) and helpless power or the power of dependency (based upon the social norm of helping those who cannot help themselves) are characterized as female. When given a choice of which form of power to use, males chose legitimate power significantly more often than females, and females chose helpless power significantly more often than males. The forms of power which each sex rejected were just as informative as those they chose. Males almost never chose to use helpless power and females almost unanimously rejected the use of expert power.

A study by Sternglanz and Serbin (1974) illustrates the way power typing may be communicated to children. They performed an observational analysis of the male and female role models presented on ten popular commercially produced children's TV programs. In addition to the expected findings that (a) there are twice as many major male as female roles and (b) that males are more often portrayed as aggressive and constructive than females, while females are more likely to be portrayed as deferent, a sex difference relating to the use of power was found. The use of "magic" was limited almost entirely to females. Four of the five female title-role stars were witches of some kind. The authors suggest that children are informed that the only way you can be a successful human if you are female is through the use of magic. "By using magic, one may manipulate others without their being aware of it, and they manipulate them effectively. One may imagine the shock to the little girls at the age of ten years or so when they realize that witchcraft is not really a viable career" (p. 714). Not only are male traits considered more socially desirable (Broverman, Vogel, Broverman, Clarkson, & Rosenkrantz, 1972), but the female trait which receives the greatest amount of attention in programming directed towards children is one which cannot be developed. Indirect power is typed as female and, under normal conditions, cannot exist at all.

Children's Perception of Status and Power

In order to demonstrate that gender differences in children can be more parsimoniously explained as status differences, it is necessary to demonstrate that children are able to perceive differences in status and power as well as they are able to perceive gender differences. Unfortunately, most studies in this area have concentrated on the perception of appropriate sex-roles. Although a child may be able to state that daddy wears a tie and is interested in sports and mommy wears a dress and is interested in sewing, how that child perceives the relative power of his or her parents is left unresolved. Nevertheless, cultures tend to allocate authority—which is legitimatized power—on the basis of age and sex. Parsons' (1955) model of family functions has provided the theoretical basis for most of the direct investigations of the perception of the relative power of various members of the family. This model assigns high power and goal-interference actions to male and low power and goal-facilitation actions to females. Emmerich (1961), for example, found that children discriminated age roles by assigning high power actions to the adult and low power actions to the child. They also assigned more high power actions to the father than to the mother figure. The amount of power attributed to the father increased between the sixth and eighth years. Gender-specific use of the power dimension generalized across role situations. Thus, perceptions of the parents' ability to contribute to family goals were unrelated to their gender, although perception of their relative authority was related to gender. The correspondence of younger and female individuals in attributions of relative powerlessness is noteworthy.

More recently, studies have focused on the perception of sibling power within the family system. Sutton-Smith and Rosenberg (1968) analyzed the consensual responses of 95 preadolescent children on two 40-item power inventories. They found that older and younger children agreed that the older sibling was more powerful and that the younger sibling showed more resentment and appealed more to the parents for help. Of note is the finding that the greatest consensual agreement was on the item indicating that firstborns were more bossy and that non-firstborns engaged in the low power tactics of going to others outside the dyad for help, crying, tale-telling, and the like. Of the possible birth-gender combinations, only a boy with an older sister perceived himself and was perceived by others as not having to seek outside help. He did not indicate the same degree of powerlessness as children in other non-first categories. Bigner (1974) has found that even among children in kindergarten the second-born child perceives himself or herself as having less control over the outcomes of social interactions and as having to be more facilitating and agreeable about group goals than eldest children. Interestingly, children who had an elder male sibling assigned more high-power items to older siblings than subjects who had a female older sibling. This gender differentiation with respect to power did not change with the increasing age of the subjects. In the age group tested, five through thirteen years, boys appeared to be more sensitive to the use of the power dimension than girls. Discrimination of sibling roles by function did not occur, although the author had predicted this finding.

Sutton-Smith and Rosenberg (1968) suggest that

> the accident of birth creates size and ability differences, and these no less than size differences in lower species lead to the institution of a pecking order. We may assume that the less powerful younger siblings will fight back with all the powers at their command. The younger brother's relative strength when he has only an older sister to contend with may be taken as an illustration of this view (p. 70).

It is noteworthy that boys have been found to be more sensitive to the evaluation of others on the basis of perceived power, since in other variables involving social judgment girls are usually found to be superior (Borke, 1973; Witryol & Kaess, 1957).

In a correlational analysis of a worldwide sample of 39 societies, Rosenblatt and Skoogberg (1974) found that, in adulthood, firstborn sons were likely to have more authority over their siblings, more control of family property, more power or influence over others, to be respected more by their siblings, and to head a kin group than other sons. Firstborn daughters, however, differed from their female siblings only in being more likely to receive respect from other siblings. Although birth-order effects appear to be a matter of controversy in investigations of our society, they may be much stronger in nonwestern societies. And, gender-birth order interactions may be even more powerful.

There is also some indication that male-female power relationships within the family system affect older as well as younger children. Firstborn males with female second siblings have higher self-esteem than those with male second siblings (Hollender, 1972). Self-esteem is lower in females than in males, but there is no differential effect of the sex of the second sibling. The effect of the male sibling probably extends beyond those behaviors which seem to be directly linked with social power. For example, both male and female children who have an older male sibling show more masculine sex-role preference as measured by the It Scale than singleton children of the same sex (Bigner, 1972). In general, children with an older female sibling do not differ from singleton children of the same sex. It can be argued that these data indicate that the male role possesses some reinforcing properties in its own right which may or may not be independent of the power dimension.

Modeling and Peer-Reinforcement Phenomena

There is evidence from a variety of studies that low-status individuals are more likely to model and/or imitate others than those with high status. Subjects who are low in competence or high in anxiety are more likely to imitate in situations where little information concerning the appropriate or expected behavior is provided (Akamatsu & Thelen, 1974). A relationship between dependency and overall and incidental imitation has been suggested (Ross, 1966). Geshuri (1975) found that high-dependent observers modeled most closely under contingent-reward conditions than under other conditions. Girls, in general, modeled more closely than boys. Since there was no interaction between sex and dependency in this study, Geshuri argues that, while children of preschool age have learned to imitate equally well regardless of gender, girls have been trained by this age to be more aware of the social sanctions that can follow noncompliance with social demands. He suggests that sex differences in this area are due to differential attention to the cue functions of the observed reward and that selective attention is mediated by dependency. Girls were found to be significantly more conforming when they were threatened by social rejection than when they were not (Carrigan & Julian, 1966). This difference was not as large for boys.

If we look at model rather than observer characteristics, we also find a gender/status effect. Bandura, Ross, and Ross (1963), in a well-known study, found that children primarily imitated the model who had the power to reward, regardless of his or her sex. They indicated, however, that the sex of the individuals involved did play a role. Despite elaborate experimental manipulations designed to establish differential power and status, a number of children actually attributed rewarding power to an uninvolved adult male bystander or to one who shared the rewards with them. Some comments indicated their firm conviction that only a male can possess resources and that a female is only an intermediary for the male. "He's the daddy, so it's his; but he shares nice with mommy. . . . He's the man, and it's all his because he's a daddy. Mommy never really has things belong to her. . . . He's the man, and the man always really has the money, and he lets ladies play too" (p. 533). These findings suggest that status and power and gender can be confounded even when attempts are made to manipulate them as separate entities.

These data are somewhat more confused when we examine the child's imitation of his or her peers. Preschool groups tend to show cleavages by such ascribed status characteristics as race and sex just as do peer groups of older children (Hartup, 1970). These cleavages are only slightly less strong in the young child's peer group. *Cleavage* is defined by the frequency with which children have play contacts with same versus different race or sex children. Data indicate that there is a relative deprivation of reinforcing stimuli from persons of the opposite sex which extends from early in the preschool years (Stevenson, 1965). Charlesworth and Hartup (1967) observed that, in the nursery school years, there is a marked tendency for boys to direct reinforcements to boys and girls to girls. There is a large difference, however, in the probability values they cite: $p < .002$ for the number of reinforcements given by boys to boys versus those given to girls, as opposed to $p < .05$ for the number of reinforcements given by girls to girls versus those given to boys. These data may indicate that boys are much more gender exclusive in their reinforcements than girls even during the earliest years of extra-familial social interactions. Such an interpretation is consistent with the findings that same-race cleavage is stronger among majority-group children than among minority-group children (Morland, 1966; Springer, 1953). The hypothesis that it is the boys who control the preference for like-sex rather than opposite-sex peers is also supported by a finding of Reese (1962) on the relationship between the status possessed by a child with his or her same- and opposite-sex peers. This investigator found that, in fifth-graders, acceptance by girls of boys was significantly associated with acceptance by other boys. Although girls who were least accepted by other girls tended to be least accepted by boys, popularity with boys did not differ for girls who were moderately or highly popular with other girls.

THE CLASSROOM AS A SOCIAL SYSTEM

Status in the Classroom

Most sociometric studies of interpersonal relations in the classroom have concentrated on social acceptance rather than social power. A number of studies using different techniques, however, have indicated the existence of dominance hierarchies in young children. Edelson and Omark (1973) directly asked children in nursery school through third grade "Who is toughest?" Nursery school children often answered "Me," but by the second and third grades there was 70% agreement on the dominance hierarchy. Boys were nominated for the top 40% of positions, while girls were generally in the bottom 40%. Girls agreed with boys on these judgments of peer status even though they had supposedly low rates of interaction with them at this stage. In a task involving judgments of one's own and other's competence on an unstructured task, first-graders of both sexes rated 80% of the female subjects at the median or below, as opposed to 31% of their male classmates (Pollis & Doyle, 1972). These status rankings were shared by the evaluated individual. There was a high significant correlation ($r = .62$) between group and own ratings. Actually, there was no real difference between boys and girls in task competence. In a study involving modeling in a naturalistic setting (Wolf, 1973), nine-year-old boys evaluated the same-sex model as much more attractive than the opposite-sex model, while no differences were found for girls.

Differences in the perception of power on the basis of ascriptive status may also account for the large number of findings showing that at every age—elementary through high school and college—girls express lower occupational aspirations than boys. Looft (1971) distinguished between preference and power by asking first and second graders two questions: "What would you like to be when you grow up?" and "Now what do you think you really will do when you grow up?" To question number one, the 33 boys nominated 18 different occupations. The 33 girls, however, nominated only 8 different occupations. In fact, 25 girls named either nurse or teacher as their first choice. Other choices included mother, stewardess, and sales clerk. One wished to be a doctor. In response to the second question, significantly fewer girls than boys changed from their original choice to some other vocation perceived as desirable. As the author comments:

> Girls, especially, learn early that certain adult statuses are open to them and that these are few in number, reflecting a recognition of traditional sex-role expectations; none expressed a desire to be a politician, a lawyer, a scientist. A few girls said they would be mothers, but no boy said he would be a father. The fact of early sex-role vocational learning was perhaps captured most poignantly by the single girl who initially expressed a desire to be a doctor; when questioned further, she commented: "I'll probably have to be something else—maybe a store lady" (p. 366).

Aspiration and Achievement: Internal versus External Barriers

At every age, nine through seventeen, the correlation between the prestige of an occupation (and its power) and preference for that occupation is higher for males than for females (Barnett, Note 3). In fact, the correlation between occupational prestige and preference is virtually zero for females. These sex differences increase with age and reach their highest level between the ages of fifteen and seventeen. In a comparison between first- and fifth-grade children, Brook and her associates (Brook, Whiteman, Peisach, & Deutsch, 1974) found a significant relationship between parental and children's vocational aspirations. White parents especially had lower occupational aspirations for their daughters. Among the younger children, girls had higher vocational aspirations than boys, but this reversed among older children. Differences in parental educational aspirations for boys and girls at the fifth grade were particularly marked. The authors noted that social-class differences were stronger among younger children, whereas sex differences were more important among the older boys and girls. They suggest that two processes, an early familial identification and a later more general acculturation process, may be at work. It is also possible that whatever characteristics make it possible to ascribe class membership may be attenuated with the child's increasing age, especially in the ideologically "classless" school situation. Gender characteristics, of course, remain unalterable and, in fact, become more salient with age.

If, as earlier indicated, status differences are internalized in the early years of life, one would expect even young girls and boys to have different expectations regarding their abiltiy to control their environments. Several attempts have been made to explore locus-of-control phenomena in young children. Nowicki and Duke (1974) suggest that a power-versus-helplessness factor contributes most of the variance in the locus-of-control scores of young children. In a large sample of white, black, and Spanish children of both sexes and of both high and low socioeconomic status from the second, fourth, and sixth grades, Gruen, Kort, and Baum (1974) present results which may show a relationship between internality (perceived ability to control one's environment) and several measures of ascriptive status. Older children make more internal responses than younger children, affluent children make more internal responses than disadvantaged children, and white children make more internal responses than either black or Spanish children. Although sex differences were found only among black subjects in this study, several studies have found adult females to be more external than males (McGinnies, Nordholm, Ward, & Bhanthumnavin, 1974; Denmark, Note 4).

Perhaps more important than findings about simple sex differences in locus of control are findings which indicate that the same scores have different implications for males and females. Hrycenko and Minton (1974) found a relationship between internal locus of control and preference for a higher power position in males but not females. Among undergraduates, subjects who reported that parents used more punishing and controlling-type behaviors were found to have greater expectations of control by powerful others (Levenson, 1973). And, finally, Nowicki and Segal (1974) found that female achievement behavior could be predicted better by asking a subject to assess her father's locus-of-control orientation rather than her own.

These data can be interpreted to indicate that locus-of-control orientation reflects a perception of power relationships as they actually exist, that these power relationships are interpreted in terms of the male, and that these perceptions are socially mediated by group membership rather than being the product of "accidental" differences in individual experience. Perceptions of one's powerlessness could also lead to self-devaluation. A belief in external control is predictive of academic cheating among girls but not among boys (Johnson & Gormly, 1972). It may also account for the persistent tendency of females to devalue the work of other females (Goldberg, 1968; Pheterson, Kiesler, & Goldberg, 1971) or to attribute competent work by females more to such outside factors as luck or accident than to internal variables such as skill or motivation (Deaux & Emswiller, 1974; Feldman-Summers & Kiesler, 1974). Recently, Etaugh and Brown (1975) found that both boys and girls as young as ten years of age are more likely to attribute a female's success on a "male-appropriate" task less to ability than the similar success of a comparable male. The authors found no consistent interaction effects (between age and sex) and suggest that differential perceptions of male and female performance appear to be well established by the fifth grade.

Sex differences based on perceived, and probably real, differences in ability to control one's life are not dissimilar from those found between black and white children. Friend and Neale (1972) investigated 120 white or black fifth graders of various social classes and found that internal forces such as ability and effort were judged as more important for their performance than task difficulty or luck (external factors) by white children, while the reverse was true for black children. Although these investigators did not break down their results by sex, Entwisle and Greenberger (1972), using the Crandall Intellectual Responsibility Scale (Crandall, Katkovsky, & Crandall, 1965), which is designed to reveal beliefs about control over one's own academic successes and failures, found that, among middle-class white children, boys of high IQ took more responsibility for their own success than comparable girls.

Group Processes in the Classroom

Unfortunately, few studies have attempted to chart gender-specific development trends in terms of small-group processes. In fact, it has been suggested that the major contributions concerning the developmental aspects of peer relations were made twenty years ago (Hartup, 1970). Hartup extensively reviewed the literature on peer-group interaction and social organization. While the entire review will not be reiterated here, a study by Zander and Van Egmond (1958) appears to be particularly relevant for understanding the relationship between social power and the interpersonal behavior of children. Measures were made of the intelligence and social power of all children in a number of classrooms. Social power was estimated by means of a sociometric-like technique: "Who can most often get you to do things for him?" Every child in these second- and fifth-grade classes also rated every other child on perceived attractiveness, academic ability, and ability to "threaten." Children were also put into standardized, small problem-solving groups, and their participation was observed. Finally, teacher evaluations were obtained.

Social power was not highly correlated with actual intelligence (.20 for boys; .28 for girls), although brighter children do have more power. Boys and girls who were attributed high social power were more attractive to their classmates than those with lower power attributions, regardless of intelligence. Girls with greater power were seen as more academically able by other children regardless of intelligence, while boys were described as able only if they were high in both intelligence and power. Boys, but not girls, with high social power were described as more threatening. There was very little difference in the behavior of girls based on degree of social power or intelligence. Boys, in general, made significantly more demands and attempts to influence their peers and engaged in more aggressive acts. Girls did not display any type of behavior significantly more often than boys.

Boys low in both intelligence and power were the only males who were passive in their groups. Low-low boys behaved very much like girls. The authors summarize:

> Girls who were high in power and intelligence were little different from those who were low in either of these qualities, because, we believe, high social power and intelligence were not needed in order to be the nurturant, obedient or responsible persons required by society. Girls could fulfill these expectations regardless of the amount of power or intelligence they possessed (p. 266).

It should be noted that it is not the sex differences in role that one would like to stress here but the lack of importance of individual capacities in the fulfillment of the female role. Their teachers were able to make less distinctions between females than males because the performance of girls or the status which they can achieve is less important than their ascribed status as females. Only the higher male status leaves room for differences in personal achievement. In analogy to a crude racist remark, "A female Ph.D. is still a broad."

It should also be stressed that some of these differential perceptions of males and females are as relatively independent of degree of social influence as they are of actual competence. Zander and Van Egmond (1958) have provided data on the number of influence attempts made within their problem-solving groups by boys and girls who vary in degree of intelligence and social power. The rank order of influence attempts clearly shows the relationship between achieved-status variables and the behavior of boys and lack of relationship for girls (see Table 1). Since they have provided data on the number of successful attempts as well, one can calculate the percentage of successful attempts which they did not provide. Although boys who were high in both

Table 1. The Relationship between the Total Number of Influence Attempts, the Percentage of Successful Influence Attempts, and Level of Intelligence and Social Power in Boys and Girls.

Group	Total Influence Attempts	Percent Successful
High intelligence, high power boys	25.55	61%
Low intelligence, high power boys	24.34	56%
High intelligence, low power boys	21.63	55%
High intelligence, high power girls	16.69	58%
Low intelligence, low power boys	16.00	49%
Low intelligence, high power girls	15.96	55%
High intelligence, low power girls	13.57	53%
Low intelligence, low power girls	13.49	41%

Data adapted from Zander and Van Egmond (1958).

intelligence and social power had the highest percentage of successful influence attempts during the problem-solving sessions and girls who were low in both intelligence and social power had the lowest percentage of successful attempts, the effects were inconsistent in terms of the other groups. For example, girls who were high in both intelligence and social power were more influential than any other group except comparable boys, yet they showed a smaller number of influence attempts than any male group except those who were low in both intelligence and social power. We are left with the unresolved question of what constitutes effective reinforcement of social power if it is not, as appears in this study, success in the use of one's power to influence.

The way children reinforce each other for particular kinds of social behaviors is not well understood. There is a high relationship between the giving and receiving of positive reinforcements (Charlesworth & Hartup, 1967). Social acceptance is significantly correlated with the frequency with which a child gives positive reinforcements, but children do not receive more negative reinforcements from disliked than from liked peers (Hartup, Glazer, & Charlesworth, 1967). Measures of sociometric acceptance and rejection are not significantly correlated. Moreover, a reinforcement may have different meanings for two individuals involved in a dyadic interaction. Patterson, Littman, and Bricker (1967) analyzed the behaviors of both the target and aggressor in aggressive interactions in nursery school. When the target child responded by withdrawing, acquiescing, or crying, the attacker in subsequent interactions was likely to perform the same aggressive act toward the same victim. The victim's low power position appeared to function as a positive reinforcer for the aggressor. Initiators of aggressive encounters were likely to be successful if there was no adult intervention, and it has been estimated that most (as many as 80%) of the aggressive incidents were not noticed or were ignored by nursery school staff (Smith & Green, 1975). Boys had a higher probability of being involved in an aggressive encounter than girls, but there was not consistent evidence that adults intervened differentially in boy-boy, boy-girl, or girl-girl encounters.

THE UNEXAMINED EFFECT OF PHYSICAL POWER UPON SOCIAL POWER

Sex Differences in Aggression

It is well accepted even among those who hold an essentially null hypothesis view of sex differences between males and females (Maccoby & Jacklin, 1974) that, as young children, males are much more aggressive than females. It has been suggested that these differences in overt aggression disappear with age, but definitive studies are unavailable. For example, it is exceedingly difficult to set up experiments which involve the infliction of bodily harm upon one individual by another. In fact, experimenters have been ɩeluctant to use manipulations which involve active treatment or arousal in the study of aggression in females (McKenna & Kessler, Note 5). When interviewed about differential treatment of male and female subjects (Prescott & Foster, Note 6), investigators indicated that they did not believe some manipulations were appropriate for or relevant to women. Self-reports of the use of physical force in the implementation of influence attempts are unlikely to come to the attention of any but the child therapist and then are likely to be dismissed as the aberrant case. It is noteworthy, therefore, that the use of physical-power tactics has been reported and does vary with sex (Sutton-Smith & Rosenberg, 1968). Beating up, belting and hitting, wrestling and chasing are ascribed to boys. Scratching and pinching and tickling are ascribed to girls. The direct physical power of older brothers upon their younger siblings apparently has a strong effect, as these second-born children are the only ones who score higher on getting angry, shouting, or yelling. In a previously cited study of college students, the authors found the same tendency for firstborns to use more physical-power tactics; the only difference was that children were more willing to admit to using direct aggressive techniques. These findings suggest a continuity of power relationships from childhood through college years.

The Role of Body Build

Body build is clearly related to the ability to use physical force effectively. Body build is also a determinant of social status in children (Felker, 1972; Johnson & Staffieri, 1971; Lerner & Korn, 1972; Staffieri, 1972). From age five through adulthood, males and females view the mesomorphic body build as "all things good." Boys, in particular, associate the mesomorph with an assertive, aggressive pattern, while ectomorphs are seen as socially submissive (Johnson & Staffieri, 1971). Both boys and girls would prefer to have mesomorphic body builds (Lerner & Korn, 1972; Staffieri, 1972). Endomorphs receive the most negative evaluations from boys and girls. They are seen as most likely to fight, cheat, worry, be teased, lonely, lazy, mean, ugly, stupid, and sloppy. These data become particularly relevant when we consider them in the light of the body types of males versus females in general. At all ages, human males are taller than females and have a larger percentage of fat-free body weight (Garn, 1966). Garn suggests that the 7% larger male body size seen after sexual maturity and the 30% greater lean body mass of adult males have their beginnings well before birth. In relative terms, males are mesomorphs and females are endomorphs. It is not improbable that the larger body size of male children gives them a significant initial advantage. Later, direct physical force is not usually necessary to maintain status; covert manifestations will do as well. Females from age six upward manifest smaller territorial boundaries than males (Aiello & Aiello, 1974). Even as adults, females, but not males, decrease their movements upon intrusion into their territories (Mahoney, 1974). As indicated earlier, boys with high social power, but not girls, were seen as more threatening (Zander & Van Egmond, 1958). Covert nonverbal behaviors may provide a source of reinforcement for masculine dominance without the awareness of any of the participants.

CONCLUSION

Although physical size is at least as obvious an ascriptive characteristic as the gender ascription to which it is highly correlated, almost no note of this variable has been made in the extensive literature on sex differences. Is it because it is socially unacceptable to admit that the use of force is more a "norm" in interpersonal behavior than psychologists would like to believe? Is physical size so "obvious" a variable that it has no psychological "value"? Or do we prefer the illusion of sex differences to the possible reality of power differences?

"The child is mother to the woman," and the high degree of correspondence between the behavior of the female as a child and her behavior as an adult is noteworthy. Adult females talk less than males within a group context (Alkire, Collum, Kaswan, & Love, 1968) and continue to have less ability to influence groups of which they are a part (Wahrman & Pugh, 1974). Their lack of influence remains unrelated to their degree of competence in the group's activities. Women who "illegitimately" attempt to influence the behavior of male-dominated groups are subject to severe social sanctions (Wolman & Frank, 1975). Independent of the behavior of the individuals involved, gender seems to serve a stimulus function which connotes low status.

It is necessary to caution against the absolute confusion of power and gender in which some feminists engage. Janeway (1974) points out: "As always, the world belongs to the powerful, and though, almost universally, the powerful are male, we can't reverse that statement. Males are not almost universally powerful" (p. 187). She suggests a new phrase: "The weak are the second sex." It is this equation of weakness and femininity, Janeway believes, which underlies a great deal of masculine reaction to a redefinition of women's role. A step up for women may be seen by men in reverse, as a step down to an inferior level, women's level. The division of the world by sex instead of power creates an alliance of both weak and powerful males by means of anatomy. The existence of such an alliance could explain why social scientists are so reluctant to admit to a confusion of gender and status.

Psychologists need to study characteristics other than gender—such as race and age—which also convey information about ascriptive status to see if they produce similar role inequalities. Relatedly, the bases for the socialization of status differences between the sexes need exploration. No one denies that some behavioral differences between some males and females exist under some conditions, but the interactional nature of socialization phenomena has been omitted from most investigations. If a child is fortunate enough to be strong, well-built, healthy, intelligent, upper-middle class, white and male, children are likely to respond positively to him. Although we know that there is a positive relationship between the giving and receiving of positive reinforcements, we do not know the causal direction. Perhaps some children are more socially accepted because they give more reinforcements to their peers, or, perhaps, they give more because they are accepted. In any case, peer regard increases self-esteem, self-evaluation and in the perception of control over one's life. Such children will engage in more attempts to control their environment and will probably succeed. Our major problem may not be that few of these children are female, but that there are so few at all. Taking into account all the ascriptive characteristics which connote low status, the powerless are the vast majority of us all.

REFERENCE NOTES

1. Unger, R.K. *Status, power and gender: An examination of parallelisms.* Paper presented at the conference "New Directions for Research on Women," Madison, Wisconsin, May 1975.
2. Johnson, P. *Social power and sex role stereotypes.* Paper presented at the meeting of the Western Psychological Association, San Francisco, May 1974.
3. Barnett, R. *The relationship between occupational preference and occupational prestige: A study of sex differences and age trends.* Paper presented at the meeting of the Eastern Psychological Association, Washington, D.C., April 1973.
4. Denmark, F. Personal communication, September 2, 1975.
5. McKenna, W., & Kessler, S.J. *Experimental design as a source of sex bias in social psychology.* Paper presented at the meeting of the American Psychological Association, New Orleans, August 1974.
6. Prescott, S., & Foster, K. *Why researchers don't study women.* Paper presented at the meeting of the American Psychological Association, New Orleans, August 1974.

REFERENCES

Aiello, J.R., & Aiello, T.D. The development of personal space: Proxemic behavior of children 6 through 16. *Human Ecology,* 1974, *2,* 177-189.

Akamatsu, T.J., & Thelen, M.H. A review of the literature on observer characteristics and imitation. *Developmental Psychology,* 1974, *10,* 38-47.

Alkire, A.A., Collum, M.E., Kaswan, J., & Love, L.R. Information exchange and accuracy of verbal communication under social power conditions. *Journal of Personality and Social Psychology,* 1968, *9,* 301-308.

Bandura, A., Ross, D., & Ross, S.A. A comparative test of the status envy, social power and secondary reinforcement theories of identification learning. *Journal of Abnormal and Social Psychology,* 1963, *67,* 529-534.

Bigner, J.J. Sibling influence on sex-role preference of young children. *Journal of Genetic Psychology,* 1972, *121,* 271-282.

Bigner, J.J. Second borns' discrimination of sibling role concepts. *Developmental Psychology,* 1974, *10,* 564-573.

Borke, H. The development of empathy in Chinese and American children between three and six years of age: A cross-cultural study. *Developmental Psychology,* 1973, *9,* 102-108.

Brook, J., Whiteman, M., Peisach, E., & Deutsch, M. Aspiration levels of and for children: Age, sex, race and socioeconomic correlates. *Journal of Genetic Psychology*, 1974, *124*, 3-16.

Broverman, I.K., Vogel, S.R., Broverman, D.M., Clarkson, F.E., & Rosenkrantz, P.S. Sex-role stereotypes: A current reappraisal. *Journal of Social Issues*, 1972, *28*, 59-78.

Carrigan, W.C., & Julian, J.W. Sex and birth-order differences in conformity as a function of need affiliation arousal. *Journal of Personality and Social Psychology*, 1966, *3*, 479-483.

Charlesworth, R., & Hartup, W.W. Positive social reinforcement in the nursery school peer group. *Child Development*, 1967, *38*, 993-1002.

Crandall, V.C., Katkovsky, W., & Crandall, V. Children's beliefs in their own control of reinforcements in intellectual academic achievement situations. *Child Development*, 1965, *36*, 91-109.

Deaux, K.K., & Emswiller, T. Explanations of successful performance on sex-linked tasks: What is skill for the male is luck for the female. *Journal of Personality and Social Psychology*, 1974, *29*, 80-85.

Edelson, M.S., & Omark, D.R. Dominance hierarchies in young children. *Social Science Information*, 1973, *12*, 1.

Emmerich, W. Family role concepts of children ages six to ten. *Child development*, 1961, *32*, 609-624.

Entwisle, D.R., & Greenberger, E. Questions about social class, internality-externality, and test anxiety. *Developmental Psychology*, 1972, *7*, 218.

Etaugh, C., & Brown, B. Perceiving the causes of success and failure of male and female performers. *Developmental Psychology*, 1975, *11*, 103.

Feldman-Summers, S., & Kiesler, S.B. Those who are number two try harder: The effect of sex on attributions of causality. *Journal of Personality and Social Psychology*, 1974, *30*, 846-855.

Felker, D.W. Social stereotyping of male and female body types with differing facial expressions by elementary school age boys and girls. *Journal of Psychology*, 1972, *82*, 151-154.

French, J.R.P., Jr., & Raven, B. The basis of social power. In D. Cartwright (Ed.), *Studies in social power*. Ann Arbor: Institute for Social Research, 1959.

Friend, R.M., & Neale, J.M. Children's perception of success and failure: An attributional analysis of the effects of race and social class. *Developmental Psychology*, 1972, *7*, 124-128.

Garn, S.M. Body size and its implications. In L.W. Hoffman & M.L. Hoffman (Eds.), *Review of child development research* (Vol. 2). New York: Russell Sage Foundation, 1966.

Geshuri, Y. Discriminative observational learning: Effects of observed reward and dependency. *Child Development*, 1975, *46*, 550-554.

Glidewell, J.C., Kantor, M.P., Smith, L.M., & Stringer, L.A. Socialization and social structure in the classroom. In L.W. Hoffman & M.L. Hoffman (Eds.), *Review of child development research* (Vol. 2). New York: Russell Sage Foundation, 1966.

Gold, M. Power in the classroom. *Sociometry*, 1958, *25*, 50-60.

Goldberg, P. Are women prejudiced against women? *Trans-Action*, 1968, April, 28-30.

Gruen, G.E., Kort, J.R., & Baum, J.F. Group measure of locus of control. *Developmental Psychology*, 1974, *10*, 683-686.

Hartup, W.W. Peer interaction and social organization. In P.H. Mussen (Ed.), *Manual of child psychology* (3rd ed.). New York: John Wiley & Sons, 1970.

Hartup, W.W., Glazer, J.A., & Charlesworth, R. Peer reinforcement and sociometric status. *Child Development*, 1967, *38*, 1017-1024.

Henley, N.M., & Freeman, J. The sexual politics of interpersonal behavior. In J. Freeman (Ed.), *Women: A feminist perspective*. Palo Alto: Mayfield Publishing Co., 1975.

Hollender, J. Sex differences in sources of social self-esteem. *Journal of Consulting and Clinical Psychology*, 1972, *38*, 343-347.

Hrycenko, I., & Minton, H.L. Internal-external control, power position and satisfaction in task-oriented groups. *Journal of Personality and Social Psychology*, 1974, *30*, 871-878.

Janeway, E. *Between myth and morning: Women awakening*. New York: William Morrow & Co., 1974.

Johnson, C.D., & Gormly, J. Academic cheating: The contribution of sex, personality, and situational variables. *Developmental Psychology*, 1972, *6*, 320-325.

Johnson, P.A., & Staffieri, J.R. Stereotypic affective properties of personal names and somatotypes in children. *Developmental Psychology*, 1971, *5*, 176.

Lerner, R.M., & Korn, S.J. The development of body-build stereotypes in males. *Child Development*, 1972, *43*, 908-920.

Levenson, H. Perceived parental antecedents of internal, powerful others, and chance locus of control orientations. *Developmental Psychology*, 1973, *9*, 268-274.

Lippitt, R., & Gold, M. Classroom social structure as a mental health problem. *Journal of Social Issues*, 1959, *15*, 40-49.

Looft, W.R. Sex differences in the expression of vocational aspirations by elementary school children. *Developmental Psychology*, 1971, *5*, 366.

Maccoby, E.E., & Jacklin, C.N. *The psychology of sex differences*. Stanford: Stanford University Press, 1974.

Mahoney, E.R. Compensatory reactions to spatial immediacy. *Sociometry*, 1974, *37*, 423-431.

McGinnies, E., Nordholm, L.A., Ward, C.D., & Bhanthumnavin, D.L. Sex and cultural differences in perceived locus of control among students in five countries. *Journal of Consulting and Clinical Psychology*, 1974, *42*, 451-455.

Morland, J.K. A comparison of race awareness in northern and southern children. *American Journal of Orthopsychiatry*, 1966, *36*, 22-31.

Nowicki, S., Jr., & Duke, M.P. A preschool and primary internal-external control scale. *Developmental Psychology*, 1974, *10*, 874-880.

Nowicki, S., Jr., & Segal, W. Perceived parental characteristics, locus of control orientation, and behavioral correlates of locus and control. *Developmental Psychology*, 1974, *10*, 33-37.

Parsons, T. Family structure and the socialization of the child. In T. Parsons & R.F. Bales (Eds.), *Family socialization and the interaction process*. New York: Free Press, 1955.

Patterson, G.R., Littman, R.A., & Bricker, W. Assertive behavior in children: A step toward a theory of aggression. *Monographs of the Society for Research in Child Development*, 1967, *32* (Serial No. 113).

Pheterson, G.J., Kiesler, S.B., & Goldberg, P.A. Evaluation of the performance of women as a function of their sex, achievement and personal history. *Journal of Personality and Social Psychology*, 1971, *19*, 114-118.

Pollis, N.P., & Doyle, D.C. Sex role, status, and perceived competence among first-graders. *Perceptual and Motor Skills,* 1972, *34,* 235-238.

Reese, H.W. Sociometric choices of the same and opposite sex in late childhood. *Merrill-Palmer Quarterly,* 1962, *8,* 173-174.

Rosenblatt, P.C., & Skoogberg, E.L. Birth order in cross-cultural perspective. *Developmental Psychology,* 1974, *10,* 48-54.

Ross, D. Relationship between dependency, intentional learning and incidental learning in preschool children. *Journal of Personality and Social Psychology,* 1966, *4,* 274-281.

Sherif, M., & Sherif, C.W. *Social psychology.* New York: Harper & Row, 1969.

Smith, P.K., & Green, M. Aggressive behavior in English nurseries and play groups: Sex differences and response of adults. *Child Development,* 1975, *46,* 211-214.

Springer, D. National-racial preferences of fifth-grade children in Hawaii. *Journal of Genetic Psychology,* 1953, *83,* 121-136.

Staffieri, J.R. Body build and behavioral expectancies in young females. *Developmental Psychology,* 1972, *6,* 125-127.

Sternglanz, S.H., & Serbin, L.A. Sex role stereotyping in children's television programs. *Developmental Psychology,* 1974, *10,* 710-715.

Stevenson, H.W. Social reinforcement of children's behavior. In L.P. Lipsitt & C.C. Spiker (Eds.), *Advances in child development and behavior.* New York: Academic Press, 1965.

Sutton-Smith, B., & Rosenberg, B.G. Sibling consensus on power tactics. *Journal of Genetic Psychology,* 1968, *112,* 63-72.

Wahrman, R., & Pugh, M.D. Sex, nonconformity and influence. *Sociometry,* 1974, *37,* 137-147.

Witryol, S.L., & Kaess, W.A. Sex differences in social memory tasks. *Journal of Abnormal and Social Psychology,* 1957, *54,* 343-346.

Wolf, T.M. Effects of live-modeled sex-inappropriate play behavior in a naturalistic setting. *Developmental Psychology,* 1973, *9,* 120-123.

Wolman, C., & Frank, H. The solo woman in a professional peer group. *American Journal of Orthopsychiatry,* 1975, *45,* 164-171.

Zander, A., & Van Egmond, E. Relationship of intelligence and social power to the interpersonal behavior of children. *Journal of Educational Psychology,* 1958, *49,* 257-268.

Physical Sex Differences:
A Matter of Degree

DOROTHY V. HARRIS
The Pennsylvania State University

Biology is the starting point for the discussion of sex differences. Biology also demonstrates the *identity* of male and female, pointing out the basic similarities and continuity in their development (Oakley, 1972). At every stage of development, the male and female share the same body ground plan. While there is a definite masculine and feminine physical prototype, envisioning a continuum from the most masculine to the most feminine is the best way to understand human physical characteristics. In the normal male and female, beyond the distinctive reproductive organs where even the anatomical difference is more apparent than real, all characteristics are shared to some degree by both sexes. In most cases, no absolute distinction can be made between the male and female characteristics; it is only a matter of degree.

PRENATAL DEVELOPMENT

Prenatally, up to a critical stage in the development of the embryo, the sex is nonspecific. Sex dimorphism is determined by either the X or the Y sex chromosome provided by the male parent, which determines the destiny of undifferentiated gonads, developing into either a pair of ovaries or a pair of testicles. From this point, the sex chromosome exerts no further influence upon subsequent sexual differentiation. This is passed on to the influence of the hormonal secretions produced by the testes (androgens) and ovaries (estrogens). In fact, further sexual differentiation is determined by the hormonal secretions of the testes because, in total absence of gonadal hormones, the fetus continues to differentiate to the development of the female gonads. It appears that, as endocrinologist LeVine (1966) expressed it, the basic human plan is female and masculinity comes about as the result of something "added."

In general, throughout the prenatal development, the male develops more slowly than the female. At twenty weeks after conception, the male is already two weeks behind the development of the female. The newborn female's physical maturity at birth is equivalent to the four- to six-weeks-old male

(Hutt, 1972), even though the average male is both larger and heavier. However, the male tends to grow faster than the female during the postnatal stage and continues to do so but with progressive deceleration until about seven months of age.

Traditionally, female infants are protected and handled with more care than male infants. This differential treatment is the beginning of the socialization process which suggests that the female is physically less tolerant of strains and stresses. This assumption is without scientific support. In fact, the female infant is physically more mature and therefore capable of withstanding as much or more than the male.

In observing the growth and development of the male and female after birth, they follow a similar pattern during infancy and early childhood, with growth curves paralleling one another. During childhood, the weight of the male exceeds that of the female, on the average, by approximately four percent and the height by approximately two percent, in spite of the greater maturity of the female. The male continues to be both heavier and taller than the average female of the same age until about eight years (Rarick, 1973).

Despite the average male's superior advantages in height and weight during infancy and early childhood, he develops much more slowly than the female. The growth speed of the male follows as much as two years behind that of the female, with even greater differences observed among some. This is most apparent during puberty. Bone ossification, dental maturity, as well as physiological and neurological maturity, are reached sooner in the female.

Although gains in height and weight proceed at fairly uniform rates during childhood, the gain in height is approximately twice that in weight. Females tend to maintain their proportionately longer leg length in relation to trunk length until the end of early childhood. During infancy and early childhood, the male has an overall width advantage of the pelvis, while the female tends to have relative or absolute larger width of the inner structure. The relative gain of shoulder width is approximately the same for both sexes during the ages of six to ten. The amount and development of muscle tissue are practically identical during the first decade of life.

The caloric intake of males exceeds that of females from the second month of life. From infancy, the male displays a consistently higher basal metabolism. In addition, he develops a proportionally larger heart and lungs, producing a greater vital capacity than that of the female. At birth, females tend to have proportionately more fat tissue, which increases with physical maturation. This, along with a lower basal metabolism, may create a greater problem in controlling weight for some females.

In general, preadolescent sex differences in physical size and ability are minor, with no significant differences observed. The female's advanced physical maturity provides her with an advantage in physical activities. Frequently, females are capable of out-performing their same-aged males at this stage of development. In the early 1970's, when the Little League was charged with discriminatory practices, the arguments for excluding girls on the basis of inferior abilities could not be supported (Torg & Torg, 1974). The

Little League was not able to demonstrate and support that significant differences exist between males and females of Little-League age that would preclude the female's participation. Judge Pressler was "persuaded by a heavy preponderance of evidence that there is no substantial physiological difference relative to athletic performance between girls ages 8 to 12 on one hand and boys 8 to 12 on the other hand" (Torg & Torg, 1974, p. 50). On the basis of the research and evidence available, there does not appear to be any support for differential treatment in sport and physical-activity programs of males and females during childhood and preadolescence.

ADOLESCENCE

Puberty begins in the female as much as two years earlier than in the male, producing a growth spurt during which the female grows faster and sometimes larger than the same-aged male. She reaches mature height soon after onset of menarche, when higher levels of female sex hormones (estrogens) cause the closure of the epiphyses in long bones. This cessation is produced by sex hormones also in the male, but much later. This provides the male with the added advantage of several growing years which contribute to his relatively larger body at maturation.

Sex hormonal differences influence other developments which have implications for sport performance. Estrogens cause deposition of increasing quantities of fat in the subcutaneous tissues of the breasts, upper arms, buttocks, hips, and thighs. This produces the broadening of the hips and the curves that are generally characteristic of the feminine figure. Thus, the relative proportion of lean body mass (muscle and bone) to total body weight is less for the female. The relatively smaller amount of muscle in the female is not caused by the inhibitory effect of estrogen but by the absence of the higher levels of male sex hormones (Lewin, 1973). Increasing levels of androgens in the male during puberty produce greater muscularity and more prominent muscle definition. The female's lesser muscle mass is further masked by greater amounts of subcutaneous fat not observed in the male. The higher percentage of fat in the female increases her ability to retain body heat in the cold; she is also more buoyant. Females appear to be less efficient in heat dissipation, however, as they do not begin to sweat until their bodies are two to three degrees warmer than the male. Further, their sweat glands are not as productive. Greater consideration should be given to the female when working or exercising in hot environments, until a better understanding of her response to heat stress is reached.

The fact that the female menstruates probably has caused more misconceptions about differences between males and females than any one other characteristic. There is little reason for concern in the healthy female, as menstruation is a normal function which should not cause any marked alteration in lifestyle. Gold medals have been won by female athletes during every phase of the menstrual cycle, and many athletes have produced their personal record while menstruating. Further, pregnant athletes have performed with success in Olympic and other competitive athletic events without problems. In general, restriction of activity in normal, healthy females does not appear warranted.

Comprehensive reviews looking at the effect of menstruation on cognitive and perceptual-motor behaviors by Sommer (1973) and Parlee (1973) revealed confusion in the findings. Sommer, in taking an overall view of the results, observed that, where a cyclic effect occurred, responses were mediated by social and psychological factors. She suggested that subjects expressed feelings and interacted with their social environment in ways consonant with their expectations about themselves and the demands and social expectations of their society. Studies which utilized objective performance measures generally failed to demonstrate any menstrual-cycle-related changes. Paige (1973) concluded that religion and society have much to do with how a female responds to menstruation. At this stage of the knowledge, it is difficult to relate with any degree of assuredness behavior or performance variables with hormonal fluctuation and menstruation in the female.

The increased production of androgens during puberty transforms the boy's body into that of an adult male. The delayed growth spurt provides the male with a longer growing period which, among other things, allows the legs and arms to grow longer proportionately to his trunk length than observed in mature females. An increase in the shoulder width occurs, accompanied by a rapid increase in height. The thickening of the skeletal structure and marked development of the skeletal musculature contribute to his greater body weight. The relatively less fat tissue is reduced even further during puberty, resulting in a higher ratio of lean body mass to fat tissue than in the female. Increased physical vigor and strength accompany the muscular growth, which reaches maximal levels soon after the end of puberty. Increase in the male's strength is probably more the result of quantitative than of qualitative change in musculature. This increase is most apparent in the upper extremities, less so in the trunk, and it appears to be absent in the lower extremities when compared to the female. Wilmore (1975) has demonstrated that females are capable of developing leg strength comparable to that of the male when participating in similar strength-training programs. Males, however, continue to develop greater shoulder and trunk strength than females on the same weight-training program. They also exhibit significant muscle hypertrophy that is not observed in females. The higher levels of androgens in males produce the greater muscle mass, greater shoulder and trunk strength, and the ability to "bulk up" with weight training, which is not characteristic of the female.

POSTPUBERTY

When comparing postpubertal males and females, the males are generally taller and heavier. Their larger size, greater vital capacity and cardiac output, along with lower heart rates, provide an advantage in strenuous activities.

Physically, the male is stronger and faster, therefore capable of generating more power. The wider shoulder and longer extremities in relation to the trunk are mechanically superior. A larger shoulder girdle results in a higher center of gravity. The male generally has a greater ability to deliver oxygen to the working muscle because of the larger lung surface, larger heart, and higher hemoglobin level in the blood. When measurements of maximal oxygen consumption are based on total body weight, the male is more efficient because he has less fat tissue to which oxygen must be supplied.

The physically smaller female generally has a longer trunk in relation to her leg length and a lower center of gravity due to her smaller shoulder girdle and increased pelvic development. The smaller chest, lungs, and heart, combined with the lesser chest strength, reduce the female's vital capacity. Her maximal oxygen uptake is less than that of the male due to the smaller heart and lungs, the lower hemoglobin levels, and the higher percentage of body fat.

The size and structural differences between and among males and females are only a matter of degree, possibly produced by the variation of the ratio of androgens to estrogens. This variation in size and structure produces marked differences in speed and strength and the ability to generate power. The higher the level of sport competition, the more selective the process is of those individuals who are stronger and faster. This is true whether the athletes are males or females. Therefore, the characteristics of the male are much more compatible with the physical demands of sport. This is not to say that females cannot participate at a high level; however, it does suggest that, for high-level sport performance, males and females should compete on separate teams. Otherwise, very few females will have the opportunity for high-level performance. It appears that "biology is destiny" when developing strength and speed and power. This, along with the fact that sport is selective of the stronger and faster athletes, suggests that the male will have an inherent advantage in any sport that involves strength and speed. This advantage often allows him to beat another who may be more skilled but have less power. Billie Jean King and Jimmy Connors are both highly skilled tennis players; however, Connors is so much more powerful than King that she would have little chance of success.

If there are positive benefits and if the experience in competitive sport is significant and meaningful, then these are human values which should not continue to be the prerogative of the male even though he holds an inherent advantage in most sports. All humans can experience the pleasures and satisfactions of participating in competitive sport and should have the opportunity if they so desire. Success reinforces a positive sense of selfhood, and competitive sport should be structured to enhance the opportunity to experience success for as many participants as possible. For much too long the single standard of performance, that of the male, has been one to which all others have been compared. Thus, the female's best performance is considered inferior. Females have continued to improve their performance with better training and coaching; however, the best of the females will never be able to out-perform the best of the males in any activity involving strength and speed.

Females have come closest to the male's performance in swimming, in which their greater buoyancy compensates to some degree for their lesser power when compared to the male.

SUMMARY

In summarizing the physical differences observed in males and females, it appears that the degree of difference may be explained by the ratio of androgens to estrogens in both sexes. Beyond that, training, coaching, and experience can alter one's inherent capacity for physical performance. The greatest differences are observed from puberty throughout the active reproductive years, when sex hormones are at their highest levels. During this period, males have higher levels of androgens, which promote greater muscle mass, larger and more dense bones, and increased power, which give them a decided advantage over females in situations demanding strength, speed, and power. Females have higher levels of estrogens, which shorten the growing period and increase fat tissue. More significantly, lower levels of androgens do not promote the same development of muscle mass. The net result is a smaller and less powerful female, as compared to the male, on the average. Nevertheless, the female has the ability to develop a high level of skill in any sport and compete successfully with other females. The hormonal difference which exists between males and females will preclude the female from developing the same degree of strength, speed, and power as her equally trained male counterpart.

REFERENCES

Hutt, C. *Males and females.* Middlesex, England: Penguin Education, Division of Penguin Books, Ltd., 1972.

LeVine, S. Sex differences in the brain. *Scientific American,* 1966, *214,* 84-90.

Lewin, R. *Hormones: Chemical communicators.* Garden City, New York: Anchor Books, 1973.

Oakley, A. *Sex, gender and society.* New York: Harper & Row, Publishers, 1972.

Paige, K.E. Women learn to sing the menstrual blues. *Psychology Today,* September 1973, pp. 41-46.

Parlee, M.B. The premenstrual syndrome. *Psychological Bulletin,* 1973, *80,* 454-465.

Rarick, G.L. *Physical activity: Human growth and development.* New York: Academic Press, 1973.

Sommer, B. The effect of menstruation on cognitive and perceptual-motor behavior: A review. *Psychosomatic Medicine,* 1973, *35,* 515-534.

Torg, B.G., & Torg, J.S. Sex and the Little League. *The Physician and Sports Medicine,* 1974, *5,* 45-50.

Wilmore, J.H. Inferiority of female athletes: Myth or reality. *Journal of Sports Medicine,* 1975, *3,* 1-6.

What Inhibits Achievement and Career Motivation in Women?

HELEN S. FARMER
University of Illinois at Urbana-Champaign

It has long been known that women do not achieve or contribute as much as men in the fields of science, the humanities, and the arts (Astin, Note 1; Commission on the Status of Women, 1970; Maccoby & Jacklin, 1974; Rossi & Calderwood, 1973) in spite of the fact that they represent over 40% of the professional labor force today (Blitz, 1974) and have represented at least 30% of the professionals since 1890. Fewer women proportionately rise to the top of their chosen profession, business, or trade. Although women represented 40% of the professional and technical workers in 1974, they represented less than 20% of the managers and administrators that year (U.S. Department of Labor, 1974), and a majority of these women were elementary school teachers.

The dilemma confronted is that women, found to be equally intelligent as men (Maccoby & Jacklin, 1974), do not contribute to society through their work in proportion to their participation. Why do women scientists, artists, writers, educators, and social scientists not contribute as much as men? What inhibits their achievement and productivity?

The growth of the feminist movement in the 1960's and its continuing expansion in the 1970's have led to a variety of intervention strategies aimed at accelerating equal opportunity for all women (Farmer & Backer, Note 2). Some of the strategies include legislation, assertiveness training, consciousness raising, multiple-role planning, women's studies programs, and encouragement to women to enter and train in the nontraditional professions (e.g., engineering, physics, law, and medicine). These intervention strategies, however, are typically provided in a "shotgun" fashion rather than on the basis of careful examination of the factors contributing to women's unequal status. The selective review of literature on achievement and career motivation that follows provides some insight into the factors inhibiting such motivation in women. Having identified the relevant factors, it seems more likely that optimal interventions can be formulated as well as most effectively applied.

ACHIEVEMENT MOTIVATION

In their review of 58 studies on achievement in women, Maccoby and Jacklin (1974) reported a series of studies indicating that women have lower levels of academic self-confidence and are less competitive compared with men. They noted that this difference in self-confidence between the sexes usually does not appear in elementary or high school students but appears first in college. It might be speculated that, since college often precipitates a marriage-career conflict (Matthews & Tiedeman, 1964), the lowered self-confidence and achievement motivation noted in college women by Drew and Patterson (Note 3) are thus fostered.

Astin (Note 1) found that girls perform as well as boys in math, science, and tests of spatial relationships up to about age 10; thereafter their performance becomes increasingly poorer. She suggested that this effect is due, as least in part, to differential reinforcement on the part of parents and teachers.

The model of achievement motivation developed by Atkinson and Raynor (1974) and McClelland (1971) identified the following factors as critical for high achievement motivation: an internal standard of excellence, independence, persistence, preference for tasks of intermediate difficulty, high academic performance, and clearly defined goals. On the basis of her separate examinations of achievement motivation for boys and girls, Bardwick (1971) suggested that this is a male model of achievement motivation. Alper (1974) refers to achievement motivation in women as the "now-you-see-it-now-you-don't" phenomenon. Her recent review of achievement motivation in women does not support Maccoby and Jacklin's (1974) conclusions that differences between the sexes do not become significant until women reach college. Rather than to clear-cut differences between the sexes during the elementary and high school years, Alper points to the illusive quality of female achievement motivation. Bardwick (1971) refers to the differences as one of "ambivalence" for women, created by their pull toward both achievement and affiliation with the opposite sex and their "fear" that success in one rules out success in the other.

Maehr (1974) recently proposed that situational variables may play a critical role in achievement motivation as it manifests itself within different racial and cultural groups. Lockheed (1975), for example, found that women had less "fear of success" when responding to cues that presented women in socially sanctioned achievement situations (e.g., Anne, a medical student in a medical class that is half female) than when responding to cues that presented women in nontraditional roles (e.g., Anne as the only female in her medical class). Providing contextual change in the stimulus cue had a dramatic effect on these women's fear of success. Monahan, Kuhn, and Shaver (1974) provided high school students with cues of both sexes. They found that girls and boys both gave more negative responses to the female cue, supporting the view that females who succeed are viewed as less attractive than males.

Alper (1974) has been studying the relationship of sex-role orientation to achievement motivation in women for more than a decade and has found that women with traditional female orientations, attitudes, and beliefs score lower on achievement-motivation measures than women with nontraditional female orientations. Entwisle and Greenberger (1972) found that high-IQ girls generally held more liberal views than average- and low-IQ girls and that high-IQ girls from blue-collar homes were the most liberal about women's roles.

ACHIEVEMENT MOTIVATION AND "FEAR OF SUCCESS"

Horner (Note 4) researched the avoidance of achievement in women, which she calls "fear of success," and documented the changing strength of this "fear" when competitive factors are changed. For most women, Horner found that they had less fear of success when they were competing against themselves than when they were competing with other students. The opposite was true for most males. Tomlinson-Keasey (1974) found that married women students with children had significantly lower fear of success than unmarried coeds. We might infer that these women had less fear of academic success, having found a husband who accepted their academic aspiration. The married women were also a more select group and were highly motivated to return to study.

Lockheed (1975) made adaptations in Horner's basic research design by providing additional prompting cues to her subjects. She required two groups of subjects, undergraduates in a small Western college, to respond to the same cues with the following additions: (1) All Anne's classmates in medical school are men. "After first-term finals, Anne finds herself at the top of her class." (Quotes indicate Horner's cues.). (2) Half of Anne's classmates in medical school are women. "After first-term finals, Anne finds herself at the top of her class." Subjects in the second condition, both men and women, had significantly less measured fear-of-success themes than those in the first condition. Lockheed concluded that the second cue provided the necessary social sanction for women to be comfortable with Anne's success in medical school.

Lipman-Blumen and Leavitt (1976) proposed an operational definition of the lower aspiration level of women through a description of a vicarious-achievement ethic; namely, many women choose indirect achievement satisfaction through the successes of important male persons in their lives (father, brother, boyfriend, husband, boss) rather than directly through their own successes. An example might be a woman saying she doesn't want to be the president (or director, etc.) but just wants to work with him. The vicarious-achievement motive suits well the woman who wants to avoid primary responsibility on the job but, at the same time, benefit from the successes of her boss through reflected glory. From a sample of married college females (N = 643), Lipman-Blumen and Leavitt (1976) found only 17% free of the vicarious-achievement motive. Twelve percent of this subgroup were pursuing a Ph.D., whereas none of those measuring high on vicarious-achievement motivation were pursuing Ph.D.'s.

Bettelheim (1969) suggested that education is an enhancement for boys whereas for girls it is a form of insurance in case they don't make it in marriage; therefore, he assumed that women who enter "direct-achievement" occupations, such as law or medicine, experience a loss of femininity. Similarly, men who enter "vicarious-achievement roles," such as nurse, elementary school teacher, or librarian, experience a loss of masculinity.

Harmon (1972) found it harder to predict the stability of career choice for college women than for college men. She found that women who aspired to high-level careers in their freshman year often changed their choices to less demanding careers by the time they were college seniors. Harmon hypothesized that lack of reinforcement for their high aspirations resulted in lowered career-aspiration level for these women. Relatedly, Hawley (1972) found that college women's choice of a traditional or nontraditional career was related, among other things, to whether the attitudes of significant men toward working women were positive or negative.

Tomlinson-Keasey (1974) found that married (older) coeds, compared to unmarried coeds, had higher levels of achievement motivation as well as lower "fear-of-success" scores. Research on the contribution of marriage plans to achievement motivation is being conducted currently by Drew and Patterson (Note 3).

EARLY SOCIALIZATION IN THE FAMILY AND ACHIEVEMENT MOTIVATION

The effect of early socialization patterns in the family has been found to affect motivation in boys differently from girls (Moss & Kagan, 1961). Results of studies are mostly limited to middle-class white families, where boys of parents who encouraged certain attitudes and behaviors were found to be highly achievement motivated. Examples of such attitudes are "hard work is good" and "the real reward comes from knowing you have performed well." Examples of behaviors are showing initiative, being independent, and delaying gratification (Rubovits, 1975). Boys exhibiting these attitudes and behaviors were found to frequently have a close warm relationship with their mothers and to identify with their fathers. In contrast, girls who exhibited both high need achievement and high academic and career performance did not exhibit a warm relationship with their mothers (Moss & Kagan, 1961; Crandall & Battle, 1970). Mothers of these girls were typically described as cool; however, they did encourage their daughters to be initiating, independent, competent, and achieving. Such women more often identified with their fathers than their mothers (Carpenter & Eisenberg, 1938; Plank & Plank, 1954). Many high-achievement-oriented women were found to view achievement as compatible with their feminine sex role (Houts & Entwisle, 1968; Mathews & Tiedeman, 1964), unlike high-ability women with lower measured achievement motivation who were in conflict about these roles (Mathews & Tiedeman, 1964).

Within the same families girls are found to receive different social-learning experiences than boys. While boys are encouraged to be competitive, initiating, achieving, and independent, girls are often encouraged to be dependent, conforming, cooperative, and unconcerned about grades (Rubovits, 1975). When women raised in such households find themselves faced with the necessity to work, they are poorly prepared for the competitive marketplace or to choose work commensurate with their potential.

As the working mother becomes more commonplace (Linden, 1973; Farmer & Backer, 1977), the socialization patterns in middle-class homes will change. How these changes will affect achievement and career motivation in women will be interesting to assess. It goes without saying that studies of the effect of socialization in the family on the motivation patterns of ethnic-minority girls and daughters of working-class parents are badly needed both to reflect changing patterns and to identify cross-cultural differences.

The stability of the effect of early socialization patterns on the motivation of women and men has been challenged by Maehr (1974), who suggests that changing the social sanctions in the environment may change achieving motivation and behavior. The work of Weiner (1974) on attribution of cause and effect related to achievement suggests that persons try harder to achieve when they view themselves as competent and in charge. The work of Weiner and Maehr suggests that less attention be paid to early socialization patterns and more attention be paid to developing contextual changes which (1) increase a woman's sense of career competence and (2) increase the social approval given the achievements of women. A better understanding of how early socialization patterns contribute to career and achievement motivation can be used, however, to redirect the efforts of parents to optimize motivation in their children of both sexes.

CAREER MOTIVATION

There are developmental and situational differences in the vocational-choice process of girls and boys. Following the Terman and Miles classic study, Tyler (1964) studied the development of sex differences in play and school and found that, whereas girls appear to be precocious in social development, they tend to lag behind boys in career development, especially at the college level. Similarly, other researchers (Campbell, 1974; Harmon, 1975) have suggested that women's vocational interests may crystallize somewhat later than men's and may be organized in a different way. Strong's (1955) earlier studies support the view that men and women in the same professions have significantly different career interests.

Ginzberg and his associates (1966) documented another important difference in the career-choice process for women. He noted that girls cannot realistically plan on a career until they know what kind of man they will marry (provided that they plan to marry). Their financial status and freedom to continue their education will be determined partially by the husband's career and his attitudes toward educated and working women. In addition, the number of children that a woman plans for or bears will affect the pattern of her career life. She may elect an interrupted career pattern or a parallel-track system, as suggested by Super (1969). Ginzberg postulated that this greater uncertainty in planning is probably the major difference between the sexes in their career development.

An interesting finding by Astin (Note 1) was that women who have high career motivation and pursue graduate-level education often show an exceptional aptitude for mathematics early in their education. In fact, mathematics aptitude was found to be the best predictor of career motivation in Astin's sample of 5000 women who had been five years out of high school. In earlier research, Astin (1969) found that women with a doctorate ($N = 1547$) were as highly motivated to work as men and that over 90% of the women graduating with Ph.D.'s in 1957 were still in the labor force eight years later. Such findings suggest that women who seek graduate-level degrees are not intellectual dilettantes but serious professionals.

Many women consider—and have the right to choose—a stable homemaking career. At the present time, about 50% of all women choose not to work outside the home (U.S. Department of Labor, 1974). Exposure to multiple-role planning early in the education of those girls and women who will choose not to work outside the home may facilitate their right to choose *freely*, having been informed of all the options.

WORK DISCRIMINATION

That women have been discriminated against in the labor force has been conclusively documented in the past few years (U.S. Department of Labor, 1974; Sweet, 1973). Discrimination takes a variety of forms—from practices at the point of obtaining training (Astin, Note 1) to practices in hiring, promoting, and providing on-the-job training, and salary increases (Fuchs, 1974; Parrish, 1974; Blitz, 1974). Attitudes of employers (Stimpson, 1973; Taylor, 1973), employees (Crowley, Levitin, & Quinn, 1973) and women themselves toward working (Hawley, 1972; Medvene & Collins, 1974) indicate widespread belief in "myths" about women, which are not verified by the facts of their behavior (U.S. Department of Labor, 1974).

The relationship between work discrimination and career motivation in women has not been clearly demonstrated. In the research of Farmer and Bohn (1970), for example, career motivation was increased for a group of employed women when they were given role-set (Sarbin, 1954) instructions to reduce attitudes about work discrimination. However, the role set also included instructions to reduce home-career conflict and fear of success (Horner, 1972), leaving the evidence on the effect of work discrimination inconclusive.

THE SOCIAL CONTEXT

At least three aspects of the social context affect the achievement and career motivation of women (Edye, 1970). One aspect is the availability of resources which support the educational and career development of women. These include nondiscriminatory educational admissions and employment practices, as well as the availability of child care and homemaking assistance. A second aspect is the expectations of significant others in the environment (i.e., parents, husbands, employers, teachers, etc.). A third aspect contributing to the motivation of women is supportive legislation related to providing equal opportunity and equal rights for all. A brief description of each of these aspects follows.

A social context which provides resources for women, making it possible for them to continue their education or employment during the childbearing years, increases the likelihood that women will continue their career development without interrupting it to raise a family. In 1940 only 4% of women with children eighteen and under were working. By 1970, 37% of these women were working and 30% of women with preschool children were working. Concurrent with this increase of women in the labor force was the growth of public, private, and employer-operated day-care facilities. Recent figures from a Department of Labor Survey (U.S. Department of Labor, 1974) indicate that present day-care facilities meet about 20% of the need in the U.S. Homemaking has been made easier by improved technology and the increasing numbers of families where husbands share some homemaking tasks (Hedges & Barnett, 1972). A third resource supporting the motivation of women to achieve is the increasing number of employers who offer permanent part-time employment and flexible scheduling for working women to help them take care of their children's and family's needs. For example, working half-time during the years when children are nursery-school age and working six-hour days when the children are in elementary school is attractive to many women. Flexible work schedules, adequate child-care facilities at reasonable cost, and husbands who share responsibility for homemaking contribute to the career motivation of women.

The expectations and behavior of significant others in a woman's life may play a critical role in determining whether or not she will be motivated to achieve and realize her career potential. Attitudes of husbands, parents, teachers, counselors, and employers, to name a few, may inhibit the achievement motivation of women. Such attitudes as "A woman's place is in the home," "Babies need their mothers when they are young," "Women were not intended to compete," "Find a husband, and he'll take care of you," and "A woman can experience success through her husband" are a few of the social myths which inhibit the full career development of some women. In contrast, when the attitudes of parents and husbands are supportive of women as persons whom they expect to contribute to society, women are found to continue in innovative career roles (Epstein, 1973; Rapoport & Rapoport, 1969).

In the past few decades, several laws have been passed which benefit employed women. In education, Title IX of the Education Amendments (1972) requires that equal access be given to both sexes in all aspects of education. This means that girls are legally equally eligible for courses in shop and mechanics in high school, for training as scientists and engineers in higher education, and for apprenticeships in the crafts (e.g., plumber, electrician) if they so desire. In employment, the Equal Employment Opportunity Act (1972), the Equal Pay for Equal Work Act (1972), and Executive Order 11246 (requiring Affirmative Action Plans by employers receiving government funding) support the eradication of sex discrimination in employment, salary scales, and promotions. Most outdated protective legislation for women (i.e., requiring special rest periods for women and eliminating them from many jobs requiring physical strength) has been repealed (U.S. Department of Labor, 1974). Maternity leave no longer interrupts seniority accumulation and is viewed legally as a temporary disability rather than as an interruption. Tax benefits are provided for child-care costs up to $400 a month, except for women whose joint income with their husband is over $18,000. The support legislation such as that described above should lead to increased participation of women in the labor force and to their increased motivation to achieve.

FUTURE DIRECTIONS

Achievement and career motivation in girls differs from that in boys as a result of several as yet poorly defined factors. Some of these factors have been identified in the research literature: (1) *reduction in academic self-confidence* for girls in college (Tomlinson-Keasey, 1974); (2) *fear of success* in college and high school women, found in varying degrees depending on the perceived social sanction given to women's careers (Horner, Tresemer, Berens, & Watson, Note 5; Katz, 1973; Monahan et al., 1974); (3) *vicarious-achievement motivation* found to contribute to women's contentment with traditional career roles, such as secretary, elementary school teacher, and nurse (Lipman-Blumen, 1972); (4) *home/career conflict* found to inhibit career motivation in both college women and working women (Morgan, Note 6; Farmer & Bohn, 1970); (5) *myths* about women and the world of work and their possible influence on the career-exploration process (Birk & Tanney, Note 7); (6) studies of academic motivation have found *risk-taking behavior* lower in girls than in boys (see review by Maccoby & Jacklin, 1974); (7) *sex-role orientation* was found to affect achievement motivation (Alper, 1974; Entwisle & Greenberger, 1972); (8) the availability of *resources* (i.e., child care) in the environment (Edye, 1970) was found to affect motivation; and (9) *family socialization* patterns in the home, especially those encouraging or discouraging independence (Crandall & Battle, 1970; Rubovits, 1975), have been found to affect both academic and career motivation. Figure 1 presents these factors, suggesting that some are behaviors and attitudes in the persons themselves and others are caused by attitudes, behaviors, and resources available to persons in their environment. This is a theoretical working model. No exact proportions are intended for any one factor, and the model should be interpreted accordingly.

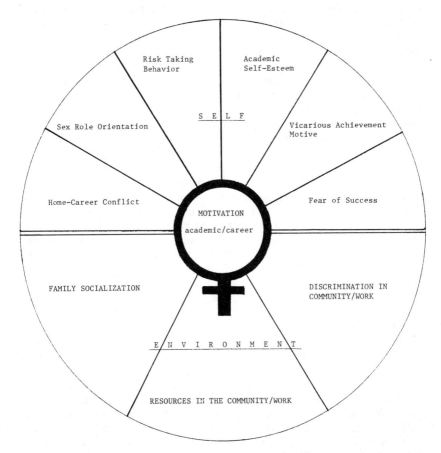

Figure 1. A conceptual model for understanding inhibited academic/career motivation in women.

Previous studies typically have looked at the effect of one of these variables and have not controlled for the possible effect of others on motivation. A current study of the author (Farmer, 1976) examines the potency of the above variables to predict both achievement motivation and career motivation in samples of high school students, college undergraduates, and women returning to higher education after an absence of at least five years.

Researchers are encouraged to undertake or continue studies aimed at a better understanding of career and achievement motivation in girls and women in terms of what increases and what decreases it. The degree of interdependence of career and achievement motivation in different subcultures could be studied. Crosscultural studies of motivation patterns in women in ethnic and geographic subgroups would be valuable. Comparative studies of the effect on motivation of various legal, economic, and social changes could potentially influence social reform as well as educational and counseling practice. Researchers might also look at coeducational interventions in the schools and elsewhere to determine how motivational patterns in both sexes are tied to changing attitudes, values, and experiences.

Although research findings to date on the career- and achievement-motivation patterns of women are not sufficient to provide highly specific direction to counseling practice, they are sufficient to suggest some general directions for counselors interested in increasing career motivation in women.

For example, early results from the author's study indicate that different factors are associated with achievement and career motivation for different age groups of girls and women. High school girls who were high in career motivation also perceived the support system in the community (i.e., equal-rights legislation, attitudes of employers and significant others, child-care facilities, etc.) as positively and significantly contributing to their career goals. On the other hand, high school girls who had *low* career motivation were less sure of such support in the community and were also more traditional in their sex-role orientation. Such girls might be helped through group discussion, through provision of information about what support they can expect from the environment, and through experiences that are designed to change their expectations.

For college women, findings from the author's study indicate that self-confidence is a critical factor in high career motivation. Also, the risk-taking behavior of these women was contrary to the generally accepted model (Atkinson & Raynor, 1974) in that women with low motivation were moderate risk takers and women with high motivation were either high or low risk takers. In a changing society, where the opportunity system is not easily predicted, the risk-taking behaviors required for taking advantage of the career opportunities may not be the usual ones. Counselors who invest time in teaching college women moderate risk-taking behavior may be wasting their time.

A third age group of women studied by the author were older women returning to school after an absence to raise a family. These women had a risk pattern similar to that of the college women studied. They were also similar to the high school group in that high career motivation was associated with nontraditional sex-role orientation and vice versa. However, these women surprised us with their scores on the fear-of-success measure. Women with high career motivation were *high* in fear of success, and women low in career motivation were low on this factor. This finding is contrary to earlier findings (Horner, 1974), in which the opposite relationships held for college and high school girls. Perhaps it is possible for older women to be highly motivated to enter a challenging career while at the same time experiencing conflict about their feminine role in society. Such age-related differences in the factors affecting achievement and career motivation are important for counselors to take into account.

Research to increase the career motivation of girls and women points to the powerful influence of exposing them to nontraditional role models (Lockheed, 1975). In a recent study, Plost (1974) found that presenting a female computer programmer in a career film significantly increased the career motivation of eighth-grade girls for that career in comparison to the interest they expressed when presented with the same film using a male model. Role models may be presented directly by inviting women in nontraditional careers to visit with students or by encouraging students to find part-time work in settings where they would interact with women in nontraditional career roles. Role models may also be presented indirectly through film, printed materials, and discussion. Women from different subcultures—such as black women, who reportedly have minimal fear of success and home-career conflict (Gump & Rivers, 1975)—may also be helpful role models for girls and women experiencing motivational conflicts.

Counselors are encouraged to be active in parent and teacher in-service education aimed at reducing sex-role stereotypic behavior. Teachers could be motivated to encourage girls to take science, shop, and math when interest and ability indicate the appropriateness of such consideration. Parents could be motivated to encourage career and achievement aspirations in their daughters and to discourage vicarious-achievement patterns. Counselors can begin to recognize biased occupational and career information (Birk, Cooper, & Tanney, Note 8, Note 9) and develop a library of nonbiased materials. The U.S. Department of Labor's Women's Bureau is a rich source of many unbiased and free publications on women and careers.

When girls and women begin to feel that it is all right to be assertive and independent, it is more likely that they will choose careers that require these attributes and will begin to contribute to society at levels more commensurate with their talents and potential. Counselors can encourage girls and women, boys and men to adopt flexible (androgynous) attitudes toward their sex roles, in opposition to the view that some behaviors and careers are feminine and others are masculine. This is a challenge, but one that must be met if society is to benefit fully from the resource potential of 51% of its population.

REFERENCE NOTES

1. Astin, H.S. *Preparing women for careers in science and technology.* Paper presented at the Massachusetts Institute of Technology Workshop on Women in Science and Technology, Boston, May 1973.

2. Farmer, H. & Backer, T. *New career options for women: A counselor's sourcebook.* New York: Human Sciences Press, 1977.
3. Drew, D. & Patterson, M. *Noah's ark in the frog pond: The educational aspirations of male and female undergraduates.* Unpublished manuscript, 1974. (Available from National Research Council, Washington, D.C.)
4. Horner, M. *Sex differences in achievement motivation and performance in competitive and non-competitive situations.* Unpublished doctoral dissertation, University of Michigan, 1968, No. 69-112, 135.
5. Horner, M., Tresemer, D., Berens, A. & Watson, R., Jr. *Scoring manual for an empirically derived scoring system for motive to avoid success.* Unpublished manuscript, Harvard University, 1973.
6. Morgan, D. *Perceptions of role conflicts and self concepts among career and non-career college educated women.* Unpublished doctoral dissertation, Teachers College, Columbia University, 1962.
7. Birk, J.M. & Tanney, M.F. *Career exploration for high school women: A model.* Paper presented at the meeting at the American Personnel and Guidance Association Regional Convention, Atlanta, Georgia, May 1973.
8. Birk, J.M., Cooper, J. & Tanney, M.F. *Racial and sex role stereotyping in career information illustrations.* Paper presented at the meeting of the American Psychological Association, Montreal, August 1973.
9. Birk, J.M., Cooper, J. & Tanney, M.F. *Stereotyping in Occupational Outlook Handbook illustrations: A follow-up study.* Paper presented at the meeting of the American Psychological Association, Chicago, August 1975.

REFERENCES

Alper, T. Achievement motivation in women: Now-you-see-it-now-you-don't. *American Psychologist,* 1974, *29,* 194-203.
Astin, H. *The woman doctorate in America.* New York: The Russel Sage Foundation, 1969.
Atkinson, J.W. & Raynor, J.O. *Motivation and achievement.* Washington, D.C.: V.W. Winston & Sons, 1974.
Bardwick, J. *Psychology of women.* New York: Harper and Row, 1971.
Bettelheim, B. *The children of the dream.* London: MacMillan, 1969.
Blitz, R. Women in the professions, 1890-1970. *Monthly Labor Review,* 1974, *97,* 34-39.
Campbell, D.P. *SVIB-SCII manual.* Stanford, California: Stanford Unversity Press, 1974.
Carpenter, J. & Eisenberg, P. Some relations between family background and personality. *Journal of Psychology,* 1938, *6,* 115-136.
Commission on the Status of Women. *Participation of women in the economic and social development of their countries.* New York: United Nations, 1970.
Crandall, V. Achievement behavior in young children. *Young Children.* New York: Russell Sage Foundation, 1969, 11-45.
Crandall, V. & Battle, E. The antecedents and adult correlates of academic and intellectual achievement efforts. In J. Hill (Ed.), *Minnesota Symposia on Child Psychology* (Vol. 4). Minneapolis: University of Minnesota Press, 1970.
Crowley, J., Levitin, T. & Quinn, R. *Facts and fictions about American working*

women. Ann Arbor: University of Michigan Institute for Social Research, Survey Research Center, January 1973.

Edye, L. Eliminating barriers to career development of women. *Personnel and Guidance Journal,* 1970, *49,* 24-36.

Entwisle, D. & Greenberger, E. Adolescents' views of women's work role. *American Journal of Orthopsychiatry,* 1972, *42,* 648-656.

Epstein, C.F. Positive effects of the multiple negative: Explaining the success of black professional women. *American Journal of Sociology,* 1973, *78,* 912-935.

Farmer, H. Why women contribute less to the arts, sciences and humanities. Paper presented at the annual meeting of the American Psychological Association, Washington, D.C., September 1976.

Farmer, H. & Backer, T. *New career options for women: A counselor's sourcebook.* New York: Human Sciences Press, 1977.

Farmer, H. & Bohn, M. Home-career conflict reduction and the level of career interest in women. *Journal of Counseling Psychology,* 1970, *17,* 228-232.

Fuchs, V. Women's earnings: Recent trends and long-run prospects. *Monthly Labor Review,* 1974, *97,* 23-25.

Ginzberg, E. & Associates. *Life styles of educated women.* New York: Columbia University Press, 1966.

Gump, J. & Rivers, L. The consideration of race in efforts to end sex bias. In E. Diamond (Ed.), *Issues of sex bias and sex fairness in career interest measurement.* Washington, D.C.: U.S. Government Printing Office, 1975.

Harmon, L. Variables related to women's persistence in educational plans. *Journal of Vocational Behavior,* 1972, *2,* 143-153.

Harmon, L. Career counseling for women. In D. Carter & E. Rawlings (Eds.), *Psychotherapy for women: Treatment toward equality.* Springfield, Illinois: Charles C Thomas and Sons, 1975.

Hawley, P. Perceptions of male models of femininity related to career choice. *Journal of Counseling Psychology,* 1972, *19,* 308-313.

Hedges, J. & Barnett, J. Working women and the division of household tasks. *Monthly Labor Review,* 1972, *97,* 4-22.

Horner, M. The measurement and behavioral implications of fear of success in women. In Atkinson, J. & Raynor, J. (Eds.), *Motivation and achievement.* New York: John Wiley and Sons, 1974.

Houts, P.S. & Entwisle, D.R. Academic achievement effort among females: Achievement attitudes and sex role orientation. *Journal of Counseling Psychology,* 1968, *15,* 284-286.

Katz, M. *Female motive to avoid success : A psychological barrier or a deviancy?* Princeton, N.J.: Educational Testing Service, 1973.

Linden, F. *Women: A demographic, social, and economic presentation.* New York: The Conference Board, Inc., 1973.

Lipman-Blumen, J. & Leavitt, H. Vicarious and direct achievement patterns in adulthood. *The Counseling Psychologist,* 1976, *6,* 26-32.

Lockheed, M. Female motive to avoid success: A psychological barrier or a response to deviancy? *Sex Roles,* 1975, *1,* 41-50.

Maccoby, E. & Jacklin, C. *The psychology of sex differences.* Stanford, California: Stanford University Press, 1974.

Maehr, M. Culture and achievement motivation. *American Psychologist,* 1974, *29,* 887-896.

Mathews, E. & Tiedeman, D. Attitudes toward career and marriage and the development of life style in young women. *Journal of Counseling Psychology,* 1964, *11,* 375-384.

McClelland, D. *Assessing human motivation.* New York: General Learning Press, 1971.

Medvene, A. & Collins, A. Occupational prestige and its relationship to traditional and nontraditional views of women's roles. *Journal of Counseling Psychology,* 1974, *21*(2), 139-143.

Monahan, L., Kuhn, D. & Shaver, P. Intrapsychic versus cultural explanations of the "fear of success" motive. *Journal of Personality and Social Psychology,* 1974, *29,* 60-64.

Moss, H. & Kagan, J. Stability of achievement and recognition-seeking behaviors from early childhood through adulthood. *Journal of Abnormal and Social Psychology,* 1961, *62,* 504-513.

Parrish, J. Women in professional training. *Monthly Labor Review,* 1974, *97,* 41-43.

Plank, E.H. & Plank, R. Emotional components in arithmetic learning as seen through autobiographies. In R.S. Eissler (Ed.), *Psychoanalytic study of the child.* New York: International Universities Press, 1954.

Plost, M. Effect of sex of career models on occupational preferences of adolescents. *Audiovisual Communication Review,* 1974, *22,* 41-50.

Rapoport, R. & Rapoport, R. The dual career family. *Human Relations,* 1969, *22,* 3-30.

Rossi, A. & Calderwood, A. (Eds.). *Academic women on the move.* New York: Russel Sage Foundation, 1973.

Rubovits, P. Early experience and the achieving orientations of American middle-class girls. In M. Maehr & W. Stallings (Eds.), *Culture, child and school.* Monterey, California: Brooks/Cole, 1975.

Sarbin, T. Role theory. In G. Lindzey (Ed.), *Handbook of social psychology* (Vol. 1). Cambridge, Massachusetts: Addison-Wesley, 1954.

Stimpson, C. (Ed.). *Discrimination against women: Congressional hearing on equal rights in education and employment.* New York: R.R. Bowker Co., 1973.

Strong, E. *Vocational interests 18 years after college.* Minneapolis: University of Minnesota Press, 1955.

Super, D. Theory of vocational choice. *The Counseling Psychologist,* 1969, *1,* 2-10.

Sweet, J. *Women in the labor force.* New York: Harcourt Brace, 1973.

Taylor, S. Education leadership: A male domain? *Phi Delta Kappan,* 1973, *55,* 124-128.

Tomlinson-Keasey, C. Role variables: Their influence on female motivational constructs. *Journal of Counseling Psychology,* 1974, *21,* 232-237.

Tyler, L. The antecedents of two varieties of interest patterns. *Genetic Psychological Monographs,* 1964, *70,* 177-227.

U.S. Department of Labor, Women's Bureau. *The myth and the reality.* Washington, D.C.: U.S. Government Printing Office, 1974.

Weiner, B. *Achievement motivation and attribution theory.* Morristown, New Jersey: General Learning Press, 1974.

Cognitive-Developmental Theory: A Guide to Counseling Women

L. LEE KNEFELKAMP
University of Maryland

CAROLE C. WIDICK
Ohio State University

BARBARA STROAD
University of Maryland

Increasingly women seem to phrase their concerns about interpersonal relationships, achievement and success, and educational and vocational goals in the vocabulary of "women's issues." This is not particularly surprising given the nature of a woman's environment. Women are currently "hot copy" in the vernacular of the media. From *Ms.* to *Redbook,* from Barbara Walters to Johnny Carson, the women's role in society is defined, dissected and debated. Everyone, it seems, attempts to tell the individual woman who she should be and how she should live. While the individual woman has perhaps more freedom to define herself now than ever before, she is also subject to a greater variety of demands. The bombardment of information about women constitutes a formidable environmental press; consequently many women see personal problems in the light of the broader social issue—what it means to be a woman. Caught up in the debates about her role, the female client often defines her concerns from the perspective and vocabulary of the "women's movement." Thus, it seems that an individual's attitudes towards "women's issues" and the "women's movement" are not a side issue but a major content area that must be addressed by the counseling profession.

Typically, literature pertaining to the counseling of women has attempted to alert the profession to the impact of sexist biases on the counseling process; for example, the need for attitude change has been demonstrated, and counseling strategies which enhance self-awareness and provide women with a broader vision of that which is possible have been advocated (Schlossberg & Pietrofesa, 1973). While these have been important contributions to the field, we are still in need of a specific conceptual framework for counseling women. The central question remains: how can we as counselors respond to the concerns of women in ways which respect individual differences and foster individual growth and development?

A FIRST STEP: CONCEPTUALIZING THE PROBLEM

As we read the literature concerning the women's issue, speak with colleagues, and counsel college students, we see an important difference in the way women's issues are discussed. Some individuals describe those issues in fairly dogmatic terms similar to the following: "We identify the agents of our oppression as men. . . . All men have oppressed women" (Redstockings Manifesto, 1970, p. 533). "It would be preposterously naive to suggest that a BA can be made as attractive to girls as a marriage license" (Kirk, 1970, p. 35). "If the older woman does not neglect her family, she can work without harm, if she limits her work to the feminine fields such as secretarial, nursing, school teaching, clerical, and many others. She should avoid the more masculine fields or executive jobs, since they will reduce her femininity" (Andelin, 1975, p. 232).

Others sound more like this:

> I'm a sympathizer, a femsymp if you will, but some feminists come on so abrasive they alarm even me. I can only lament the impression they must make on the undecided. Some of these zealots remind me of Pentecostal Christians who grab your elbow and stare you down and demand, "Do you know the Lord?" when everyone else in the church is keening and writhing and speaking in tongues. Since I'm there too, having heard the sermon and the altar call and the hymn, I am accountable: why am I too not seized with ecstasy? But Pentecostal fervor happens not to be my style, nor does evangelical feminism. There are ways and ways of being saved. I have heard the message, sorores. I agree. But I'd rather be in the woodwind section than the percussion, and I don't think you can afford to alienate the piccolos, or to forget that there are other contexts in which to view life. Is not your cause more important than that? (Howard, 1973, p. 380) *

or

> With slavery, those who enslaved were damaged, if in a different way from those they enslaved. So it is with men and women, who are people first, before they are men and women. There are as many points of difference between men and men and women and women as there are between men

* From *A Different Woman*, by Jane Howard. Copyright © 1973 by Jane Howard. Reprinted by permission of the publishers, E.P. Dutton & Co., Inc., and The Sterling Lord Agency, Inc.

and women. For either sex to use these differences against the other sex is self-defeating for both sexes (Calderone, 1974, p. 72).

Interestingly, these individuals seem to be more adequately differentiated by the process with which they think about women's issues than by the particular content of their beliefs. Some individuals think in categorical absolutes (see Andelin and Redstockings), some recognize the legitimacy of all points of view (see Calderone), and some acknowledge different points of view yet are committed to a position, stance, or life style (see Howard). The pattern that emerges has striking similarities to the cognitive-developmental theories. Accordingly, these theories should offer us fertile ground for developing guidelines in the area of counseling women.

COGNITIVE-DEVELOPMENTAL THEORY: A GUIDE TO COUNSELING WOMEN

Several theorists have proposed stage models, referred to as cognitive-developmental (Schroder & Suedfield, 1971) or hierarchical-stage theories (Loevinger, 1966), which share a particular set of assumptions and central constructs explicated below. The most important commonality for our purposes is the attempt to conceptualize and describe individuals in terms of their thought processes and the influences of these cognitions upon behavior. Three central ideas form the basis of these theories: structural organization, developmental sequence, and interactionism (Rest, 1973). These concepts give the cognitive models a unique power to provide the counselor with a framework from which to recognize individual differences within the counseling process. Because they are crucial to a counseling framework, they are explicated below.

Structural Organization

Cognitive developmental theories take an information-processing view of the individual. The person is seen as an active interpreter of the world outside of herself; she selectively attends to stimuli, imposes a "meaningful" order onto the stimuli she comprehends, develops and uses principles and rules to guide her behavior and to solve problems. Bieri (1971) suggested that the individual's way of processing information is determined by "relatively fixed patterns for experiencing his world . . . patterns which we may refer to as cognitive structures" (p. 178). The thought processes, or cognitive structure, of the individual will define not only how the self is viewed but also how others and the environment are perceived. The way an individual thinks dictates what she will do; for example, the structural organization linked to "women's identity" dictates how a woman sees her role and, ultimately, the behavior she feels to be appropriate.

Developmental Sequence

Stage theorists view development as a progression through an invariant sequence of hierarchical stages where each stage is characterized by a qualitatively different way of thinking. Each stage represents a more differentiated and integrated structural organization subsuming that of the previous stage. Once the cognitive structure is expanded to incorporate a wider, more complex range of experiences, the individual views the world through the new, more differentiated structure.

Interactionism

From the cognitive-stage point of view, development is seen as a product of the interaction between the person and the environment. Both a maturity or readiness within the individual and certain elements in the environment are assumed necessary for growth to occur. In describing the nature of the change process, the developmentalists emphasize the role of the environment in creating dissonance or disequilibrium; the individual is confronted by environmental stimuli which cannot be handled by existing constructs, thus challenging the individual to alter the cognitive structure to accommodate more complexity. It should be noted, however, that too much disequilibrium or challenge can become overwhelming and result in fixation at a stage rather than progression to the next stage (Maves, 1971). Thus, cognitive-developmentalists attempt to promote growth by providing a delicate balance of support and disequilibrium for the individual.

Patterns of Qualitative Change

Kohlberg (1970), Perry (1970), and Loevinger and Wessler (1970) are among the theorists who adhere to the assumptions listed above. Each of the theorists attempts to explain human development by focusing upon a particular facet of the person. Kohlberg has emphasized the development of the individual's thought processes with respect to moral reasoning; Perry has proposed a stage model of reasoning about knowledge and learning; and Loevinger and Wessler have outlined a stage theory of ego development. Despite their differences in focus, the three theories are highly correlated (Kohlberg, 1971). Each of the theories shares similarities in theoretical assumptions, namely that development proceeds in certain distinct and measureable ways, that the plateaus along the developmental sequence are categorized as stages—each one representing a more complex and integrated system than the previous—and that the elements of each stage imply prescriptions for movement to a higher level.

Most importantly, the three theorists have hypothesized and found empirical support for a pattern of qualitative changes that make up the developmental sequence. These theories formulate the following generic statements about the nature of development:

1. Development proceeds from cognitive simplicity to cognitive complexity. Individuals at "lower" stages of development tend to be more absolute, stereotypic, and dogmatic in their perceptions.

2. Individuals become less externally oriented and more inner-directed as higher stages of development are attained. Individuals at higher stages are less bound by any external authority—whether it be a teacher, a counselor, or their peer group. Moreover, as one moves upward on the developmental scale, the ability to accept responsibility for the consequences of one's actions increases.

3. Tolerance for ambiguity and stress appear to increase as individuals reach higher stages of development. Individuals at higher stages seem to have a grasp of means-ends relationships that allow them to be more adaptable in pursuit of goals.

4. The pattern of development proceeds toward a greater capacity to empathize with others, particularly with those individuals who hold conflicting points of view.

5. As an individual moves towards higher stages of development, the orientation to others changes from a strong self-focus to a posture of conformity to the group and then to a mature focus of mutual interdependence on others. The individual is truly autonomous and inner-directed when she arrives at the point of acknowledging her interdependence on others in her life.

Despite the similarities and degree of correlation among the cognitive-developmental theories, a basic difference does exist. Kohlberg and Perry have outlined development of one facet of an individual; they limit what they attempt to explain. In contrast, Loevinger and Wessler have attempted to describe personality development in a holistic way. It is beyond the scope of this article, however, to describe each theory in detail. At this point, it seems most useful to take a representative theory and show its utility as a framework for understanding female clients and their view about "women's issues" and themselves.

THE PERRY MODEL—A MODIFICATION

On the basis of research conducted with Harvard undergraduates, Perry and his associates (1970) derived a cognitive-stage framework that presents nine positions or stages, each representing a qualitatively different mode of thinking about the nature of knowledge. Students at different stages are hypothesized to conceive "knowledge" and "learning," the teacher's role, and one's own role as a learner in different ways and to respond differently to the demands of a given learning environment. Recent work has supported the hypothesis that the stages do indeed exist (Knefelkamp, Note 1) and that students at different phases of cognitive development require different instructional modes in order to achieve maximally (Widick, Note 2).

While the Perry schema was designed to describe the way students developed in their reasoning about knowledge, it is quite possible that the schema can be seen as a metatheory or process model. In that sense, it may provide a general framework for viewing an individual's development in reasoning about many aspects of the world. Support for this idea is provided by the work of Harvey, Hunt, and Schroder (1961). They postulated a cognitive-development model of "conceptual systems." In their view, an individual has numerous conceptual systems or cognitive structures for different "content" areas—for example, religion, knowledge, child-rearing. Harvey et al. assumed that each conceptual system of an individual goes through a pattern of developmental stages. It is the writers' contention that individuals have a conceptual system for "woman's role in society" and that the Perry schema describes the developmental pattern of an individual's thinking about that issue. We believe it is feasible to substitute "woman's role" where Perry used "learning task" and "counselor" where Perry used "teacher."

The following modification of Perry's system describes nine steps which move the woman client from a simplistic, categorical view of herself and her role in the society to a more complex pluralistic view in which she can no longer equate her own personal view of that role with the truth. A woman's concept of the female role determines the way she will interpret the pressures of the societal environment, will view the role of the counselor, and will view herself. If sufficiently challenged, the woman will move upward along the schema to a point where there is a personal confrontation with the meaning of her existence and with questions such as "What is my role?" and "What is to be valued?" In this sense, intellectual development with respect to this particular issue and identity formation are intertwined: intellectual progress leads to the task of examining one's place and commitments in the world.

The nine positions may be grouped into three more general categories:

Dualism

The first three positions are characterized by simplistic, dichotomous thinking about the role of women. The individual believes there is only one right role for women in society and that those who differ with that view are wrong. Thus, for the dualistic individual, concepts such as "truth," "importance," and "correctness" with respect to a view of women are external givens. The individual is a receptacle ready to receive "truth" from the correct authority figure or peer-group norms. At all three positions, women view themselves as having only a minimal right to hold and express their own opinions and look to some legitimate external authority for the correct opinions to hold. They also have developed little capacity to recognize the legitimacy of conflicting points of view. In fact, those who differ are often viewed as the enemy. Movement from position one to three does represent a sequential preparation for the acceptance of diversity of opinion with respect to woman's proper role.

Relativism

Positions four, five, and six represent a relativistic perspective. Truth, or the right role for women, exists only in the context of a particular individual's life. The legitimacy of diversity or relativism is recognized. At first, "truth" is relegated to a small corner of the broad and uncertain realm of knowledge about women's roles. Then, with position five, all knowledge, opinions, and values are disconnected from a concept of truth or absolute correctness. The individual becomes capable of empathy, of genuinely understanding that another may hold an entirely different perspective from one's own and that such diversity is to be not only recognized but sought and celebrated. The individual gains the capacity to detach herself from an issue and think about it in an unemotional manner. The individual can also examine herself with that same capacity for detachment and weigh evidence and arguments and evaluate them. At this point the individual often confronts questions about the meaning of existence. If there is no one right role for a woman, how is one to determine one's own beliefs, values, and goals? To what can one anchor oneself—is there no right answer for anything? Thus, a relativistic view of one's role as a woman may be accompanied by an enormous amount of disequilibrium. All the old rules and regulations suddenly disappear, and the woman is confronted with making her own way in a world that offers a wide array of conflicting perspectives. However, the individual often continues to develop due to the support that comes from the realization that one can create one's own truth, one's own role in the world, independent of old authorities. At position six, the individual is looking toward the creation of such a role, toward a genuine commitment.

Commitment in Relativism

During positions seven, eight, and nine, the individual gradually accepts the responsibility of creating her own identity in a pluralistic world and acts through commitment to establish, experience, and elaborate her identity. Perry found two components to commitment, both particularly applicable to women and women's role. First, he saw a crystallization of the substance of one's commitment through selection of a career, a set of values, a stance toward sex role, and a stance toward life style. He further expanded the notion of commitment to include the individual's recognition that within the self there are many diverse personal themes and that these may be in conflict with one another or integrated but that they all must be considered in a personal definition of identity. During this phase, the woman will undertake to find her own particular balance point in a relativistic world. She will find it, experience it, and commit herself to living it.

This adapted model provides an understanding of the relationship between the woman's mode of thinking and her behavior in a particular situation. For example, a dualist and a relativist will react differently to the demand that they take a stand on an issue such as women's role. The dualist will be only too happy to comply if she is certain that the stand is the "right" stand; while the relativist will balk at making a commitment amid so many valid and viable alternatives. In yet another instance, two individuals may come to identical decisions but from very different perspectives—one being simplistic and dogmatic in nature, the other representing a thoughtfully committed stance.

In summary, there are basic and important differences in the sense of self and in the behaviors enacted among those who think in categorical absolutes, those who recognize the legitimacy of differences, and those who are committed to a position, stance, or life style. The adapted cognitive model offers a view of the interrelatedness of the individual's sense of identity and thought processes. The general model proposes a sequential and hierarchical developmental process in which the individual moves from the lower stages, characterized by narrow-minded, stereotypic thinking, authoritarianism, and a defensive sense of self, to the upper stages, characterized by open-mindedness, an ability to accept responsibility for the consequences of one's actions, and a commitment built on a positive self-identity.

If indeed a developmental pattern exists in the reasoning about women's issues, what are the implications? How does one translate the theoretical model into useful counseling strategies for the practitioner?

IMPLICATIONS FOR COUNSELING

Counselor, Know Thy Client

Implicit in the cognitive-developmental models are counseling goals and strategies; the purpose of counseling is conceived as fostering movement along the developmental hierarchy. Moreover, the concept of stages provides a useful way to conceptualize individual differences and adapt counseling strategies to meet individuals "where they are" and to help them move to a more complex view of the world and a more integrated and fully developed sense of self. Listening to clients verbalize their perceptions of women's roles and women's issues, as well as how the thought processes define the client's sense of self, will provide the basis for systematically helping the client move along the developmental hierarchy. It is important that counselors understand three additional concepts about cognitive-stage theory in order to truly understand their clients and how the development of the clients may be positively affected.

1. Adherence to a *content* belief is not the equivalent of developmental stage; therefore dualists can be both feminists and anti-feminists. Committed individuals can similarly span the spectrum of beliefs with respect to women's

issues. The key is not the content of a belief; the clue to the sense of identity is to be found in how the client reasons about issues, how the client perceives self interacting with environment, and how conforming the client is to external control of thoughts and actions.

2. Individuals do not skip stages as they progress developmentally. A dualist must move into relativism before commitment can be understood and experienced. It is the counselor's work to facilitate the developmental process, and the intervention cannot be developmental unless it takes into consideration the client's initial position and individual pattern of growth— that which Tyler (1969, p. 37) calls the "perceptual task" of counseling.

3. Just as individuals cannot skip stages, there is evidence that they cannot understand reasoning that is more than one stage level above their own (Rest, 1973). Hence it is important for the counselor to use language that the client will understand and not try to move the client along the continuum too rapidly. The client must be given time to assimilate new ways of thinking about herself and her world, and she should not be forced into choices whose implications she cannot fully comprehend and accept.

Counselor, Know the Process

Developmental counseling, interpreted from a cognitive-developmental perspective, has generally defined the developmental interventions necessary to move an individual upward along the hierarchy. In developmental counseling, more attention is paid to the process than to the content.

The emphasis is on the cognitive aspect of the process. Deliberate efforts are made to cause the client to think increasingly more complexly about herself and her world. The counselor interacts with the client at the stage level she can understand and then provides sufficient cognitive dissonance to cause the client to expand her thought processes. This process, known as "plus-one staging," results in the client's moving upward to the next stage of development. Hence, the cognitive-developmental model does not promote adjustment to the status quo, but rather it deliberately seeks to promote greater complexity on the part of the client. Plus-one staging is one of the most effective techniques to that end. It is based on the central concept of cognitive-development counseling: support and challenge. The counselor must always be involved with designing and utilizing interventions that will provide the appropriate challenge and support variables for the client's particular stage of development. Obviously, the variables will vary with clients; however, general types of challenges and supports conform to the characteristics of the stages themselves.

Support and Challenge

The crucial intervention concept of developmental counseling is the use of *challenge and support* factors to promote growth. The client will move along the continuum to a more examined life only if she is challenged sufficiently to do so; however, she must be provided sufficient support to enable her to take the risk of growth.

The task of the counselor is to identify what specific factors will provide challenges and supports for individuals at different developmental stages. Hence, the counselor must be very careful to work with a client in such a way that fosters the client's growth rather than arrests development at a lower stage. For example, a young dualistic woman needs to be provided with diversity—a variety of perspectives on women's role and the way in which she might create her own role—rather than be encouraged to make a too-soon commitment to a particular life role. It is important to remember that the dualistic-thinking client will very much want the counselors to show her "the right way," and this is a temptation that counselors can easily fall into. But it does not foster development to relativism. The relativist client, on the other hand, may well need to be helped to make an initial commitment and to accept the responsibility for having made that choice.

The concept of challenge and support stimulates consideration of current issues in counseling. For example:

1. Should a woman who requests a female counselor always be granted that request? Might she not instead benefit from the additional perspectives that the male counselor will provide? Under what circumstances do we grant such a request? Is it a considered decision on the part of counseling centers, an automatic one, a political one?

2. Are consciousness-raising groups counter-developmental for certain clients? The dualistic militant feminist may well need to be without the support of such a group and be encouraged to explore the legitimacy of opinions that differ from hers. The dualistic traditional female might well find such a group overwhelming—and, hence, counter-developmental—and would need careful preparation before being placed in such groups. Do we place in groups clients who are best able to use them as a source of positive growth and development? Do the groups themselves promote individual differences? When are the groups developmental and when might they be dysfunctional?

3. What is the reality base of vocational counseling? The developmental perspective requires that vocational counseling not be guided by feminist or anti-feminist ideology. A dualistic feminist may believe that her only "right" vocational path lies in the professions; for her, careful consideration of reality factors—ability, time, demands of work—is crucial. A relativist may meander from vocation to vocation, fearful of cutting off options; for this student, counseling may need to force her to look at her definition of herself as a woman in the world of work and challenge her to realize the necessity of commitment. For the forty-five-year old "just a housewife" who has discovered and replaced one dualistic belief (my place is in the home) with another, the task is complex. This woman needs to be able to understand that Nirvana does not necessarily exist in the B.A. and that there are multiple

perspectives with respect to her being able to lead a more fulfilling life. She needs to fully comprehend the societal and economic realities of her choice before she decides on whether or not to return to school.

In summary, challenges and supports are modes, practices, or verbal interactions that the counselor uses to move the client toward cognitive restructuring at a higher level. It is the counselor's responsibility to carefully analyze the needs of the client, to define the crucial support and challenge variables for the particular client circumstance, and to developmentally carry out the use of variables. Briefly, the counselor will work to enable the dualistic client to gain a greater appreciation of the legitimate options that are open to her and will work to foster a movement towards commitment on the part of the relativist.

Counselor, Know Thyself

Upon reflection, the implications of cognitive-developmental theory for the counselor are serious. Clearly, the counselor cannot help to move a client upward along a developmental continuum if she is not very far along the continuum herself. The logical question follows: what are the implications of the model for counselors and counselor education? Several things need to be considered:

1. Counselor education programs need to provide a learning atmosphere that promotes students' developmental growth. It is important that such programs foster the development of relativism and commitment as a basic approach to the profession. Such a program would present alternative ways of working with a wide variety of clients and would encourage students to develop their own perspectives on counseling after they have been well educated in their field. It would be important to ask the following questions of any training program. Does the program foster only one right way of working with clients? Does it allow a biased view of men and women to exist implicitly? Does it provide challenge and support so that the students will be enabled to examine themselves, their own attitudes, stereotypes, and values? Does it foster a sense of commitment to the profession? Does the training provided expose students to all types of clients—age, race, sex, religion? Does the training foster a deep respect for individual differences and an ability to legitimize even the opinions of those who disagree with one's own views?

2. Counselors need to have a thorough understanding of the many alternative perspectives related to counseling women and women's issues. There is no simple answer to Freud's famous "What do women want?" Counselors need to avoid the dangers of defining and prescripting the client on the basis of her sex alone. Rather, they need to become aware of the many and varied perspectives with which individual women will aproach their identity concerns. Continuing individual study and staff training in this area will do much to reduce the "if you've seen one, you've seen them all" attitude of the discriminatory and ill-prepared counselor.

3. Counselors need to have a thorough and realistic analysis of their own view of the role of women in the society and of the many and complex issues that are raised with respect to women. They need to seriously examine the effects their personal views about women have on their counseling interventions. It is just as important for counselors to recognize and control their perceptions of the issues as it is for the counselors to recognize how their clients are perceiving themselves. The same type of self-examination that was deemed necessary for students in counselor education programs is every bit as necessary for practitioners in the profession.

Clinician, Not Politician

The counselor needs a theoretical framework from which to approach counseling women clients. The framework should postulate a schema of development, provide a methodology for promoting that development, and emphasize the importance of each individual's unique journey to a more complex sense of identity. All too often theory is replaced by political stance. The writers submit that that is not an adequate state of affairs for the profession. Women and women's issues are not just a current fad that is not to be taken seriously. The challenge to the profession is as long lasting as it is real.

We believe that the goal of counseling women is the development of individuals who are cognitively complex, autonomous, and able to make clear commitments. We believe that the counseling profession can do more to foster the advancement of women by promoting development rather than pounding rhetorical drums. Recently, the counselor's response to these issues has sounded more like that of a politician than a clinician. The counseling profession might well benefit by investigating and further developing counseling implications from cognitive-developmental theory.

REFERENCE NOTES

1. Knefelkamp, L. *Developmental instruction: Fostering intellectual and personal growth in college students.* Unpublished manuscript, University of Minnesota, 1974.
2. Widick, C. *An evaluation of developmental instruction.* Unpublished manuscript, University of Minnesota, 1975.

REFERENCES

Andelin, H.B. *Fascinating womanhood.* New York: Bantam Books, 1975.
Bieri, J. Cognitive structures in personality. In H.M. Schroder & M. Suedfield (Eds.), *Personality theory and information processing.* New York: Ronald Press, 1971.

Calderone, M.S. Physician and public health educator. In R.B. Kundsin (Ed.), *Women and success: The anatomy of achievement.* New York: William Morrow and Company, Inc., 1974.

Harvey, O.J., Hunt, D.E., & Schroeder, H.M. *Conceptual systems and personality organization.* New York: Wiley, 1961.

Howard, J. *A different woman.* New York: Avon Books, 1973.

Kirk, G. Quotation. In R. Morgan (Ed.), *Sisterhood is powerful.* New York: Vintage Books, 1970, p. 35.

Kohlberg, L. Stages of moral development as a basis for moral education. In C. Beck & E. Sullivan (Eds.), *Moral education.* Toronto: University of Toronto Press, 1970.

Kohlberg, L. The concepts of developmental psychology as the central guide to education: Examples from cognitive, moral, and psychological education. In M. Reynolds (Ed.), *Psychology and the process of schooling in the next decade: Alternative conceptions.* Washington, D.C.: Leadership Training Institute, U.S. Office of Education, 1971.

Loevinger, J. The meaning and measurement of ego development. *American Psychologist,* 1966, *21,* 195-206.

Loevinger, J., & Wessler, R. *Measuring ego development* (Vol. 1). San Francisco: Jossey-Bass, 1970.

Maves, P.B. Religious development in adulthood. In M.P. Stronment (Ed.), *Research on religious development.* New York: Hawthorne Press, 1971.

Perry, W., Jr. *Intellectual and ethical development in the college years.* New York: Holt, Rinehart and Winston, 1970.

Redstockings. Quotation. In R. Morgan (Ed.), *Sisterhood is powerful.* New York: Vintage Books, 1970, p. 533.

Rest, J. Developmental psychology as a guide to value education: A review of Kohlbergian programs. *Review of Educational Research,* 1973, *44*(2), 241-259.

Schlossberg, N.K., & Pietrofesa, J.J. Perspectives on counseling bias: Implications for counselor education. *The Counseling Psychologist,* 1973, *4*(1), 44-53.

Schroder, H.M., & Suedfield, M. (Eds.). *Personality theory and information processing.* New York: Ronald Press, 1971.

Tyler, L. *The work of the counselor.* New York: Appleton-Century-Crofts, 1969.

Counseling
for the Strengths
of the Black Woman

DORIS JEFFERIES FORD
Atlanta University

The Civil Rights movement of the late sixties profoundly impacted far more than legislative decision-making. It also challenged those engaged in the various branches of psychology to examine their philosophies, practices, and research regarding the study of black people (King, 1969). The myriad of data published prior to the seventies describe black people as functioning from a deficit model (Allport, 1954; Clark & Clark, 1950; Goodman, 1952; Grier & Cobbs, 1968; Hernton, 1965; Kardiner & Ovesey, 1962; Pettigrew, 1971; Silberman, 1970; Super, 1957). This perspective is under review because the data do not account for the metamorphosis of black consciousness and self-assertiveness. Silverstein and Krate (1975) contend:

> The changes in black identity that emerged during the sixties both reflect and are determined by the black protest movement. . . . The black movement is possibly the single most powerful force today fostering the development of new racial self-esteem and self-confidence in the children of the black underclass (p. 250).

Davis (1971) earlier made the same observation regarding positive changes in blacks toward themselves while at the same time criticized the negligible research on the black woman:

> The paucity of literature on the black woman is outrageous on its face. But we must also contend with the fact that too many of these rare studies must claim as their signal achievement the reinforcement of fictitious clichés. . . . She has been labelled "aggressive" or "matriarchal" by white scholars and "castrating female" by some blacks (p. 3).

It is understandable that most writers find it difficult to describe the black woman beyond a negative theoretical orientation, since available personality and behavioral postulates provide limited positive options. An acceptable

This article was originally published under the name Doris Jefferies. The author is currently at Valpar Corp., Tucson, Arizona.

theory, therefore, must account for the observation that, in spite of the academic arguments and studies that operate against them, black women of different economic statuses continue to progress and make significant contributions to the quality of life. Although the nation's responses to their being both black and women serve as a common denominator, black women differ widely in their economic, social, and political powers. Economically, black women range from millionaire status to well below the poverty line. Socially, some can trace their ancestral heritage back several generations, while others may be knowledgeable of only one immediate parent. Politically, the first woman to run for President of the United States was black, while there are those black women who are unaware of their voting rights. Regardless of their status in life, black women have strengths which can be observed when the counseling psychologist operates from a theoretical frame of positivism.

The strengths of black women will be the focus of this paper, with the hope that from it will grow a more inclusive theory for counseling which will in turn generate new perspectives for research and practices.

THE BLACK FEMALE CHILD

Because of the socioeconomic status of the black family in the United States, the black child has had to contribute economically to the well-being of the family. Ladner (1971) recognized that "the social canon of 'childhood' is often unobserved to varying degrees because it is a luxury which many parents cannot afford" (p. 61). The black female child living in poor circumstances often assumes family responsibility at a far earlier age than her middle-class counterpart. She works to maintain the home and family in order to free the mother to work outside the home. Jefferies (1971) noted that the child culture requires children to be dependent on other children for meeting their physical and psychosocial needs. Additional observations were made by Silverstein and Krate (1975), who noted that children living in Harlem were self-reliant and independent, thus equipping them for survival.

The capacity to nurture, the sense of responsibility, the independence, and the self-reliance that the black female child living in poor communities has developed can be utilized effectively in counseling. The counseling psychologist must not insist on client-dependent behavior but must reinforce the strengths of the black child. The principle is basic to most existing counseling theories, but the lack of understanding of the strengths of the black female child may have limited its utilization in the past.

THE BLACK FEMALE ADOLESCENT

The most intensive and recent study of the black female adolescent that reflects contemporary black ideology is that of Ladner (1971). Her sociological study of over 100 black females from a poor and urban environment attempted to redefine the psychosocial phases of black female development. "Adolescence," according to Patterson (1962), "is a time when the individual is expected to become increasingly independent of the family; yet is not allowed complete independence" (p. 356). Ladner's study revealed that the black female adolescent had experienced Patterson's descriptors of adolescence during late childhood and that the black female is socialized into womanhood at a faster rate than her non-black peers. Furthermore, Ladner noted that the preoccupation with confusion, rebellion and the "generation gap" was not as characteristic of the impoverished black adolescent females in the study as with middle-class adolescent females. Although both groups share the stage of self-definition, the subjects in Ladner's study were preoccupied mainly with the vital issues of survival. An analysis of peer-group behavior led Ladner to conclude, "Perhaps the most vital function of the peer group in this regard was its role as a clearinghouse for ideas and as a judge or evaluator for sifting various ideas as to the best or most appropriate form of behavior in specified situations" (p. 115).

The counseling psychologist who works with black female adolescent clients similar to the subjects in Ladner's study can use the strength of peer-group relations to facilitate problem solving. The counseling psychologist can be supportive of the self-reliance and independence of the group by being available to assist the group as a "visiting consultant" when such services are requested.

THE BLACK FEMALE EMPLOYEE

Historically, the entry of the black woman into the world of work began as a subhuman act rather than as an act of equal rights for women. The black woman came to America in chains for the purpose of attending to the slave master's property and family. Because of the structure of the economic system into which she was thrust, the black woman worked outside of her home, thereby placing her in an egalitarian status with her man. Unpampered, the slave woman was able to develop the capability to work and handle demanding tasks over lengthy periods of time and under difficult conditions. "During her pregnancy a slave wife usually continued her back-breaking labor until a few weeks before her child was born. . . . The mother carried the infant to the field with her or returned to the cabin at intervals during the day to nurse it" (Blassingame, 1972, p. 93).

Even at the time when "cotton was king," small numbers of black women began to diversify within the labor force, moving beyond agricultural tasks. In 1772 Fenda Lawrence as a free black woman was certified to work as a trader in the state of Georgia. Some black women were appointed to become teachers of black children, while others who had been fathered by white slaveowners were given property ownership and themselves became entrepreneurs (Bennett, 1966). Consequently, participation in the labor force by the black woman became an economic tradition that remains prevalent in the black community today.

Epstein (1973) found that the black woman is much less bound by stereotypic wifely roles than her white counterpart, because the black woman historically has accepted her participation in the labor force. Her survey also indicated that even though the black woman may marry a college-educated man, she still cannot consider total withdrawal from the marketplace. She is aware that the black man's education does not guarantee financial success. Thus, the black woman has adapted an egalitarian position; the slavery system unintentionally produced willingness-to-work responses in the black woman as an equal labor participant with her man. Scanzoni (1975) also found supportive evidence for the egalitarian theory. He reported that the black woman and black man develop a more egalitarian marital relationship than do whites and that the black woman sees herself as more task-capable than other women.

The counseling psychologist would rarely have to work with the black female client in a consciousness-raising group to help her convince herself that she is capable of joining the labor force. Instead, the view of herself as a worker can be expanded upon to help her discover a career that will be personally satisfying and enriching. Epstein (1973) observed a paradox for the black woman. Although her sex and race are evaluated negatively by society, for the competent black woman these attributes, in combination, can work positively in her career planning. Many organizations prefer to "kill two birds with one stone" by hiring a black woman to meet federal regulations. The study by Epstein also showed that the black woman is seen as more professionally serious than her white counterpart. The counseling psychologist can, therefore, assist the black female client to increase her competencies and take advantage of her "double negative equals positive" position on the job market.

HIGH SELF-ESTEEM IN THE BLACK WOMAN

Many of the strengths of the black woman have been reviewed thus far to assist the counseling psychologist in developing a new and more positive orientation toward her. Perhaps it can be hypothesized that recognition of these strengths would positively affect the self-esteem of the black woman. Some researchers are beginning to investigate the positive psychological attributes of the black woman. Rosenberg (1972) compared 14 ethnic groups on measures of self-esteem. He found that, although black people are exposed to the most intense, humiliating, and crippling forms of discrimination in virtually every institutional area, they do not particularly have low self-esteem. Results of Rosenberg's study are supported by six other studies reviewed by Guterman (1972) which suggest that the level of self-esteem among blacks does not differ significantly from that of whites and that in some instances it is actually higher than that of whites.

More specific to black women is a study by Fichter (Note1), who found that black women have a high degree of self-confidence. Epstein (1973) similarly observed from her study of 31 professional black women that they displayed a high level of confidence in their competence and ability.

BLACK DEVELOPMENTAL STAGES AND SELF-ESTEEM

Kirk (1975) synthesized the stages, suggested by several black psychologists, that lead to high self-esteem within the context of black consciousness. The schema may be useful in helping the counseling psychologist understand the black female client's developmental stage in relationship to black ideology.

Stage One: Self-Hate

Blacks in the first stage spend most of their time criticizing others who may sound better or disagree with their point of view. Their behavior is deficiency motivated and characterized by hate, prejudice, low self-esteem, hostility, and fear.

Stage Two: Self-Pity

Blacks in the second stage are still denying the self and wondering how to affirm their blackness. Should they burn cities? Grab guns? Their behavior is usually self-indulgent. The world seems an evil and hostile place.

Stage Three: Self-Examination

At the third stage, blacks begin to explore their cultural heritage from Africa to America. With this knowledge comes self-recognition and self-help. They learn to interpret the negative and positive feedback from the cultural environment. These blacks try out new roles and images, searching for the one which fits them best.

Stage Four: Self-Knowledge

Blacks at stage four of growth are less ambivalent and more confident. They are oriented toward working with others and unifying the total black experience. They will talk more openly and assertively about unity, politics, and racism and show fewer negative and irrational behaviors. They are also working toward the development of individual identities.

Stage Five: Self-Esteem

Blacks in the fifth stage have realized their own identity and the dignity of their blackness. They have learned how they are a part of society, and they are optimistic about themselves. They feel they are useful, productive, and necessary citizens, and they relate effectively to the external world.

Although the stages of development toward black self-esteem offered by Kirk reflect the ambiguity of self-concept theory, the framework can serve as a general guide when working with the black female client. Greater specificity is necessary, however, for systematic assessment of the maturation process.

CONSIDERATIONS FOR COUNSELING PSYCHOLOGISTS

In order to more fully understand the self-esteem of the black woman, research models and designs more appropriate than many of the current ones must be used. The heretofore dominant emphasis on the deficit model creates limitations for the counseling psychologist working with the black female client. The assumption that the black woman is operating from the weakest social position in society, and consequently has low self-esteem, prevents the psychologist from helping her to rally her positive qualities and thus decreases her ability to resolve her presenting problem.

It is the responsibility of counseling psychologists not only to conduct research that identifies the weaknesses of the black woman but also to more clearly identify her strengths so that those strengths can be utilized in mental-health programs in the black community. The positive perspectives presented in this paper can function as departure points for future research designed to reveal the healthy aspects of the black woman.

REFERENCE NOTE

1. Fichter, J.H. *Graduates of predominantly Negro colleges—Class of 1964* (Public Health Services Publication No. 1571). Washington, D.C.: 1970.

REFERENCES

Allport, G.W. *The nature of prejudice.* Garden City: Doubleday and Company, 1954.
Bennett, L., Jr. *Before the Mayflower: A history of the Negro in America.* New York: Penguin Books, 1966.
Blassingame, J.W. *The slave community.* New York: Oxford Press, 1972.
Clark, K.B., & Clark, M.P. Emotional factors in racial identification and preference in Negro children. *Journal of Negro Education,* 1950, *19,* 341-50.
Davis, A.Y. Reflections on the black woman's role in the community of slaves. *Black Scholar,* 1971, *3,* 2-11.
Epstein, C.F. Positive effects of the multiple negative: Explaining the success of black professional women. *American Journal of Sociology,* 1973, *78,* 912-935.
Goodman, M.E. *Race awareness in young children.* New York: Collier Books, 1952.
Grier, W.H., & Cobbs, P.M. *Black rage.* New York: Basic Books, Inc., 1968.
Guterman, S.S. *Black psyche.* Berkeley: The Glendessary Press, Inc., 1972.
Hernton, C.C. *Sex and racism in America.* New York: Grove Press, Inc., 1965.
Jefferies, D. Counseling ghetto children in groups. In M.M. Ohlsen (Ed.), *Group counseling with children.* New York: Holt, Rinehart & Winston, 1971.

Kardiner, A., & Ovesey, L. *The mark of oppression.* Cleveland: The World Publishing Company, 1962.

King, M.L. The role of the behavioral scientist in the Civil Rights Movement. In N.D. Glenn & C.M. Bonjean (Eds.), *Blacks in the United States.* San Francisco: Chandler Publishing Company, 1969.

Kirk, W. Where are you? Black mental health model. *Journal of Non-white Concerns,* 1975, *3,* 177-188.

Ladner, J.A. *Tomorrow's tomorrow: The black woman.* Garden City: Doubleday & Company, 1971.

Patterson, C.H. *An introduction to counseling in the school.* New York: Harper & Row, 1962.

Pettigrew, T. Negro American personality: The role and its burdens. In E.P. Hollander & R.G. Hunt (Eds.), *Current perspectives in social psychology.* New York: Oxford Press, 1971, pp. 159-165.

Rosenberg, M. Race, ethnicity and self esteem. In S. Guterman (Ed.), *Black psyche.* Berkeley: The Glendessary Press, Inc., 1972, pp. 87-99.

Scanzoni, J. Sex roles, economic factors, and marital solidarity in black and white marriages. *Journal of Marriage and the Family,* 1975, *37*(1), 130-144.

Silberman, C.E. *Crisis in the classroom.* New York: Random House, 1970.

Silverstein, B., & Krate, R. *Children of the dark ghetto.* New York: Praeger Publishers, 1975.

Super, D.E. *The psychology of careers.* New York: Harper & Row, 1957.

Psychotherapy and Women's Liberation

JEAN HOLROYD

Neuropsychiatric Institute, UCLA

I look at myself and ask: "What do the others say is visible?" (Porchia)

Personality theories and scientific data on women frequently contribute negatively to the psychotherapy of female clients. This article examines some of the background factors which have shaped our information about women and then reviews some contemporaneous approaches to the therapy of women.

Pervasive androcentrism noted in 1926 by Horney (1973)—for example, woman's personality characteristics a consequence of dealing with her castration, her sexual fulfillment a result of identifying with the man's orgasm, and her masochism inferred from the reports of male homosexuals (Thompson, 1973)—continues to this day in Erikson's developmental theory (Doherty, 1974). Gender bipolar characterizations of personality are found in psychoanalysis and in Jungian psychology, though the latter gives more serious consideration to the female principle within individuals and societies (de Castillejo, 1973; Harding, 1970; Jung, 1957; Neumann, 1955). Attempts to derive psychological traits from biological characteristics to the exclusion of historical and social influences (Menaker, 1974; Mitchell, 1974) were at the outset somewhat misogynic: loss of penis led to envy, masochism, narcissism, and weak superego. Other biocentric theorizing has been more idealistic but equally misleading: presence of uterus led to "the blissful consciousness of bearing a new life within one's self" (Horney, 1973, p. 10) or concern with "inner space" (Erikson, 1974).

Contemporary psychoanalysts agree that personality traits of masculinity and femininity can be established by psychological influences in opposition to a biological state (Chodoff, 1973; Stoller, 1973a). Paradoxically, it is biological discoveries about sexual response (Masters & Johnson, 1966), embryology (Sherfey, 1973), brain physiology, and intersexuality (Stoller, 1973a) which promise the most profound impact on androcentric theories. (For example, it seems the genitals of both sexes are embryologically female and behavior is female in experimental animals unless the fetal brain is organized by androgen, according to Stoller, 1973a.) Yet "Biology is destiny" dies hard. An analyst who has published articles sympathetic to women's liberation recently wrote, "There must be a division of work and responsibilities [in marriage], and this dichotomy must be responsive to the all-important biological needs served by women. Theirs is to bear and nurture, and there can be no adequate substitute for this—nor should one be sought" (Seidenberg, 1973a, p. 313).

Current personality theories tend to rest with biological and cultural dualities rather than provide understanding of the shifting dynamics within succorance and power relationships, particularly as related to the hypothesized fear or hostility between sexes (Hays, 1964; Kovel, 1974; Zilboorg, 1973). Radical feminists expect these dualities will be transcended and harmonized by technology (Mitchell, 1971), but others suggest technology will only subserve yet poorly understood powerful, erotic, conflictful forces between men and women (Kovel, 1974). Both Mitchell (1974) and Kovel (1974) view psychoanalysis as the most promising approach to understanding these complex relationships, despite previous political abuse or Freudian theory.

A critical question is, how do personality theories and related psychotherapies deal with the impact of exponential social changes? The data for female development will differ for a girl raised with coeducational home-economics classes, well-funded sports opportunities, and effective contraception. Gelb (1972) suggests replacing theories of intrapsychic mechanisms (Id, Ego) with the concept that mental development is dependent on ever-changing social institutions. Weisstein (1972), citing the studies of Schachter, Rosenthal, and Milgram, points out that feelings and behavior are determined more by the social surrounding than by inner traits.

The basic data available on women may be shaped more by the scientific social surrounding than by inner traits also. To some extent scientists create what they observe (Burtt, 1965), and new information which does not fit a present theory may simply be abandoned (Quen, 1975). Measurement of achievement motivation is an example of the first influence (Mednick & Weissman, 1975), and pre- and post-menstrual sexual arousal ascribed to intervening abstinence rather than to hormones an example of the second (Ford & Beach, 1975). It will be years before the influence of scientists' preconceptions on behavioral data is appreciated.

I also suspect that woman's self-report has been disregarded.

> Did women, until Masters and Johnson, believe they were having two different kinds of orgasm? Did their psychiatrists cow them into reporting something that was not true? If so, were there other things they reported that also were not true? If clinical experience means anything at all, surely we should have been done with the double orgasm myth long before the Masters and Johnson studies (Weisstein, 1972, pp. 237-238).

The apparent impotence of female patients in making themselves heard is articulated by two different women about different therapies.

The female patient

> knows that Freud's discovery of the unconscious workings of the mind was one of the greatest breakthroughs in man's pursuit of knowledge. . . . She has been taught that only after years of analytic training is one capable of understanding Freudian truth. She may even know how the human mind unconsciously resists that truth. How can she presume to tread the sacred ground where only analysts are allowed? (Friedan, 1965. pp. 91-92)

And a Jungian mused, "To be told, as she often is told by psychologists, that man represents the spirit and she the earth, is one of those disconcerting things a woman tries hard to believe, knowing all the time that they are not true; knowing that the pattern does not fit" (de Castillejo, 1973, p. 77). Exploring and publicizing how women think and feel—through feminist literature, consciousness-raising groups, and the like—is a major contribution of the Women's Movement to psychology and psychotherapy.

I will help you to approach if you approach and to keep away if you keep away. (Porchia)

Feminism and women's liberation interact with a multitude of other influences which affect the psychotherapy of women: secularization, population growth, war, socialist theories, urbanization, advances in health care, economic vicissitudes, and perhaps soon a guaranteed right to equal treatment under the law. In the following pages I review how women's issues are being addressed in psychotherapy, recognizing I thereby arrogate for the Women's Movement important influences originating elsewhere. The recent literature has been concerned particularly with the interactions between therapy and women's changing concepts of self (sexuality, femininity, economic role, and relationship to the family); consciousness raising; and treatment of behaviors or symptoms deemed sex-role typed or secondary to the traditional female role (phobias, passivity, dependency, depression, underachievement).

Sexuality

Within a span of 20 years women have experienced changes in sexual self-concept. Women wish to be more active in approaching males, yet they still demonstrate much confusion about their own sexuality and sexual relationships (Fried, 1974). Their confusion may be merited. Instead of the passive-receptive stereotype, recent writers have described an active, almost hypersexual female.

> The truly receptive vagina is grasping, secreting, and pleasure-giving through its own functions. . . . In the female, wider areas are involved in

erotic stimulation and vasocongestion is more extensive. Arousal may
thus take longer and necessitates more imagination; resolution and return
to a resting state may also be more lengthy. When these factors are taken
into account, it may be possible for the woman to maintain arousal for
long periods, thus putting her in the position of being more sexual than
the man rather than less so, as has been commonly assumed (Moulton,
1973, p. 245).

It has been hypothesized that "if women's sexual drive has not abated,
and they prove incapable of controlling it, thereby jeopardizing family life and
child care, a return to the rigid, enforced suppression will be inevitable and
mandatory. Otherwise the biological family will disappear, and what other
patterns of infant care and adult relationships could adequately substitute
cannot now be imagined" (Sherfey, 1973, p. 152). We wonder whether this
hypothesis will replace the discredited hypothesis of female sexual passivity in
misogynic popularization of personality theory. Reich viewed sexual
liberation as the primary task of therapy but thought it was impossible within
the present structure of capitalistic, patriarchal society (Mitchell, 1974).
Certainly, the present social conditions which support liberated female
sexuality are tenuous, as evidenced by repeated attempts to circumvent the
Supreme Court decision on abortion, lack of significant progress in male
contraception, and slow acceptance of the Equal Rights Amendment. This
social ambivalence will be reflected in different ways by females in therapy.

In spite of institutionalized ambivalence about sexual liberation, progress
in the treatment of sexual dysfunction is reflected in major treatment
programs (Kaplan, 1974; Masters & Johnson, 1970). Kaplan (Note 1)
reported that in past research 25% of non-orgasmic patients achieved coital
orgasms after 3 years of psychoanalytically oriented psychotherapy, while
Masters and Johnson have reported 80% of patients become orgastic after a
few weeks of treatment. With treatment combining sexual experiences and
psychotherapy, prognosis is 100% remission for patients with vaginismus
after *in vivo* desensitization of the phobic element (and most patients are
highly orgastic). For patients unresponsive to arousal with no vaginal
secretions, prognosis is very good following treatment which moves the
patients through natural stages they may have skipped—for example,
teaching them to masturbate. Prognosis seems not so good for patients for
whom orgasm hasn't occurred despite a high degree of arousal, and
psychoanalytically oriented psychotherapy is continued in an effort at gaining
better understanding.

A feminist psychoanalyst treating sexual dysfunction would help the
patient acquire positive concepts of womanhood rather than focus on
competition and negative attitudes toward men (Moulton, 1975). She also
would explore specific sexual fears and fantasies and broaden the patient's
concepts of what is normal sexual activity. Realization of the superordinate
goal of becoming a competent woman, with appropriate self-assertion,
valuing of inner feelings, and active productivity, leads to sexual liberation.

Fried (1974) believes the new self-concept of being a sexual equal facilitates shedding of resistances. In analytically oriented heterosexual group therapy, interpretations and short discussions may be enriched by the therapist modeling spontaneity and providing here-and-now experiences—for example, teaching female patients to feel pelvic sensations while they are in the group. The goal is to make the woman aware of her own body's responsiveness in everyday situations.

Several female sexual "problems" have been discarded, or at least should be. Actively homosexual women rarely come to therapy because they are unhappy with their sexual-object choice (McDougall, 1975), and homosexuality has finally been removed from the list of mental illnesses. Sexual double standards and the vaginal orgasm as an index of emotional maturity have been repudiated by female psychologists surveyed as practitioners and consumers of therapy (APA, Note 2). And "frigidity" has been redefined as several more specific types of dysfunction.

Femininity

Women today insist that their femininity be taken for granted because they *are* female and that stereotyping definitions be abandoned (APA, Note 2). Awareness of "I am a girl" is achieved very early, not by coming to terms with her castration but by her responding to social expectations. Stoller noted that "even in the neuter (XO) child who is not biologically female, a feminine gender identity develops if the infant is unquestioningly assigned to the female sex" and "as with males [gender sense] is fixed in the first few years of life and is a piece of identity so firm that almost no vicissitudes of life can destroy it" (1973b, pp. 265-66). Patients have been critical of therapists who emphasize the old-fashioned virtues of beauty, receptivity, dependence, and non-assertiveness to demonstrate their femininity and attractiveness to men (Kronsky, 1975; APA Note 2). McDougall (1975) cautioned that the masculinized or virile (opposite of female stereotyped) woman entering treatment should not be confused with the homosexual woman, as their dynamics are quite different.

Economic Role and the Family

Radical and socialist books readily available in paperback editions have made women aware of the socio-economic, political, and "male ego satisfaction" functions of their traditional roles within the nuclear family (Firestone, 1970; Hole & Levine, 1971; Mitchell, 1971, 1974). Radical therapy appeals to the resulting dissatisfaction because it facilitates awareness of social oppression (by men, capitalism, sex-role stereotypes, marriage), the experience of appropriate anger, and movement away from destructive elements in the environment toward new orientations and activities which offer personal fulfillment and lead to social change (Gelb, 1972; Hermes, 1972). Radical therapy cites the case of women as "the classic example of the oppressive role of psychiatry" (Steiner, 1972, p. 304). Female patients have become convinced that cultural factors hold them back (Fried, 1974) and that psychotherapists have acted as agents of the culture. Some therapists now publicize their freedom from traditional values to counteract this consumer prejudice (Elias, 1975; Harmon, 1973).

The crux of the problem is that women, whatever their work in society, are defined in kinship terms as wives or mothers or simply in terms of their relationships with men, and women clients object (Kronsky, 1975; Mitchell, 1974). Female psychologist respondents (APA, Note 2) criticized a wide variety of therapist attitudes or behaviors which forced them into a kinship role: suggesting that getting married would solve problems, that a woman's attitude toward having children is a sign of her emotional maturity, that child rearing and a child's problems are primarily the mother's responsibility in family therapy, that a husband's needs are primary; or simply being insensitive to the women's career, work, and role diversity. When women report they have been mistreated in such a fashion, Kronsky (1975) believes it is important to verify their experience of sex-role stereotyping even from a member of the mental-health establishment.

Some contemporary analysts see their goal as helping women decide whether they wish to combine motherhood and a fulfilling life in the outside world or not (Marmor, 1973). Menaker (1974) noted that the issue is much deeper than work role because many women do not have a strong sense of self. They have inherited society's demeaning attitudes about women (hence themselves) by introjecting their mothers' attitudes, and some have also been rejected by their own mothers. Hence they will experience ego growth and an enhanced sense of self to the extent that women with better self-concepts are available as models and to the extent that they can internalize new experiences. Obtaining employment outside the home is only a partial, though perhaps preliminary, step (since society values it). Psychoanalytic therapy should free a woman to permit incorporation of those new values and experiences.

When it comes to kinship role and work role, radical feminists view the nuclear family as a prime example of *mystification*—being told a lie (that it is the ultimate good life arrangement for women) and being asked to integrate that lie with the reality (that it is oppressive and non self-actualizing). Stephenson (1973) suggests therapists should look critically at the nuclear family and ask whether roles should be diluted or whether other supports could be provided. Radical therapists state that the task of therapy is to make a woman free so she may engage in constructive social change, not only for her own sake but for society's benefit as well. "The effects of the social system in which a client lives are not seen as givens but as part of a process which can be changed by action as easily as one can change one's attitudes or feelings about it" (Clark & Jaffe, 1972, pp. 221-22). Radical feminists urge therapists to capitalize on a rapidly changing society to liberate men as well as women from the illusion of cultural entrapment (Mitchell, 1971). There is a major egalitarian emphasis both in clients learning to value their own personal experience to achieve their own identity and in use of non-authoritarian groups for problem-solving and for mutual support when meeting resistance from other parts of society (Hermes, 1972; Steiner, 1972). In fact, radical therapists who consciously reject certain traditional values (e.g., the nuclear family) recognize that those values are deeply entrenched within themselves, interfering with their therapy of liberation (Clark & Jaffe, 1972).

Whether one speaks of social role in the community, conscious role values, or unconscious material, there is an energized competition between old and new paradigms. During therapy the struggle may appear between client and family, or community, client, and therapist, or within the client or the therapist. It is important for the therapist at least to be aware of which values are in the ascendency in various parts of the system and aware of where the struggle is occurring.

Consciousness Raising and Feminist Therapy

One of the primary contributions of the feminist movement to the understanding of role problems has been the consciousness-raising (CR) group. Women come together to "discuss the politics of their lives . . . the terrible afflictions women endure . . . learn how to trust each other . . . learn [how] their experiences fit into a political pattern—a pattern best described as sexism . . . [and] invent their own tactics for social change" (Dreifus, 1973, pp. 5-7). They discuss such things as childhood training for sex roles, adult sexuality, education, work, marriage, pregnancy and childbirth, aging, appearance, and a variety of other topics.

The CR groups, by definition, are not therapy, although Brodsky (1973) suggested they might be used as a model for therapy with women, and consciousness raising serves many functions of psychotherapy: catharsis, exploration of personal history, opportunity for a close relationship with an understanding listener, and examination of interpersonal relationships. But, according to Elias (1975), unlike therapy CR is egalitarian and prohibits confrontation and criticism (differences which might fade for some therapies and some consciousness-raising groups). Kirsch (1974) summarized research on the changes which occurred after consciousness raising. Women became more independent, confident, ambitious, self-aware; showed increased self-esteem and self-acceptance, including body image; had less guilt and self-doubt, more anger (at least initially); became more trusting and intimate with other women, more egalitarian with men, and more sensitive to sex-biased incidents such as divisions of labor and language usage.

Feminist therapy seems to be a combination of radical-therapy philosophy with humanist-therapy techniques (e.g., Gestalt and transactional analysis) and behaviorism, but it focuses on one particular type of oppression which has retarded the growth of women—sexism. Like radical therapists, feminists have criticized traditional therapy for helping the individual adjust to a "sick" society, and especially helping women accept their traditional feminine role (Hole & Levine, 1971; Rice & Rice, 1973). Feminist therapy is also non-authoritarian and specifically promotes the use of groups and therapy contracts with group members. It requires clients to explore how they have been conditioned by sex-role stereotypes into low self-expectations; to learn what they are doing to perpetuate the situation (and why); and to overcome their conditioning (Elias, 1975). Its goal is the development of autonomous individuals valued in their own right (Barrett, Berg, Eaton, & Pomeroy, 1974).

It is an oversimplification to conceptualize the difference between psychoanalysis and feminist therapy or consciousness raising in terms of "where the action is"—in the head or in the community. Many female therapists feel modified Freudian theory to be harmonious with their feminist therapy, and some analysts report that the number of patients specifically requesting women therapists has increased (Fried, 1974; Kronsky, 1975; Sherfey, 1973; Symonds, Note 3). Beesly wrote, "Psychoanalytic theories and psychotherapists have been and are concerned with understanding intrapsychic processes in an effort to *help people achieve the psychological freedom to explore and define their social-sexual, economic, political and biological roles,* rather than reinforcing social-sexual roles which exist at any given time" (1973, pp. 83-84, emphasis added). Glatzer suggested CR for those who wish to work on various aspects of the women's movement rather than character reconstruction but noted that, even in traditional group therapy, women's issues come up as reality problems behind which lie emotional conflicts. "If the group therapist analyses the anxieties, defenses, transference, and resistances as they manifest themselves around this cultural problem, there is little need to modify the psychodynamic approach in group psychotherapy to include woman's changed role" (1974, p. 286). Mitchell's (1974) sympathetic analysis and commentary on Freud's theory concluded with a call for political action.

Women's liberation potentially could be used as a psychological defense against personal growth or change (Mintz, 1974), and in fact one small subgroup of radical feminists took the extreme position that men are the oppressors and therefore only men need to change. Actually, feminist therapists of several different orientations discourage rationalization and denying of responsibility as part of their therapeutic intervention. They confront women for playing the role of victim and may challenge, in Eric Berne fashion, such games as "Ain't it awful?" "Rescue me," "The marriage's success depends on me," or "I am the only parent" (Elias, 1975). "In spite of how her environment leans on her, a woman, nevertheless, has to know how to engage with it in ways which will be nourishing and zestful, not just successive acts of self-betrayal. She is creating her own life, bit by bit" (Polster, 1974, pp. 249-250).

They owe you a life and a box of matches, and they want to pay you a box of matches, because they don't want to owe you a box of matches. (Porchia)

Levenson (1972) hypothesized that neurotic problems may be considered an index of the underlying social conflicts of the time, and the neurotic a person who is sensitized to the directions of change. Dora was a psychological bellwether of Freud's era, and Portnoy acted out of the conflicts of our day. In this framework women's neurotic problems may be viewed as consequences of contemporary cultural conflict and constraints on women. Phobias, passive dependence, underachievement, and depression have received special attention in the literature.

Phobias—especially *agoraphobia,* which has a much higher incidence in women than in men—represent an extreme of the "female" traits of helplessness and dependency. Agoraphobia has been variously explained as stemming from a sex-role conflict response to feeling trapped, in marriage or some other situation not permitting assertion (Fodor, 1974b); a feared loss of self experienced when a woman sees a pointless future with no choice about what will happen to her (Seidenberg, 1973b); and a "declaration of dependence" of women who paradoxically had come from families stressing self-reliance (Symonds, 1973).

In analytic therapy the women's anger, frustration, and fear of conflict responded reasonably quickly (with consequent lessening of depression), but Symonds (1973) observed an underlying fear of taking their life into their own hands (of participating, growing, enjoying, and discovering) which was very slow to respond to therapy. Altering the dependent, avoidant lifestyle of phobic patients by eclectic behavioral techniques was advocated by Fodor, who quoted Freud as writing, "One can hardly ever master a phobia if one waits till the patient lets the analyst influence him to give it up . . . one succeeds only when one can induce them through the influence of the analysis to . . . go about alone and to struggle with their anxiety while they make the attempt" (Fodor, 1974b, p. 156). A behavioral program involves: (a) desensitization—not only of the agoraphobic activities (shopping, driving, etc.) but also of hierarchies having to do with being independent, sexual, achieving, and assertive, (b) behavior rehearsal—of the avoided activities, (c) group therapy—for discussing roles, feminist literature, goal setting, encouraging outside interests (going to work, etc.), dealing with realistic problems in achieving autonomy (e.g., economic dependency on men), providing a laboratory for the practice of assertive behavior, and social reinforcement for change, (d) modeling (based on Bandura's demonstration that phobic people will approach a feared object after exposure to a model who is comfortable with the object)—of a confident female therapist and also of other patients who are not so very different in terms of overall achievements and life pattern, and (e) family consultation—for family members who maintain the phobic's behavior by compliance with dependency demands.

Both *passivity* and *dependency* have been discussed in recent feminist literature. Frequently assertion is confused with aggression and connotes lack of femininity to the patient. An analytic therapist claims that partial identifications with male figures are normal and healthy in a patriarchal culture and clients may be helped to deal with feelings of guilt and shame such identifications engender (Kronsky, 1975). Clients have a right to their feelings, beliefs, and opinions and may be taught to support and justify them through assertion training (Jakubowski-Spector, 1973). Whatever the therapy model, women's pervasive guilt about their own assertiveness, even when the assertion is repressed, calls for special awareness on the part of the therapist. "They are burdened with such sensitivity to the judgments of others that they can be expected to read into most remarks of the therapist the negative self-evaluations which they most fear. What they need is a permissive atmosphere in which they can release their pent-up feelings of rage, helplessness and inadequacy, and explore their strivings towards healthier assertiveness which are commingled with feelings of competitiveness, hatred and envy towards men. . . . I believe that interpretations or even 'mirrorings' of such negative attitudes can imply to the already over-sensitive woman patient that there is something neurotic or unhealthy about such attitudes" (Kronsky, 1975, p. 62). Therapists making inappropriate responses to women's assertive behavior (failing to appreciate its adaptive and self-actualizing potential or attributing it to "penis envy") were cited for sex bias in the APA survey (APA, Note 2).

Many of the conflicts and issues relating to inappropriate passivity, kinship role, and work role also have implications for neurotic *dependency*. Symonds (Note 3) differentiated the woman with an insatiable need to be cared for (who *must* have a man and who may respond poorly to a female analyst because she devalues all women) from the woman who is successful in many areas of life but appears dependent because she is trying to exert power with her impotence. She suggested that the latter is out of touch with her repressed rage and remains an object rather than a subject because she is afraid of alienating the person to whom she has given over her care. Prognosis for greater autonomy and independence is good because she has not rejected her femaleness, and in therapy she can learn that the more she speaks for herself the less she needs others' approval. Prognosis is poor for the first type because she has essentially rejected herself in devaluing all women.

Feminists assert that *depression* is a normal response to a repressive sexist society (Beck & Greenberg, 1974), but few feminist therapists would go so far as to advocate social revolution in lieu of treating the depressed female patient. Depressed women can be viewed alternatively as lacking sufficient reinforcers, suppressing anger over not getting what they think they deserve, experiencing role loss, or turning anger against themselves (Fodor, 1974a). Or their affective symptoms may be secondary to a triad of negative cognitive perceptions of themselves, the world, and the future (Beck & Greenberg, 1974).

Some of the contemporary approaches to treating depression in women teach active coping methods to the patient. Lewinsohn characterized behavioral treatment as changing the patient's behaviors in order to increase the level of positive reinforcement she receives (cited in Beck & Greenberg, 1974). It includes: (a) keeping records to discover relationship of mood to expectation of reinforcement, (b) consciousness-raising contact with other women, (c) assertion training to express anger and to take independent action, (d) initially setting easily achieved goals with high rewards (graded task assignments), and (e) discouraging dependency on the therapist by providing strong positive reinforcement for a change in a positive direction (Fodor, 1974a).

Cognitive therapy helps the patient identify misconceptions and thought patterns leading to depressive affect but also includes behavioral techniques, such as graded assignments and fantasy techniques (vividly imagining oneself in a better situation) (Beck & Greenberg, 1974). Intervention helps the patient: (a) identify the thought which mediates between event and affect (e.g., "occupation—housewife" leads to the thought "I am worthless," which leads to depression), (b) distance herself emotionally from those automatic thought sequences to clarify reality perceptions, (c) identify stereotyped themes which relate to her personal history, and (d) expose and evaluate her misconceptions, prejudices, and unrealistic fantasies.

While *fear of success* (Horner, 1969) and general career *underachievement* (Vetter, 1973) are recognized by-products of the socialization of women, there is not much written on treatment of these problems specifically. Can the reader imagine a Masters-and-Johnson-size research effort on behalf of female occupational dysfunction? Fodor (1974a) reports using a desensitization hierarchy for achievement and fantasy of an idealized self-image to prepare a woman to accept her success. Consciousness-raising groups of professional women (Whiteley, 1973), assertion training (Jakubowski-Spector, 1973), and enlightened vocational counseling are probably also helpful.

The flower that you hold in your hand was born today, and already it is as old as you are. (Porchia)

Increasingly therapists are being held accountable for considering the impact of sex-role stereotyping and sexism on their clients. The following principles derive from the foregoing material and may be useful, regardless of your preferred treatment model and where you fall on the conservative to radical-feminist spectrum.

1. There is an abundance of conflicting information about women, much of it generated to support someone's research hypothesis, clinical theory, or political stance. Psychologically and biologically there is no "typical" woman and often not even a "type" of response pattern. Your client's self-report should be respected above all.

2. Relate to your client as a person valued in her own right rather than focusing on her wife-role, mother-role, feminist identity, or whether she looks and acts like what you think a woman should be.

3. Share your attitudes about woman's role, so that both of you are

aware of your relative positions. This assumes social awareness on your part—not just self-awareness but where you fit into the overall system of shifting values. If your client has experienced more consciousness raising than you have, at least that is somewhat better than when both of you are "blind" to the issues.

4. Recognize that society's ambivalence about sexuality and about woman's role may cause your client a lot of confusion and personal grief. Discourage her from claiming problems which are someone else's (frigidity vs. premature ejaculation; vocational incompetence vs. unjust occupational restrictions). On the other hand, reinforce her for taking responsibility, for actively seeking solutions, for changing the system which constrains her, and for not taking the role of the victim. In considering her struggle to know herself or give up symptoms, "listen with the fourth ear" for evidence of the subtle pull of her environment, the social pressures large and small which impinge on her decisions.

5. Women's groups (consciousness-raising or otherwise) permit formation of new identifications with other women who view themselves as competent and provide mutual support as women undergo rapid social changes, especially for the female client who has not experienced belonging to a group of other women. Female therapists may or may not be beneficial as models, depending on their level of consciousness and whether they are similar enough to the client to permit identification.

6. Supplement therapy with specific training to counteract deficiencies in socialization skills due to sex-role stereotyping during the developmental period: assertion training, desensitization of achievement fears, vocational guidance, and the like. It would almost seem to be poor practice not to advise the new sex therapies for women with sexual dysfunction by referral to an appropriate clinic if necessary (with or without continuing therapy).

REFERENCE NOTES

1. Kaplan, H.S. *The female sexual dysfunctions: Psychoanalysis or sex therapy?* Paper presented at the 19th annual meeting of the American Academy of Psychoanalysis, Los Angeles, May 2-4, 1975.
2. American Psychological Association Board of Professional Affairs. *Report of the Task Force on Sex Bias and Sex-Role Stereotyping in Psychotherapeutic Practice.* Unpublished, 1975.
3. Symonds, A. *Neurotic dependency in successful women.* Paper presented at the 19th annual meeting of the American Academy of Psychoanalysis, Los Angeles, May 2-4, 1975.

REFERENCES

Barrett, C.J., Berg, P.I., Eaton, E.M., & Pomeroy, E.L. Women's liberation and the future of psychotherapy. *Psychotherapy: Theory, Research and Practice,* 1974, *11,* 11-15.

Beck, A.T., & Greenberg, R.L. Cognitive therapy with depressed women. In V. Franks & V. Burtle (Eds), *Women in therapy*. New York: Brunner/Mazel, 1974.

Beesly, M.G. Critical evaluations: Modern woman: Implications for psychotherapy. *Canadian Psychiatric Association Journal*, 1973, *18*, 83-86.

Brodsky, A. The consciousness-raising group as a model for therapy with women. *Psychotherapy: Theory, Research and Practice*, 1973, *10*, 24-29.

Burtt, E.A. *In search of philosophic understanding*. N.Y.: The New American Library, 1965.

Chodoff, P. Feminine psychology and infantile sexuality. In J. Miller (Ed.), *Psychoanalysis and women*. Baltimore: Penguin Books, 1973.

Clark, T., & Jaffe, D.T. Change within a counter-cultural crisis intervention center. In H.M. Ruitenbeek (Ed,), *Going crazy*. New York: Bantam Books, 1972.

de Castillejo, I. *Knowing woman: A feminine psychology*. New York: Harper Colophon Books, 1973.

Doherty, M.A. Sexual bias in personality theory. *The Counseling Psychologist*, 1974, *4*(1), 67-74.

Dreifus, C. *Woman's fate*. New York: Bantam Books, 1973.

Elias, M. Sisterhood therapy. *Human Behavior*, April 1975, 56-61.

Erikson, E. Woman and the inner space. In J. Strouse (Ed.), *Women and analysis: Dialogues on psychoanalytic views of femininity*. New York: Grossman Publishers, 1974.

Firestone, S. *The dialectic of sex: The case for feminist revolution*. New York: William Morrow, 1970.

Fodor, I. Sex role conflict and symptom formation in women: Can behavior therapy help? *Psychotherapy: Theory Research and Practice*, 1974, *11*, 22-29. (a)

Fodor, I. The phobic symptom in women: Implications in treatment. In V. Franks & V. Burtle (Eds.), *Women in therapy*. New York: Brunner/Mazel, 1974. (b)

Ford, C.S., & Beach, F.A. Feminine fertility cycles. In S. Hammer (Ed.), *Women: Body and culture*. New York: Harper & Row, 1975.

Fried, E. Does woman's new self-concept call for new approaches in group psychotherapy? *International Journal of Group Psychotherapy*, 1974, *24*, 265-272.

Friedan, B. *The feminine mystique*. New York: Penguin Books, 1965.

Gelb, L.A. Mental health in a corrupt society. In H.M. Ruitenbeek (Ed.), *Going crazy*. New York: Bantam Books, 1972.

Glatzer, H. Discussion (of Fried and Mintz papers). *International Journal of Group Psychotherapy*, 1974, *24*, 281, 287.

Harding, M.E. *The way of all women*. New York: G.P. Putnam's Sons, 1970.

Harmon, L. . . . And soma. *The Counseling Psychologist*. 1973, *4*(1), 87-90.

Hays, H.R. *The dangerous sex: The myth of feminine evil*. New York: Pocket Books, Inc., 1964.

Hermes, J. On radical therapy. In H.M. Ruitenbeek (Ed.), *Going crazy*. New York: Bantam Books, 1972.

Hole, J., & Levine, E. *Rebirth of feminism*. New York: Quadrangle/The New York Times Book Co., 1971.

Horner, M.S. Fail: Bright women. *Psychology Today*, 1969, *3*, 36-41.

Horney, K. The flight from womanhood: The masculinity complex in women as viewed by men and women. In J. Miller (Ed.), *Psychoanalysis and women*. Baltimore: Penguin Books, 1973.

Jakubowski-Spector, P. Facilitating the growth of women through assertive training. *The Counseling Psychologist*, 1973, *4*(1), 75-86.

Jung, C.G. *Animus and anima.* New York: The Analytical Psychology Club of New York, Inc., 1957.

Kaplan, H.S. *The new sex therapy.* New York: Brunner/Mazel, 1974.

Kirsch, B. Consciousness-raising groups as therapy for women. In V. Franks and V. Burtle (Eds.), *Women in therapy.* New York: Brunner/Mazel, 1974.

Kovel, J. The castration complex reconsidered. In J. Strouse (Ed.), *Women and analysis: Dialogues on psychoanalytic views of femininity.* New York: Grossman Publishers, 1974.

Kronsky, B.J. Feminism and psychotherapy. In S. Hammer (Ed.), *Women: Body and culture.* New York: Harper & Row, 1975.

Levenson, E. *The fallacy of understanding.* New York: Basic Books, 1972.

Marmor, J. Changing patterns of femininity: Psychoanalytic implications. In J. Miller (Ed.), *Psychoanalysis and women.* Baltimore: Penguin Books, 1973.

Masters, W., & Johnson, V. *Human sexual response.* Boston: Little, Brown, 1966.

Masters, W., & Johnson, V. *Human sexual inadequacy.* Boston: Little, Brown, 1970.

McDougall, J. Homosexuality in women. In S. Hammer (Ed.), *Women: Body and culture.* New York: Harper & Row, 1975.

Mednick, M.T., & Weissman, H.J. The psychology of women—Selected topics. *Annual Review of Psychology.* Palo Alto: Annual Reviews, Inc., 1975.

Menaker, E. The therapy of women in the light of psychoanalytic theory and the emergence of a new view. In V. Franks & V. Burtle (Eds.), *Women in therapy.* New York: Brunner/Mazel, 1974.

Mintz, E. What do we owe today's woman? *International Journal of Group Psychotherapy,* 1974, *24,* 273-280.

Mitchell, J. *Woman's estate.* New York: Random House (Vintage), 1971.

Mitchell, J. *Psychoanalysis and feminism.* New York: Random House (Vintage), 1974.

Moulton, R. A survey and reevaluation of the concept of penis envy. In J. Miller (Ed.), *Psychoanalysis and women.* Baltimore: Penguin Books, 1973.

Moulton, R. Multiple factors in frigidity. In S. Hammer (Ed.), *Women: Body and culture.* New York: Harper & Row, 1975.

Neumann, E. *The great mother: An analysis of the archetype.* New York: Pantheon Books, 1955.

Polster, M. Women in therapy—A Gestalt therapist's view. In V. Franks & V. Burtle (Eds.), *Women in therapy.* New York: Brunner/Mazel, 1974.

Porchia, A. (Tr. by W.S. Merwin). *Voices.* Toronto: The Ryerson Press, 1969.

Quen, J.M. Case studies in nineteenth century scientific rejection: Mesmerism, Perkinism, and acupuncture. *Journal of the History of the Behavioral Sciences,* 1975, *11,* 149-156.

Rice, J.K., & Rice, D.G. Implications of the women's liberation movement for psychotherapy. *American Journal of Psychiatry,* 1973, *130,* 191-6.

Seidenberg, R. Is anatomy destiny? In J. Miller (Ed.), *Psychoanalysis and women.* Baltimore: Penguin Books, 1973. (a)

Seidenberg, R. The trauma of eventlessness. In J. Miller (Ed.), *Psychoanalyis and women.* Baltimore: Penguin Books, 1973. (b)

Sherfey, M.J. On the nature of female sexuality. In J. Miller (Ed.), *Psychoanalysis and women.* Baltimore: Penguin Books, 1973.

Steiner, C. Radical psychiatry. In H.M. Ruitenbeek (Ed.), *Going crazy.* New York: Bantam Books, 1972.

Stephenson, P.S. Modern woman: Implications for psychotherapy. *Canadian Psychiatric Association Journal,* 1973, *18,* 79-82.

Stoller, R.J. The "bedrock" of masculinity and femininity: Bisexuality. In J. Miller (Ed.), *Psychoanalysis and women.* Baltimore: Penguin Books, 1973. (a)

Stoller, R.J. The sense of femaleness. In J. Miller (Ed.), *Psychoanalysis and women.* Baltimore: Penguin Books, 1973. (b)

Symonds, A. Phobias after marriage: Women's declaration of dependence. In J. Miller (Ed.), *Psychoanalysis and women.* Baltimore: Penguin Books, 1973.

Thompson, C. Some effects of the derogatory attitude toward female sexuality. In J. Miller (Ed.), *Psychoanalysis and women.* Baltimore: Penguin Books, 1973.

Vetter, L. Career counseling for women. *The Counseling Psychologist,* 1973, *4*(1), 44-54.

Weisstein, N. Kinder, kuche, kirche. In H.M. Ruitenbeek (Ed.), *Going crazy.* New York: Bantam Books, 1972.

Whiteley, R. Women in groups. *The Counseling Psychologist,* 1973, *4*(1), 27-43.

Zilboorg, G. Masculine and feminine: Some biological and cultural aspects. In J. Miller (Ed.), *Psychoanalysis and women.* Baltimore: Penguin Books, 1973.

Women Counselors for Women Clients? A Review of the Research

MARY FAITH TANNEY
JANICE M. BIRK
University of Maryland

Few issues so arouse women in psychology as passionately as the question of sex-role stereotyping or sex bias by the counselor/therapist (terms to be used interchangeably) and its implications for clients (American Psychological Association, 1975; Chesler, 1971, 1972; Gardner, 1971; Rice & Rice, 1973). A complete review of this question would involve evaluating the four possible counselor-client combinations by sex on relevant process and outcome dimensions. Since most counselors and therapists are men, however, and most of the consumers of psychological services are women (Boulware & Holmes, 1970; Chesler, 1971; Gove & Tudor, 1973; Howard & Howard, 1974; Siassi, 1974), the most relevant initial approach to examining the impact of counselor gender on clients is to focus on the woman client and how she is affected by male and by female counselors.

Until fairly recently, practitioners in the helping professions have operated within the belief system that they do not respond differently to clients merely on the basis of client sex (Meltzoff & Kornreich, 1970). Fabrikant (1974) observed:

> There has been exploration of the relative advantages of the patient having a male or a female therapist, depending on the parental figure considered to be the focus of the difficulty. The assumption made seems to be that the sex of the patient is less important than the sex of the therapist. The therapist of choice for young children was usually a female on the assumption that the mother figure is more important to the child in early years. Later in childhood, and particularly for the male child, the male therapist becomes more important. The explanation was that the male child needed a male model with whom to identify (p. 83).

Currently this viewpoint is questioned, and the proposal is made that women could utilize female counselors more effectively than male counselors (Rice & Rice, 1973). Kronsky (1971) proposed that a feminist-oriented therapist (who will probably be a woman) will be able to offer significant sensitivity to a woman client's experiences in a male-dominated society. Chesler (1972) adopts the strongest stance: a woman client can be understood and helped only by a woman therapist who is herself a feminist.

The most current empirical literature related to the impact of therapist/counselor sex on clients (in individual counseling) can be divided into those studies examining the attitudes of women clients toward male and female therapists and those focusing on therapists' reactions to women clients.

CURRENT RESEARCH ON CLIENT REACTIONS

An investigation by Fuller (1964) was one of the few studies to examine whether counseling-center clients have counselor preferences based on sex, whether such preferences vary with client sex and presenting problem, and whether such preferences change after counseling. She found that female college clients with personal-social problems expressed preferences significantly more often for female counselors. Relatedly, Boulware and Holmes (1970) asked university students, not clients, to view slides of the faces of potential therapists and to indicate how much they would like to talk to each individual if they had a personal or vocational problem. The women in the sample preferred the older male therapists for vocational problems, but, when speculating about a personal problem, the older women therapists were preferred. This preference seemed to the researchers to be based on variables other than just sex similarity, such as expected understanding.

As part of a broader investigation, Howard, Orlinsky and Hill (1970) measured the extent to which personal characteristics of patients and therapists influence patients' feelings of satisfaction following therapy. On the basis of a sample of female patients, combinations of marital status and age of both patients and therapists were found to influence ratings of therapy satisfaction. In general, patients rated psychotherapy sessions with female therapists more satisfying than those with male therapists.

Does sex of the therapist influence client behaviors during the interview? Fuller (1963) found female clients generally to be more likely than male clients to express feelings. Additionally, client-counselor pairs which included a female, regardless of whether she was client or counselor, produced significantly more client self-disclosure than did all-male dyads. Brooks (1974) studied the interaction of client and counselor sex and counselor status on self-disclosure and found that female subjects were not, in general, more disclosing than men, although they did reveal more to male counselors than to female counselors. Supporting Fuller's (1963) results, she found that dyads containing a female (client or counselor) produced more client self-disclosure than all-male dyads. Female clients also revealed more to female interviewers of lower status, although high-status male interviewers elicited greater self-disclosure than low-status male interviewers. The fact that these results were found only in the initial segment of the interviews suggests that the effects of counselor sex and status on client self-disclosure may dissipate quite rapidly.

A small body of research has examined the impact of counselor sex as it interacts with additional variables. Hill (1975), for example, investigated the effects of experience level as it interacted with counselor sex. Although some of her findings pertain more to counselor behavior as it is affected by the sex of the client, female subjects paired with female counselors produced more discussion of feelings than mixed sexual dyads. Scher (1975) studied the interaction of the counselor-client sex pairing with verbal activity, counselor experience and success in counseling. Neither counselor sex nor client sex was found to be a significant predictor of counseling outcome.

Grantham (1973) examined within initial interviews the effect of counselor sex, race and language style on black students and found that clients were able to explore themselves more extensively in interviews with female counselors. The presence of a female counselor, rather than racial similarity, was the significant variable in stimulating personally relevant material.

In summary, empirical evidence of female clients' preferences for same-sex or other-sex counselor is sparse. Research studying the impact of pairing client and counselor on the basis of sexual similarity is uncommon as well. Where research does exist, frequently the results are contradictory and confusing due to the selection of different populations and the use of different instruments.

RESEARCH ON COUNSELOR REACTIONS

In contrast to the small number of studies examining client reactions to counselor gender, far more attention has been focused on applied psychologists' attitudes about sex-role stereotypes and their judgments of mental health. The classic, heuristic study of Broverman, Broverman, Clarkson, Rosenkrantz and Vogel (1970) demonstrated that clinicians' judgments about the mental health of individuals differed as a function of the sex of the person evaluated. All mental-health professionals in the sample, regardless of sex, maintained a double standard of mental health; that is, a diferent standard of mental health was applied for women than for men and for adults, sex unspecified.

Other researchers have explored how therapists' sex and therapeutic-training experiences influence their clinical judgments about male and female clients. Slechta (Note 1) interviewed 15 professional counselors and found marked similarities between the terms they used to describe the "typical women" and those used to describe neurotic symptoms. Although the sample size warrants cautious generalization of the results, it is noteworthy that the interviewed subjects maintained they did not ascribe to sex role differences. Indeed, over two-thirds of the subjects maintained that there are no personality differences between men and women! It would seem that the expressed attitudes of mental-health professionals regarding sex-role stereotypes should be accepted cautiously.

Goldberg (Note 2) studied the attitudes of 184 urban, practicing clinical psychologists towards women. All subjects completed questionnaires tapping attitudes towards men in general, women in general, the mental-health standards for women, the mental-health standards for men and the mental-health standards for adults in general. Also investigated were subjects' attitudes towards men and women who need psychotherapy, who are successful or unsuccessful in psychotherapy, as well as other issues related to psychotherapy in which differential attitudes towards the sexes might be expected. The data were analyzed according to age, sex and experience level of the subjects. Results of this study did not reveal any markedly prejudiced sex-linked attitudes, although some differences appeared between some groupings. Younger therapists were less likely to express traditional views of women as the weaker sex, while the older male therapists appeared to hold traditional ways of thinking about females. Women therapists in general seemed to hold attitudes toward men and women which were more egalitarian than those of men therapists. Goldberg concluded that the expressed attitudes of clinical psychologists towards women and men were multifaceted and complex and that simple statements of unqualified prejudice against women among this population were unfounded.

Neulinger, Schillinger, Stein and Welkowitz (1970) found differences in the responses of 114 therapists to questions about the optimally integrated person. Analyses of a personality questionnaire based on Murray's need system revealed that female therapists described achievement as more necessary for males than for females. Male therapists rated abasement as more necessary for women than did the female therapists. In general the subjects rated dominance, achievement, autonomy, aggression and counter-action as more indicative of mental health in men than in women, while patience, nurturance, play, deference, succorance and abasement were rated as higher needs for the optimally integrated female than for the male. In a survey of mental-health workers, Fabrikant, Landau and Rollenhagen (Note 3) found that their subjects' view of females was quite negative. More female than male therapists contended that the role of wife/mother was the appropriate goal for their female patients.

According to the literature reviewed thus far, the judgments of mental-health professionals regarding the appropriateness of certain behaviors and needs oftentimes are affected by the sex of the subject. For example, Abramowitz, Abramowitz, Jackson and Gomes (1973) presented 71 professional counselors with bogus clinical profiles varying in the testees' political inclination and sex. Greater psychological maladjustment was attributed to the politically active women leaning toward the "left" than to the male, but only by the less politically liberal examiners. The authors concluded that males are allowed a wider range of normal behaviors than females.

Larson (1970) studied how sex and symptoms affected the diagnosis, therapy and referral patterns of clergymen. Unlike Abramowitz and associates (1973), sex of patient did not unilaterally affect the clergymen's perception of the normal personality or of most of the clinical syndromes described.

Other studies have revealed significant differences between the perceptions of male and female therapists. Duplicating the Broverman et al. (1970) study with counselor trainees, Maslin and Davis (1975) found that the males continued to hold somewhat more stereotypic standards of mental health for females than for adults. The female counselors in training, however, unlike the Broverman professionals, held approximately the same set of expectations for all healthy persons, regardless of sex.

In a partial replication of the study by Broverman and associates (1970), Aslin (Note 4) examined the mental-health expectations for women held by feminist therapists and by male and female psychotherapists from community mental-health centers (CMHC). Specifically, she studied the effects of several variables on the psychotherapists' judgments of normal mental health, the sex and feminist identification of the psychotherapists, and the sex (adult vs. female) and social role (wife vs. mother) of the person being judged. Using a bipolar adjective list, subjects indicated the pole to which normal adults, females, wives and mothers would be closer. No significant differences were found on any role evaluations made by the feminist therapists when compared with the women CMHC therapists. Male and female therapists were found to differ in their judgments of mental health for female versus mother, and the male CMHC therapists' judgments of adult differed significantly from their judgments of female, wife and mother.

Reversing the trend described earlier, Haan and Livson (1973) discovered that women Ph.D. psychologists ascribed more favorable characteristics to the female than to the male subjects they were assessing. The male psychologists did not rate the women as positively, nor did they rate men and women in general as favorably as their female colleagues. Specifically, the female subjects were seen as more calm and as having wide interests by women judges, while the male subjects were rated as more bothered by demands, self-defensive, rebellious and as arousing nurturance.

All of the above studies examined attitudes towards the mental health of men and women and assume that attitudes, whether or not they are prejudicial to women, will be conveyed within the counseling session (Stevens, 1971). Only one study was found which attempted to measure behavioral correlates of therapists' attitudes toward women. Gross, Herbert, Knatterud and Donner (1969) studied the impact of race and sex not only on diagnosis but also on the disposition of patients in a psychiatric emergency room. They found that treatment decisions made concerning women were likely to be significantly affected by race. Specifically, behavior that required hospitalization of a female patient was more often perceived as neurotic when the female was white, and schizophrenic when the female was nonwhite. It is noteworthy also that criteria for hospitalization differed between women and men.

SEX BIAS IN CAREER COUNSELING

Counseling psychologists often assist clients to make decisions regarding vocational choice, career entry and re-entry. An excellent review of literature relevant to career-counseling theories as well as the factors affecting career choices among women was provided by Vetter (1973). Even when the counseling contract does not focus explicitly on career matters, counselor-client attitudes concerning the value of work for women are likely to emerge in any significant helping relationship with a female.

Friedersdorf (Note 5) attempted to determine the attitudes of counselors towards the educational and vocational aspirations of high school girls and to determine the nature and extent of attitudinal differences among counselors. In this study the male and female counselors rated both college-bound and non-college-bound high school girls. Several differences were found between the male and female counselors. The male counselors (a) associated college-bound girls with traditionally feminine occupations at the semi-skilled level, (b) tended to think of women in feminine roles characterized by feminine personality traits, and (c) perceived the college-bound girl as having positive attitudes toward traditionally feminine occupations, regardless of the classification of the occupation. The female counselors, by comparison, perceived the college-bound girl as interested in occupations requiring a college education. Additionally, the female counselors tended to expand the traditional image of female work roles and projected women's roles into careers presently occupied predominantly by men.

Thomas and Stewart (1971) examined secondary school counselors' responses to female clients with traditionally feminine (conforming) and traditionally masculine (deviate) career goals. Although the female counselors gave higher acceptance scores to both deviate and conforming clients than did the male counselors, these differences washed out when counselors indicated the appropriateness of the two types of goals for the women clients. Counselors, regardless of sex, rated female clients with deviate career goals to be more in need of counseling than those with conforming goals.

In a related study, Cline-Nafzinger (1971) explored the difference in attitudes that male and female counselors, counselor educators and teachers expressed towards women's roles. Although both men and women rejected the notion of limiting women to intra-family activities, women counselors in particular rejected traditional roles for women. Relatedly, women in this survey were more supportive of working mothers than were the men. An additional finding was that counselors, regardless of sex, described women as supportive and vicariously achieving, whereas counselor educators supported the achievement motivation in women.

Persons (1972) evaluated the impact of client sex and race on the occupational predictions made by male and female counselor trainees. Equivalent information on test scores, age, grade point average and personality variables was provided for all clients, with the sex and race of client varied. The counselor trainees predicted the occupation that the bogus clients would most likely enter, and then the prestige of the predicted occupations was evaluated. Although male counselor trainees consistently predicted higher prestige occupations for male clients and for white clients, female counselor trainees did not demonstrate either racial or sexual bias in the prestige levels of their occupational predictions.

Counselors' attitudes toward women and work were assessed by Bingham and House (1973). Their survey revealed that, in general, male counselors were not uniformly supportive of women working. The authors noted that this ambivalent attitude could be problematic for female clients.

Schlossberg and Pietrofesa (1973) arranged for male and female counselor trainees to interview a coached woman client who was undecided about choosing a traditionally masculine (engineering) or a traditionally feminine (teaching) occupation. Regardless of sex of the counselor, the client received active discouragement for her nontraditional career consideration.

Not all research has found counselors to be consistently biased toward traditional career choices for women. Smith (1973) disputed Schlossberg's and Pietrofesa's methodology and reported (Smith, 1974) that she found no sexual or ethnic discrimination among counselors in her study. She asked secondary school counselors to predict the academic success and to choose an appropriate career for four hypothetical cases. The results showed that variation in client sex and ethnic designation did not produce variations in counselor evaluations. Counselor sex was not related to any systematic variance in evaluation.

The research just cited indicates that sex bias frequently occurs in career counseling. The bias, however, seems to be operative in both male and female counselors.

CONCLUSION AND IMPLICATIONS

What then can be concluded about the impact of the sex of the counselor on women clients? On the basis of the literature reviewed here it seems clear that examiners of this question are becoming more sophisticated, more sensitive, and following a pattern akin to early psychotherapy outcome research. After initially examining the global issue of whether or not psychotherapy helped patients, therapy outcome research gradually evolved into an examination of various contextual variables, such as the effect of therapist experience level, age, race, orientation and type of client problem. The examination of the impact of therapist sex on clients is demonstrating a similar development. No longer is therapist sex the main independent variable; race, age and experience level are but a few of the interactive therapist dimensions which are being evaluated. Although client self-disclosure (Brooks, 1974; Fuller, 1963; Hill, 1975) and client satisfaction (Howard et al., 1970) are important considerations, additional areas of measurement need to be explored to assess how women clients react to therapists and to measure more than therapist attitudes toward women. Until these investigations are complete, it is impossible to describe clearly the impact of the gender of the therapist on women clients.

In spite of the lack of conclusive empirical findings, psychologists continue to theorize about the possible impact of the gender of the therapist on the woman client, and that, perhaps, is as it should be, for the counseling interactions themselves continue. It can be conjectured, for example, that in long-term therapy the sex of the therapist merely stimulates the patient to discuss her conflicts in a particular order (Kopp, Note 6). Whereas a male therapist may initially draw a client's memories of social repression in a male-dominated world, a female therapist at the beginning may arouse the patient's longings for nurturance. In the give and take of good psychotherapy, however, both areas of repression will be addressed. It is possible also that the sex of the counselor may transcend the prescribed role in vocational counseling and that women professionals may be utilized by their clients less for their counseling assistance, per se, and more as role models of women who have "made it." Plost (1974) documented the impact of a female career model on the occupational preferences of women.

Few areas of investigation are so reactive. It may be that the social desirability (Aslin, Note 4) of positively evaluating male characteristics as the mental-health standard is being replaced by the intention among therapists to be seen as not sexually stereotyping clients. Although this development may make measurement of such phenomena difficult, the fact that therapists are becoming more sensitive makes the experimental complications worthwhile.

Women clients' perceptions and preferences for sex of counselor need to be monitored carefully. Rising social consciousness may create among women clients a greater demand for women counselors and therapists. In the interim, training programs need to emphasize the new knowledge of the psychology of women (Rice & Rice, 1973). Practicing counselors, too, need to sensitize themselves continually to the sex-role stereotypes inherent in language (Farb, 1974), career information (Birk, 1974), personality theories (Doherty, 1973) and practice (Fabrikant, 1974).

REFERENCE NOTES

1. Slechta, J.B. *Women in therapy as perceived by mental health personnel or down the primrose path with a "blind" therapist.* Paper presented at the meeting of the Rocky Mountain Psychological Association, 1971.
2. Goldberg, L.H. *Attitudes of clinical psychologists toward women.* Unpublished doctoral dissertation, Illinois Institute of Technology, 1973.
3. Fabrikant, B., Landau, D., & Rollenhagen, J. *Perceived female sex role attributes and psychotherapists' sex role expectations for female patients.* Paper presented at the meeting of the American Psychological Association, Honolulu, 1972.
4. Aslin, A.L. *Feminist and community mental health center psychotherapists' mental health expectations for women.* Unpublished doctoral dissertation, University of Maryland, 1974.

5. Friedersdorf, N.W. *A comparative study of counselor attitudes toward the further educational and vocational plans of high school girls.* Unpublished paper, Purdue University, 1969.
6. Kopp, S. Personal communication, September 16, 1975.

REFERENCES

Abramowitz, S.I., Abramowitz, C.V., Jackson, C., & Gomes, B. The politics of clinical judgment: What non-liberal examiners infer about women who don't stifle themselves. *Journal of Consulting and Clinical Psychology,* 1973, *41,* 385-391.
American Psychological Association, Report of the Task Force on sex bias and sex role stereotyping in psychotherapeutic practice. *American Psychologist,* 1975, *30,* 1169-1175.
Bingham, W.C., & House, E.W. Counselors view women and work: Accuracy of information. *Vocational Guidance Quarterly,* 1973, *21,* 262-268.
Birk, J.M. Interest inventories: A mixed blessing. *Vocational Guidance Quarterly,* 1974, *22,* 280-286.
Boulware, D.W., & Holmes, D.S. Preferences for therapists and related expectancies. *Journal of Consulting and Clinical Psychology,* 1970, *35,* 269-277.
Brooks, L. Interactive effects of sex and status on self-disclosure. *Journal of Counseling Psychology,* 1974, *21,* 469-474.
Broverman, I.K., Broverman, D.M., Clarkson, F.E., Rosenkrantz, P., & Vogel, S.R. Sex role stereotypes and clinical judgments of mental health. *Journal of Consulting and Clinical Psychology,* 1970, *34,* 1-7.
Chesler, P. Patient and patriarch: Women in the psychotherapeutic relationship. In V. Gornick & B.K. Moran (Eds.), *Women in sexist society: Studies in power and powerlessness.* New York: Basic Books, 1971.
Chesler, P. *Women and madness.* New York: Doubleday, 1972.
Cline-Nafzinger, C. A survey of counselors' and other selected professionals' attitudes toward women's roles (Doctoral dissertation, University of Oregon, 1971). *Dissertation Abstracts International,* 1971, *32,* 3021A. (University Microfilms No. 72-955)
Doherty, M.A. Sexual bias in personality theory. *Counseling Psychologist,* 1973, *4*(1), 67-74.
Fabrikant, B. The psychotherapist and the female patient: Perceptions, misperceptions and change. In V. Franks & V. Burtle (Eds.), *Women in therapy.* New York: Brunner/Mazel, 1974.
Farb, P. *Word play.* New York: Alfred A. Knopf, 1974.
Fuller, F.F. Influence of sex of counselor and of client on client expressions of feeling. *Journal of Counseling Psychology,* 1963, *10,* 34-40.
Fuller, F.F. Preferences for male and female counselors. *Personnel and Guidance Journal,* 1964, *42,* 463-467.
Gardner, J. Sexist counseling must stop. *Personnel and Guidance Journal,* 1971, *49,* 705-714.
Gove, W.R., & Tudor, J.F. Adult sex roles and mental illness. In J. Huber (Ed.), *Changing women in a changing society.* Chicago: University of Chicago Press, 1973.
Grantham, R.J. Effects of counselor sex, race and language style on black students in initial interviews. *Journal of Counseling Psychology,* 1973, *20,* 553-559.

Gross, H.S., Herbert, M.B., Knatterud, G.L., & Donner, L. The effect of sex and race on the variation of diagnosis and disposition in a psychiatric emergency room. *Journal of Nervous and Mental Disease,* 1969, *148*(6), 638-6.

Haan, N., & Livson, N. Sex differences in the eyes of expert personality assessors: Blind spots. *Journal of Personality Assessment,* 1973, *37,* 486-492.

Hill, C.E. Sex of client and sex and experience level of counselor. *Journal of Counseling Psychology,* 1975, *22,* 6-11.

Howard, E.M., & Howard, J.L. Women in institutions: Treatment in prisons and mental hospitals. In V. Franks & V. Burtle (Eds.), *Women in therapy.* New York: Brunner/Mazel, 1974.

Howard, K.I., Orlinsky, D.W., & Hill, J.A. Patients' satisfaction in psychotherapy as a function of patient-therapist pairings. *Psychotherapy: Theory, Research and Practice,* 1970, *7,* 130-134.

Kronsky, B.J. Feminism and psychotherapy. *Journal of Contemporary Psychotherapy,* 1971, *3*(2), 89-98.

Larson, R.F. The influence of sex roles and symptoms on clergymen's perception of mental illness. *Pacific Sociological Review,* 1970, 53-61.

Maslin, A., & Davis, J.L. Sex-role stereotyping as a factor in mental health standards among counselors in training. *Journal of Counseling Psychology,* 1975, *22,* 87-91.

Meltzoff, J., & Kornreich, M. *Research in psychotherapy.* New York: Atherton Press, 1970.

Neulinger, J., Schillinger, K., Stein, M.I., & Welkowitz, J. Perceptions of the optimally integrated person as a function of therapists characteristics. *Perceptual and Motor Skills,* 1970, *30,* 375-384.

Persons, W.E. III. Occupational prediction as a function of the counselor's racial and sexual bias (Doctoral dissertation, University of Florida, 1972). *Dissertation Abstracts International,* 1973, *34,* 139A-140A. (University Microfilms No. 73-15, 533)

Plost, M. Effect of sex of career models on occupational preferences of adolescents. *Audio Visual Communication Review,* 1974, *22,* 41-50.

Rice, I.K., & Rice, D.E. Implications of the women's liberation movement for psychotherapy. *American Journal of Psychiatry,* 1973, *130,* 191-196.

Scher, M. Verbal activity, sex, counselor experience, and success in counseling. *Journal of Counseling Psychology,* 1975, *22,* 97-101.

Schlossberg, N.K., & Pietrofesa, J.J. Perspectives on counseling bias: Implications for counselor education. *Counseling Psychologist,* 1973, *4*(1), 44-54.

Siassi, I. Psychotherapy with women and men of lower classes. In V. Franks & V. Burtle (Eds.), *Women in therapy.* New York: Brunner/Mazel, 1974, 383-408.

Smith, M.L. Notes on "Perspectives on counseling bias: Implications for counselor education." *Counseling Psychologist,* 1973, *4*(2), 93.

Smith, M.L. Influence of client sex and ethnic group on counselor judgments. *Journal of Counseling Psychology,* 1974, *21,* 516-521.

Stevens, B. The psychotherapist and women's liberation. *Social Work,* 1971, *16,* 12-18.

Thomas, A.H., & Stewart, N.R. Counselor response to female clients with deviate and conforming career goals. *Journal of Counseling Psychology,* 1971, *18,* 352-357.

Vetter, L. Career counseling for women. *Counseling Psychologist,* 1973, *4*(1), 54-67.

Supermoms Shift Gears: Re-entry Women

LINDA BROOKS
Converse College

Thirty-three year old Catherine entered assertiveness training feeling restless and discontent, as well as irritated with her husband's assumption that she would handle all the home responsibilities. Through assertiveness training, she was encouraged to express her irritation, but her husband's lack of response made her feel guilty and depressed. During a trial separation, Catherine sought the help of a counselor. As she began exploring her options, she realized she had some talents, as well as a need to achieve outside the home. More importantly, self-esteem and a sense of her own power began to emerge. She became excited about possible achievements in the work force. Her husband returned, and she sank back into depression as she refocused her energy on the marital relationship.

Forty-two year old Jennifer came to a counselor for help in selecting a field from one of her many interests and talents. She was not interested in any more "women's jobs" such as she had filled in the past. On one level, she knew she was intelligent and multi-talented. On another, in spite of her many past accomplishments, she lacked self-confidence. Yet she considered her wish to achieve outside the home valid and was psychologically prepared to handle multiple roles. Her husband's occasional sulking, therefore, failed to mobilize any guilt. Jennifer terminated counseling with intentions of returning to graduate school.

Catherine and Jennifer represent women at two different stages in the "re-entry" process. Catherine was emerging from a dependent relationship, feeling resentful, goalless and guilty, and focused at first entirely on her discontent in her marriage, unaware that establishing her own identity and self-worth might help her marriage. Jennifer, on the other hand, was ready to explore her options and needed help with value clarification and decision making. For all their differences, Catherine and Jennifer shared a lack of confidence, an uncertainty about personal worth, and a keen intelligence. Both also had extensive volunteer experience and had spent several years of marriage being a "Supermom" (Bedell, 1973)—that is, attending to their family needs while submerging their own.

Hundreds of adult women similar to Catherine and Jennifer are seeking the services of counselors attuned to their special needs. Most present a paradoxical appearance: an impressive set of talents and abilities and past achievements combined with an acute lack of confidence; mature cognitive ability and a strong sense of responsibility combined with "lack of depth and specificity in thinking, and fantasy more appropriate to a college-aged person" (White, Note 1).

In addition to a paradoxical psychological appearance, women returning to school or work outside the home represent varied personal situations. For older women, the departure of the last child has created the "empty-nest" stage and a "pressure for self-development, accompanied by anxiety approaching old age" (Pincus, Radding, & Lawrence, 1974, p. 193). For younger women, enrolling the last child in nursery school has prompted a search for new roles. A great sense of urgency to update skills or explore job options has occurred for many separated, divorced, or widowed women.

Many returning women are well-educated; most are middle class and economically comfortable. They have had extensive volunteer experiences and have been vicarious achievers through filling enabling, facilitating, and back-up roles (Lipman-Blumen, 1975). Various personal situations as well as greater societal permission for women to think about themselves have created a transitional situation that prompts a search for personal fulfillment and a consideration of direct, rather than vicarious, achievement roles.

Yet, few women consider new options and roles outside the home without difficulty. Some experience intense role conflict; others are unfamiliar with opportunities in education and the labor market. Counselors cognizant of the special needs of adult women are in increasing demand. Through presenting a stage model, this article will provide guidelines for counselors working with adult women who "re-enter" through school or work outside the home and will focus on married, middle-class women who have been primarily wives and mothers for a number of years. These women will be referred to as "re-entry women," although it is recognized that some will be engaged in an initial entry, never having worked outside the home or attended classes past high school.

COUNSELING AND THE RE-ENTRY PROCESS

Viewing the re-entry process as a series of stages has the benefit of providing the counselor with a framework for both assessment and intervention. While the re-entry process will seldom occur in such an orderly progression, awareness of issues involved in each stage will help the counselor assess unresolved issues, anticipate future stresses, and plan effective interventions. The schema of stages discussed below is a compilation of Matthews' (1969) model for vocational counseling with adult women, career development theory, and the author's experience with re-entry women.

The stages of re-entry fall within two broad categories: (a) preparation and (b) decision-making. Tasks of the preparation phase involve removing psychological blocks that prevent commitment to exploring new roles and options. Tasks of the decision-making phase involve assessing abilities and interests and generating, selecting, and implementing goals and options. The preparation and decision-making framework recognizes that self-exploration is necessary before the individual can begin to investigate possible directions and make choices that implement a preferred life-style (Seay, 1973; Driver, Note 2).

The preferred mode of treatment is group counseling with specific objectives and structured activities, supplemented with the availability of individual sessions. The reader is referred to several group models available in the literature (Blimline, 1974; Goodman, Walworth, & Walters, 1975; Hiltunen, 1968; Manis & Mochizuki, 1972; and Seay, 1973).

Preparation Phase

Stage 1: Vague discontent. Many women begin the re-entry process feeling a confusing discomfort about their present life. They may feel bored and depressed but unable to pinpoint the difficulty. "Sometimes the individual questions her personality, blaming herself rather than understanding the factors contributing to her vague or inarticulated discontents" (Manis & Mochizuki, 1972, p. 595).

Friedan (1963) wrote about this "problem with no name" over ten years ago. Since then, women have gained greater societal permission to fill multiple roles. Discontent may thus be seen as the result of dependency and a failure to develop an individual identity apart from or in addition to wife and mother rather than a failure to adjust to an expected role. Still, the middle-aged client housewife who retreats into depression, alcohol, or physical illness is well known to counselors.

It is tempting to view this depressed, middle-aged client as someone with deep-seated neurotic problems. Alternatively, such clients may be viewed as women in a transitional stage, who primarily had been vicarious achievers and who currently need new avenues for gaining a sense of achievement and fulfillment. Significantly, one study found an association between depressive symptoms and difficulty finding employment after a relocation due to the husband's job. Symptoms markedly decreased four months later, following brief job counseling and success in locating employment (Weissman, Pincus, Radding, Lawrence, & Siegel, 1973).

Some counselors readily recognize that a woman's source of self-esteem may be external and too dependent on her husband and family but fail to actively encourage her to take specific steps toward gaining an internal source of self-esteem. The counselor who recognizes role questioning as healthy and independent achievement as an important basis for self-esteem can effectively intervene with women experiencing vague discontent by clarifying their feelings and assisting them in actively exploring new alternative roles.

Many women in Stage 1 will not initiate contact with counselors but might be members of a community group that requests speakers from local women's counseling centers. Speakers can effectively intervene with Stage-1 women by discussing the phenomenon of vague discontent, the underlying psychological factors, and some viable solutions, thereby helping the woman label her feeling and letting her know she is not unusual or abnormal. Thus, the woman may be stimulated to begin the needed reevaluation of her life in a positive way.

Stage 2: Inner preparation.[1] The potential re-entry woman tentatively decides she wants to become involved in new roles outside the home. She then faces such questions as: "Do I really want to enter the competitive world?" "What if I don't make it?" "How will my family and friends react?" "I'm not sure what I want to do—is it worth the risk of trying to find out?"

Matthews pointed out that Stage 2 cannot be fully resolved without actual experience in school or work. A support group for adult women, however, can provide the climate to facilitate the process. "When the woman can say with reasonable security, 'I am ready to risk reordering the pattern of our lives,' she is ready for the next stage" (Matthews, 1969, p. 118).

Stage 3: Intensive family involvement. Before a woman can fully commit herself to serious exploration of her options, she needs to share her new thinking with her family, a process which can prevent later conflicts. "Many a woman's misunderstanding and conflicts stem from her family's lack of qualitative involvement in the decision-making process" (Matthews, 1969, p. 118). The counselor should urge family discussions revolving around "why the wife/mother is thinking about work or education; what kind of plans she is mulling over; what kind of changes this may bring about in the home; and what ideas each family member has about possible occupations for her to look into. In this way the family gradually becomes accustomed to the whole idea, has a real feeling of participation, and reaches toward a synthesis of views and plans" (Matthews, 1969, p. 118).

Clearly, it is necessary for a woman to understand and share her own motivations. Counselors of adult women may encounter the nonsupporting and sometimes hostile husband who was inadequately prepared for the inevitable adjustments at home. Owing to faulty communication, the husband may inaccurately conclude that his wife's new aspirations indicate plans to leave him.

Decision Phase[2]

Although some issues involved in the three preparation stages cannot be resolved without ensuing experience, the re-entry woman now faces the

---

[1]Stages 2 and 3 are identical to Phases 1 and 2 in Matthews' (1969) model of vocational counseling for adult women.

[2]Appreciation is extended to David Mahrer for clarifying the stages involved in the Decision Phase.

decision-making process. Rather than narrowly focusing on possible career choices, however, the process should be broadened and viewed as choosing a life style. The woman should be encouraged to take a long-range view of her life, something she has perhaps never attempted previously (White, Note 1). The organizing questions become: "What kind of person do I want to be?" "What life style would be satisfying?" rather than "What kind of job should I look for?"

The counselor must guard against the tendency of women in the decision-making phase to make premature decisions to reduce anxiety. Explaining the life-planning process will provide reassurance that her confusion can be reduced through a logical process, as well as give permission to be in a transition stage, one which involves seeing the self as in process (White, Note 1).

Stage 4: Assessment. Career-development approaches recognize the need to identify abilities and interests. Yet, such identification is no easy task for a woman who has few experiences outside the home, who views her successful years as wife and mother as requiring no special talents, and who downgrades her many accomplishments in various community organizations or in her husband's business because she did not receive payment for these activities. The circular reasoning of "I did this on a volunteer basis without pay; therefore, the skills carry no monetary value" is supported by society's tendency to devalue volunteer activities and work in the home.

A further difficulty of the assessment stage is that women are trained to be modest. Identifying strengths feels like "bragging." Occasionally, low self-esteem women, when asked to specify their own abilities, will, without thinking, point to the talents of their family instead. Such women need concentrated assistance in identifying specific skills. Careful perusal of past and present activities is necessary to help them extract ability areas. Feedback from family and friends is frequently enlightening. Many women who enter the assessment stage with the statement "I'm just a housewife" experience a boost in self-confidence as they begin to identify the specific skills utilized in their family management and volunteer activities. Additionally, they become excited about experimentation activities designed for reality testing.

Stage 5: Generating alternatives. With a clearer assessment of abilities and interests, the re-entry woman is ready to generate options. "What activities will allow me to pursue my interests and use my talents?" During Stage 5, the re-entry woman needs to be encouraged to dream and fantasize. Schlossberg noted that "women, like all groups whose vocational development has been arrested, need special help in stretching, in raising their aspiration level, in raising consciousness," because society has limited their dreaming (1972, p. 137). Similarly, Matthews stated, "Most women need ideas and encouragement in order to experiment in fantasy with the new role of student or worker" (1969, p. 118). Some authors have suggested reasons for the various difficulties women experience in generating alternatives—namely, lack of self-confidence (Shishkoff, 1973; White, Note 1); ability exceeds aspiration level (Fleck, 1968; Hiltunen, 1968); unfamiliarity with the labor market, training opportunities, educational programs (Berry, 1972; Fleck, 1968; Manis & Mochizuki, 1972). It is important that the counselor urge the woman to dream and fantasize as if all things were possible.

Stage 6: Narrowing alternatives and value clarification. Having generated alternatives, the re-entry woman is ready to reduce her options through clarifying life and work values. The basic question is "What alternatives will allow me to implement my preferred life style?"

Value clarification is particularly important for women who have multiple talents and interests. Frequently, they feel confused and view their indecisiveness as a personal inadequacy. While inability to make decisions may be due to dependency and unwillingness to take risks, it may also be the result of lack of knowledge concerning the decision-making process. Teaching the steps in decision-making, particularly noting the relationship between personal values and choices, is essential as well as reassuring (see Friel & Carkhuff, 1974, and Gelatt, Varenhorst, Carey, & Miller, 1973, for excellent discussions of this relationship). A clear assessment of personal values, which includes implicitly a preferred life style, allows each alternative to be evaluated according to specific criteria.

An additional process helpful to Stage 6 is reviewing decisions the person has made in the past:

> Women have often forgotten their earlier motivations and goals set forth for them by other people, including boy friends, girl friends, teachers, and relatives, and it is beneficial to use methods which will recall these memories so that they may lose their power and become simply an out-dated appraisal that may no longer be effective.
>
> Often the woman herself had self-expectations in her younger days that were possibly romantic and unrealistic but, because they were never put to the test of reality, still have an adolescent appeal to them. These, too, must be dealt with by recalling them to memory and examining them in the light of present-day reality (White, Note 1).

Stage 7: Implementation and goal setting. Some women enter Stage 7 with a clear goal. "I want to seek a job in public relations." "I'm going to school and major in business." "I'm going to do volunteer work." Others will have a broad sense of direction but will need to engage in trial experiences. They may audit a course if they anticipate a return to school. They may try out a volunteer job prior to actively seeking paid work. It is important that the woman remain actively engaged in the planning process. Long-range goals may overwhelm her unless she is able to reduce them to manageable short-term goals requiring continuous activity.

Continued support from the counselor and peers also is essential. Those who have participated in a special seminar for adult women have access to supportive peers. Some colleges and universities offer special academic packages for groups of mature students (Anderson, 1974; Brooks, Hines, Davis, & Fleishel, Note 3; Hansot, 1973; Taines, 1973). These special group programs offer the opportunity for the re-entry woman to discover that others share similar concerns. The relief and reinforcement women gain from realizing the commonality of their concerns cannot be over-emphasized. Rarely have they talked in any depth to other women. It is surprising how often they believe that their feelings are unusual and, consequently, that they are abnormal. The impact of sharing concerns with other women is so positive and encouraging that the counselor would do well to make sure some kind of sharing with the other women is arranged.

Less support may be necessary for the re-entry woman who has previously clarified and established her life goals. Her commitment may urge her on regardless of her shaky self-confidence. If she is unclear as to how a difficult or perhaps boring job fits into her life goals other than getting her out of the house, then she not only needs support but also needs help reevaluating her reasons for returning to work.

Bailyn (1965) wrote lucidly about the difficulties women experience with making commitments to work and career. Her thesis is that society has not created the decision to work for women, as it has for men, but rather has created the necessity for a choice. While many women work outside the home because of economic need (U.S. Department of Labor, 1974), the married middle-class re-entry woman may not need to work for financial reasons:

> The fact that a woman functions in a situation in which she may or may not work decreases the likelihood that the choice to work, when made, will be definitive. Commitment may be seriously undermined. All serious work entails drudgery and unrewarding effort, and there are times when anyone—regardless of sex—would welcome a legitimate excuse to stop. When faced with discouragement in her work, it is not difficult for her to discover that her children really do need her all the time or that dilettantism is quite as acceptable as the serious intellectual effort that has bogged down. And, as a matter of fact, a decision to desist would surely have strong social support (Bailyn, 1965, p. 239).

Exposure to other women who have successfully combined homemaking with roles outside the home will provide encouragement. Many women have been exposed only to role models representing one of two extremes—traditional wives and mothers, or full-time career women. Seventy percent of a sample of adult women clients said they could not identify a woman in their lives who had served as a role compromise model (Pincus et al., 1974).

Because of a lack of skills, some women will need further help with implementation: preparing resumes, applying and interviewing for jobs, assertiveness and communication skills frequently are deficit areas. Counselors must be able to not only assess deficit areas but also facilitate their development if the adult woman is to follow her plan through to completion.

The counselor also needs to strike a balance between being an advocate in reducing environmental blocks and encouraging the woman to take active responsibility for her own life.

SPECIAL PROBLEMS OF WOMEN RETURNING TO SCHOOL

Very often women return to school with inadequate preparation. Their motivations and goals may be confused. Some return because they are seeking relief from boredom. Others return because of marital difficulties or as an act of compulsion—i.e., "I must go to school or my life won't be complete (Letchworth, 1970). Family involvement may be incomplete, role conflict may be acute. These women are bound to experience adjustment difficulties. Even the more adequately prepared woman will face fears and doubts as new questions occur with the actual experience of attending classes.

Three issues are particularly salient for women re-entering school: low self-confidence, time management, and role conflict. While the following discussion of these issues is confined to women returning to school, it may be assumed that women entering work outside the home face similar issues.

Low Self-Confidence

The adult woman student may be afraid she cannot compete with the younger student, may be afraid "you can't teach an old dog new tricks," and may not be sure of her academic ability. She truly feels rusty. She does not know what to expect, particularly if she previously had not attended a post-secondary institution.

Intervention. Providing a forum for expressing these anxieties can help disperse the feeling, as well as let the woman find comfort in knowing that others share her concern. While feelings of confidence will gradually develop, interventions in addition to group support will help the process. Study-skill sessions may help the re-entry woman feel more confident; providing interactions with adult students who have "made it" provides encouragement. Simply informing the student that the research indicates adults not only are quite capable of learning but usually do better academically than the younger student (Richter & Whipple, 1972) often is reassuring.

Time Management

Without a doubt, management of time is one of the primary difficulties of the re-entry woman. Many simply attempt to add the additional responsibilities of school to an already full schedule of family and social activities. They begin to feel overwhelmed and at a great loss as to how to manage their time more effectively.

Intervention. Principles of planning ahead and determining priorities can be presented. Some items are essential—for example, sleep and study—and some are preferences but not necessities—for example, keeping the house spotless. The re-entry woman can be urged to consider how time can be saved by using small snatches and by combining tasks. One woman makes her grocery list while waiting for a late professor. Another realizes she can save a car trip by buying groceries on the way home from picking up her pre-school child. Gradually, "They learn to abstract the essentials from the traditional family role and to ignore or allocate to others many other responsibilities" (Katz & Knapp, 1974, p. 108). Women who are willing to share their schedules and needs with their family frequently are surprised at the family cooperation they receive.

Role Conflict and Guilt

A woman may feel conflicted and guilty if unable to attend to her family needs as fully as she had in the past. She may feel selfish and thus question whether she has a right to meet her own needs. At the same time, she feels a strong need to do well academically to prove to both herself and her family that her new venture is worthwhile. Such feelings frequently create conflicting goals—being a Supermom versus getting all A's.

Intervention. Again, open discussion of the issues with peers helps to view the situation realistically. Being a Supermom, for example, could possibly prevent the children's independence. Emphasizing all humans' right to pursue their own interests and redefining selfishness as *always* putting your needs first help the person recognize that no one person's needs are more important than any other's.[3] Re-entry women tend to resolve the role-conflict issue by flexible time scheduling and by assuming the attitude that the roles of wife, mother, and student are not in conflict (Likert, 1967). Assertiveness training and communication-skills training can be especially helpful with women who encounter resistance from their husbands. Sharing self as a person with feelings and needs instead of always playing wife and mother helps involve the family and win their cooperation.

Resistance from husbands can take many forms, from overt hostility to subtle behaviors, such as asking for affection when the wife is studying. Some husbands feel quite supportive until they realize their wife views school more seriously than bridge club and is not as readily available as before. Westervelt (1969) noted that one sample of adult women students all stated their husbands were supportive of their return to school, yet only one-third received active help at home.

---

[3]The author is indebted to Patricia Jakubowski for clarifying this distinction.

CONCLUSIONS AND GUIDELINES

One day in the future, when sex-role stereotypes are minimal and both males and females are encouraged to think in terms of multiple roles, special counseling services and continuing education programs for the re-entry woman will no longer be necessary. Society will have accepted and will allow choices on the basis of individual interests and abilities rather than sex. In the meantime, re-entry women face special issues and can profit from interaction with counselors attuned to their unique needs.

The theme of this article has been that re-entry women are involved in a normal, transitional state that is resolved through a series of stages. Counselors should be prepared to facilitate women who enter counseling at any stage, from vague discontent to lack of knowledge concerning the labor market. For women who do not seek services voluntarily, preventive outreach programs geared to issues representative of the various stages are both appropriate and effective. Preventive programs that emphasize "efforts to decrease people's vulnerability to specific stresses and . . . to reduce these stresses at their source" can effectively inhibit the aggravation of later symptoms (Bloom, 1973, p. 14).

One frequent type of preventive program is a special group offered to women in the community. Re-entry women, seriously considering potential role changes, can benefit perhaps most from group experience with other women sharing similar concerns. Such an approach provides a supportive socialization aid necessary for successful role changes (Brim, 1968). It is noteworthy that women tend to prefer group seminars over individual counseling (White, Note 1).

As counselors plan services, they need to keep in mind that re-entry women may be leery of services associated with "women's liberation" or feminism. While they are seeking change, most want to "embrace traditional as well as self-fulfilling roles" (Manis & Mochizuki, 1972, p. 599). An approachable counseling service, consequently, must be nonideological and at the same time encourage women to seek fulfilling roles based on their individual needs and abilities. Counselors who readily recognize the influence of sex-role stereotypes on women's choices must be careful not to be biased against choices that retain traditional roles. Biased counseling, both positive and negative in nature, may effectively restrict viable choices and inhibit the freedom to explore a wide range of options.

In addition to a nonideological service, counselors also need to recognize that the confusion and depression that many re-entry women experience are not neurotic or deep-seated in nature. Rather, they may stem from situational stresses that can be alleviated by a counseling approach that focuses on current problems, is reality based, and encourages realistic self-appraisal and goal-setting (Manis & Mochizuki, 1972). The overriding counseling goal may be conceived of as choosing a life style. "A life style is an overall way of looking at the world . . . it provides a framework for choices throughout a life span. . . . In using this concept, the counselor assists each client in learning how to make choices whenever she is confronted with them rather than selecting a single course of action" (Eason, 1972, p. 132).

In summary, effective counseling for re-entry women is nonideological, is nonbiased in nature, and is prepared to facilitate the woman at every stage in the re-entry process. Additionally, the counselor views her as "in transition" and accordingly offers services focusing on effective decision-making toward choosing a life style.

REFERENCE NOTES

1. White, M.S. *Intervention in women's transitional stages.* Paper presented at Conference on Human Development: Issues in Intervention, Pennsylvania State University, College of Human Development, May 30-June 2, 1973.
2. Driver, E. *Self-exploration: The necessary first step.* Paper presented at Multi-Faceted Women's Center Conference, Continuum Center, Oakland University, October 26, 1973.
3. Brooks, L., Hines, R., Davis, B., & Fleishel, P. *Recycling lives: Meeting the developmental needs of mature students.* Paper presented at American College Personnel Association Convention, Atlanta, March 1975.

REFERENCES

Anderson, D. DeAnza builds a "Wreputation." *American Education,* 1974, *10*(4), 30-33.
Bailyn, L. Notes on the role of choice in the psychology of professional women. In R.J. Lifton (Ed.), *The woman in America.* Boston: Houghton Mifflin, 1965.
Bedell, M. We are never tired; we are never afraid; but, oh, the guilt! *Ms.,* 1973, *1*(11), 84-87.
Berry, J. Educational innovation and an era. In National Vocational Guidance Association, *Counseling girls and women over the life span.* National Vocational Guidance Association Monograph, 1972, 75-87.
Blimline, C.A. The emerging woman: A profile. *Journal of National Association of Women Deans, Administrators, and Counselors,* 1974, *38,* 38-40.
Bloom, B.L. *Community mental health: A historical and critical analysis.* Morristown, N.J.: General Learning Press, 1973.
Brim, O.G., Jr. Adult socialization. In J.A. Clausen (Ed.), *Socialization and society.* Boston: Little, Brown and Company, 1968.
Eason, J. Life style counseling for a reluctant leisure class. *Personnel and Guidance Journal,* 1972, *51,* 127-132.
Fleck, H. Changing patterns for women. *Forecast for Home Economics,* 1968, *14,* 71.
Friedan, B. *The feminine mystique.* New York: Dell Publishing Co., 1963.
Friel, T.W., & Carkhuff, R.R. *The art of developing a career: A helper's guide.* Amherst: Human Resource Development Press, 1974.
Gelatt, H.B., Varenhorst, B., Carey, R., & Miller, G.P. *Decisions and outcomes: A leader's guide.* New York: College Entrance Examination Board, 1973.
Goodman, J., Walworth, S., & Walters, E. "Down with the maintenance stage": Career development for adults. *Impact,* 1975, *3*(6), 44-51.
Hansot, E. A "second-chance" program for women. *Change,* 1973, *5*(1), 49-51.

Hiltunen, W.A. A counseling course for the mature woman. *Journal of National Association of Women Deans and Counselors,* 1968, *31,* 93-96.

Katz, J.K., & Knapp, N.H. Housewife, mother, other: Needs and helpers. *Personnel and Guidance Journal,* 1974, *53,* 105-109.

Letchworth, G.E. Women who return to college: An identity-integrity approach. *Journal of College Student Personnel,* 1970, *11,* 103-106.

Likert, J.G. (Ed.). *Conversations with returning women students.* Ann Arbor: University of Michigan Center for Continuing Education of Women, 1967.

Lipman-Blumen, J. Editorial statement. *Personnel and Guidance Journal,* 1975, *53,* 680.

Manis, L.G., & Mochizuki, J. Search for fulfillment: A program for adult women. *Personnel and Guidance Journal,* 1972, *50,* 594-599.

Matthews, E.E. The counselor and the adult woman. *Journal of National Association of Women Deans and Counselors,* 1969, *32,* 115-122.

Pincus, C., Radding, N., & Lawrence, R. A professional counseling service for women. *Social Work,* 1974, *19,* 187-195.

Richter, M.L., & Whipple, J.B. *A revolution in the education of women: Ten years of continuing education at Sarah Lawrence College.* Bronxville, N.Y.: Sarah Lawrence College, 1972.

Schlossberg, N.K. A framework for counseling women. *Personnel and Guidance Journal,* 1972, *51*(2), 137-143.

Seay, R. (Ed.). *The continuum center for women: Education, volunteerism, employment.* Battle Creek, Mich.: W.K. Kellog Foundation, 1973.

Shishkoff, M.M. Counseling mature women for careers. *Journal of National Association of Women Deans and Counselors,* 1973, *36,* 173-177.

Taines, B. Older women, newer students. *Community and Junior College Journal,* 1973, *44,* 17.

U.S. Department of Labor, Employment Standards Administration, Women's Bureau. *Twenty facts on women workers,* 1974.

Weissman, M., Pincus, C., Radding, N., Lawrence, R., & Siegel, R. The educated housewife: Mild depression and the search for work. *American Journal of Orthopsychiatry,* 1973, *43,* 565-573.

Westervelt, E. From evolution to revolution. In proceedings of *An imperative for the seventies: Releasing creative woman power,* June 15-27, 1969. St. Louis, Mo.: University of Missouri at St. Louis, Extension Division, 1969.

Counseling "Single-Again" (Divorced and Widowed) Women

ALICE L. ASLIN
University of Missouri—St. Louis

While it is widely known that the divorce rate in this country is growing, there is also a pervasive anti-divorce tradition. Indeed many divorcing people are faced with being judged as either "adulterous, criminal, neurotic, immature, or at best frivolous and unfortunate" (Gettleman & Markowitz, 1974, p. 15). Psychotherapists have advanced an additional assumption—namely, that divorce and the death of a spouse are analogous. Fisher (1973) summarizes this perspective: "Divorce is the death of the marriage: the husband and wife together with the children are mourners, the lawyers are the undertakers, the court is the cemetery where the coffin is sealed and the dead marriage is buried" (p. 55).

The death analogy is used to explain the traumatic process of divorce for both men and women. To understand the reasons women apparently find divorce more traumatic, theoreticians proposed that the woman's identity is traditionally tied to the family and marriage (Bardwick, 1971; Lopata, 1971), thus she experiences greater loss. Recently, however, humanists and feminists have cast divorce in the perspective of a creative, growth-oriented process. They point out the personal strength required to separate and to endure the social consequences of divorce. Gettleman and Markowitz (1974) predicted that the social expectation that divorce will be traumatic and devastating results in people actually experiencing it that way.

These perspectives seem to each have some validity but cannot explain the traumatized divorcing woman seen in therapy, whose accustomed ways of acting as a wife and mother are no longer adequate. She may be experiencing the mourning process of a marital death, the negative reflection from a social anti-divorce tradition and the growing process of self-examination and change. But many women experience much more; they respond to the loss of their wife role and the demands of a new single-woman role for which they are

The author gratefully acknowledges the valuable assistance received from Sue and Joe Ruebel.

unprepared. In this regard divorced women's experiences are identical to those of widows and can be treated similarly. This perspective maintains that divorce and widowhood are traumatic for women primarily because their accustomed ways of coping as a wife are no longer appropriate and they have not been socialized to function unmarried.

Woman's traditional socialization focused on gaining all her sense of identity from the wife and mother roles. These roles were summarized by Stevens (1971) as essentially the role of nonbeing: "These roles are intrinsically passive. They require the subjugation of oneself to the needs of others—a husband and children" (p. 13). In addition to overtly not developing her own identity via a career or other important involvements with society, she is programmed to find her identity covertly through her man. Specifically the division of marital sex-roles has meant that the wife is dependent on her husband for economic support, for social status, for all interactions with societal institutions, for emotional satisfaction and for companionship and conversation. Thus traditional female socialization yields women unprepared to function as autonomous adults. "Women have been taught to feel ashamed of their own self-seeking, to feel guilty if they do something significant for themselves. . . . Women need help in learning to think about and plan for themselves, having so long been considered the mirror of men's experience" (Walstedt, 1971, p. 9). Additionally, traditional socialization conditions women to be nonassertive and indecisive. Through an extensive examination of specific personality and behavioral items reported by women and through surveys of mental-health impairment, Bernard (1971) found that married women appear to be more psychologically damaged than single women. She concluded that the role of wife, traditionally conceived as a sexual object and helpmate, is dysfunctional for women.

Lopata (1973) pointed out that most wives do not develop their lives for single status. "None of the research indicates that women who enter marriage organize their plans with the expectation of having to phase out of this role through divorce or widowhood" (Lopata, 1973, p. 41). Thus, in counseling divorced or widowed women, it is crucial to be alert to the multiplicity of the separating process and the ways women may not be prepared to be single. Bohannan (1970) suggested that at least six processes are occurring: emotional, legal, economic, parental, community or social, and psychic. Focusing on any one or a combination of these six areas, the counselor assists the single-again woman in working through the trauma of losing her wife identity and coping autonomously (summarized in Table 1).

EMOTIONAL ISSUES

The emotional phase of terminating the wife role and gaining a psychological maturity as a single woman may occur at different times in the divorcing process. Some women will have completed emotional separation before the legal or even physical separation occurs. Others may be emotionally dependent long after contact with the former husband ceases and

Table 1. Loss of "Wife" Role.

PROCESS[1]	Stereotypic Wife Behavior	Disorganization Caused by Loss of Role (Divorce and Widowhood)	Counseling Needs	Single-Again Role
EMOTIONAL	Cheerful, childlike, tender, sympathetic, accommodating.	Hurt, anger, abandonment, rejection.	Contact with others to share feelings and gain sense of personal emotional identity.	Emotionally mature and autonomous functioning.
LEGAL	Uninformed about and uninvolved in legal process.	Bewilderment, loss of control, experiencing of discrimination or intimidation by lawyers or legal process.	Assertiveness training, support to gain legal information.	Active, informed, participant in securing her legal rights.
ECONOMIC	Unthinking consumer, dependent on husband as "bread winner," credit reference, and financial planner.	Division of money and property, feeling cheated, unprepared to be self-supporting.	Job training and finding; financial skills, recognition of her financial contribution to marriage.	Independent, financially self-directed and skilled.
PARENTAL	Nurturing, overly responsible and protective.	Guilt and worry about children. Using children to fight marital battles.	Consultation to assist children adjust. Workable relationship with father and paternal family.	Empathic and loving relationship with children.
COMMUNITY (SOCIAL)	Status and relationships dependent on husband or children. Homebound	Loss of or new relationship with friends. End of couple contacts.	Understanding others' reactions. Options for new relationships.	Friendships and social support system.
PSYCHIC	Non-assertive.	Afraid, lonely, mourning.	Griefwork. Beginning "new" life.	Purposefulness, security, and confidence.

[1]Column 1 is adapted from *Divorce and After*, by Paul Bohannan. Copyright © 1970 by Paul Bohannan. Reprinted by permission of Doubleday & Company, Inc.

will probably remarry rapidly. Likewise, some widows, particularly those whose husbands experienced lengthy illness, will have emotionally terminated their wife role, while others may not.

Both widows and divorcées, however, experience similar feelings at some point in the process. There may be much hurt and pain at the death of the relationship and at the loss of the wife's familiar duties and habits. Some feel abandoned and rejected and are angry at the former husband regardless of whether he died or was divorced. Often women generalize, distrusting and withdrawing from other intimate relationships.

Counseling within a homogeneous group is often indicated for divorced and widowed women with psychological concerns. Sharing helps the counselee overcome the sense that her pain, loneliness and fear are unique. She gains support from the strengths obvious in the other women and can begin to understand that she will again feel happy and purposeful. Women's groups seem to allow for free verbalization of feelings of isolation, worthlessness, loneliness and helplessness, as well as feelings of independence, strength, power and identity. Since women are socialized to validate their worth through being accepted and loved by others, their identification with other women may facilitate development of a powerful sense of self.

Although society supposes that divorced people will be enemies, this is not always the case. Some women may be neutral toward former husbands and able to formulate viable relationships with them. Society also predicts that both divorcées and widows will feel abandoned and rejected, while in fact some may feel liberated and happy. Gettleman and Markowitz (1974) stated that in their experiences "after an initial period of confusion or depression, almost without exception [people] look and feel better than ever before. They act warmer and more related to others emotionally" (p. 45).

LEGAL ISSUES

The changing legal status of the single-again woman may arise as an issue in counseling. While it is not advisable for counselors to dispense legal advice, it is important that they be informed of state laws and encourage clients to gain accurate information. Thus, by uncovering the mysteries of the law, single-again women may feel and behave with more assertiveness and control. Many women will initially be reluctant to question their lawyer. If the lawyer is male, the woman may feel that he is identifying more with the husband. The counseling psychologist may use assertive-training techniques and role playing to encourage the client to be an active participant in the legal system. Counselors must be particularly alert to legal issues regarding child custody with lesbian divorcées or women with unconventional life styles. Counselor and client may explore together potential legal impediments to distinguish them from rationalizations or feelings of being victimized. Since the counselor "cannot artificially separate, for example, a divorced mother's emotional concerns from the legal 'danger' she may be in" (Gettleman & Markowitz, 1974, p. 145), professional legal consultation may be indicated.

ECONOMIC ISSUES

The economic divorce for many women will be based on the reality of ending a marriage where the husband contributed the monetary support while the wife performed the domestic duties. Initially many women will feel that they did not earn a share of the marital profits (savings, stocks, and other financial assets). The counselor may encourage the woman to consider the value of her work as a homemaker—identifying the tasks she performed and estimating their value on the open market may illustrate this point. The worksheet presented in Table 2 may aid women to re-estimate their financial contribution to the marriage.

Table 2. Worksheet: My Worth as a Housewife.

Occupation	Time per Week	Hourly Rate	Total
Food buyer			
Nurse			
Tutor			
Waitress			
Seamstress			
Maintenance worker			
Lover			
Nanny			
Cleaning woman			
Cook			
Housekeeper			
Laundress			
Chauffeur			
Gardener			
Counselor			
Errand runner			
Bookkeeper			
Interior decorator			
Caterer			
Animal caretaker			
Purchasing agent			
Receptionist			
Social secretary			

Adapted from *The Washington Post,* March 17, 1974, Potomac section, p. 13. Copyright © 1974 The Washington Post. Reprinted by permission.

Secondly, the counselor may assist divorced women in dealing with feelings of being vulnerable and trapped if they remain financially dependent on their ex-husbands. The possibility that this may not be a workable long-term solution should be examined in view of the observation that within one year only 38% of ex-husbands are providing fully the court-ordered child support and/or alimony and 79% make no payments at all by the tenth year (Gettleman & Markowitz, 1974, p. 225). Though the Uniform Reciprocal Support Act makes it possible for a woman to find a former husband who has moved to another state and stopped paying, the procedure is complicated, costly and does not guarantee payment. Some may elect to remain dependent only for the time period necessary to be trained, re-trained or secure a job. Career-planning workshops or certainly vocational and educational guidance are indicated. Since employers may consider the divorced woman a "bad risk"—"she'll marry again and quit her job"—information about recourses to job discrimination against women may be pertinent. Since society tends to view women's financial status in terms of their marital status, women need to be particularly assertive in convincing lenders that they are creditworthy and referred to legal resources when discrimination occurs. Educating women to establish independent credit ratings, file income tax, budget, invest and purchase insurance may be accomplished in workshops with consultation from a financial manager.

PARENTAL ISSUES

Perhaps one of the most difficult areas of adjusting to the single-again role is the adjustment to being mother without father, as is the case for widows; being mother without "full-time" father, when the divorced woman gains custody; or mother without "full-time" children, when father is granted custody. The basis for much difficulty lies in the myth that children are damaged by a one-parent upbringing regardless of the quality of the parenting and the assistance provided the child in coping. Again the societal anti-divorce indoctrination creates problems for that child if he or she experiences isolation, disapproval or the expectation that he or she will be disturbed or delinquent.

Initially the counselor may provide consultation to the single-again woman to make the children's adjustment as untraumatic as possible. The counselor may provide support and guidance to the widow as she copes with her children's mourning. Additionally, the counselor may alert a single-again widow to the reality that her duties as mother change with the loss of the father. Lopata (1973) suggests that

> the void caused by his absence could be filled by the mother attempting to undertake all his duties and rights, by the children undertaking segments of the father's roles, by people outside of the nuclear family serving as substitutes or by some aspects of the father's role being dropped completely (pp. 97-98).

In contrast, the divorced woman needs merely to help her children understand that the "child's parents are divorced from each other—not from the child" (Bohannan, 1970, p. 45). Children tend to mirror their parents' emotions, so that the best prognosis is for the child with psychologically strong parents who are empathic and loving.

More divorcing women today are considering whether they or the child's father should take custody, even though the cultural policy endorses mother-custody. The counselor may be particularly supportive in sorting out the feelings of guilt and failure, the realities of what is best for both child and parent and the social pressures that may make it impossible for the mother to relinquish custody.

Additionally the counseling psychologist may assist the divorced mother to develop and maintain a workable relationship with the ex-husband. This does not mean disguising feelings just to be overtly friendly for the sake of the children. It does mean to refrain from sabotaging the other parent's relationship with the child and to not use the child as a weapon or pawn in the parental struggles. Instead, the formerly married can be guided to support the child's attachment to each parent even though the parents have differences. Similarly, children should not be deprived of existing relationships with grandparents and other paternal or maternal relatives. In essence, divorcing parents should be guided to support the child's pre-existing ties and support systems.

COMMUNITY OR SOCIAL ISSUES

A woman whose social relationships were established on her wife role will usually experience much disruption in her "couple" contacts. Those who maintained their own identities and relations will find many of their involvements continuing. As Goode (1956) noted, "the post divorce (or post-wife) adjustment process, then, is one by which a disruption of role sets and patterns, and of existing social relations, is incorporated into the individual's life pattern" (p. 19). Most single-again women will experience that there are "no clear directives, external or internal, as to . . . her appropriate behavior or feelings" (Hunt, 1966, p. 40). Family and friends may be sympathetic, jealous of her new freedoms, or project that the single-again woman is a failure, crazy or inadequate. Likewise, male acquaintances may be seductive, fatherly, frightened that she's husband-hunting or angered if she isn't. Most women will need much time to sort out the numerous and conflicting responses they receive. Since the single-again status is ambiguous and non-institutionalized, the woman will experience conflicting expectations and perceptions of her. She also may feel left out or like the "fifth wheel" as she attempts to participate as a single person in our couple-oriented society.

Most single-again women gain insight and learn coping strategies from sharing these experiences with other women. Hunt (1966) predicted that

> they will shortly find that they are part of a large, half-hidden society in
> which they will rapidly become comfortable and at ease—an underground

subculture of which they knew nothing in advance, a veritable World of Formerly Married, with its own rules of conduct, its own mechanisms for bringing people together, . . . its own opportunities for friendship, social life and love (p. 4).

The counselor should be aware of and point out the possible traps to successful social adjustment as a single person. Krantzler (1973) suggested that such traps include unwarranted generalizations, unreal expectations, self-fulfilling prophecies, disasterizing, attempting to live through others, attempting to escape oneself, and using another person to make one feel whole again (pp. 109-116).

PSYCHIC ISSUES

The psychic process according to Bohannan (1970) includes reactions of fear, despair and loneliness. This may be experienced by the widow months after the death of the spouse as the process of mourning ends and the realization of her single condition strikes. The divorced woman who did not want or was ambivalent about the separation may experience much anguish and loneliness over the loss of companionship. Such feelings occur most strongly during traditional family-oriented times—holidays, weekends, anniversaries and other special occasions. Counselors alert to these crisis periods may assist the client in initiating special plans or events to support her during these times.

While much of the process of losing the wife role and gaining a single-again identity is similar for divorced and widowed women, some differences are noteworthy. Obviously the finality of death makes the widow's reactions less ambiguous than those of the divorcée who, with some reality, may entertain ideas of reuniting with the husband. Thus, the grief and bereavement process may be part of the counseling process with widows. Parks (1965) found that the "typical reaction to bereavement" starts with phases of numbness, followed by wave-like attacks of distress and yearning interspersed with depression and feelings of futility. Some widows may report no feelings of grief.

Lyman (1971) reported that the recovery time is faster at first for the divorced woman, as she is pushed by the need to prove herself. However, it may take longer for her to re-establish a fulfilling life with satisfying social relationships. In contrast, the widow may initially need much encouragement to face the task of planning a new life.

While most single-again women will go through a period of readjusting to the facts of single life, some will not cope so readily. The counselor must be alert to signs of severe psychological stress and failure to cope, such as extreme withdrawal, obsessive or compulsive behavior and severe depression. Such signs may suggest psychological dysfunction beyond the potentially debilitating trauma of being single again. Thus, for some, more traditional modalities such as intensive individual psychotherapy, chemotherapy or hospitalization may be indicated. For counselors unfamiliar with the stresses experienced by persons becoming single again, it may be difficult to discriminate between typical behavior associated with this personal crisis and the behavior characterizing severe psychological problems. Consultation with professionals attuned to the being-single-again process seems indicated, since misjudgment either way may have debilitating effects. Clearly the unrecognized and untreated psychological problems will have negative repercussions for the client. Conversely, the woman experiencing the universal trauma of being divorced or widowed needs to recognize the "normalcy" of what she is experiencing, which includes her getting the message that she'll make it through the process and that she isn't a failure, crazy or inadequate in human relationships.

ISSUES FOR COUNSELORS

The counseling psychologist's attitudes are particularly important in dealing with women who have lost the wife role. A therapist who supports the normative expectation that a female be primarily wife and mother will at least subtly communicate this attitude to her. Thus, the therapist may reinforce the client's sense of failure and lost identity and even encourage her to desperately find another mate rather than to be assertive and develop herself socially and intellectually.

Additionally, many therapists are trained to view crisis and unhappiness as a product of individual disorder. They may project that the client has basic personality and character faults rendering her incapable of maintaining a marital relationship. Likewise, they may view a woman's struggle to overcome her sex-role socialization and to function autonomously as her inability to have an intimate interaction (i.e. dependence) with a man. Such person-oriented perspectives ignore the social content and prejudice affecting the single-again woman's growth. As Whiteley (1973) pointed out, therapy is not to help women adjust to their "femininity" as traditionally defined but rather to help women to develop their individuality.

The therapist's marital status (unmarried, married or single-again) may significantly affect perceptions and treatment of the single-again woman. Some may feel threatened by realizations that divorce or death of a spouse may happen to them. Others may be repelled by the struggles for autonomy of the single-again woman. Others may realize their own insecurity or aloneness and may feel inadequate and fearful in comparison to the woman's situation, feelings, or strengths.

DIVORCED WOMEN'S WORKSHOP—ONE APPROACH

Across the country, counseling centers and programs for women are offering workshops and groups focused on women becoming single again. Some, such as the Divorced Women's Workshop offered by the University of

Missouri—St. Louis Extension Division, utilize a one-day format and employ lawyers and accountants to provide specialized information. Additionally, group members are encouraged to share personal feelings and to develop action plans for their future lives. Participants seem to benefit particularly from sharing information about opportunities and alternatives available to single-again women.

The more homogeneous the group is, the more effective such workshops tend to be. Thus, if the women's ages, educational backgrounds, employment experiences, and presence and ages of children are similar, the discussions can be more focused, productive and cover a wider range of issues. For example, the divorce experience of a 30-year-old PhD with a career and no children will be considerably different from those of a 60-year-old woman who has never been employed and who has grown children. Likewise, issues for a woman considering divorce will differ from those confronting a woman who has completed the legal aspects of divorce and is already coping with the realities of being alone. To achieve homogeneity, workshops may be focused toward particular populations such as working women or divorcées who have completed the legalities of divorce.

SUMMARY

Counseling psychologists intervening with divorced and widowed women should recognize the trauma associated with losing the wife role and the failure of traditional female socialization to prepare most women for more assertive, autonomous functioning. From this theoretical perspective, counseling approaches and programs should prepare "single-again" women to replace stereotypic female behavior with emotional, legal, economic, parental, social and psychic coping behaviors. Specific programs for "single-again" women may range from women's groups and divorced women's workshops to career planning, legal information and financial-management programs. The counselor can assist women to develop from the wife role, through the traumatic "no role" state of divorce or widowhood, to the establishment of independent personal identity.

REFERENCES

Bardwick, J.M. *Psychology of women: A study of bio-cultural conflicts.* New York: Harper & Row, 1971.

Bernard, J. The paradox of the happy marriage. In V. Gornick, & B. Moran (Eds.), *Women in sexist society: Studies in power and powerlessness.* New York: Basic Books, 1971.

Bohannan, P. (Ed.). *Divorce and after.* New York: Doubleday, 1970.

Fisher, E.O. A guide to divorce counseling. *The Family Coordinator,* 1973, *22*(1), 55.

Gettleman, S., & Markowitz, J. *The courage to divorce.* New York: Simon and Schuster, 1974.

Goode, W.J. *Women in divorce.* New York: The Free Press, 1956.

Hunt, M.M. *The world of the formerly married.* New York: McGraw-Hill, 1966.

Krantzler, M. *Creative divorce*. New York: M. Evans and Co., 1973.

Lopata, H.Z. *Occupation: Housewife*. New York: Oxford University Press, 1971.

Lopata, H.Z. *Widowhood in an American city*. Cambridge, Mass.: Schenkman Publishing, 1973.

Lyman, H.B. *Single again*. New York: David McKay, 1971.

Parks, C.M. Bereavement and mental illness: A clinical study. *British Journal of Medical Psychology*, 1965, *38*, 1-26.

Stevens, B. The psychotherapist and women's liberation. *Social Work*, 1971, *16*,12-18.

Walstedt, J.J. *The anatomy of oppression: A feminist analysis of psychotherapy*. Pittsburgh, Pa.: KNOW, Inc., 1971.

Whiteley, R.M. Women in groups. *The Counseling Psychologist*, 1973, *4*(1), 27-43.

The Myth of the Perfect Mother

BOBBIE L. WILBORN
North Texas State University

The female in our culture must make many decisions regarding the bearing and rearing of children, and the primary decision, of course, is whether or not to become a mother at all. Many women now have the freedom to make that decision, some do not. Children come into families in various ways, such as by birth, by adoption, and by marriage. Once there is a mother-child dyad established, however, many mothers exhibit a belief in a peculiarly contemporary myth that it is possible—in fact, necessary—to be a perfect mother. If she achieves that perfection, the mother raises a perpetually cooperative, happy, and perfect child.

The popular literature which has bombarded mothers in recent years has brought about an awareness that mothers greatly influence their child's personality, and that realization appears to have led to the belief that mothers carry full responsibility for every aspect of their child's development and behavior. The mother may understand that she serves as a model for her child's life, but she must project an unswerving image of perfection and control of every situation (Dinkmeyer & McKay, 1973). The mere sight of a child who is less than perfect becomes for the mother a message of her own failure and leads to self-blame (Dreikurs & Soltz, 1964).

In truth, there is no perfect mother; but, even if perfection were attainable, the mother and child would experience many moments of pain and frustration as new feelings and experiences come into the life of the developing child. The mother must learn to acknowledge and accept the child's right to experience these developmental processes and to receive the ultimate learning from them without undue parental expectations of perfection.

It is the concept of development itself which counselors are often called upon to help mothers understand; development means becoming, not being. Many mothers need help to understand that, as development takes place, there are peaks of happiness and good behavior and depths of sadness and misbehavior, and neither can be counted on. When a child does not live up to expectations, the mother may feel guilt and disappointment, but, in taking so much blame for the child, the mother is giving herself and her child needless pain. The mother needs to understand her developing child and how to establish a relationship with the child that permits freedom and growth for both of them and yet maintains order in their environment.

Lack of knowledge of how to develop a warm and understanding relationship as she also learns to understand and control the behavior of another developing individual is of concern to many mothers. Problems which children present are increasing in frequency and intensity, and many mothers do not know how to cope with them. They somehow know that children cannot be treated as they were in the past, but they do not know what else they can do. The ability to cope with this crisis must be resolved in a satisfactory manner, or it is a continuing source of frustration for the mother who attempts to fulfill the myth of perfection. The author's experience and that of others (Dinkmeyer & McKay, 1973; Dreikurs & Soltz, 1964; Grey, 1974; Satir, 1972) indicate it is this crisis of mother-child relationship which brings many mothers to counseling centers. It is a crisis sometimes unrecognized by a mother on her initial contact with a counselor, because she often does not distinguish the disruptive effect of this stressful and faulty relationship from her general feelings of helplessness or anxiety.

It is not fair to identify such a major crisis of motherhood and isolate the problem from the crisis of parenthood. The relationships of both parents with their children are crucial, and the myth of perfect parenting also affects fathers. It is imperative that fathers, too, understand how to develop positive relationships with their children and that they realize that expectations of perfection are unfair and detrimental to parent and child. Our society, however, puts the greater pressure on women to be perfect mothers owing to the still existing cultural expectations of the female's role in child rearing; therefore, the focus of this article will be on the mother's role as a parent.

SOCIETAL PRESSURES

It is society's expectation of what good mothers should be that is the basis for many of the problems of mothers, and this in turn is related to the myth of the perfect mother. The modeling that girls have received in preparation for motherhood has been from their mothers and their perceptions of their mothers; child rearing always has been based on tradition. In past generations mothers were the essence of the home they wove around the family. Even if they had special skills beyond baking, cleaning, and sewing, they put them aside to raise their families.

As our present generation of women have become mothers, many of them have discovered that what they thought a mother should be and the kind of mother they are capable of being are quite different. If there is one thing motherhood seems to have taught those mothers who seek counseling it is that a mother has little status in her own right. The value of what used to be some of mother's most important work has been drastically curtailed by modern technology. Some mothers find satisfaction within the boundaries of the home by pursuing individual interests which are beyond family care and which are personally enhancing. Other mothers come from an environment which allows or requires them to seek employment outside the home. All of these women share the fact that motherhood may be frustrating unless the mother can perceive herself as a worthwhile person apart from motherhood.

Our present generation of mothers appears to be the most confused that our society has known (Dinkmeyer & McKay, 1973; Dreikurs & Cassel, 1972; Dreikurs & Grey, 1970; Grey, 1974). It is a common assumption that the only training most mothers have had for becoming a parent is to have been a child. The typical mother today, therefore, may tend to be a relatively autocratic parent who is attempting to use techniques for child control that were effective when she was a child. Most mothers seem vaguely aware that in our present democratic social system children have quickly caught on to the idea that they can and do share in the quest for equal rights—equality meaning equal worth with equal claims of dignity and respect. We find mothers speaking and behaving from a position of authority, while children are listening and acting from a position of equality. Thus there is a great gap in communicating and understanding. When these old methods of authority intensify rebellious behavior rather than bring children's behavior under control, mothers feel like failures and realize they are not living up to the myth of the perfect mother (Dreikurs & Soltz, 1964). The attempt to adhere to an outmoded model of family roles and of child rearing often leads to the labeling as pathological of what is actually a transitional situation of family conflict.

FAMILIES IN TRANSITION

Our society is in a state of change, and, therefore, the role and expectations of the family, which must always accommodate to society, are changing with it. Owing to transitional difficulties, the family's major psychosocial task—to nurture its members—has become more important than ever. Only society's smallest unit, the family, can change and still maintain enough continuity to raise children who will be able to adapt to society's demands.

The structure of the family is an open sociocultural system which adapts to changed circumstances to enhance the psychosocial growth of each member (Minuchin, 1974). The family structure is a set of interaction patterns which organize the transactions among family members. Repeated transactions establish the patterns that are fundamental to the system, and these regulate the family members' behavior. Individual behavior of the family members is best understood in terms of its pattern and its results. The individual's decisions about what is deemed necessary to gain importance in the family are displayed in transactions with other family members (Adler, 1957).

Our current societal expectations of equality have brought about changes in the levels of power within a family. The old tradition of autocratically raising children is no longer effective in a democratic society. Parents have to learn new ways of dealing with children because relationships have changed. The unquestioned authority that once characterized the parental role is being replaced by a flexible and rational authority. Parents are expected to understand children's developmental needs and to explain the rules they impose. Parenting is an extremely difficult process which is seldom experienced with complete personal satisfaction. In today's complex, fast-developing society, in which generation gaps occur at smaller and smaller intervals, parenting difficulties have increased.

MOTHER'S ROLE

As society and the family are in transition, so is the role of the mother in transition. The role of the mother in our society is often misunderstood (Dreikurs & Soltz, 1964). A mother may feel that, in order to fulfill her role, she must dominate family affairs and be able to control her children. She may feel personally responsible for everything they do and believe her child's misbehavior or lack of success is a reflection on her abilities as a mother and her worth as a person. The mother's need for personal prestige prevents her from letting the child fail or make mistakes and thereby robs the child of opportunities for experiencing personal strength and self-sufficiency.

The mother may feel that to be successful she must do everything for the sake of the child. If her motives were purely altruistic, however, she would be less concerned about her image as a perfect mother and more devoted to promoting feelings of adequacy in her children. Rather than applying pressures that only prove her self-worth, she would try to stimulate a sense of cooperation and responsibility within the children. A child learns responsibility by experiencing it, by being given the opportunity to make a decision within the limits of age and experience and to live with the consequences of that decision. The child's freedom to choose and the feelings of satisfaction from a job well done, or the realization of the consequences of a poor choice or failure at a task, will help the child attain the long-range goal of responsible adulthood.

Many mothers may feel they must protect their children, even though children can cope with many more areas of life than the mother is able to allow. A mother who overprotects and unnecessarily does things for her child views the child as incapable of dealing with life. She not only prevents the child from accepting responsibility but is actually dependent on the child for her own feelings of importance. Mothers may feel they are useless unless they keep themselves constantly in the service of their children (Dinkmeyer & McKay, 1973).

Most children react with discouragement to the standards and methods of the mother who tries to be perfect. Since they cannot live up to the mother's standards, they lose confidence in themselves and become irresponsible, or they feel defeated and become helpless.

Mothers, too, frequently feel inadequate, since they experience little success in influencing their children to behave and to perform as they believe they should. Mothers often feel ineffective and unappreciated. Discouraged mothers further discourage children, and the discouragement leads to faulty interactions which disrupt the mother-child relationship. It is these discouraged mothers who seek help in understanding their problems.

STRATEGIES FOR BEHAVIOR CHANGE

The personality theory and therapeutic system of Individual Psychology as developed by Alfred Adler have proven to be an effective counseling model for working with mothers who are struggling to free themselves from the myth of perfection.

> Adlerian Psychology . . . is socio-teleological and views man holistically as a creative, responsible, "becoming" individual moving toward fictional goals within his phenomenal field. It holds that man's self- and life-perceptions, his life-style, are sometimes self-defeating because of inferiority feelings. The individual with "psychopathology" is discouraged rather than sick, and the therapeutic task is to encourage him, to activate his social interest and to develop a new life-style through relationship, analysis, and action methods (Mosak & Dreikurs, 1973, p. 35).

The strategies recommended in this article are based on a specific philosophy of life and a distinctive concept of man as it has been presented by Alfred Adler and his co-workers, principally Rudolf Dreikurs. The methods have proven effective for many years while in use in counseling centers, therapeutic social clubs, multiple psychotherapy, group therapy, marriage therapy, family therapy, parent study groups, educational settings, and community outreach programs (Dreikurs, 1946, 1948; Mosak, 1973; Mosak & Dreikurs, 1973). The methods have proven effective for the solution of family conflicts and for helping mothers learn to free themselves of the overpowering burden of assuming the total responsibility for their family and their children (Dreikurs, 1948; Dreikurs & Grey, 1970; Dreikurs & Soltz, 1964). The methods are not meant to suggest that mothers be either permissive or punitive. What mothers need to learn is how to become a match for their children, wise to their ways and capable of guiding them.

The process of psychotherapy as practiced by the Adlerian counselor has four phases: establishing a relationship, uncovering the dynamics and goals of the client, interpretation culminating in insight, and reorientation through action methods (Dreikurs, 1956, 1961). Since the Adlerian holds that the client suffers from discouragement, a primary technique of the therapist lies in encouragement.

Encouragement and understanding are the immediate needs of mothers who have become discouraged. The first goal of counseling with these mothers, then, is to establish and maintain a good relationship between the mother-client and the therapist. Such a relationship is a friendly one between equals. The therapy process is structured so that the mother begins to understand that she is a creative person who plays a basic role in creating her problems. Furthermore, she is responsible for her own actions, and her problems are based upon her own faulty perceptions, inadequate or faulty learnings, and faulty values. If this is so, she can also assume responsibility for change. As the mother understands these concepts, she is able to realize that what she has not learned can be learned and that her faulty learning and perceptions can be altered and modified. From the beginning of counseling with the mother, any efforts of the client to remain passive are discouraged. The client must be active and responsible for contributing to the relationship, the analysis, and the reorientation.

The relationship process increases the understanding and education of the mother. For many mothers, it is the first opportunity they have had to experience a good interpersonal relationship based on trust, mutual respect, and cooperation. The survival of the relationship even under stress helps the mother to understand that good or bad relationships do not merely happen; they are the product of people's efforts. Too often the mother has come to accept misbehavior or poor relationships as normal, and she despairs of ever being able to change them. The problem, however, is in her personal discouragement and her faulty understanding of human behavior. Poor interpersonal relationships are produced by misperceptions, unwarranted anticipations, and inaccurate conclusions on the part of those involved in the relationship. Through the continuous process of participation in a cooperative relationship with the therapist, the mother develops the freedom and courage (a) to explore her personal transactions with members of her family, (b) to interpret the purposes of those transactions, and (c) to redirect her behavior if she wants change to take place.

During the analysis phase of counseling the mother explores with the counselor her current life situation as she views it and develops insight into the pattern of her behavior. She begins to understand that as a parent she does not cause the behavior of her children; she simply provides the atmosphere which makes the behavior possible. Children decide how to use their potentialities and their environment in the way that will gain them the most recognition. Children have the creative capacity to put their own meaning on events and to act according to their own perceptions. Children do not merely react, they interpret situations and decide. The mother is helped to realize that the child's behavior acts upon the parent just as the parent's behavior acts upon the child. A behavior pattern is changed when one party to the transactional agreement fails to act as expected by the other party.

In the interpretation phase of counseling, emphasis is characteristically put on the goals of the mother's behavior. She is confronted with her feelings and the purpose of her feelings. She is confronted with the idea that her behavior, as well as the behavior of her children, is purposive and goal-directed; the goal of the psychological action becomes the final explanation for the behavior (Adler, 1957). The mother must become aware of the decisions she makes relative to her psychological direction and the part those decisions play in her interactions with her children.

In essence, counseling is a deliberate effort to encourage the mother, to increase her self-confidence and to further her understanding of human behavior. She can function as an effective human being only after she believes in herself and her personal worth. Exposure of the contradiction between what the mother believes she should do and what she realistically can do ultimately encourages her. She sees that her failures, or perceived failures, have not been due to personal weakness, but that she has been mistaken as to the nature of her intentions.

As the mother begins to understand the nature of the transactions in which she is involved with her children, she is able to give up some of her feelings of guilt or inferiority related to not having perfect children. The counselor encourages the mother to face the problems of her situation and to develop new behaviors and transactions. The mother's difficulty does not lie in the tasks which she faces but arises out of anxiety about her prestige and her dread of failure. As the mother begins to realize that perfection in the mother role is a societal myth, she is able to work toward accepting herself as a person of worth. She is then able to accept her children in the same way and to provide the climate which will allow her children to be unique and autonomous but also able to accept responsibility.

A NEW ROLE FOR MOTHER

Understanding the purposes and goals of her own behavior leads the mother to the knowledge that she can free herself from the tyranny of her children. She no longer must take the responsibility for everything they do nor believe their misbehavior is a reflection of her capability. She can give up her illusion of proving her worth through service to her children.

The first step in the reorientation phase of counseling with the mother is to encourage her attempts to change her part in the interactions with her children. The mother may want to acknowledge the equal claims of parent and child to dignity and respect, but often there is confusion about the application of democratic principles. Learning to work with the democratic principles of child rearing is a major challenge for many mothers. Without continued encouragement from the counselor, mothers may become permissive anarchists rather than democratic leaders. A democratic atmosphere must be based on the premise of equal rights and responsibilities. Freedom is followed in natural order by responsibility.

Before she can implement democratic procedures of child rearing, the mother must first be able to understand her child's present behavior. The behavior a child uses to gain importance in the family will reveal the child's perceptions. If the behaviors are disturbing or antisocial, the child has developed negative ideas about how to find a significant place within the family. These mistaken goals reflect an error in the child's comprehension of the environment. If the mother can identify and understand the purposes behind the child's behavior, she is in a position to help correct misbehavior. When the mother is not aware of the meaning of the child's behavior, she responds to the mistaken assumptions of the child and further convinces the child that the mistaken goal is the way to be significant. Nearly all of children's misbehavior is a bid for recognition.

Dreikurs and Soltz (1964) identified four goals of children's misbehavior: (a) attention—wanting attention and service, the child assumes that keeping others involved is the way to gain status; (b) power—wanting to be the boss, the child assumes that being in control is the way to gain status; (c) revenge—wanting to hurt others and to get even, the child assumes that one cannot be loved and accepted to gain status; and (d) display of inadequacy—wanting to avoid any demands which might be made, the child assumes that helplessness is the way to avoid competition and keep others in one's service. The child's behavior may seem illogical to others, but it is consistent with the child's own orientation and perceptions.

To help children give up their mistaken goals and to redirect their behavior, the mother must learn to effectively use the skill which the counselor has modeled throughout therapy—the skill of encouragement. Encouragement implies demonstrating respect for the child under current conditions, not as the mother would ideally have the child to be. Encouragement is a continuous process aimed at giving the child a sense of self-respect and a sense of accomplishment. Encouraging mothers express pleasure with any positive effort made by the child and limit critical remarks. It is important for the child to understand that, whether or not the task is successfully completed, the child is worthwhile in the mother's estimation (Dreikurs & Soltz, 1964).

As a mother learns to use encouragement with her children, she can follow some basic rules to help the child acquire a sense of responsibility (Dreikurs & Soltz, 1964). One cannot teach responsibility; one can only give it to a child and let the child learn how to handle it.

A mother must provide honest and real learning situations which will allow her child to experience the logical consequences of behaviors. It is important when using logical consequences that the mother use words which will convey her belief in the child's power to take care of the problems which will be encountered. The mother does not have the right to assume the responsibilities of her children, nor does she have the right to take the consequences of their acts. These belong to the children, and through the use of logical consequences children relate their pleasure or pain to their behavior and decisions and not to the intervention of someone else. If the mother wants her children to become responsible, she gives up the desire to control or to protect or to pity and allows the logical consequences of the child's behavior to take their course (Dinkmeyer & McKay, 1973; Dreikurs & Soltz, 1964).

As democratic leaders, mothers must be firm without being dominating. If no limits are set, the child keeps reaching to see just how far s/he can go. The usual result of permitting violation of order at one time and "blowing up" at another is that the child learns to mind only when mother gets violent. Firmness without domination requires practice in mutual respect. The mother gains respect by her refusal to be placed at the mercy of an unruly child. Only when the mother has confidence in the child's ability can she show respect for the child, meaning that the mother regards the child as an individual with the same rights to make decisions as she has. Similar rights, however, do not mean that children may do what adults do. Everyone in the family has a different role to play, and each has the right to be respected in that role (Dreikurs & Soltz, 1964).

CONCLUSION

Establishing a positive mother-child relationship requires that both mother and child change. The mother who is retraining herself and her child may have to try new methods several times. It takes a considerable length of time and a fundamental change in the mother's concept of the relationship between adults and children before mothers can use the techniques of encouragement and logical consequences to end the faulty mother-child interactions. Those mothers who have learned to use these techniques, however, no longer expend great amounts of their time and effort in negative interactions and conflict with their children and, for perhaps the first time, are able to really enjoy being with their children. Changing behavior requires courage and practice, but those mothers who have succeeded encourage others to persevere.

REFERENCES

Adler, A. *Understanding human nature.* New York: Premier Books, 1957.

Dinkmeyer, D., & McKay, G. *Raising a responsible child.* New York: Simon and Schuster, 1973.

Dreikurs, R. *The challenge of marriage.* New York: Duell, Sloan & Pearce, 1946.

Dreikurs, R. *The challenge of parenthood.* New York: Duell, Sloan & Pearce, 1948.

Dreikurs, R. Adlerian psychotherapy. In F. Fromm-Reichmann & J.L. Moreno (Eds.), *Progress in psychotherapy.* New York: Grune & Stratton, 1956.

Dreikurs, R. The Adlerian approach to therapy. In M. Stein (Ed.), *Contemporary psychotherapies.* Glencoe, Ill.: The Free Press, 1961.

Dreikurs, R., & Cassel, P. *Discipline without tears.* New York: Hawthorn Books, 1972.

Dreikurs, R., & Grey, L. *A parent's guide to discipline.* New York: Hawthorn Books, 1970.

Dreikurs, R., & Soltz, V. *Children: The challenge.* New York: Meredith Press, 1964.

Grey, L. *Discipline without fear.* New York: Hawthorn Books, 1974.

Minuchin, S. *Families & family therapy.* Cambridge, Mass.: Harvard University Press, 1974.

Mosak, H. (Ed.). *Alfred Adler: His influence on psychology today.* Park Ridge, N.J.: Noyes Press, 1973.

Mosak, H., & Dreikurs, R. Adlerian psychotherapy. In R. Corsini (Ed.), *Current psychotherapies.* Itasca, Ill.: Peacock Publishers, 1973.

Satir, V. *Peoplemaking.* Palo Alto, Calif.: Science and Behavior Books, 1972.

Psychosocial Issues in Counseling Mastectomy Patients

WENDY S. SCHAIN
Jewish Social Service Agency
Rockville, Maryland

With about 89,000 new cases and 33,000 deaths expected in 1975, breast cancer (mammary carcinoma) is the foremost site of cancer and cause of death in American women (*75 Cancer Facts and Figures,* 1974). Until just recently, most of the attention paid to mammary carcinoma was primarily of a medical-biological nature. Little or no mention has been made of the psychosocial problems a woman faces when confronted with a diagnosis of breast cancer and its treatment.

Over the next 10 years about a million women will need to face the changes in self-concept, self-worth, the differences in expectations and life style, the alterations in sexual interaction, and perhaps the fear of death and dying which follow a mastectomy. The population of breast-cancer patients is diverse, and the mental-health profession must recognize the multitude of problems related to the particular age, marital status, socioeconomic level, and degree of psychosocial strength associated with each individual. For example, the worries and fears of a 30-year-old Caucasian woman who has had one breast amputated and would like to become pregnant are significantly different from those of a 62-year-old black menopausal woman who is a recent widow and is suffering from a recurrence of her breast cancer. To be helpful to the diversity of women who may be in need of psychosocial support systems, the mental-health professional must become aware of: (a) accurate medical and epidemiological facts about mammary carcinoma, (b) possible options available to breast-cancer patients, and (c) the specific problems and issues faced by women who have undergone radical breast surgery.

THE PROBLEM

Recovery can be defined as successful adaptation to the various emotional and physical crises precipitated by breast cancer; therefore, to help a woman recover, the counselor must know the specific problems to be addressed at the various stages of the disease. Some of these problems are: (a) the specific psychosocial issues a woman must work through to regain her original emotional equilibrium, (b) the identification and coordination of tasks among the various helping professions, (c) the sequencing of appropriate treatment plans, and (d) the most effective therapeutic techniques to help the woman become fully rehabilitated.

Women who develop breast cancer go through various stages: (a) detection of a breast problem and the diagnosis, (b) pre-surgical period, (c) surgery and subsequent treatment(s), (d) rehabilitation, and (e) continuing care. At each of these stages the woman experiences new concerns and important decision-making. Ideally, psychological support should be available during each stage, but unfortunately many women do not receive any emotional help until after the mastectomy. In reviewing the literature and interviewing breast-cancer patients, a glaring absence of good mental-health principles is apparent in the current treatment of the mastectomee. Additionally, little information exists about the psychosocial and psychosexual factors associated with this disease. Much research is necessary to build a reliable clinical base for the development of comprehensive care programs.

After breast surgery, a woman faces feelings of mutilation, concerns about her worth and value as a female, fears of dying, and oftentimes the dread of the ravages of a cancer death. The particular problems each woman faces vary among individuals. For example, the threat of imminent death may not only be the initial crisis of the terminal patient but will probably remain her major preoccupation, whereas a younger woman whose disease has been arrested by the surgery would perhaps dwell more on the loss of the breast and the implications for her social and sexual life.

Counselors in various health settings may be required to help one or both types of women and therefore must have the necessary information and skills to assist them. The population of mastectomy patients can be dichotomized into those who primarily are afraid of dying and those whose predominant concern is feeling like an emotional or sexual cripple. Treatment of a dying patient is a specialized skill (Abrams, 1974); this article is restricted to those women whose surgery, allegedly, has arrested their cancer.

BASIC FACTS AND TERMS RELATED TO BREAST CANCER

Counselors must be familiar with basic facts and with the terminology of this disease, since these are crucial to the perceptions and experiences of mastectomees.

1. The incidence of breast cancer is most frequent between the ages of 37 and 55. If detected and treated early enough (before cancer cells have spread to other parts of the body), the survival rate after 10 years is about 85% Factors which are significant in the identification of high-risk groups include prevalence of the disease in one's family, age, prior history of benign breast diseases, racial and ethnic ancestry, and reproductive life (see Kushner, 1975, pp. 100-101).

2. A biopsy is the removal of the entire growth or a part of it for microscopic examination to determine whether or not it is cancerous.

3. Metastasis occurs when cells from a malignant tumor spread to other parts of the body and cause another cancer to grow. This can take place by direct invasion to adjacent organs or via the blood and lymph fluids.

4. "Reach to Recovery" is a rehabilitation program operated by former mastectomy patients who work as volunteers for the American Cancer Society. These women visit newly mastectomized patients (generally while in the hospital) to assist them with physical, psychological, and cosmetic concerns related to their surgeries.

5. Mammography, xerography, and thermography are three different detection methods for evaluating breast tissue without surgery. Thermography is the least risky because it does not use radiation, but it is also the least accurate. None is yet reliable enough for accurate diagnosis without biopsy.

6. Reconstructive mammoplasty for cancer patients may restore the cosmetic attributes of the breast by using various techniques and synthetic implants. The "uninvolved nipple" can often be "banked" (attached temporarily to another part of the body) until it can be placed on the reconstructed breast (Millard, Devine, & Warren, 1971).

7. Surgical procedures vary in methodology and the amount of tissue removed. Kushner (1975, p. 187) describes the differences between a Halsted radical, a modified radical, a simple mastectomy, and a subcutaneous mastectomy.

POSSIBLE FACTORS PRECIPITATING BREAST CANCER

Psychosocial Variables

Studies exploring psychological variables in cancer were reported as early as 1926, when Elida Evans found that cancer patients had a tendency to form close dependent attachments. For the last half century, however, there have been few studies employing psychological testing of cancer patients, their samples have been small, and their results are questionable. Nevertheless, while many of these studies are two decades old, their findings should be known to counselors who wish to understand the possible psychodynamics of breast-cancer patients.

Tarlau and Smalheiser (1951), using traditional psychodiagnostic instruments such as the Rorschach and the Draw-A-Person test, compared terminal-cancer patients with an equal number of cervical-cancer patients. They found that certain personality patterns seemed more likely to be related to the pathogenesis of cancer rather than to the progress of the disease itself. Breast-cancer patients were found to be functioning at an oral level with inhibited emotional responsiveness. They had difficulty in accepting their inner drives, they rejected their feminine roles, and were less likely than the cervical-cancer patients to have experienced early sexual intercourse.

Studies by Wheeler and Caldwell (1955) and Bacon, Renneker, and Cutler (1952) failed to reveal consensus regarding psychodynamic factors affecting breast-cancer patients. Nevertheless, certain trends did occur, such as problems in the mother-daughter relationship, subjective experiences of deprivation, difficulties in expressing overt aggression, and inhibited sexuality. Reznikoff (1955), LeShan and Worthington (1956), and a group of researchers from the Chicago Institute (Renneker, Cutler, Hora, Bacon, Bradley, Kearney, & Cutler, 1963) support a connection between emotional reactions leading to depression and the onset of this disease.

Bahnson and Bahnson (1966) attempted to transcend a purely descriptive etiological theory and hypothesized that a dynamic relationship exists between repression and regression in the predisposed cancer patient. Regression, for example, could produce an increase of kinetic energy in the somatic system that eventually could stimulate the growth of tumor cells. These investigators acknowledge a multicausal process in etiology of cancer and make it quite clear that, while depression theories and psychogenic components contribute to incidence of breast disease, they are not sufficient variables to account entirely for the development of cancer.

A new area of interest (viz., that of interpersonal interaction) needs to be added to psychological factors and to psychophysiological variables as an important condition in breast cancer. Jamison and Wellish (Note 1) reported findings of a pilot study of breast-cancer patients and their spouses. This study employed a personality inventory, a marital-adjustment scale, a measure of internal versus external locus of control, and a questionnaire about a number of intrapsychic and interpersonal issues. Responses revealed a number of important demographic features as well as: incidence of suicidal thoughts in these women, experience of phantom breast sensations, changes in sexual satisfaction and activity after surgery, and a relationship between the husband's hospital visitation pattern and the wife's emotional adjustment after discharge. More definitive description of these interactional variables is crucial to understand the emotional and sexual sequelae to breast surgery, but at least this study provides a focus on dyadic variables. It would be helpful if future research would standardize the amount of time between the surgery and the psychological evaluation and control for differential prognoses.

In summary, studies examining psychological factors of breast-cancer patients are minimal and suffer from small samples, poorly controlled variables, and questionable methodology. Findings suggest that certain psychological variables may play a facilitative role in the development of cancer in those individuals who may be biologically predisposed.

Sociocultural Factors Indirectly Contributing to Breast Cancer

For decades, the media have mirrored the myths of a sexist society and have exalted for women the qualities of submission, acceptance, and physical beauty. Men in our society are bombarded from childhood with messages that a sultry, sensuous sex object will be a fair reward for the purchase of X, Y, or Z automobile, "Savage" aftershave cologne, and other products advertised in *Penthouse* or *Playboy* magazine. American women are conditioned to believe their value resides firmly in being beautiful (of which the breasts are symbolic). It is understandable, therefore, that the prospect of mastectomy would be devastating for women who have been thus socialized. Loss of the breast, so highly prized and publicized, is often experienced (at least temporarily) as loss of identity.

A study by Bart (1971), which examined depression in middle age, might provide some clues to the social and emotional factors interacting in the pre-breast-cancer patient. Bart combined sociological theory with psychoanalytic and existential views to explain the relationship between loss of role, diminished self-concept, and possible predispositions to psychosomatic illness.

> When their husbands or children leave them, their lives may seem meaningless; their world may no longer "make sense." Thus introjected anger leads to "proper" behavior which in turn leads to expectations of reward; when this reward does not materialize, but in fact tragedy strikes, they suffer from a loss of meaning and become depressed (p. 173).

Bart further elaborates that women's anger has been habitually internalized, and this anger could become somatized and might ultimately precipitate cancer. One can speculate that certain conditions of our culture can combine with certain factors affecting the development of the feminine personality and ultimately effect a predisposition to disease. Such an assumption has implications for rehabilitation programs to help breast-cancer patients channel aggression outward to the appropriate objects.

The relationship between the loss of physical attribute, the conspicuousness of its absence, and the impact of this loss on the self-system is highly culturally conditioned. The impact is dependent on how relevant that characteristic is to a woman's self-concept and how high the status value of that characteristic is in her society (Wright, 1960). At present, in our society a woman's breasts are more crucial to her identity and self-evaluation than almost any other personal attribute. As Stannard (1971) implies,

> And though at present women increase the size of their breasts with internal or external falsies, if it became fashionable to be flat-chested women would, as in the 1920's, flatten their breasts with bandages, or, if rich, have a plastic surgeon transform their breasts into the fashionable size (p. 190).

Because a woman's view of her breasts and her self-concept are highly related, a mastectomy has a significant impact. To experience unexpected breast surgery is a social stigma, a physical insult, and an emotional trauma.

REACTIONS FOLLOWING SURGERY

What might be a woman's reaction to this trauma? How does she acknowledge her lack of symmetry, her altered body image, her anxiety about the remaining breast, and her recognition that the loss was due to a cancerous condition? Although this problem has not yet been scientifically studied, the range of psychological states after a mastectomy probably parallels the range of defense mechanisms and coping behaviors that are described in the literature. The major question is whether her reactions were primarily dependent upon (a) presurgical personality pattern, (b) the extent of disability and disfigurement, (c) prognosis and additional treatment(s), (d) support systems available at the time of trauma, (e) major life tasks interfered with as a result of this loss, and (f) the kind and degree of unresolved issues elicited by this crisis. Post-mastectomy reactions range from fear, anxiety, jealousy, complaints, confusion, irritability, depression, and relief to such positive behaviors as courage, inventiveness, and adaptability. Guilt can pervade all stages, from detection through the post-surgical period.

Shands, Finesinger, Cobb, and Abrahams (1951) as well as Kushner (1975) investigated the various circumstances, events, and people which women blamed for their cancer. Frequently mentioned conditions were husbands, nursing babies, venereal disease, past sins, trauma such as a blow to the breast, personal negligence, and not being intelligent enough to recognize symptoms.

Some women directly acknowledge the loss of their breasts, while other women deny the loss or tend to diminish the significance of the functional or symbolic value of that organ. For example, a woman may claim that she would not miss it much because originally it had been small. A woman who perceived her value to be primarily associated with body integrity (e.g., dancer, model, etc.) might feel especially deprived and defective after a mastectomy. On the other hand, a woman whose identity is independent of physical attributes (for example, teacher or writer) may have less difficulty in adapting to a breast amputation, since her major life style is relatively unchanged.

THE HELPING PROCESS

An important issue which must be kept in mind when working with mastectomy patients is to understand the perceived personal and social connotations of the surgery. What will she be unable to do as a result of the surgery? What real changes in physical activity are a direct result of the amount of tissue excised and resulting loss of strength? Is there a discrepancy between the real and imagined set of limitations? What is this woman afraid to do, to wear, to feel, to fantasize because she experiences her body and herself as suddenly different? What is she plainly incapable of doing?

Unfortunately, supportive help is often unavailable to the patient until after her mastectomy. What is the most critical problem for the woman at this time? The major issue is similar to that described by Bach (1974) in reference to counseling divorced women: to attempt to turn a traumatic situation into a potentially growth-producing experience. Counseling should not only be reparative; it should be integrative in helping these women understand their current reactions in light of their past psychological and social histories.

A woman who has lost one or both breasts must be helped to deal with the diminished feelings of self-worth, to explore fears of death and dying, to externalize her anger, ask questions about cosmetic concerns, fantasize about reconstructive surgery, rehearse what communications to share with her family and friends, talk about her sexual concerns, such as her loved one's reaction to her amputation. As a result of increased awareness about women's options and their right to "informed consent" (Kushner, 1975), the emphasis for mental-health professionals will be on pre-surgical intervention (after biopsy)—that is, helping women (a) make more rational and informed decisions about the type of treatment and surgery they want, (b) help them prepare for hospitalization (e.g., finding assistance for children and household chores), and (c) discuss some of the anticipated psychological reactions to the loss of a breast.

The Work of the Client

Certain psychological tasks must be performed by the breast-cancer patient in order to return to a functional and stable way of life or possibly to move on to a more sensitive and better integrated level of experience. The following issues are common to breast-cancer patients:

1. Threat to life, fear of pain, dying, and manner in which they assume they will die.
2. Physical-rehabilitation exercises and prevention of or treatment for lymphedema.
3. Breast prostheses—types, availability, cost, and proper fitting.
4. Loans and financial support for rehabilitation efforts and / or time lost from work.
5. Obstacles in obtaining health and life insurance policies after a cancer diagnosis.
6. Side effects of chemotherapy and radiation therapy.
7. Employment problems (e.g., job discrimination) and legal recourse.
8. Techniques in breast reconstruction and attendant fantasies and fears.
9. Sexual attitudes and behaviors related to the breast surgery.
10. Cosmetic concerns and alterations in styles of dress (low-cut halters and sleeveless clothes can be problematic).
11. Feelings of being de-valued and less feminine.
12. Communications with family members, especially adolescent daughters who may be struggling with sexuality and their own image.

13. Pregnancy, abortion, and possible sterilization for the pre-
menopausal woman.
14. The physician-patient relationship.

The relative priority of each concern varies with each woman, her age, the
severity of her disease state, her personality and major defense mechanisms,
and the amount of time which has elapsed since the initial crisis. If the woman
was fortunate enough to receive some professional assistance in the hospital
or shortly thereafter, she may be able to cope more effectively with the
problems in less time. Most women, however, are not so fortunate.

Klein (1971) outlined the psychological problems a mastectomy patient
needs to work through in order to return to psychological equilibrium: (a)
accepting the loss of the breast by fully mourning that loss, (b) reintegrating a
self-image worthy of love and the rewards of life, and (c) accepting the threat
of potential recurrence with which she will have to live for 5-10 years, and
perhaps for the rest of her life. The woman who can deal with these issues may
find strengths she did not know she had and adapt to the physical loss with
increased self-understanding and self-esteem. Often, as a result of confrontation with catastrophe, a woman reassesses her basic philosophy of life and
realigns values and priorities in a new and more meaningful manner.

The Work of the Counselor

Just as the breast-cancer patient has certain psychological tasks to
manage after mastectomy, so does the counselor. Mastectomy—and any life-
threatening, body-mutilating experience—demands that involved professionals examine their own feelings of mortality, vulnerability, and sexuality.
Counselors in this situation must combine their basic theoretical orientations
with an understanding of principles unique to rehabilitation counseling, sex
therapy, assertiveness training, and medical data about breast cancer. Only
then can they move on to the major tasks inherent in the helping process:

1. Clarify with the patient her presenting concern (e.g., job discrimination) as well as more subtle apprehensions. Often a woman will have multiple
concerns—for example, the fear of dying, grief over the loss of her breast, the
pain and agony associated with viewing her incisional area, and feelings of
being lopsided or asymmetrical.

2. Help the woman decide what to tell her children or how to ask her
physician about reconstructive mammoplasty. The counselor can provide the
opportunity to rehearse certain anxiety-provoking communications. In
addition, the counselor can provide meaningful feedback to the breast-cancer
patient about these critical issues which may help her to express her feelings
and concerns in a more effective way. For example, a common concern is how
to encourage adolescent daughters to be alert to warning signals about breast
cancer without developing an incapacitating preoccupation with the problem.
Dialogues between the woman and her counselor can be an excellent role-
playing rehearsal to work through some of these concerns.

3. Do not get enmeshed in the medical, health issues of the woman's problem, or report to her new kinds of treatment (but do be aware of what the controversial issues and possible options are). Assurances obviously must be avoided, for they may be proven false and then be construed as deceitful.

4. Be flexible to different needs of the patient. Changes in her behavior and communications may mean she has regressed under the stress of this trauma to a level where support is the primary therapeutic modality she needs. Self-exploration or value clarification are not useful at this time. On the other hand, be sure to know when the woman has moved out of the "crisis intervention stage" and exhibits a readiness to integrate this new experience into her larger life in a creative and adaptive manner.

5. Help the woman express and examine her sexual concerns. She may have concerns about delayed orgasm especially if her breast(s) was a highly sensitive and erogenous area of her body. New techniques and combinations of pleasurable activities may be necessary. Many women fear they will become sexually inhibited or withdraw because they do not wish to risk what their partner's reactions will be. Some women may want to experiment with several partners to confirm their femininity or to test some newly discovered sexual appetites.

6. Evaluate what types of therapeutic involvement will be most useful to the woman. Select or combine (a) individual treatment, (b) group counseling, (c) marriage counseling, (d) family intervention, and (e) sex therapy. Decide whether your client would be most responsive to (a) supportive therapy intended to re-establish her former level of functioning, (b) insight therapy with re-educative goals and a desire to achieve a higher level of functioning than that which existed prior to surgery, (c) behavior modification to recondition attitudes and/or perhaps desensitize certain aversive reactions, (d) relaxation techniques for individuals whose somatic complaints are primarily a result of anxiety but whose capacity for insight is limited, or (e) traditional psychoanalytic technique for motivated women who have a high level of unimpared ego strength but who have experienced a reactivation of unresolved psychosexual conflicts because of their mastectomies.

7. Be alert to your own underlying fears and needs. The female therapist, in particular, must examine what the threat of breast amputation evokes in her. What are her own fantasized reactions and concerns? How are they related to her work with this client? For counselors of both sexes, is it difficult to talk about death? Does the issue of cancer and its reported ravages and pain inhibit even the use of the name of this disease with the client? Is it possible that the counselor may be attempting to compensate for some of these concerns in a way that is not useful to the client (e.g., by avoiding discussion of certain topics)?

A male counselor working with a mastectomized woman must recognize what a mastectomy stimulates in him. Since this surgery is rare in males, does the counselor view this amputation as a castration concern? Does the male therapist see this woman (as she may see herself) as diminished in status because she has lost a breast? What value does he place on breasts, symbolically or actually?

8. This particular loss may re-activate in the patient a previous experience of loss (a parent, child, spouse). Since many of the mastectomees are middle-aged women, the surgery may precipitate a reliving of old pains.

In summary, counselors must be informed about the facts of breast cancer and the women most often affected. They must also know the options and choices available to women in both the medical and psychological treatment of the disease. In addition, mental-health professionals must be flexible in their theoretical orientation and be in touch with their own dynamics. Furthermore, the counselor working with mastectomy patients must be prepared to help all those people who are indirectly affected by the woman's breast cancer (viz., children and spouses or lovers). Husbands and lovers may need the time and support of trained professionals to sort out ambivalent reactions such as anger, guilt, feared impotence, and worries about the death of their loved one. Breast cancer often threatens a young woman's life style more than it threatens her life. Thus, there is an obvious need for the counseling profession to intervene (in addition to early medical and surgical treatment) to help resolve the fear, trauma, and emotional disability that the loss of a breast frequently causes. Effective cure for breast cancer demands treatment for the woman's psyche as well as for her body.

REFERENCE NOTE

1. Jamison, K., & Wellisch, *Psychological effects of mastectomies on women* and *Reactions of the mastectomy patient's significant other.* Papers presented at the meeting of the American Psychological Association, Chicago, September 1975.

REFERENCES

Abrams, R. *Not alone with cancer.* Illinois: Charles C Thomas, 1974.

Bach, G.R. Creative exits: Fight-therapy for divorcée's. In V. Franks & V. Burtle (Eds.), *Women in therapy.* New York: Brunner/Mazel, 1974, 307-326.

Bacon, C.L., Renneker, R., & Cutler, M. A psychosomatic survey of cancer of the breast. *Psychosomatic Medicine,* 1952, *14,* 453-460.

Bahnson, C.B., & Bahnson, M.B. Role of the ego defense: Denial and repression in the etiology of malignant neoplasia. *Annals of the New York Academy of Sciences,* 1966, *125,* 827-845.

Bart, P.B. Depression in middle-aged women. In V. Gornick & B.K. Moran (Eds.), *Women in sexist society.* New York: Basic Books, 1971, 163-186.

Evans, E. *A psychological study of cancer.* New York: Dodd, Mead & Co., 1926.

Klein, R. A crisis to grow on. *Cancer,* 1971, *28,* 1660-1665.

Kushner, R. *Breast cancer.* New York: Harcourt Brace Jovanovich, Inc., 1975.

LeShan, H.L., & Worthington, R.E. Personality as a factor in the pathogenesis of cancer: A critical review of the literature. *British Journal of Medical-Psychology,* 1956, *29,* 49-56.

Millard, D.R., Devine, J. Jr., & Warren, W.D. Breast reconstruction: A plea for saving the uninvolved nipple. *American Journal of Surgery,* 1971, *122,* 763-764.

Renneker, R.E., Cutler, R., Hora, J., Bacon, C., Bradley, G., Kearney, J., & Cutler, M. Psychoanalytic explorations of emotional correlates of the breast. *Psychosomatic Medicine,* 1963, *25,* 106-123.

Reznikoff, M. Psychological factors in breast cancer. *Psychosomatic Medicine,* 1955, *17,* 96-108.

75 cancer facts and figures. New York: American Cancer Society, 1974.

Shands, H.C., Finesinger, J.E., Cobb, S., & Abrahams, R.D. Psychological mechanisms in patients with cancer. *Cancer,* 1951, *4,* 1160-1470.

Stannard, U. The mask of beauty. In V. Gornick & B.K. Moran (Eds.), *Women in sexist society.* New York: Basic Books, 1971, 187-207.

Tarlau, M. & Smalheiser, I. Personality patterns in patients with malignant tumors of the breast and cervix. *Psychosomatic Medicine,* 1951, *13,* 117-121.

Wheeler, J.I., & Caldwell, B.M. Psychological evaluation of women with cancer of the breast and cervix. *Psychosomatic Medicine,* 1955, *17,* 256-268.

Wright, B. *Physical disability: A psychological approach.* New York: Harper, 1960.

An Intervention Model for Rape and Unwanted Pregnancy

PATRICIA FREIBERG
American University

MARGARET W. BRIDWELL
University of Maryland

The analytic grief process is one framework within which one can understand and help a woman who is dealing with feelings surrounding unwanted pregnancy or rape. Though the grieving process is most commonly related to death, other losses may also be appropriately applied to the concept of grief or mourning (Freud, 1917/1957). The experience of patients who have undergone amputations, for example, is a loss which has been studied and described as part of the grief reaction (Parkes, 1972). From the analytic grief framework one can formulate a philosophy related to counseling the rape victim or the woman facing unwanted pregnancy. This article will describe such a philosophical orientation and the counseling interventions which emerge from it.

THE CONCEPT OF LOSS AS RELATED TO UNWANTED PREGNANCY AND RAPE

An unwanted or terminated pregnancy may be characterized as a loss because there is a fetus which she will lose. Those ascribing to a strict medical model would see the loss as a biological one and consider it analogous to the same process as postpartum depression. Although a biological loss is certainly one consideration in a terminated pregnancy, the loss may be viewed in a number of ways. In a sense, the woman loses an aspect of herself. It may be immediately felt upon losing the baby/fetus, felt at a later date, or experienced in various stages both in anticipation of the loss or later. For example, a client recently spoke of her "nine-month anniversary," having noted the time when she would have delivered. Though she had had an abortion after nine weeks, she found herself in a state of depression much later. Thoughts centering around "What kind of child would I have had?" "Did I kill a human?" "What would I be doing today?" were all running through her mind.

A rape victim also experiences a sense of loss. It has been our observation that the loss may be regarded as a loss of self-respect, as a temporary loss of power, or sometimes as a loss of virginity. Even more dramatically, however, for some rape victims there may be, additionally, the threat of loss of life. Although the threat of death may only last a few moments, the shock that follows such a trauma may be devastating. A University of Maryland co-ed who had been raped at knifepoint experienced such an emotional reaction. When one of the authors approached this woman in her dormitory room, she was found surrounded by a pile of clothing and overturned bureau drawers. With a glazed look in her eyes she asked, "Did you come to talk to me about my death?"

A cogent discussion of the relationship between mourning and melancholia has been provided by Freud (1917/1957). We view that framework as applicable to some women who experience a loss around rape or unwanted pregnancy. It must be stressed, however, that, although we are outlining a counseling orientation as applied to a mourning framework, all women involved in rape or unwanted pregnancy do *not* necessarily experience those feelings of loss or trauma. The grief process refers to four interrelated feelings: denial, depression, anger, and resolution (reconstruction). When a person cannot experience the complete grief process, she may have subsequent psychological difficulty. As the grief process is more explicitly described with respect to unwanted pregnancy and rape, case examples will be used to illustrate the four stages.

UNWANTED PREGNANCY AND THE GRIEF PROCESS

Denial may be characterized by a woman behaving as though the pregnancy had not occurred or assuming a very nonchalant posture toward the entire process. The decision of whether or not to carry a child to term is done almost mechanically, and one may observe a woman arranging for an abortion in the same manner as planning a trip to the grocery store. A more clear-cut example of a woman trapped in the denial stage is a patient who came to the gynecologist at a time when she was five months pregnant, obviously large, and who insisted she had no child inside her.

There is a possible danger that a woman who sustains denial may experience serious emotional trauma after the abortion or delivery of the child. A counselor at an abortion clinic in the Washington, D.C., metropolitan area described a woman appearing for her abortion in a very calm, rational, and accepting stance toward the procedure she had elected. Once the abortion had been completed and the woman was in the recovery room, however, she reacted with uncontrollable sobbing. She subsequently required hospitalization.

The second stage of the mourning process is *depression*. Once a woman becomes aware of an unwanted pregnancy, she may become sad and unhappy. Often the sadness or feelings of depression result in an inability to think as clearly and effectively as is required to make an important decision. Depression may last only very briefly and may simply be weeping or depressive feelings of a very fleeting nature. At the opposite extreme, the depression may drag on for a long time. Tinnin and Bridwell (1972) observed that this process may be even more pronounced if the patient has experienced an earlier loss such as the death of a close relative. Again, as in the previous stage of denial, the problem of unresolved depression may reactivate itself in many forms.

A sophomore woman came into the counseling center frightened about some hallucinations she was experiencing. The sounds and pictures she described were those of a baby crying. When asked whether she had ever been in counseling, the woman responded that she had seen a counselor during a brief stay in a home for unwed mothers. Upon closer examination, it was found that this woman had remained for a long time at a stage of denial before she slid into a low level of depression. The woman's general style of handling problems was denial. Partly as a result of that, and partly because of strict and punitive parents, she was unable to directly acknowledge or understand her feelings about her pregnancy. The depression had finally culminated in the hallucinatory expression.

The third stage, *anger*, is especially difficult for many women in our society to accept or express. A display of anger or assertion has become synonymous, in many respects, with negative feelings (Alberti & Emmons, 1970, pp. 10-12). Many women, therefore, feel at an impasse from the standpoint of expressing their protests about the situation. In our experience, anger may be associated with a number of things. It may be that the woman is angry at herself for committing an error in the use of birth control; or a woman may feel anger toward her boyfried for "forcing her to have intercourse." Anger at the process of the abortion (or going into a home for unwed mothers, and the like) is another possibility. Last, the inconveniences and discomfort associated with carrying a child to term or with having an abortion are both things about which the woman can become justifiably upset. Tinnin and Bridwell (1972) assert that failure to complete the basic task of anger could result in a later reaction of anger unjustifiably projected onto others.

A university co-ed seen by the psychologist illustrates the dilemma of becoming trapped in this third stage of reaction. She became quite angry (and remained so) at her boyfriend for what *he* had gotten her into—he had assured her that she would not become pregnant and that the use of birth control was unnecessary! Her anger remained so great that only with psychological intervention could she function in heterosexual activity without feeling a constant resentment toward whomever she was dating.

Reconstruction or *resolution* is the final phase of the grief process. In this phase a person experiences and integrates all her feelings, and there is evidence of a genuine acceptance of the pregnancy.

In all these feelings, the time span associated with each stage is individual in nature. A majority of women anticipate pregnancy long before receiving the results of their pregnancy test. For these women, most or all of the grief cycle may have been completed by the time they receive the test results. Hearing that they are pregnant may or may not reactivate the grief cycle. It is thus important for anyone working with such women to inquire very closely into the woman's *total* reaction and method of handling the process, including when she first suspected the pregnancy. It should also be noted that the grief process is not necessarily a step-by-step set of feelings and that a woman may move back and forth within that chain before resolution is reached. Additionally, a reminder years later could reactivate the feelings in a milder form. Finally, as with any paradigm, and as stated earlier, there are also cases for which this grief process may be irrelevant.

COUNSELING WITH UNWANTED PREGNANCY

The reaction of society to abortion and unwanted pregnancy has produced a number of problems. Until recently abortion was illegal in many states. There continues to be controversy among politicians, and organizations such as "Birthright" actively oppose abortion. Recently an abortion clinic in Maryland was picketed by representatives of "Right to Life." Television cameras were present, and that evening a local news station showed films of a sixteen-year-old woman going into the clinic. The unsuspecting woman experienced much trauma around the television coverage of what she had intended to be a personal medical concern. Additionally, the possible shame of discussing the topic with some people has created many barriers which result in a number of women feeling constricted and unable to complete the grieving process. The appearance of legal and competent abortion clinics has begun to alleviate this problem.

We feel it is extremely important to establish a counseling process for women who first discover they are pregnant. The decision to have an abortion or not is a weighty matter, yet must be resolved quickly because of risks associated with abortion at an advanced stage of pregnancy. Because of the finality of either choice, feelings must be faced early in the discovery of unwanted pregnancy. An unfortunate example is of a college junior who was not seen until she had already undergone an abortion. She was a practicing Catholic, who felt that the consequence of her abortion was mortal sin. She believed she had killed a child, and that was entirely unpardonable to her. The intensity and irreversibility of her feelings eventually resulted in a psychotic break.

Tinnin and Bridwell (1972) delineated some tenets involved in an early decision-making process. First, encourage a woman to verbalize her feelings surrounding the pregnancy, from both the standpoint of her physical sensations and also her feelings and fantasies about the unborn child. Second, even though a woman has made a decision to have an abortion or to carry the child to term, encourage her to verbalize the pros and cons that relate to the decision. Third, the person who is counseling with the woman about to undergo an abortion should describe the setting and procedure for the actual abortion process. Last, alert the woman that she may possibly experience conflicting feelings following the abortion (for example, relief, anger, detachment, and the like). The majority of unmarried women at the University of Maryland elect an abortion. A similar guidance process would be appropriate, however, for a woman choosing to carry the child to term.

There are a number of ways of aiding a woman who appears trapped in any of the stages of the grief process. If, for example, she is in a state of denial, one might ask her about bodily sensations. This is done by becoming quite graphic in a descriptive inquiry concerning enlarged breasts, morning sickness, and the like. Or one might directly inquire about the feelings associated with carrying a child inside of her. Often, even if the woman does not respond immediately, many will think about such questions later and thus move toward a more integrated realization of the pregnancy.

It is also important to include the boyfriend in the counseling process if possible. There are a number of cases in which the woman has had less difficulty than the man in dealing with the unwanted pregnancy, and a counseling program which is equally attentive to the male is highly recommended.

In addition to the male partner, the patient's problem invariably has an effect on significant others. Parents should be considered, and patients asked if they feel they can include their parents in their initial decision regarding the pregnancy. In our experience, patients seem to know when they can confide in their parents. Though the families are a more obvious aspect, friends often have difficulties too. The gynecologist saw a freshman woman who came in very confused and upset because her best friend had had an abortion and had not confided in her. She had learned of the abortion from someone else and was concerned about how she had failed her friend.

There are predisposing factors which can increase the likelihood of post-abortion problems. Some variables to note are: (a) the repeater, or woman who has had previous abortion(s), (b) previous history of psychiatric or psychological problems, (c) unresolved state of denial, (d) failure to use contraception, (e) unassertive behavior with respect to contraception, (f) strict religious or family values, (g) absence of any supportive relationships, or (h) unstable relationship with boyfriend. One word of caution must be made in that abortion is seen by some women as a form of birth control. This should be considered when dealing with the repeater.

RAPE AND THE GRIEF PROCESS

In the past few years, popular media have done much to highlight the realities of the rape victim's situation. A woman may experience fears of talking with medical or legal personnel, or she may anticipate upsetting reactions by significant others. Societal forces such as those may thus operate to cause a woman to suppress or deny the rape or may keep a woman from reporting the rape at all. The first stage of the grief process, *denial,* may therefore be even more exacerbated.

Threats of pregnancy, venereal disease, or other medical repercussions may be the precipitants of finally seeking help, although those problems may also escape medical attention because of fear of the physician's reaction. A gynecological patient took two years to finally work through her feelings about a rape experience. The patient had been complaining of abdominal pains and had seen a number of physicians, all of whom could find no physical basis for her symptoms. She was referred to the author/gynecologist, who also examined the woman and eliminated the medical possibilities which might cause the pain. As the patient and gynecologist then explored the possibilities of other types of precipitating events, the conversation turned to a discussion of body image and feelings about self. Finally the patient revealed that she had been raped two years previously and she had never had an opportunity to talk with anyone about her feelings surrounding the rape.

In our review of the literature it appeared that little had been written on the effect of rape on the victim. Those studies which do concern themselves with the psychological components of the victim either make reference to the grief process (Zuspan, 1974) or speak of stages and reactions which are very analogous to the grief process (Sutherland & Scherl, 1970). Both of those articles point out the strong tendency to deny the event of rape.

During the period of *depression,* the woman will often react with shame, guilt, fear, humiliation, and hate. Women may ask themselves questions which take the form of self-blame: "Why did I submit? . . . I should have fought him," or "I shouldn't have been walking alone on that dark street."

The *anger* stage of the grief process presents a different set of emotions for the rape victim. As mentioned earlier, under many circumstances, anger is not a socially acceptable emotion for a woman. It is important for the woman to allow herself to become angry at the rapist. The guilt, shame, and humiliation involved with rape, plus the blaming attitudes sometimes thrust upon the woman by others, however, are inherent difficulties which contribute to the problems associated with the expression of anger.

The last stage which must occur for a rape victim is *resolution,* which involves integration of the previous stages. We have noted that one unique way of resolving feelings may occur for some women who volunteer on the Rape-Crisis telephone hot lines. Some of the women involved in such work have themselves been raped. Talking and empathizing with other women seems to be helpful for some rape victims. Although working in the rape-crisis centers has been useful, one danger, however, may be in the lack of resolution of anger. The pitfall of remaining only angry at the rapists may, in fact, prevent a woman from resolving her rape experience.

COUNSELING WITH A RAPE VICTIM

Even though the woman may not see the need for any psychological help, there is much benefit in establishing a relationship and providing support immediately after the reported rape. Initially, the state of shock or denial may mean that a woman will refuse help after one interview. In our experience, however, some women who immediately refused help did seek out the psychologist a week or so later. Another strong recommendation is to provide follow-up psychological services at the time the woman returns for a subsequent medical check-up. Some patients will have questions about the state of their body and whether others will ever be able to detect signs of rape. Apprising the woman of her physical condition, plus explaining that others, including physicians, cannot see evidence of rape, is a very important role of the gynecologist.

Unfortunately, many therapists appear preoccupied with trying to assess whether or not a rape actually has occurred. This preoccupation may be at the expense of ignoring more immediate emotional needs of the woman and may also contribute to a patient's already shaky feelings of having caused the rape. Werner (1972) described a patient whom he had been seeing in an ongoing therapeutic relationship. She had been raped while he was on vacation, and he made a slightly frustrated reference to the fact that he could not get his patient to see the connection between the rape and his vacation. Although one could question Werner's interpretation of the precipitants to the rape, nonetheless, in describing the reactive phases of this patient, he corroborated many of the previously described aspects of the grief process. He also illustrated the traumatic consequences which often occur for the woman, especially at a later date, when the event is reopened for legal purposes.

Other points should be considered when counseling the rape victim. Some women are fearful of seeing a gynecologist—especially a male. Helping the victim with the feelings which are preventing her from seeking a physician may be the first step in any rape counseling.

Supportive family or friends can be very helpful for a woman who has just been raped. Some women, however, experience fear over telling someone close. A second aspect of counseling, then, would be in helping the rape victim explore any anticipatory concerns with respect to family, friends, and self and likewise assisting family or friends deal with their own reactions to the rape, so that they may be consequently more supportive toward the victim.

Negative effects of rape are often heightened by condemnation, and the like, by others. A freshman woman whom we saw told her mother about her rape experience, and her mother's reply was, "I told you you shouldn't have worn those short skirts!" Lewis (cited in Zuspan, 1974) indicated that 25% of the rape victims with whom he had worked were involved in a relationship where the victim perceived the rape as being a threat to that relationship. He cited one instance of a woman who did not resist the rapist. As a result, she was afraid to tell her husband because there was no evidence of bodily harm to "prove" the incident.

As soon as the rape victim is able to consider the issue of legal involvement, the decisions of whether or not to report the rape and/or press charges against the rapist are all matters which may be of major consequence to the woman. Possible personal repercussions need to be carefully examined, and in so doing the counselor who works with the rape victim needs to be aware of some legal facts.

Forcible rape is a definition employed in legal circles. The word "forcible" is the clue to the illegality of the act. Evidence of forcible rape generally is confirmed by bodily injury that is most likely detected via medical examination. Hayman (cited in Zuspan, 1974) delineated some additional factors which lend credibility to the assessment of forced rape. Those are: age (under 10 and over 60), history of previous sexual *in*experience, evidence of emotional stability, known good character, and testimony by witnesses to the event (a rare phenomenon!).

Although proof of rape is important for legal authorities, the unfortunate aspect is that a woman often has difficulty proving forcible rape. Under threat of knife, gun, or bodily assault, most women display sound judgment by being submissive to the rapist. A woman who has been submissive generally will not show evidence of bodily injury.

One of the single most important components of psychological intervention is in helping the rape victim review and verbalize the situation surrounding the rape, as well as the rape itself. The woman will most likely need encouragement to discuss what has happened, and that rehashing is important lest powerful and obsessional feelings build. There are strong feelings associated with the traumatic event which usually need to be expressed. Some of those feelings have been researched by Skirnick. She conducted interviews with 26 former rape victims who had been treated at the University of Chicago Hospital. She cited figures indicating that women report feelings of shame (73%), fear (92%), anger (62%), guilt, humiliation, hate, and uncleanliness (cited in Zuspan, 1974, p. 144).

As in the case of unwanted pregnancy, later problems may present themselves. Some predisposing factors which may increase the likelihood of post-rape problems are: (a) severe trauma associated with the actual event, such as extreme brutality, perversity, and the like, (b) previous history of psychiatric or psychological problems, (c) unresolved state of denial, (d) strict religious or family values, (e) an absence of any supportive relationships, or (f) the presence of severe guilt about the rape.

Incest is a form of rape often overlooked in the literature and often having a powerful effect on a woman. This problem is occasionally brought to the attention of the gynecologist and has been an occasion for cross-referral to the psychologist. In our experience, the concept of grief has also been useful in dealing with the patient who presents incest as a problem.

In a previous article (Freiberg & Bridwell, 1975) the importance of the interdisciplinary approach (medical and psychological) in working with sexual problems was stressed. In our experience, many problems which might require psychological intervention seem to come first to the attention of the gynecologist. The reverse is also true where those students who may need medical help see the psychologist instead, although that seems to happen with less frequency. The analytic grief process has been a useful framework in our work with university students. Most of those students are white, middle-class women. Generalizations to other populations may be appropriate if the counselor keeps in mind that there may need to be modifications in the framework. Additionally, as has been stated earlier, there are some women for whom this model does not apply.

REFERENCES

Alberti, R.E., & Emmons, M.L. *Your perfect right: A guide to assertive behavior.* San Luis Obispo, Calif.: Impact, 1970.

Freiberg, P., & Bridwell, M.W. An interdisciplinary approach to female sexuality. *The Counseling Psychologist,* 1975, *5,* 106-111.

Freud, S. [*Mourning and melancholia*]. In J. Strachey (Ed.), *Standard edition, Vol. 14.* London: Hogarth Press, 1957.

Parkes, C.M. *Bereavement: Studies of grief in adult life.* New York: International Universities Press, Inc., 1972.

Sutherland, S., & Scherl, D.J. Patterns of response among victims of rape. *American Journal of Orthopsychiatry,* 1970, *40,* 503-511.

Tinnin, L.W., & Bridwell, M.W. Anticipatory guidance for abortion. *Maryland State Medical Journal,* 1972, *21,* 73.

Werner, A. Rape: Interruption of the therapeutic process by external stress. *Psychotherapy: Theory, Research, and Practice,* 1972, *9,* 349-351.

Zuspan, P. Alleged rape: An invitational symposium. *The Journal of Reproductive Medicine,* 1974, *12,* 133-152.

A Research Perspective on Counseling Women

CLARA E. HILL
University of Maryland

Counseling of women is a subset of psychotherapy and counseling in general. As such, many of the issues applicable to psychotherapy research are relevant also for research in counseling women. Of particular relevance is Bergin's (1971) challenge that the effects of therapy are not uniform but that research should take into account which treatment by what therapist is effective for what client with what problem under what conditions. In examining the preceding articles, then, the traditional criteria of psychotherapy research will be used: client variables, counselor variables, independent or treatment variables, and dependent or criterion variables.

CLIENT VARIABLES

One of the factors that are evident in examining the data from counseling research is the high variability among clients in their response to treatment. In Bergin's (Note 1) most recent analysis of outcome data of psychotherapy, he estimated that 40% of the improvement could be accounted for by spontaneous remission, an additional 25% of the improvement was due to the specific effects of treatment, 25% of patients did not change, and 10% of the patients actually deteriorated during therapy. Some of the variability in response to treatment is due both to individual differences in clients prior to treatment and to different reactions of clients to the same treatment.

The rationale for viewing the counseling of women as a separate domain is that (a) counselors have been biased in their attitudes and treatment of women and (b) women have different problems than men (Holroyd; Tanney & Birk). Most of the research, however, has not actually measured how male and female clients do respond in counseling sessions. Tanney and Birk point out in their article that the studies which examined how male and female clients react in counseling settings resulted in somewhat conflicting data. Female clients may self-disclose and discuss feelings more than males, but this effect seems to be a result of an interaction with sex of counselor. No generalizations can be made at this point to substantiate that female clients in general react differently than male clients or that counselors treat male and female clients differently during a counseling session.

It still seems possible, however, that counselors do respond differently to men and women as clients and that perhaps we are just not studying the relevant variables. One explanation could be that the differences are not due simply to the sexual gender of clients, since there is a large amount of individual variability among women. In fact, Mischel (1966) has found that there are more differences among women than between women and men. A counselor may respond in certain ways to certain personality types, behaviors, or problems, rather than responding to sexual gender. For example, if a particular counselor is less empathic with and terminates hostile clients sooner than other clients, and if more of the male clients than female clients this counselor sees are hostile, males would be terminated sooner. It would be the hostility, however, rather than the sexual gender to which the counselor responded. The implication of this for the researcher is to identify specific characteristics which may differentiate women not only from men but also from each other in the counseling situation.

Several of the articles in this section examined subcategories of women in terms of specific problem areas: the single-again women (Aslin), the rape victim (Freiberg & Bridwell), the mastectomy patient (Schain), the supermom (Brooks), and the perfect mother (Wilborn). These authors raise some interesting issues about women undergoing these particular problems, but again they seem to make the same, previously discussed mistake of assuming that all women react the same way to these particular problems. There is probably high variability in responding to these issues, such that different women react differently. For example, a passive, dependent woman may not react or feel the same way following a rape as an assertive, self-confident woman would feel. Indeed, probably no problem has the same characteristics or the same effects, because of both individual and situational variables.

Some of the authors took demographic or personality variables into consideration. Jefferies Ford points out that black women face different problems than white women. Unfortunately, as Tanney and Birk noted, the race variable often leads to as many conflicting results as the sex variable in research. Knefelkamp, Widick, and Stroad, in their application of the cognitive-developmental stages for females, did go a step further than just considering women as one category. Several of the other authors also postulated stage theories, although in response to particular problems (Aslin; Freiberg & Bridwell; and Jefferies Ford). Taken together, these articles suggest that all women undergo a certain set of stages to reach maturity and perhaps, as new problems arise, they go through a similar subcycle of stages. The individual variability of women could thus be accounted for by determining the stage of development at which the woman was currently situated. This leads directly to the development of treatment strategies based on moving the woman to the next higher stage of development; however, these models still ignore the rich variability of clients which would probably be encountered at each stage. Nor do the theories account for individual variability in order of progress through the stages. Furthermore, it is not clear how to reliably and validly identify what stage an individual is currently in. Stage theory appears to offer considerable conceptual clarification to the study of women, but it would probably need to be studied in relationship to the individual differences between women.

Of further concern when discussing client variables in research is a clear definition of the client population. Many of the terms used are ambiguous and hard to measure. Even the terms male and female can be interpreted in different ways, depending on whether the criteria are hormonal balance of androgens and estrogens, assigned versus chosen sexual gender, or sex-role characteristics. Perhaps some of the conflicting results are due to differences in client samples. A careful discription of the client sample used for research would enable more comparison and replication of results.

In summary, client variables need to be specified more clearly. Research has focused too much on women as a homogeneous group rather than as a group with many different characteristics and problems. Of crucial importance for research in counseling women is not just that there are different identifiable groups of women but how these differences affect the process and outcome of counseling.

COUNSELOR VARIABLES

Just as individual differences between clients affect the process and outcome of counseling, counselor variables also influence the results. Truax and Mitchell (1971), in their review of therapist variables in psychotherapy research, reported that a large amount of the variability in counseling outcome could be accounted for by therapist empathy, warmth, and genuineness. Other variables have produced conflicting results in therapy process and outcome. More recent research has examined the effects of sex of counselor on the counseling interaction. Although many researchers have looked at counselor attitudes (see Tanney & Birk), few have actually measured what happens in the counseling process. One study which did examine process variables (Hill, 1975a) found that counselor sex interacted with experience level and client sex. The results of this study indicated no straightforward effects of sex variables on various counselor and client behaviors. Tanney and Birk also reported that the effects of sex of counselor in outcome research are conflicting. Thus, it is difficult to generalize about the effects of the sex of counselor either on actual behaviors in a counseling session or on the outcome.

Again however, as with the sex of client, it appears intuitively that there are differences in the way male and female counselors react in a counseling session. Often, it is recommended that female clients be assigned female counselors (Rice & Rice, 1973; Kronsky, 1971; Chesler, 1972), presumably because they will react more sensitively and empathically with them. Yet some female counselors are probably more empathic and effective with males than with females, and a female counselor may be more sensitive only with certain females but not with others. For example, a counselor who happens to be a lesbian may be more empathic with and feel less threatened by a lesbian client than would a counselor who was heterosexual. This points to the need for specifying more clearly not only counselor and client variables but also the definitions of sensitivity and empathy.

Perhaps one of the variables counselors differ in is in their cognitive development, as noted by Knefelkamp, Widick, and Stroad. Just as clients may pass through cognitive-developmental stages, counselors might also pass through such stages. One issue which might particulary affect behavior is the counselor's cognitive stage in terms of attitude to women. At the dichotomous level such a counselor may view women in either traditional versus nontraditional, passive versus aggressive, nurturant versus nurtured, helpless versus powerful, or feminist versus nonfeminist terms. At a relativistic stage, they may begin to view different alternatives for women. And at a commitment stage, they may be able to view all clients as total human beings, with individual personalities, goals, and problems, who need to be treated separately. The stage of the counselor and the counselor's views about women might be influential in predicting sexism and bias in counseling.

As with clients, the effects of different counselor characteristics in a counseling situation need to be studied. Such variables as masculinity-femininity-androgyny, feminism, attitudes to women, experience level, psychological adjustment, cognitive-developmental stage, race, and status level may interact with the sex of counselor in predicting the process and outcome of counseling with women. These variables need to be operationally defined so that specific counselor effects can be identified.

Some literature has suggested that prior to counseling both male and female clients prefer male counselors (Chesler, 1972; Fuller, 1964), presumably because males are perceived of as having greater ability. Collins and Sedlacek (Note 2) observed that fewer clients assigned to female counselors showed for the first session; however, after the first session, clients of women counselors stayed longer. Perhaps, as Tanney and Birk noted, sex of counselor may result in differential timing effects, so that different issues are discussed at different times in the counseling process. Although most of the articles in this section offer implications for counselors, no mention is made of how to train counselors to become more aware of and to change behaviors which may be inappropriate or harmful for women clients. Relatedly, to this author's knowledge, there are no graduate training programs in counseling women. Much research is needed to determine effective methods for training counselors to counsel specific subgroups of women, if this proves justified.

INDEPENDENT OR TREATMENT VARIABLES

Once it is documented that women have specific problems, treatment programs can be developed to deal with these problems. The treatment interventions discussed in this section of the book include: rape and abortion counseling (Freiberg & Bridwell), treatment of mastectomy patients (Schain), helping supermoms (Brooks), counseling the single-again woman (Aslin), and dealing with the perfect mother (Wilborn). Holroyd, in her article, further discussed how feminism has affected and altered a variety of different types of treatments used for counseling women.

Unfortunately, none of these authors reported empirical evidence for the efficacy of their treatment approaches with their specific populations. Without such research, there is no scientific way of knowing if the treatment programs are more effective than either traditional treatments or no treatment at all. Further, we have no idea of the spontaneous remission of any of these problems without treatment, change with treatment, or deterioration of the problems and clients with treatment.

Even if a research project does find that, for example, Adlerian therapy is more effective than a consciousness-raising group in helping women overcome their perfectionistic strivings as mothers, there is no way of knowing what it was about that treatment that caused the change. Studying the components of treatments is necessary to determine the specific aspects of treatment which help women. In a scientific approach, those specific components which help women change would be identified and then put together to form interventions. The present literature on treating women takes the opposite approach of first developing entire treatment programs and looking at global effectiveness. For example, a discussion of feminist therapy without clear definition of the terms and components makes research difficult.

Several of the authors established areas of specific differences between women and men: physical characteristics (Harris), lower achievement and career motivation (Farmer), and use of power (Unger). An in-depth discussion of the research in relationship to the therapeutic interventions would be helpful. Counselors need to know how to make use of these sex differences in the counseling process in order to encourage women to use their potential.

A factor which could affect the efficacy of any treatment intervention for women is the amount of support she receives from significant others. For example, a married woman's response to rape counseling will be dependent not only on her own level of self-esteem but also on her husband's level of acceptance of her. Thus, in looking at the treatments, it would be important to assess the impact of, and perhaps solicit the cooperation of, significant others in the counseling process.

In summary, research needs to be done to determine what treatment can effectively produce changes for different women. Furthermore, the components of these treatments need to be tested to see what factors are accounting for the changes and how these differ across problems, clients, and counselors. Other factors, such as reactions of significant others, which may influence the process of treatment also need to be identified. Until we can empirically establish that our treatments are effective, we cannot be sure that women would not be better off receiving no treatment.

DEPENDENT OR CRITERION VARIABLES

Of crucial importance in a discussion of research on counseling of women is how to measure the effects of the treatment interventions. Throughout this article, it has been noted that the results of sex effects in counseling are conflicting. Some of this confusion lies in issues of measurement.

Available measures for evaluating counseling effectiveness have serious limitations for use with women. Holroyd noted that many measures have relied on male scientists' preconceptions of behavioral data and have ignored women's self-reports, thus making erroneous assumptions about women.

Additionally, many measures used to detect "sexism" in counseling may be reactive, as suggested by Tanney and Birk. Since counselors and clients seem to be highly sensitized to appearing "sexist," they may not respond honestly to some instruments. This is especially true when attitudes rather than behaviors are measured and when research is obtrusive.

The use of any measuring instrument for evaluating counseling makes some assumptions about desirable outcomes. For example, since one desirable outcome for assertiveness training is more assertive behavior, an appropriate measuring instrument is one which measures assertive behavior. For any treatment program, the desirable outcomes must be specified so that the appropriate measure can be chosen. In discussing treatment interventions for women, it is somewhat difficult to determine what the desirable outcomes would be. Most of the articles specify no desirable outcomes. Those interventions which describe developmental stages (Knefelkamp, Widick & Stroad; Aslin; Freiberg & Bridwell; and Jefferies Ford) would probably have the highest stage as the desirable outcome. However, no means are indicated for measurement of stage attainment.

As discussed earlier, individual clients respond uniquely to treatments, so they undoubtedly also have different goals. If this is true, a single measuring instrument would obscure individual change toward goals. Perhaps one woman would desire to be more assertive, whereas another would want to be less assertive. Instruments, such as Hill's (1975b), can be used to measure attainments of behaviors and goals which an individual designates as important. An individual focus also eliminates the danger of an outsider's values being used as the criteria for success.

Instruments which focus on individual goals and changes are difficult to formulate and to validate, since the individual focus yields no external criteria for comparison. Although it is much easier for research purposes to have universally desirable goals and behaviors, such instruments are not valid for individuals with unique goals in counseling. These are challenges to be faced by researchers so that the effects of counseling interventions for women can be studied.

REFERENCE NOTES

1. Bergin, A.E. *A ten-year follow-up of psychotherapy research.* Presidential address: Society for Psychotherapy Research, Boston, 1975.
2. Collins, A., & Sedlacek, W.E. *Counselor ratings of male and female clients.* University of Maryland Counseling Center, Research Report #8-72.

REFERENCES

Bergin, A.E. The evaluation of therapeutic outcome. In A.E. Bergin & S.L. Garfield (Eds.), *Handbook of psychotherapy and behavior change.* New York: Wiley, 1971.

Chesler, P. *Women and madness.* New York: Doubleday, 1972.

Fuller, F.F. Preferences for female and male counselors. *Personnel and Guidance Journal,* 1964, *42,* 463-467.

Hill, C.E. Sex of client and sex and experience level of counselor. *Journal of Counseling Psychology,* 1975, *22,* 6-11. (a)

Hill, C.E. A process approach for estimating client goals and outcome of counseling. *Personnel and Guidance Journal,* 1975, *53,* 571-576. (b)

Kronsky, B.J. Feminism and psychotherapy. *Journal of Contemporary Psychotherapy,* 1971, *3,* 89-98.

Mischel, W. A social-learning view of sex differences in behavior. In E. Maccoby (Ed.), *The development of sex differences.* Stanford: Stanford University Press, 1966, 56-81.

Rice, I.K., & Rice, D.E. Implications of the women's liberation movement for psychotherapy. *American Journal of Psychiatry,* 1973, *130,* 191-196.

Truax, C.B., & Mitchell, K.M. Research on certain therapist interpersonal skills in relation to process and outcome. In A.E. Bergin & S.L. Garfield (Eds.), *Handbook of psychotherapy and behavior change.* New York: Wiley, 1971.

Seeking the Holy Grail, or The Status of Women in Counseling

ANNETTE M. BRODSKY
University of Alabama

Many of the issues addressed in this book regarding the counseling of women clients have been generally recognized as problems for the last several years. That the dilemmas they present are now being documented by research, clarified in the counseling process, and developed into plans for remediation represents the current stage of our progress. Slowly, the widely held theoretical positions based on myths about women that lead to sexist practices are being exposed and replaced. Tanney and Birk, as well as Holroyd, effectively summarize where we are regarding research and theory. It has been a painful, eye-opening realization to discover that we and our colleagues, both male and female, operate with prejudices even in the light of verbal awareness of the issues.

In spite of the overall findings that our helping professions are moving much slower than our knowledge about inadequate practices regarding women clients, individual counselors have undergone dramatic changes in the last several years with regard to their own level of consciousness about women's issues. The openness with which prejudices against women have been dealt with by those women counselors who have responded to the impetus of the women's movement has been encouraging. In their writings and, more recently, in their teachings, a new assertiveness has been promoted to attempt new programs.

Fifteen years ago, when I first started counseling, I tried to help women suppress or compromise some of their role conflicts. My rationale was that they would not survive by complaining unduly about a situation that no one was willing to let them change. So when a bright, ambitious, college woman sought a vocation that could be done part-time so that she could lead a "normal" family life—raising children and housekeeping—I saw this as realistic, even though I knew that she was capable of becoming intensely involved in a full-time career. One student decided to go into elementary education because it fitted her needs for an off-again, on-again possibility (she could keep in touch as a substitute) around her primary homemaking career, even though she admitted she did not really *like* education courses or job prospects. Her biology major was more exciting but not worth the sacrifice of her future personal life.

Today I would handle the situation quite differently. A young woman with such goals would find them soon outdated in terms of the current social environment. I would be doing her a disservice to let her so easily dismiss her vocational interests in deference to a practical, convenient solution. Her options would be so much greater today, and her conflicts on choosing between the alternative options would be much less dependent on stereotyped expectations that she be a full-time wife and mother.

In the last fifteen years, the state of the art of counseling women has moved quietly but surely along many dimensions. We have made strides in our theory development, documentation of research, and specific new techniques for new problems. But we are still only part of the way to finding the Holy Grail—a comprehensive theory of therapy for women.

IMPEDIMENTS IN THE SEARCH FOR THE HOLY GRAIL

The highly achieving female still is not believed to be fulfilled unless this is merely an adjunct to her major role of wife and mother. The Holroyd article brings out the illogic of this stereotype and its sexist perpetuation by clinicians. The reality of the continuing stereotype, by women and their counselors, that careers cannot be a major fulfillment for professional women has been shown by Farmer's data on achievement, by the American Psychological Association Task Force on Sex Bias and Sex Role Stereotyping in Psychotherapeutic Practice (in press), and in reported difficulties encountered by professional couples in psychology who find subtle obstacles in the environment (Bryson, Bryson, Licht and Licht, 1975).

Another barrier in the road to the Holy Grail is the continuing stereotyping in the educational process with young children. The Unger article documents some very disturbing evidence that young children are not changing their stereotypes about masculinity and femininity. The Harris article demonstrates that, while women indeed have to concede that men as a group are physically stronger, great physical strength has not often been seen in its true perspective in terms of its lack of meaningfulness for the majority of activities required in our current mechanized society. There is no legitimate reason for power to be associated with physical strength. If, as Unger suggests, a division of sex aligns powerful and non-powerful males by means of their anatomy against the less powerful females, then part of the solution requires a break into the coalition of weak and powerful males by integrating women into the power hierarchy.

In the final analysis we must be concerned primarily with the integration of all women into the society at large—i.e., the male society. Thus, as Knefelkamp, Widick and Stroad point out, the way a woman thinks about herself dictates what she will do. Her identity of her role determines the behavior she sees as appropriate. Knefelkamp's conceptual schema for women's roles in society presents a very interesting possibility for aiding women to move from defining themselves as having a single social role to a period of relativism in which an individual woman's role choices are seen in context of her own life plans. Ultimately she must make a commitment to a particular role, which then encourages her to assume responsiblity for creating and maintaining her own identity. The latter point is probably the most difficult for women clients to attain. It is easy for counselors to jump on the bandwagon of soliciting support for injustices done to a woman client through the various prejudices and discrimination that she probably has experienced. But, after granting that she has legitimate grievances, our job as counselors is to move such clients beyond their anger and to creating livable solutions. Somewhere in this process, the client has to make herself vulnerable to succeeding and failing on her own merits or inadequacies. We cannot do our clients a service by stopping the forward process after agreeing with them that we see the discrimination and stereotyping which they have had to endure. Taking the next step is critical. If a woman chooses to leave an oppressive husband, then she also chooses to meet the complex challenges that single life presents. She needs to become assertive, but she also needs to be responsible for dealing with the consequences of her assertiveness. The old supporters of her passive martyrdom will not be able to rescue her.

We may have much to learn from the insights of Jefferies Ford on the self-awareness of black women, who have trod a longer path and may well be further toward realistic self-realization than many white women.

If we can agree that middle-class white women probably start from Kirk's stage 2 (self-pity) as opposed to stage 1 (self-hate), then the process is not far-fetched in its application to whites. White women, however, seem to get stuck longer at stage 3 (self-examination) perhaps because, as Knefelkamp proposes, they can't make the leap from reevaluation to commitment to an individual style of their own. As adolescents, middle-class white girls are less likely to rely on peers for support than black girls, who are typically prepared for independence and responsibility at a younger age.

Knefelkamp states that vocational counseling should not be guided by a feminist or antifeminist ideology of therapy. I wonder if it would be more accountable for the therapist to state what his or her ideology is. The APA *Standards for Providers of Psychological Services* (1975) states that a written contract of services be used. The guidelines on non-sexist therapy for women (APA Task Force on Sex Bias, 1975) suggests that clients be free to question the views of the therapist on the women's movement in order for the client to judge compatibility of philosophies.

Personally I see no conflict between feminism and vocational counseling. Sexist psychotherapy is extremely damaging to women because it implies restriction of options through stereotyping, whether direct or covert. On the other hand, feminist philosophy, as practiced by competent practitioners, would encourage considering a broader range of careers for women but not condemn the traditional role where the client chooses this through self-examination in the light of alternatives. At this stage of the status of counseling women, we need to move from treating women as a kind of creature different from men to treating women as individuals who are as different from each other as they are from men.

Harris notes that we are increasingly discovering less physical differences between the sexes while finding more social differences, the latter being more resistant to change. Thus, I have a disagreement with Freiberg and Bridwell, who strive to find a common theory with which to explain with one paradigm rape victims and abortion seekers. The clinical evidence is much more complex and contradicts such a simplification. The only parallels I have noted between rape-victims counseling and pregnancy counseling is the crisis nature of the problem and its relationship to sexuality—a generally inhibited area of discussion for women.

In pregnancy counseling, we see as much of the fear of reprisal, either external or due to internal religious values against having abortions, as we do the more dynamic sense of loss of a real child. Our culture instills in women that they should have a maternal instinct and, thus, guilt at having an abortion performed. Certainly there is no personal attachment to a growth within one's body, or cancer patients would also experience grief after an operation. It is the fantasy of the future child that the woman mourns, just as one could mourn an expected award or degree that was not received or the knight on the white horse who does not arrive on the scene as expected.

As for the rape victim, I think it is destructive to see her suffering from a sense of loss. I think that accepts uncritically a faulty, male-oriented view of the victim as having something precious to lose. A sense of shock or unreality that a victim often exhibits is more likely associated with the unexpectedness of the trauma itself. Many victims report (Burgess & Holmstrom, 1974; Medea & Thompson, 1974) a sense of the unpredictability of the world and a fear that they cannot maintain control of the environment. There is also the fear that a rape will happen again. The anxiety may be overwhelming, but I cannot see it being interpreted as a sense of loss—except as the fear of loss of control over one's body.

The counselors of rape victims would do better to seek out the individual reactions to the trauma than to focus on common themes among them. Fears of the victim are often fear of the expected reactions of others if they find out that the victim has been molested, guilt over whether she did everything she could to avoid rape, fear of what might be exposed about her character should the incident come to trial if she prosecutes, and fear that others might think that she provoked the rape. Also, a knowledge of the medical and legal procedures with regard to rape in the state in which one is practicing is as essential a first step in dealing with rape victims as the psychological crisis aspects.

Two other crisis situations concerning women are discussed in this section of the book. Schain's article on mastectomy patients and Aslin's article on divorce and widowhood bring out some of the increasingly complex and situation-specific conflicts that are relevant to such women. An understanding of the trauma itself, with its medical and sociological components, offers valuable insights in dealing with these patients.

Most counselors, particularly women, are accustomed to dealing with feelings about pregnancy and childbirth and, more recently, with the realities of the female situation in divorce and widowhood. Most female counselors can readily identify with women going through these crises, as they have probably considered their own relationship to these possible events. However, very little has been said until now about psychological counseling with mastectomy patients. While there is not the negative moral implication that one has to be aware of in rape and abortion, there is the question of the counselor's potential repulsion toward a seriously ill or mutilated individual, as well as toward being involved with the client's confrontation with dying. Schain certainly makes an enlightening presentation to familiarize counselors with mastectomy patients' issues.

One final area this section addresses is that of the relationship between women and children. The articles presented here lead one to the depressing conclusion that most of the socialization of women is indeed a case of arrested development. Many women never reach the adolescent self-identity and striving for independence that men do, let alone a higher level of development in which a unifying philosophy of life is achieved. So we see women in their forties, after completing child-rearing, finally asking themselves, "What do I want to be when I grow up?" Some women go directly from child-rearing to retirement. Pauline Bart (1971) notes that the depressive consequences of the "empty-nest syndrome" for women who have no other purpose in life occur frequently enough for us to attend more closely to the process of how this happens and to do some primary prevention.

Brooks suggests that the vicarious achievement many women experience through their husbands' occupations could be made real achievement. The "role compromise" model that she suggests offers perhaps the best of what we have to offer at this stage of social awareness about women's needs. Brooks notes that women entering careers or school at a late date have low self-confidence, problems with time management, and role conflict. In the re-entry process the woman feels not only intellectually inferior but also a social misfit. Indeed, some continuing education programs teach very basic re-entry skills, such as how to use the library and how to talk to young people.

Unlearning to keep the house spotless is a suggested source of more time. The goal is a noble pursuit, but one of the difficulties is trying to disavow previous long-standing beliefs that one's self-esteem is based on the spotlessness of one's house. Admitting that those previous values were wrong or foolish is not an easy posture for a client to accept beyond the verbal level. Turning over the task of taking out the garbage to the husband may be agreeable on the surface to all concerned, but, if the husband does not adopt the same value system that the garbage at some point or another has to be emptied, then the transfer of responsibility will not work.

Another major value which many women have to reappraise in order to find a specific self-identity is that of the perfect mother, as noted by Wilborn. A critical task is to separate the role of mother from the identity as a person who also happens to have children. The notion of the perfect mother is based on the related notion of a universal maternal instinct, which implies a universal, innate knowledge about child-rearing.

I am inclined to think that we take the specifics of child-rearing practices much too seriously, and I would disagree with Wilborn that the counselor should pay so much attention to the amount of control and guidance in the parent-child interaction. I think we are finally coming to see the schizophrenogenic mother being let off the hook as a causative agent for psychosis. One wrong move does not make your child schizophrenic, and children are resilient enough to take a lot of honest mistakes in parenting. Firstborn children do fairly well, considering that they were raised by naive parents. I think Gersch (1966) had the right perspective when he titled his child-care book "How to Raise Children at Home in Your Spare Time."

The reality I would like to see communicated to mothers is to see their children as human beings with personalities of their own that interact with the mother's personality. Both parties have to come to terms with the limitations of the other. The relationship is not equal, but neither is the mother all-important. Referring again to Unger's review, one becomes impressed with all the conditioning that goes on outside the home and the impossibility of taking all the credit or all the blame for the way a child turns out—unless that child never leaves the house.

Not all women biologically capable of having children like children. Those who do often don't like *all* the aspects of child-rearing that a mother must do. Mothers need to communicate to children and to fathers and teachers that mothers are people too. To the discouragement that Wilborn talks about with regard to children, I would add that mothers also become discouraged. They need praise and forgiveness, and they need to see that their children care about them. If mother blows up when she reaches the limits of her patience, then the child needs to know that this is a temporary reaction, that mother will apologize later when she's calm, and that it is not such a terrible thing. Until mothers feel that they have a legitimate right to privacy, their own friends, time off, and the expression of anger, we are going to see a continuation of the current trend of the most productive, intelligent, stereotype-free, professional women not choosing to have children—a trend that Bernice Lott (1973) predicts will lead to future generations raised only by the more traditional women, who buy all the restrictions of the stereotyped mother role and teach them to their own female children. This will assure that we will not overcome the sexist ideology prevalent in our society.

CONCLUSION

What do we really need to do next? It is evident from the preceding articles that new models for therapy with women are beginning to influence the development of new theoretical positions. What is not yet evident is what effect these models will have on the improvement of the condition of women as a result of their use in counseling. Outcome research is needed to assess the comparative value of the new models over the traditional, existing therapy frameworks. We desperately need to test the efficacy of alternative approaches to the treatment of women clients—with immediate feedback and long term follow-up. The reanalysis by sex of old studies on outcome of psychotherapy is one step that is already being implemented (Waskow, Note 1).

We are moving beyond the protests that something has been dreadfully wrong with the treatment of women in therapy to a point where we are able to identify specific sources of the problems in therapy, and now we can follow the guidance of new models that are being developed along the path of the Holy Grail—a fully developed theory of therapy for women.

REFERENCE NOTE

1. Waskow, I. Personal communication, October 18, 1975

REFERENCES

American Psychological Association. Standards for providers of psychological services. *American Psychologist,* 1975, *30*(6), 685-694.

American Psychological Association Task Force. Report on sex bias and sex role stereotyping in psychotherapeutic practice. *American Psychologist,* in press.

Bart, P. Depression in middle-aged women. In V. Gornick & B. Moran (Eds.), *Women in sexist society.* New York: Basic Books, Inc., 1971, 99-117.

Bryson, R.B., Bryson, J.B., Licht, M.H., & Licht, B.G. The professional pair: Husband and wife psychologists. *American Psychologist,* 1975, *30*, 1-22.

Burgess, A.W., & Holmstrom, L.L. *Rape: Victims of crisis.* Bowie, Maryland: Brady Co., 1974.

Gersch, M.J. *How to raise children at home in your spare time.* Greenwich, Connecticut: Fawcett Publications, Inc., 1966.

Lott, B. Who wants the children? *American Psychologist,* 1973, *28*, 573-582.

Medea, A., & Thompson, K. *Against rape: A survival manual for women.* New York: Farrar, Straus and Giroux, 1974.

Emerging Truths on the Psychology of Women, as through a Glass Darkly

DOROTHY A. EVANS
Alexandria Community
Mental Health Center
Alexandria, Virginia

The articles under review contain a wide variety of perspectives on how sex-role stereotyping limits the psychological growth and development of women and on how the apparent limitations may be redressed by different kinds of intervention strategies. The breadth of fact and informed opinion provides a valuable bedrock for refining what is now an incomplete state of knowledge about the psychology of women.

The incomplete state of knowledge may be attributed to the fact that earnest inquiry has just begun. Only recently has the Zeitgeist supported women as suitable subject matter for scientific investigation. Even now, the search is being carried out in a social-cultural context which serves to keep women in the background and, as such, to keep their self-definitions unclear. It can be assumed, then, that the results of early efforts to bring into the foreground what has always been kept back will be uneven, sometimes contradictory, and sometimes inchoate. The truths about the psychology of women will emerge mixed with some errors and distortions, for at first we will have to look through a glass darkly—a glass made dark by the historical place women have occupied and by the limitations of our methods to come to grips with the complexities of the phenomena we are now trying to study. We are products of the very sex-role stereotyping we seek to investigate and to clarify. Therefore, we probe in what are still sore places for many of us.

It is noteworthy that all of the contributors to this section of the book are women. Nonetheless, we seem to be at the first steps of that proverbial thousand-mile journey and can expect that the early fruits will sometimes be

The author is now at Howard University Hospital, 2041 Georgia Avenue, N.W., Washington, D.C. 20060.

284

brilliant insights, but perhaps more often, fragments of data with some inconsistencies, ambivalences and vagueness.

For this reviewer, the challenge is to maintain an active and open search in which we tolerate the ambiguities and contradictions of our early efforts without premature foreclosure. Thus, we can find the truths and look at them face to face—that is, not as through a glass darkly. This reviewer is engaged primarily in the practice and supervision of intensive psychotherapy, wherein by twists and turns the therapist helps the client find the fullest and deepest truths possible. My principal interest in the articles is to comment on how their assumptions, strategies, and outcomes clarify the psychological realities dealt with by therapist and client in intensive psychotherapy. It is acknowledged that from this vantage point only one vista may be illuminated among the many that are important.

RESEARCH CONSIDERATIONS

Unger, Farmer, and Harris, in their survey of empirical studies, compel one to recognize that sex-role stereotyping is a powerful socializer of women's attitudes and motivations and to realize how women evaluate and express power and competitiveness socially, career-wise, and athletically. It is clear that sex-role stereotyping affects males and females in dramatically different ways. As Harris' article makes clear, sex differences extend beyond the limitations imposed on females by their having less physical strength than males.

The data seem to show that in school and in work situations, women are less competitive, less self-confident and less powerful when compared to men, according to the evaluations of both men and women. Three lines of reaction occur to me: (a) The data need to be interpreted in terms of whether the constructs guiding the data collection reflect the values of women. (b) If the attributes women desire for themselves have been suppressed by sex-role stereotyping, systematic study is needed to determine what has happened to these attributes. (c) The developmental pattern of sex-role stereotyping and its effects need to be studied in depth.

Specifically, apropos the validity of the constructs, Unger and Farmer do not analyze whether women value power and competitiveness. Farmer mentions that women who are in the same professional careers as men have different career interests than men. Unger makes the intriguingly cryptic remark that the powerless are the vast majority of us all. Whether intrinsically or by virtue of blocked access, it may be that women value attributes other than power and competitiveness. The point is that empirical investigations may continue to show women rated as deficient if they are studied only on dimensions that are, or have been, treated as the exclusive province of men. If all humans are fairly powerless, do all women find their exclusion from the search for power burdensome or a relief from an onerous weight? Other than power, what are women seeking? What are the differential career interests of women?

As revealed in the Farmer and Unger articles, the prevailing method of study (correlational analysis) and the variables studied (e.g., power and competition) seem to delimit the attributes of women too narrowly and too simply. For example, Unger reports findings on internality-externality showing women more externally oriented than men. What does this finding mean? Data on blacks initially showed the same pattern; however, more recent factorial studies have found that blacks tend to value internality (similar to whites), but blacks (unlike whites) perceive that instrumental expressions of internality are blocked by race discrimination. It has been found that black adolescents who are able to value internality and to discriminate situations in which they can give it expression from those in which they cannot show creative and nontraditional job aspirations (Gurin, Gurin, Lao & Beattie, 1969; Vance, 1973). Tanney and Birk make the worthy point that, in looking at the effects of sex bias on counselor-client interactions, the first reports of the global effects on the female client of counselor's gender have not held up. Alternative experimental methods may uncover similar changes in women's external-internal orientation.

The data reported by Farmer point out additional difficulties in not critically examining the constructs guiding research. For example, a study by Ginzberg is cited in which women are portrayed as not foreclosing on career decisions because their career-choice process is complexly determined and involves career and personal-marital-family planning issues. What is described as a multi-determined process is labeled by Ginzberg *and* Farmer as an issue of uncertainty in career planning! Are women necessarily uncertain (unconfident?) when they do not readily decide among a complex array of considerations and options?

Regarding whether and how attributes important to women have been suppressed, it is not clear what these attributes are. Assuming that women do yearn for what has been denied them (e.g., social power, freedom to compete), it seems necessary to study how these attributes work covertly in women. Unger, for example, asserts that indirect power is typed as female but that under normal conditions it cannot exist at all. She then makes the point that a woman's individual capacities are not important in her being nurturant, obedient and responsible. This is a perplexing statement in that it seems to deny the social reality that people who are oppressed will find covert ways to express themselves. Research needs to be guided by strategies that will allow for the portrayal of all of women's attributes, overt and covert. If women's expression of power and intelligence is blocked by societal pressures, what happens to them? How can one do anything in a nurturant or responsible manner without bringing to bear one's assets, overt and covert, whether they be power and intelligence, or other attributes as yet unmeasured?!

Jefferies Ford attempts to identify the attributes of black women that are important for research and counseling. By highlighting this important area of concern, the article serves a great need; however, the assertion that black women are strong seems to be substituted unreflectively for the more traditional one that black women are weak. Both seem equally erroneous. Women are! Our task is to be extremely interested in what they are and to critically question all assertions as to what women are. Many black men have been severely discriminated against in the job market. This reviewer has encountered as many black female clients who have been anguished by their work experience as have been truly gratified by work. It has been found repeatedly that the quality of the work experience is a powerful determiner of whether it adds to the competence of the individual: Engel's (1967) study of indigent children who worked, Evans and Tyler's (in press) study of black low-income women, and Fago and Evans' (Note 1) study of black adolescent males.

Some black women who have had to work from early childhood have experienced distortions in their capacities to be both assertive and passive-dependent. So, while the counselor-researcher needs to be sensitively aware of strength wherever it is, as Jefferies Ford notes, it will not do justice to any women to classify them or any of their attributes in a fixed niche of health or illness.

In relation to the developmental sequencing of the effects of sex-role stereotyping, much work is needed. When do the damaging effects first appear? Few longitudinal studies of this question seem to have been launched, and available results of cross-sectional studies seem somewhat contradictory. For example, Unger reports that girls at a young age show higher vocational aspirations than boys but that in later childhood the pattern is reversed. Farmer cites data from Maccoby and her associates suggesting that on related dimensions, such as self-confidence and competition in relation to academic goals, females do not lag behind males until college age.

One needs to study infants to clarify whether there are critical ages for the effects of sex-role stereotyping. As Harris notes, female infants are protected more than males, even though the female infant is physically more mature. Cohen, however, reports a finding by Moss that "mothers tend to be more responsive to male infants, holding them proportionately more time than do mothers of female infants" (1966, p. 5). How strange, in that females more than males seem to be socialized for affiliation, contact comfort, and the giving and receiving of affection. These early infant care-giving methods occur during the time that the infant is developing object constancy (a crucial underpinning to a feeling of security). If this apparent discrepancy has any merit, it suggests that a strongly enforced set of sex-role stereotyping practices may hide and conflict with patterns set down at a critical period in early infancy. In any case, the systematic exploration of what happens, beginning with infancy, seems an important part of the effort to understand the origins of sex-role stereotyping and the degree to which its effects may be changeable.

INTERVENTION CONSIDERATIONS

Research and service efforts seem to be developing along parallel rather than explicitly cooperative or adversary lines. However, several of the theoretical and data articles (Tanney & Birk; Holroyd; and Knefelkamp, Widick & Stroad) offer some guidelines within which to review service issues. Tanney and Birk make it clear that no definitive answer exists as to whether women or men should provide service to women, since the question is too global. Additionally, they report confusing findings; for example, they cite a study by Cline-Nafzinger in which female counselors more than male counselors rejected traditional roles for women; females more than male counselors supported working mothers; and, irrespective of sex, counseling educators more than counselors supported achievement motivation in women. Are new, more liberal biases being substituted for older ones? Tanney and Birk suggest that female therapists may be eager to present themselves as *not* sexually stereotyping their clients. Not only does this present problems in research design, as noted by the authors, but also it may imply that counselors are merely replacing one set of stereotypes for another.

The range of problems possibly encountered by the practitioner who is motivated to oppose sex-role stereotyping (as a therapeutic strategy) is brought into some relief by Holroyd and Knefelkamp and her associates. Holroyd alludes to the danger of the therapist's intervention strategies being guided by her political interests or social-political formulations; specifically, the particular problems of the client may go unattended. Knefelkamp, Widick and Stroad expand this issue more explicitly with the point that the therapist and client can arrive at a content statement that seems to reflect a highly developed level of personal integration in the client. However, the client's statement may be rendered unreflectively or as a result of passive surrender to a persuasive therapist. As noted by M. Polster (see Holroyd), it is the therapist's job to help provide the context in which the client can become who she truly is "bit by bit." Unhumanitarian values or other "hang-ups" in the therapist will block this development, but so might the therapist's preoccupation or anxious concern with the "right attitudes."

The following two clinical examples illustrate how the therapist's "right" attitudes and political positions may lead to paradoxical effects in the client. First, this reviewer has worked with some male homosexual clients who have become saddened and less trusting of therapists as a result of the American Psychiatric Association's decision to delete homosexuality as a diagnostic category. These clients have felt that the decision is a "cop-out"—that is, that therapist and patient have colluded to avoid mutually facing and working through the client's hurt, anger, and anguish stemming from feelings of having been alienated from society. Therapists who present a closed, quasi-political, personal attitude toward the affronts women have endured may eliminate the exploration of the client's personal sorrows. Second, some black clients have commented that the "black is beautiful" movement has provided *in part* a mechanism for a defensive retreat from developing a sense of personal responsibility and integrity in a social-cultural climate hostile to blacks. Almost uniformly these patients have needed to test out the safety of sharing such reflections lest they offend the presumed militancy of the reviewer. Women counselors need to be sensitive to the stereotyping clients may do regarding female service providers. Notions of what the therapist will and will not entertain as viable areas for discussion (e.g., the desire for a traditional life style) can seriously affect therapy, particularly in the early, tender stages of the process.

Taken together, the service-oriented articles seem to reflect sensitivity to the need for a non-ideological approach to clients and to the potential of the therapist to develop a countertransference reaction in relation to the female client's struggle to freedom. The articles stress treatment of isolated problems. This orientation may obscure the need for evaluating carefully the client's presenting problem in the context of that client's total character. The therapist needs to know the forces in the client which the therapist and client can use to combat the client's problem and also to know whether the presenting problem stands alone, or is part of, or masks other problems. In these terms, the Knefelkamp, Widick and Stroad article is the most fully developed in that it presents a well-reasoned model of assessment and treatment enabling the therapist to gauge the direction and flow of the work. The model presented by these authors is clear and crisp, but, in its exclusive focus on cognition, it leaves affect and other ego operations unexamined for their possible importance in achieving personal integration. In varying degrees, the other intervention articles slight the role of diagnosis but are richly detailed and clear in sequencing the stages involved in treatment.

A brief clinical vignette from the reviewer's practice illustrates the need for careful assessment of a client's problem in terms of how she experiences it cognitively and affectively and how it fits into her total character.

A 30-year old black single female sought therapy, with the chief complaint that she had been raped seven times and that the rape experience had led to an overall lack of interest and pleasure in sexual activity. She was perplexed that she should have suffered this experience so many times. Over several months, careful exploration of the client's life experiences led to the revelation that she herself felt rapacious and devouring; she traced these subjective attributes to early childhood, at which time she developed food fetishes that helped her feel well nurtured. They also permitted her to repress her guilt and anger-laden perceptions that her parents were neglectful of her dependency needs. The client recalled that, with the onset of menstruation (age 12), her mother warned her anxiously and repeatedly not to have intercourse and not to get pregnant. She then reconstructed that she began to withdraw from social contacts and, in her withdrawal, did not perceive accurately the signals from others about what they wanted from her. She came to recognize that she projected her feelings of being rapacious and devouring onto others, including men who approached her sexually. To acknowledge free participation in intercourse was to experience emotionally the wrath of mother.

The client finally came to a position that several of the seven sexual experiences intially presented were rape and several were experienced as such based on the fact that she was operating under the sway of the ghosts of mother's prohibitions and her own faulty perceptions and defenses.

The discoveries about her symptoms and her character freed this woman to enjoy genital sex and, overall, to function at a higher level of integration.

Schain profiles the mastectomy patient's crisis in the context of the patient's character and recognizes that a mastectomy may mean significantly different things to different women. A highly differentiated scheme of treatment possibilities is offered based on these individual differences. Freiberg and Bridwell recognize that personal reactions to rape and unwanted pregnancies vary depending on the client's capacity for a healthy grief reaction (vs. melancholia) and depending on the strengths existing in the client's familial-social context. In Brooks' article, a very clear schema of intervention strategies is offered for helping women return to school and careers. A particular strength of the paper is the encouragement to counselors to help avoid premature foreclosure in the client, by helping her to be curious about and to explore many alternatives. The article is possibly misleading, however, in that the author presumes that return to the labor force or to school is a normal transitional state and that the goal of counseling in this area is one of (the client) choosing a life style. Intuitively, it seems more parsimonious to assess individual differences among women in terms of how normal the transition is and the degree to which they need assistance in incorporating this shift into a new life style. Aslin, in her article on counseling problems related to divorce and widowhood, brings our attention to the network of social, emotional, and economic factors that must be integrated into the counseling strategy. Aslin seems to suggest that mourning is a process more appropriate for widowed women than divorced women. It is the experience of this reviewer that personal integration following any significant loss depends on the capacity to mourn. Aslin also seems to disallow that a woman can be married and, in that role, achieve an independent personal identity.

Wilborn's article clarifies the need to investigate how sex-role stereotyping affects women in their role as mothers. She notes that, even though the cultural context and expectations for mothers and children are changing, mothers tend to persist in autocratic mothering practices. This reviewer believes that mothers frequently get stuck in this mode of mothering because of misalignments in marital relationships. That is, women develop "unholy alliances" with their children and try to hold them in such alliances when marital difficulties are not being resolved. For example, in the vignette cited above, the mother's intensified interest in the client's sex life seemed to be a displacement away from the mother's frustrated relationship with her husband. This brings our attention to an important intervention strategy not emphasized in the articles—namely, marital and family therapy. Women who suffer the effects of sex-role stereotyping do so not only in the context of society at large but, of equal importance, in the context of their families. It is doubtful that women can change in areas involving sex-role stereotyping without family members being involved in the treatment. The stereotyped behaviors and attitudes are just part of a dynamic equilibrium to which all family members contribute. Any isolated attempt to change the woman may well increase the motivation of other family members to maintain the equilibrium.

However radical and comprehensive the treatment approach, for many women it is a tough struggle to give up their stereotypic behaviors, even in the search for truth and greater life-loving capacities. Freud clearly understood that distorted solutions have their own passion which is hard to give up and that the battle to do so will be carried out in the transference with the therapist.

> This is the ground on which the victory must be won, the final expression of which is lasting recovery. . . . It is undeniable that the subjugation of the transference-manifestations provides the greatest difficulties for the psychoanalyst; but it must not be forgotten that they, and they only, render the invaluable service of making the patient's buried and forgotton love-emotions actual and manifest; for in the last resort no one can be slain *in absentia* or *in effigie* (1912, p. 108).

Part of the therapist's difficulty is to face the full expression of the woman's hostilities as she makes discoveries about how she has been duped and duped others in her stereotyed sex role. Female therapists will not be exempted from this issue. As to its management, one can extrapolate from Wohlberg (1975, p. 556), "The need for patience . . . and the capacity of the therapist to tolerate his patient's aggression and sense of hopelessness, as well as the patient's difficulty in utilizing proffered help [are] vital for all successful therapies."

There is a need to understand male and female humanity beyond sex-role stereotypes. Cohen put it well:

> For the woman, emphasis on dependency, passivity, and even inadequacy interferes with her functioning as homemaker, wife, and mother just as severely as with her functioning in a career. . . . Doing [any] job well requires competence, good judgment, and ability to take responsibility. . . . For the man, the overemphasis on strength, courage, initiative, and leadership does violence to his appropriate needs for rest, receiving emotional support, and getting rid of the tensions of the market place. . . . I would not be thought to be an advocate of abolishing maleness and femaleness in favor of one uniform sex. . . . Rather, my aim would be to encourage a more critical scrutiny of our assumptions about sex-typical behavior (1966, p. 14).

When the scrutinizing is complete and when efforts such as those represented herein are more complete, hopefully, we will all be free to be "more simply human than otherwise" (Sullivan, 1953, p. 32).

REFERENCE NOTE

1. Fago, D., & Evans, D. *Psychosocial competence in black adolescent males from father-absent homes.* Unpublished manuscript, 1975. (Available from D.A. Evans, Howard University Hospital, Washington, D.C.)

REFERENCES

Cohen, M. Personal identity and sexual identity. *Psychiatry,* 1966, *29*(1), 1-14.

Engel, M. Children who work. *Archives of General Psychiatry,* 1967, *17,* 291-297.

Evans, D., & Tyler, F. Is work competence enhancing for the poor? *American Journal of Community Psychology,* in press.

Freud, S. The dynamics of transference. *Standard Edition,* 1912, *12,* 97-108.

Gurin, P., Gurin, G., Lao, R., Beattie, M. Internal-external control in the motivational dynamics of Negro youth. *Journal of Social Issues,* 1969, *25,* 29-53.

Sullivan, H. *Interpersonal theory of personality.* New York: Norton, 1953.

Vance, E. Social desirability. *American Psychologist,* 1973, *28*(6), 498-511.

Wohlberg, G. A black patient with a white therapist. *International Journal of Psychoanalytic Psychotherapy,* 1975, *4,* 537-562.

A Bibliography

BEVERLY A. BELSON
Michigan State University

Abardanel, K., & Siegel, C.M. *Woman's work book*. New York: Praeger Publishers, (Information House Book), 1975.

Abramson, J. *The invisible woman: Discrimination in the academic profession*. San Francisco: Jossey-Bass, 1975.

Acker, J. Women and social stratification: A case of intellectual sexism. *American Journal of Sociology*, 1973, *78*(4), 936-945.

Altback, E.H. *Women in America*. Lexington, Massachusetts: D.C. Heath, 1974.

American Alliance for Health, Physical Education and Recreation. Research studies on the female athlete. *Journal of Physical Education and Recreation*, January 1975, *46*(1).

American women 1963-1968: Report of the Interdepartmental Committee on the Status of Women. Washington, D.C.: U.S. Government Printing Office, 1968.

Amundsen, K. *The silenced majority: Women and American democracy*. Englewood Cliffs, New Jersey: Prentice-Hall, 1971.

Andreas, C. *Sex and caste in America*. Englewood Cliffs, New Jersey: Prentice-Hall, 1971.

Angrist, S.S., & Almquist, E.M. *Careers and contingencies: How college women juggle with gender*. New York: The Dunellen Publishing Company, 1975. (For sale by Kennikat)

APA Task Force on Issues of Sexual Bias in Graduate Education. Guidelines for nonsexist use of language. *American Psychologist*, June 1974, *30*, 682-684.

Ashley-Montague, M.F. *The natural superiority of women*. New York: Macmillan, 1953.

Astin, H.S. *The woman doctorate in America*. New York: Russel Sage Foundation, 1969.

Astin, H.S. Achieving educational equity for women. *Journal of the National Association for Student Personnel Administrators*, Summer 1976, *14*, 15-24.

Astin, H.S., Parelman, A., & Fisher, A. *Sex roles: A research bilbliography*. Washington, D.C.: Center for Human Services, 1975.

Astin, H.S., Suniewick, N., & Dweck, S. *Women: A bibliography on their education and careers*. New York: Human Sciences Press, 1974.

Babcock, B.A., Friedman, A.E., Norton, E.H., & Ross, S.C. *Sex discrimination and the law: Cause and remedies*. Boston: Little, Brown, 1975.

Bardwick, J.M. *Psychology of women*. New York: Harper & Row, 1971.

Bardwich, J.M. *Readings in the psychology of women*. New York: Harper & Row, 1972.

Bardwick, J.M., Douvan, E., Horner, M.S., & Gutmann, D. *Feminine personality and conflict*. Monterey, California: Brooks/Cole, 1970.

Barr, H., & Sherif, C. *A topical bibliography on psychology of women.* Washington, D.C.: JSAS/American Psychological Association, n.d.

Barrón, P. Counseling the Chicanito. *Journal of Non-White Concerns,* October 1972, *1,* 24-30.

Beard, M.R. *Women as force in history.* New York: Macmillan, 1946.

Becker, G.S. *The economics of discrimination.* Chicago: University of Chicago Press, 1957.

Beeson, D. Women in aging studies: A critique and suggestions. *Social Problems,* October 1975, *23,* 52-59.

Bem, S. Sex-role adaptability: One consequence of psychological androgyny. *Journal of Personality and Social Psychology,* 1975, *31*(4), 634-643.

Bem, S., & Bem, D. Training the woman to know her place: The power of an unconscious ideology. *Women: A Journal of Liberation,* Fall 1969, *1,* 8-14.

Bernard, J.S. *Academic women.* University Park: The Pennsylvania State University Press, 1964.

Bernard, J.S. *Women and the public interest: An analysis of policy and protest.* Chicago: Aldine Publishing Company, 1971.

Bernard, J.S. *Women, wives, mothers: Values and options.* Chicago: Aldine Publishing Company, 1975.

Bernard, S. Aggression in women. In J. Agel (Ed.), *The radical therapist.* New York: Ballantine Books, 1971, 188-191.

Bernstein, M.D., & Russo, N.F. The history of psychology revisited or, up with our foremothers. *American Psychologist,* Fall 1974, *29,* 130-134.

Berry, J.B. The new womanhood: Counselor alert. *Personnel and Guidance Journal,* 1972, *51,* 105-108.

Berry, J.B. Women: Clients and counselors. In C.E. Warnath et al. (Eds.), *New directions for college counselors.* San Francisco: Jossey-Bass, 1973, 173-190.

Berry, J.B. Counseling older women: A perspective. *Personnel and Guidance Journal,* 1976, *55,* 130-131.

Bertle, V., & Franks, V. (Eds.), *Women in therapy: New psychotherapies for a changing society.* New York: Bruner/Mazel, 1974.

Bingham, W.C., & House, E.W. Counselors' attitudes toward women and work. *Vocational Guidance Quarterly,* September 1973, *22,* 16-23.

Bird, C. *Everything a woman needs to know to get paid what she's worth.* New York: David McKay Company, 1973.

Bird, C. Enterprising women. New York: W.W. Norton, 1976.

Bird, C., & Briller, S.W. *Born female: The high cost of keeping women down.* New York: Pocket Books, 1971.

Black Enterprise. *Black women in business and public life,* August 1974, *5.*

Black women's aspirations dampened by sexism, racism. *ISR Newsletter,* Spring 1975, *3,* 3, 5.

Borgese, E. *Ascent of women.* New York: George Braziller, 1963.

Boulding, E. Familial constraints on women's work roles. *Signs: Journal of Women in Culture and Society,* Spring 1976, *1,* Part 2, 95-117.

Brandenburg, J.B. The needs of women returning to school. *Personnel and Guidance Journal,* September 1974, *53,* 11-18.

Broverman, I.K., Broverman, D.M., Clarkson, F.E., Rosenkrantz, P., & Vogel, S.R. Sex role stereotypes and clinical judgments of mental health. *Journal of Consulting and Clinical Psychology,* 1970, *34*(1), 1-7.

Broverman, I.K., Vogel, S.R., Broverman, D.M., Clarkson, F.E., & Rosenkrantz, P.S. Sex role stereotypes: A current appraisal. *Journal of Social Issues*, 1972, *28*(2), 59-78.

Browne, J.M. *The black woman*. Washington, D.C.: ERIC Clearinghouse on Higher Education, American Association for Higher Education, 1974.

Brownmiller, S. *Against our will: Men, women and rape*. New York: Simon & Schuster, 1975.

Bruemmer, L. The condition of women in society today: A review—Part 1. *Journal of the National Association of Women Deans and Counselors*, Fall 1969, *33*, 18-22.

Bruemmer, L. The condition of women in society today: Annotated bibliography—Part 2. *Journal of the National Association of Women Deans and Counselors*, Winter 1970, *33*, 85-95.

Bullough, V.L. (with assistance of B. Bullough). *The subordinate sex: A history of attitudes towards women*. Urbana: University of Illinois Press, 1973.

Burton, G. *I'm running away from home, but I'm not allowed to cross the street*. Pittsburgh: Know, 1972.

Byham, W.C., & Katzell, M. (Eds.). *Women in the work force: Confrontation with change*. New York: Behavioral Publications, 1972.

Cade, T. (Ed.). *The Black Woman—An anthology*. New York: Signet Paperbacks, 1974.

Callahan, S.C. *The working mother*. New York: Macmillan, 1971.

Carden, M.L. *The new feminist movement*. New York: Russel Sage Foundation, 1974.

Carlson, R. Understanding women: Implications for personality theory and research. *Journal of Social Issues*, 1972, *28*(2), 17-32.

Carnegie Commission on Higher Education. *Opportunities for women in higher education: Their current participation, prospects for the future, and recommendations for action*. New York: McGraw-Hill, September 1973.

Carnegie Council on Policy Studies in Higher Education. *Making affirmative action work in higher education*. San Francisco: Jossey-Bass, 1975.

Carson, J. *Silent voices: The southern Negro woman today*. New York: Delacorte, 1969.

Cassara, B. *American women: The changing image*. Boston: Houghton Mifflin, 1963.

Chafe, W.H. *The American woman: Her changing social, economic and political roles, 1920-1970*. New York: Oxford University Press, 1972.

Chamj, B.E. *American women and American studies*. Pittsburgh: Know, 1971.

Chapman, D.W. *Known sex differences and their implications for higher education*. Poughkeepsie, New York: Vassar College, 1968.

Chasseguet-Smirgel, J. *Female sexuality: New psychoanalytic views*. Ann Arbor: University of Michigan Press, 1970.

Chesler, P. Women as psychiatric and psychotherapeutic patients. *Journal of Marriage and the Family*, 1971, *33*(4), 746-759.

Chesler, P. *Women and madness*. New York: Doubleday, 1972.

Chesler, P., & Goodman, E.J. *Women, money and power*. New York: William Morrow, 1976.

Christenson, S.J., & Swanson, A.O. Women and drug use: An annotated bibliography. *Journal of Psychedelic Drugs*, October-December 1974, *6*, 371-414.

Clements, K. *Emotional characteristics of mature women students in education*.

Washington, D.C.: ERIC Clearinghouse on Higher Education, American Association for Higher Education, 1974.

Cline-Naffziger, C. Women's lives and frustration, oppression, and anger: Some alternatives. *Journal of Counseling Psychology,* 1974, *21*(1), 51-56.

Cole, J.B. Black women in America: An annotated bibliography. *Black Scholar,* 1971, *3*(4), 42-53.

Cook, B. Role, labels, stereotypes: A counselor's challenge. *Journal of the National Association of Women Deans and Counselors,* Spring 1971, *34,* 99-105.

Cook, B.I., & Stone, B. *Counseling women.* Boston: Houghton Mifflin, 1973.

Cotera, M. A Chicana bibliography. *Magazine,* September 1973, *1,* 39.

Cowan, B.H. (Ed.). *Women's health care: Resources, writings, bibliographies.* Ann Arbor, Michigan: Belita Cowan, n.d.

Current research on sex roles. Berkeley, California: Sociologists for Women in Society, 1972.

Curtis, J. *Working mothers.* Garden City: Doubleday, 1976.

Daniels, A.K. *A survey of research concerns on women's issues* (pamphlet edited by Laura Kent). Washington, D.C.: Association of American Colleges, May 1975.

Dannett, S.G.L. *Profiles of Negro womanhood.* Yonkers, New York: Educational Heritage, 1964.

Davidson, K.M., Ginsburg, R.G., & Kay, H.H. *Sex-based discrimination: Test, cases and materials.* St. Paul, Minnesota: West Publishing Company, 1974.

Davidson, K.M., Ginsburg, R.B., & Kay, H.H. *Sex-based discrimination: Text, cases materials on sex-based discrimination.* St. Paul, Minnesota: West Publishing Company, 1975.

Deaux, K. *The behavior of women and men.* Monterey, Calif.: Brooks/Cole, 1976.

deBeauvoir, S. *The second sex.* New York: Bantam Books, 1961.

deBeauvoir, S. *The woman destroyed.* New York: Putnam & Sons, 1969.

Deckard, B.S. *The women's movement, political, socioeconomic and psychological issues.* New York: Dodd, Mead, 1975.

DeCrow, K. *Sexist justice.* New York: Random House, 1974.

Deutsch, H. *Psychology of women: A psychoanalytic interpretation.* New York: Grune & Stratton, 1944.

Diamond, E.E. (Ed.). *Issues of sex bias and sex fairness in career interest measurement.* Washington, D.C.: National Institute of Education, HEW, 1975.

Dingwall, E.J. *The American woman.* New York: Holt, Rinehart, & Winston Company, 1956.

Drake, S. Sources of information about women. *Community and Junior College Journal,* December/January 1976, *46,* 24-25.

Dreifus, C. *Woman's fate.* New York: Bantam Books, 1973.

Eason, J. Life style counseling for a reluctant leisure class. *Personnel and Guidance Journal,* October 1972, *51,* 127-132.

Eastman, P.C. Consciousness-raising as a resocialization process for women. *Smith College Studies in Social Work,* June 1973, *43,* 153-183.

Education Commission of the States. *Digest of Federal laws: Equal rights for women in education.* Denver: ECS, Report No. 61, 1975.

Education Commission of the States. *A handbook of state laws and policies affecting equal rights of women in education.* Denver: ECS, Report No. 62, 1975.

Education Commission of the States. *An overview of Federal court decisions affecting equal rights of women in education.* Denver: ECS, Report No. 70, 1975.

Epstein, C.F. Encountering the male establishment: Sex-status limits on women's career in the professions. *American Journal of Sociology,* 1970, *75,* 965-982.

Epstein, C.F. *Woman's place: Options and limits in professional careers.* Berkeley: University of California Press, 1970.

Epstein, C.F. Positive effects of the multiple negative: Explaining the success of black professional women. *American Journal of Sociology,* 1973, *78*(4), 912-935.

Epstein, C.F. *Reflections on the women's movement: Assessment of change and its limits.* New York: Institute of Life Insurance, 1975.

Epstein, C.F., & Goode, W. (Eds.). *The other half: Roads to woman's equality.* Englewood Cliffs, New Jersey: Prentice-Hall, 1971.

Falk, W.W., & Cosbey, A.G. Women and the status attainment process. *Social Science Quarterly,* September 1975, *56,* 307-314.

Farber, S., & Wilson, R.H.L. (Eds.). *The potential of women.* New York: McGraw-Hill, 1963.

Feldman, S.D. *Escape from the doll's house* (a Carnegie Commission on Higher Education report). New York: McGraw-Hill, 1974.

Ferber, M.A., & Lowry, H.M. Women: The new reserve army of the unemployed. *Signs: Journal of Women in Culture and Society,* Spring 1976, *1,* Part 2, 213-232.

Ferriss, A.L. *Indicators of trends in the status of American women.* New York: Russell Sage Foundation, 1971.

Figes, E. *Patriarchal attitudes.* Boston: Stein & Day, 1970.

Firestone, S. *The dialectic of sex: The case for feminist revolution.* New York: William Morrow, 1970.

Flexner, E. *Century of struggle* (Rev. ed.). Cambridge, Massachusetts: Harvard University Press, 1975.

Fogarty, M., Rappoport, R., & Rappoport, R. *Sex, career and family.* Beverly Hills, California: Sage Publication, 1971.

Freeman, J. *The politics of women's liberation.* New York: David McKay Company, 1975.

Fried, E. Does woman's new self-concept call for new approaches in group psychotherapy? *International Journal of Group Psychotherapy,* July 1974, *24,* 265-272.

Friedan, B. *The feminine mystique.* New York: W.W. Norton, 1963.

Friedan, B. *It changed my life: Writings on the women's movement.* New York: Random House, 1976.

Gager, N. (Ed.). *Women's rights almanac.* Bethesda, Maryland: Elizabeth Cady Stanton Publishing Company, 1974.

Gardner, J. Sexist counseling must stop. *Personnel and Guidance Journal,* May 1971, *49,* 705-714.

Garskof, M.H. (Ed.). *Roles women play: Readings toward women's liberation.* Monterey, California: Brooks/Cole Publishing Company, 1971.

Geisler, M.P., & Thrush, R.S. Counseling experiences and needs of older women students. *Journal of the National Association for Women Deans, Administrators and Counselors,* Fall 1975, *39,* 3-8.

Gettleman, S., & Markowitz, J. *The courage to divorce.* New York: Simon & Schuster, 1974.

Gillespie, J.B. *Rebellion in the marriage mart: Inquiry into a changing norm.* Madison, N.J.: Drew University, Society for the Study of Social Problems, 1975.

Ginzberg, E., & Associates. *Life styles of educated women.* New York: Columbia University Press, 1966.

Ginzberg, E., & Yohale, A. *Educated American women: Self portraits.* New York: Columbia University Press, 1966.

Glazer-Malbin, N., & Wachrer, H.G. (Eds.). *Woman in a man-made world.* Chicago: Rand McNally, 1972.

Goldberg, D. *The creative woman.* Washington: Robert B. Luce, 1963.

Goldberg, P. Are women prejudiced against women? *TransAction,* 1968, *5*(5), 28-30.

Goldman, G.D., & Milman, D.S. *Modern woman: Her psychology and sexuality.* Springfield, Illinois: Charles C Thomas, 1975.

Goodall, K. Garden variety sexism: Rampant among psychologists. *Psychology Today,* 1973, *6*(9), 9.

Gornick, V., & Moran, B. (Eds.). *Woman in sexist society: Studies in power and powerlessness.* New York: Harper & Row, 1970.

Greer, G. *The female eunuch.* New York: Bantam Books, 1972.

Grimstad, K., & Renniel, S. (Eds.). *The new woman's survival sourcebook.* New York: Alfred A. Knopf, 1975.

Grosz, R.D., & Joseph, C.D. *Vocational interests of black college women.* Washington, D.C.: ERIC Clearinghouse on Higher Education, American Association for Higher Education, 1973.

Group for the Advancement of Psychiatry. *The educated woman: Prospects and problems.* New York: Charles Scribner's Sons, 1975.

Gump, J.P. Sex-role attitudes and psychological well-being. *Journal of Social Issues,* 1972, *28,* 79-92.

Haener, D. The working woman: Can counselors take the heat? *Personnel and Guidance Journal,* October 1972, *51,* 109-112.

Hall, D.T. Pressures from work, self, and home in the life stages of married women. *Journal of Vocational Behavior,* 1975, *6,* 121-132.

Hall, D.T., & Gordon, F.E. Career choices of married women: Effects on conflict, role behavior and satisfaction. *Journal of Applied Psychology,* 1973, *58*(1), 42-48.

Hansen, L.S. We are furious (female) but we can shape our own development. *Personnel and Guidance Journal,* October 1972, *51,* 87-93.

Hansen, L.S. Counseling and career (self) development. *Focus on Guidance,* December 1974.

Harbeson, G.E. *Choice and challenge.* Cambridge, Massachusetts: Schenkman Publishing Company, 1967.

Harding, M.E. *The way of all women: A psychological interpretation* (1st rev. ed.). New York: G.P. Putnam's Sons for the C.G. Jung Foundation for Analytical Psychology, 1970.

Harmon, L.W. Anatomy of career commitment in women. *Journal of Counseling Psychology,* 1970, *17,* 77-80.

Hartsook, J.E., Olch, D.R., & deWolf, V.A. Personality characteristics of women's assertiveness training group participants. *Journal of Counseling Psychology,* 1976, *23,* 322-326.

Hawley, P. What women think men think: Does it affect their career choice? *Journal of Counseling Psychology,* 1971, *18,* 193-199.

Hays, H.R. *The dangerous sex: The myth of feminine evil.* New York: G.P. Putnam's Sons, 1964.

Henderson, A.G., & Henderson, J.G. *The liberated woman in college.* Berkeley, California: University of California, 1972.

Herschberger, R. *Adam's rib: A defense of modern women.* New York: Harper & Row, 1970.

Hilberman, E. *The rape victim.* Washington, D.C.: American Psychiatric Association, 1976.

Hogan, B. Blacks vs. women: When victims collide. *Business and Society Review/Innovation,* Summer 1974, *10,* 71-77.

Hohenshil, T.A. Perspectives on career counseling for women: 1884—1974. *Vocational Guidance Quarterly,* December 1974, *23,* 100-103.

Hole, J., & Levine, E. *Rebirth of feminism.* New York: Quadrangle Books, 1971.

Horne, A.M., & Graff, R.W. Married student concerns: Who counsels the married population? *Journal of Counseling Psychology,* 1973, *20,* 384-385.

Horner, M.S. Fail: Bright women. *Psychology Today,* November 1969, *3,* 36-41.

Horner, M.S. Sex differences in achievement motivation and performance in competitive and non-competitive situations (Doctoral dissertation, University of Michigan, 1968). *Dissertation Abstracts International,* 1969, *30,* 407B. (University Microfilms No. 69-12, 135)

Horner, M.S. Toward an understanding of achievement-rated conflicts in women. *Journal of Social Issues,* 1972, *28,* 129-155.

Horney, K. *Feminine psychology* (H. Kelman, Ed.). New York: W.W. Norton, 1967.

Hottel, A.K. (Ed.). Women around the world. *Annals of The American Academy of Political and Social Science,* 1968, *375,* 1-175.

Hough, K.S., & Bem, P.A. Is the "women's movement" erasing the mark of oppression from the female psyche? *Journal of Psychology,* March 1975, *89,* 249-258.

Howe, F., Rich, A., Hochschild, A., & Wallach, A. *Women and the power to change.* New York: McGraw-Hill, 1975.

Huber, J. (Ed.). *Changing woman in a changing society.* Chicago: University of Chicago Press, 1973.

Hughes, M.M. *The sexual barrier: Legal and economic aspects of employment.* San Francisco: University of California, Hastings College of the Law, 1970.

Hutt, C. *Males and females.* Harmondsworth, England: Penguin Books, 1972.

Hyde, J.S., & Rosenberg, B.G. *Half the human experience.* Lexington, Massachusetts: D.C. Heath, 1976.

Indiana University. *Women's films—A critical guide.* Bloomington: Indiana University, Audio-Visual Center, 1975.

Jacobson, D. Rejection of the retiree role: A study of female industrial workers in their 50's. *Human Relations,* May 1974, *27,* 477-492.

Janeway, E. *Man's world, woman's place: A study of social mythology.* New York: William Morrow, 1971.

Janeway, E. *Between myth and morning: Women awakening.* New York: William Morrow, 1974.

Jeghelian, A. Surviving sexism: Strategies and consequences. *Personnel and Guidance Journal,* February 1976, *54,* 307-311.

Jongward, D., & Scott, D. *Women as winners: Transactional analysis for personal growth.* Reading, Massachusetts: Addison-Wesley, 1976.

Kanowitz, L. *Women and the law: The unfinished revolution.* Albuquerque: University of New Mexico Press, 1969.

Kaser, J. How to get along with career women: Guidelines for career men. *Phi Delta Kappan,* 56(7), 486-488.

Katzell, M.E., & Byham, W.C. (Eds.). *Women in the work force: Confrontation with change.* New York: Human Sciences Press, 1972.

Keller, S. The future role of women. *American Academy of Political and Social Science—Annals,* July 1973, *408,* 1-12.

Kinsey, A.C., Pomeroy, W.B., Martin, C.E., & Gebhard, P.J. *Sexual behavior in the human female.* Philadelphia: W.B. Saunders, 1953.

Kitchener, K.S., Corazzini, J.G., & Huebner, L.A. A study of counseling center hiring practices: What does it take for a woman to be hired? *Journal of Counseling Psychology,* 1975, *22,* 440-445.

Klein, C. *The single parent experience.* New York: Walker, 1973.

Knox, B.S. *Trends in the counseling of women in higher education, 1957-1973* (Ruth Strang Research Award Monograph Series No. 1). Washington, D.C.: National Association for Women Deans, Administrators and Counselors, 1975.

Kohen, A.I., Breinich, S.C., & Shields, P. *Women and the economy: A bibliography and a review of the literature on sex differentiation in the labor market.* Columbus, Ohio: Center for Human Resource Research, The Ohio State University, n.d.

Komarovsky, M. *Women in the modern world: Their educations and their dilemmas.* Boston: Little, Brown, 1953.

Kraditor, A. *Up from the pedestal: Selected documents from the history of American feminism.* Chicago: Quadrangle, 1968.

Kreps, J. *Sex in the marketplace: American women at work.* Baltimore: Johns Hopkins Press, 1971.

Kreps, J. *Women and the American economy: A look to the 1980's.* Englewood Cliffs, New Jersey: Prentice-Hall, 1976.

Kundsin, R.B. *Women and success: The anatomy of achievement.* New York: William Morrow, 1974.

Ladner, J.A. *Tomorrow's tomorrow: The black woman.* New York: Doubleday, 1971.

Laws, J.L. Work aspiration of women: False leads and new starts. *Signs: Journal of Women in Culture and Society,* Spring 1976, *1,* Part 2, 33-49.

Lederer, W. *The fear of women.* New York: Grune & Stratton, 1968.

Leppaluoto, J.R. (Coord. Ed.). *Women on the move: A feminist perspective.* Pittsburgh: Know, 1973.

Lerner, G. (Ed.). *Black women in white America.* New York: Vintage Books, 1972.

Lewis, E.C. *Developing women's potential.* Ames: Iowa State University Press, 1968.

Lewis, J.A. Counselors and women: Finding each other. *Personnel and Guidance Journal,* October 1972, *51,* 147-150.

Lifton, R.J. (Ed.). *The woman in America.* Boston: Houghton Mifflin, 1964.

Lopata, H.Z. Self-identity in marriage and widowhood. *The Sociological Quarterly,* Summer 1973, *14,* 407-418.

Ludovici, L.J. *The final inequality: A critical assessment of woman's sexual role in society.* New York: W.W. Norton, 1965.

Maccoby, E. (Ed.). *The development of sex differences.* Stanford, California: Stanford University Press, 1966.

Maccoby, E., & Jacklin, C.N. *Psychology of sex differences.* Stanford, California: Stanford University Press, 1974.

Mander, A.V., Rush, A.K. *Feminism as therapy.* New York: Random House; Berkeley, California: Bookworks Publishing Company, 1974.

Markus, H. *Continuing education for women: Factors influencing a return to school and the school experience.* Washington, D.C.: ERIC Clearinghouse on Higher Education, American Association for Higher Education, 1973.

Martin, D. *Battered wives.* San Francisco: Glide Publications, 1976.

Maslin, A., & Davis, J.L. Sex-role stereotyping as a factor in mental health standards among counselors-in-training. *Journal of Counseling Psychology,* 1975, *22,* 87-91.

Masters, W.H., & Johnson, V.E. *Human sexual response.* Boston: Little, Brown, 1966.

Matthews, E.E., Feingold, S.N., Berry, J., Weary, B., & Tyler, L.E. *Counseling girls and women over the lifespan.* Washington, D.C.: National Vocational Guidance Association, 1972.

McBride, A.B. *A married feminist.* New York: Harper & Row, 1976.

McClure, G.T. *Sex role stereotyping and evaluation: A systems approach.* Washington, D.C.: ERIC Clearinghouse on Higher Education, American Association for Higher Education, 1973.

McCoy, V.R. Student wives: Lives in limbo. *Vocational Guidance Quarterly,* September 1976, *25,* 35-42.

McEwen, M.K. Counseling women: A review of the research. *Journal of College Student Personnel,* 1975, *16*(5), 382-388.

McGinley, P. *Sixpence in her shoe.* New York: William Morrow, 1964.

Mead, M. *Male and female.* New York: William Morrow, 1949.

Meador, B., Solomon, E., & Bowen, M. Encounter groups for women only. In N.A. Solomon & B. Berzon (Eds.), *New perspectives on encounter groups.* San Francisco: Jossey-Bass, 1972.

Mednick, M.T. *Motivational and personality factors related to career goals of black college women* (a final report). Washington, D.C.: ERIC Clearinghouse on Higher Education, American Association for Higher Education, 1973.

Mednick, M.T., & Tangri, S.S. The new social psychological perspectives on women. *Journal of Social Issues,* 1972, *28,* 1-16.

Merriam, E. *After Nora slammed the door.* Cleveland: World Publishing Company, 1964.

Mill, J.S. *On liberty, representative government, the subjection of women: Three essays.* London: Oxford University Press, 1969.

Mill, J.S. *On the subjection of women* (1869). New York: Fawcett Publications, 1971.

Miller, J.B. *Psychoanalysis and women.* Baltimore, Maryland: Penguin Books, 1973.

Millett, K. *Sexual politics.* New York: Doubleday, 1970.

Mitchell, J. *Woman's estate.* New York: Pantheon Books, 1971.

Mitchell, J. *Psychoanalysis and feminism.* New York: Pantheon Books, 1974.

Money, J., & Ehrhardt, A. *Man & woman, boy & girl: The differentiation and dimorphism of gender identity from conception to maturity.* Baltimore: Johns Hopkins University Press, 1972.

Morgan, R. *Women in revolt.* New York: Random House, 1969.

Morgan, R. (Ed.). *Sisterhood is powerful.* New York: Random House, 1970.

Mueller, K.H. *Educating women for a changing world.* Minneapolis: University of Minnesota Press, 1954.

Murphy, I.L. *Public policy on the status of women: Agenda and strategy for the 70's.* Lexington, Massachusetts: Lexington Books, 1973.

Murphy, K. (Ed.). Sexism in counseling. *Counseling and Values,* April 1975, *19,* 144-204. (Entire issue devoted to this topic.)

Naffziger, K.G. *A survey of counselor-educators' and other selected professionals' attitudes toward women's roles* (Doctoral dissertation, University of Oregon, 1972). Ann Arbor, Michigan: University Microfilms, 1972, No. 72-956.

National Commission on the Observance of International Women's Year. *"To form a more perfect union"* . . . *justice for American women.* Washington, D.C.: U.S. Government Printing Office, June 1976.

Newcomer, M. *A century of higher education for women.* New York: Harper, 1959.

Nieto, C. The Chicana and the women's rights movement. *Civil Rights Digest,* Spring 1974, *6,* 469-496.

O'Brien, P. *The woman alone.* New York: Quadrangle Books, 1973.

Olesker, W., & Balter, L. Sex and empathy. *Journal of Counseling Psychology,* 1972, *19*(6), 559-562.

Oliver, L.W. Counseling implications of recent research on women. *Personnel and Guidance Journal,* 1975, *53,* 430-437.

O'Neill, W.L. *Everyone was brave: The rise and fall of feminism in America.* Chicago: Quadrangle Books, 1969.

Packard, V. *The sexual wilderness: The contemporary upheaval in male-female relationships.* New York: David McKay Company, 1968.

Parelius, A.P. Emerging sex-role attitudes, expectations, and strains among college women. *Journal of Marriage and the Family,* 1975, *37,* 146-153.

Peck, E. *A funny thing happened on the way to equality.* Englewood Cliffs, New Jersey: Prentice-Hall, 1975.

Pheterson, G.I., Kiesler, S.B., & Goldberg, P.A. Evaluation of the performance of women as a function of their sex, achievement, and personal history. *Journal of Personality and Social Psychology,* 1971, *19,* 114-118.

Pietrofesa, J.J., & Schlossberg, N.K. *Counselor bias and the female occupational role.* Washington, D.C.: United States Department of Health, Education and Welfare, Office of Education, 1970. (ERIC Document Reproduction Service No. ED 044 749, CG 006 056)

Pogrebin, L.C. *Getting yours: How to make the system work for the working woman.* New York: David McKay Company, 1975.

Prentice, B., & Sandman, P. *Five hundred back to work ideas for housewives.* New York: Macmillan Company, 1971.

Presidential Task Force on Women's Rights and Responsibilities (Virginia R. Allan, Chairman). *A matter of simple justice.* Washington, D.C.: U.S. Government Printing Office, 1969.

Project on the Status and Education of Women. *Women's centers: Where are they?* Washington, D.C.: Association of American Colleges, September 1975.

Puryear, G.R., & Mednick, M.S. Black militancy, affective attachment, and the fear of success in black college women. *Journal of Consulting and Clinical Psychology,* 1974, *42*(2), 263-266.

Raza women: A bibliography related to the Spanish-speaking woman. San Francisco: Concilio Mujeres, n.d.

Reed, E. *Woman's evolution.* New York: Pathfinder Press, 1975.

Reeves, N. *Womankind: Beyond the stereotypes.* Chicago, New York: Aldine Atherton, 1971.

Rheingold, J. *The fear of being a woman.* New York: Grune & Stratton, 1964.

Rice, J.K. Continuing education for women, 1960-1975: A critical appraisal. *Educational Record,* Fall 1975, *56,* 240-249.

Riegel, R.E. *American feminists.* Lawrence: University of Kansas Press, 1963.

Riegel, R.E. *American women: A story of social change.* Rutherford: Fairleigh Dickinson University Press, 1970.

Roach, R.M. "Honey, won't you please stay home." *Personnel and Guidance Journal*, October 1976, *55*, 86-89.

Robinson, L.H. *Women's studies: Courses and programs for higher education.* Washington, D.C.: American Association for Higher Education, 1973.

Rosaldo, M.Z., & Lamphere, L. (Eds.). *Woman, culture and society.* Stanford, California: Stanford University Press, 1974.

Rose, C. (Ed.). Meeting women's new educational needs. *New Directions for Higher Education*, Autumn 1975, No. 11.

Rosenberg, M.B., & Bergstrom, L.V. (Eds.). *Women and society: A critical review of the literature with a selected, annotated bibliography.* Beverly Hills, California: Sage Publications, 1975.

Ross, S. *The rights of women.* New York: Discus/Avon, 1973.

Rossi, A.S. *Academic women on the move.* New York: Russell Sage Foundation, 1973.

Rossi, A.S. *The feminist papers.* New York: Bantam Books, 1974.

Roszak, B., & Roszak, T. (Eds.). *Masculine-feminine.* New York: Harper & Row, 1969.

Rothschild, C.S. (Ed.). *Sociology of women.* Boston: Finn-Blaisdell, 1971.

Ruble, D.N., Frieze, I.H., & Parson, J.E. Sex roles: Persistence and change. *Journal of Social Issues*, 1972, *32*(3).

Ryan, M.P. *Womanhood in America: From colonial times to the present.* New York: New Viewpoints, 1975.

Safilios-Rothschild, C. *Toward a sociology of women.* Lexington, Massachusetts: Xerox College Publishing, 1972.

Sargent, A.G. *Beyond sex roles.* St. Paul, Minnesota: West Publishing Company, 1977.

Sawhill, I. Discrimination and poverty among women who head families. *Signs: Journal of Women in Culture and Society*, Spring 1976, *1*, Part 2, 201-211.

Schaeffer, D.L. (Ed.). *Sex differences in personality.* Monterey, California: Brooks/Cole Publishing Company, 1971.

Schlossberg, N.K. A framework for counseling women. *Personnel and Guidance Journal*, October 1972, *51*, 137-143.

Schlossberg, N.K. *Liberated counseling: A question mark.* Washington, D.C.: Office of Women in Higher Education, American Council on Education, 1973.

Schlossberg, N.K. The right to be wrong is gone: Women in academe. *Educational Record*, Fall 1974, *55*, 257-262.

Scholz, N.T., Prince, J.S., & Girdon, P.M. *How to decide: A guide for women.* New York: College Entrance Examination Board, 1975.

Scott, A.F. (Ed.). *The American woman: Who was she?* Englewood Cliffs, New Jersey: Prentice-Hall, 1971.

Scott, P.B. *The black female athlete: Another neglected area in black and women's studies.* Knoxville: University of Tennessee, Association of Social and Behavioral Scientists, 1975.

Scott, P.B. *Professional black women.* Paper delivered at the Second Pan-African Conference on the Black Family, Louisville, Kentucky, March 28, 1975.

Seifer, N. *Absent from the majority: Working class women in America.* New York: National Project on Ethnic America, 1973.

Seifer, N. *Where feminism and ethnicity intersect: The impact of parallel movements.* New York: Institute on Pluralism & Group Identity, 1976.

Seward, G.H., & Williamson, C. (Eds.). *Sex roles in changing society.* New York: Random House, 1970.

Sexton, P. *Women in education.* Bloomington, Indiana: Phi Delta Kappa, 1976.

Sexton, P.C. *Minority group women.* Washington, D.C.: ERIC Clearinghouse on Higher Education, American Association for Higher Education, 1974.

Shapiro, J. *Socialization of sex roles in the counseling setting: Differential counselor behavioral and attitudinal responses to typical and atypical female sex roles.* Washington, D.C.: ERIC Clearinghouse on Higher Education, American Association for Higher Education, 1975.

Sheehy, G. *Passages: Predictable crises of adult life.* New York: E.P. Dutton, 1976.

Sherfey, M.J. *The nature and evolution of female sexuality.* New York: Random House, 1972.

Sherman, J. *On the psychology of women: A survey of empirical studies.* Springfield, Illinois: Charles C Thomas, 1975.

Shishkoff, M.M. Reachout: Treating mental health problems in middle-age women. *Journal of the National Association for Women Deans, Administrators and Counselors,* Fall 1975, *39,* 32-36.

Showalter, E. (Ed.). *Women's liberation and literature.* New York: Harcourt Brace Jovanovich, 1971.

Shulman, C.H. *Affirmative action: Women's rights on campus.* Washington, D.C.: ERIC Clearinghouse on Higher Education, American Association for Higher Education, September 1972.

Smith, J.A. For God's sake, what do these women want? *Personnel and Guidance Journal,* October 1972, *51,* 133-136.

Smith, M.L. Notes on "Perspectives on counseling bias: Implications for counselor education." *The Counseling Psychologist,* 1973, *4*(2), 93.

Smith, P. *Daughters of the promised land: Women in American history, being an examination of the strange history of the female sex from the beginning to the present, with special attention to the women of America.* Boston: Little, Brown, 1970.

Staines, G., Tavris, C., & Jayarante, T.E. The queen bee syndrome. *Psychology Today,* January 1974, *7,* 55-60.

Staples, R. *The Black woman in America: Sex, marriage and the family.* Chicago: Nelson-Hall Publishers, 1973.

Steinmann, A. Female-role perception as a factor in counseling. *Journal of the National Association of Women Deans and Counselors,* Fall 1970, *34,* 27-33.

Stewart, A.J., & Winter, D.G. Self-definition and social definition in women. *Journal of Personality,* June 1974, *42,* 238-259.

Stimpson, C.R. The new feminism and women's studies. *Change,* September 1973, *5,* 43-48.

Stoll, C.S. *Female and male,* Dubuque, Iowa: Wm. C. Brown Company, 1974.

Stoller, R.J. *Sex and gender.* New York: Science House, 1968.

Strouse, J. (Ed.). *Women and analysis.* New York: Grossman, 1974.

Stuart, M., & Liu, W.T. (Eds.). *The emerging woman, the impact of family planning.* Boston: Little, Brown, 1970.

Sullerot, E. *Women, society and change.* New York: McGraw-Hill, 1971.

Switzer, E., & Susco, W.W. *The law for women: Real cases and what happened.* New York: Charles Scribner's Sons, 1975.

Tanner, L.B. *Voices from women's liberation.* New York: Signet Book Division, New American Library, 1970.

TenElshof, A., & Searle, S.E. Developing a women's center. *Journal of the National Association for Women Deans, Administrators and Counselors,* Summer 1974, *37,* 173-178.

Tennov, D. *Psychotherapy: The hazardous cure.* New York: Abelard-Schuman, 1975.

Theodore, A. (Ed.). *The professional woman.* Cambridge, Massachusetts: Schenkman Publishing Company, 1971.

Thomas, H., & Stewart, N. Counselor response to female clients with deviate and conforming career goals. *Journal of Counseling Psychology,* 1971, *18,* 352-357.

Thompson, C.M. *On women* (M.R. Green, Ed.). New York: New American Library, 1971.

Thorne, B., & Henley, N. (Eds.). *Language and sex: Difference and dominance.* Rowley, Massachusetts: Newberry House Publishing, 1975.

Tibbets, S.L. Sex role stereotyping: Why women discriminate against themselves. *Journal of the National Association for Women Deans, Administrators and Counselors,* Summer 1975, *38,* 177-183.

Tidball, E.M. On liberation and competence. *Educational Record,* Spring 1976, *57,* 101-110.

Tomlinson-Keasey, C. Role variables: Their influence on female motivational constructs. *Journal of Counseling Psychology,* 1974, *21*(3), 232-237.

Trent, J.S., & Trent, J.D. *The National Women's Political Caucus: A rhetorical biography.* Washington, D.C.: ERIC Clearinghouse on Higher Education, American Association for Higher Education, 1973.

Unger, R.K. (Ed.). *Woman: Dependent or independent variable?* New York: Psychological Dimensions, 1975.

Vetter, L., and others. *Career guidance materials: Implications for women's career development.* Washington, D.C.: ERIC Clearinghouse on Higher Education, American Association for Higher Education, Research and Development Series No. 97, 1974.

Walstedt, J.J. *The psychology of women: A partially annotated bibliography.* Pittsburgh: Know, 1973.

Walstedt, J.J. Women as marginals. *Psychological Reports,* 1974, *34,* 639-646.

Weissman, M.M. The depressed woman: Recent research. *Social Work,* 1972, *17*(5), 19-25.

Weissman, M.M. *The depressed woman: A study of social relationships.* Chicago: University of Chicago Press, 1974.

Weisstein, N. *Kinder, Kuche, Kerche as scientific law: Psychology constructs the female.* Chicago: Voice of the Women's Liberation Movement, n.d.

Weisstein, N. Woman as nigger. *Psychology Today,* October 1969, pp. 20 ff.

Welch, S. Support among women for the issues of the women's movement. *Sociological Quarterly,* Spring 1975, *16,* 216-227.

Wesley, C. The woman's movement and psychotherapy. *Social Work,* March 1975, *20,* 120-125.

Westervelt, E.M. Essay review of opportunities for women in higher education: Their current participation, prospects for the future, and recommendations for action (report and recommendations by the Carnegie Commission on Higher Education). *Harvard Educational Review,* May 1974, *44,* 295-313.

Witt, S.H. Native women today: Sexism and the Indian woman. *Civil Rights Digest,* Spring 1974, *6,* 29-35.

Wolfson, K.P. Career development patterns of college women. *Journal of Counseling Psychology,* March 1976, *23,* 119-125.

Wollstonecraft, M. *A vindication of the rights of woman.* New York: W.W. Norton, 1967.

Women in Transition, Inc. *Women in transition: A feminist handbook on separation and divorce.* New York: Charles Scribner's Sons, 1975.

Women on campus: The unfinished liberation. New Rochelle, New York: Editors of *Change* magazine, 1975.

Woody, T. *A history of women's education in the United States* (2 vols.). New York: The Science Press, 1929.

Yates, G.G. *What women want: The ideas of the movement.* Cambridge, Massachusetts: Harvard University Press, 1975.

Yates, M. Coping: *A survival manual for women alone.* Englewood Cliffs, New Jersey: Prentice-Hall, 1975.

Zuckoff, A.C. *Bibliography on the Jewish woman* (5th ed.). New York: Jewish Feminist Organization, 1975.

INDEX

Abortion, 125, 126, 196, 261, 263, 265,
    280
  clinic, 264
Acceptance, 146
  vs. power, 136
Acculturation, 142
Achievement, 5, 6, 21, 29, 43, 48, 142-144,
    274
  age and, 168
  fear of, 204
  motivation, 102-103, 159-172, 194
  vicarious, 161-162, 166, 167, 213, 219,
    281
Activism, 2
Adjustment, 62
Adler, A., 243, 245, 246, 249
Adolescence, 13, 155-156
  of Black female, 187-188
Affirmative action, 128
Age, 5-6
  and aggression, 146
  of client, 209
  at marriage, 15
  of therapist, 209
Aggression, 24, 103, 108-110, 137
  and age, 146
  and breast cancer, 253, 254
  in females, 147
  mode of, 25
  and sex, 146-147

Ambiguity, 177
Ambivalence, 160
American College Testing Program, 68
American Psychiatric Association, 288
American Psychological Association,
    216, 278, 279, 283, 293
Androgen, 11, 153, 155, 156, 158
Anger, 57, 201, 254, 256, 262, 263, 266,
    268, 282
Anniversary, 237
Antidivorce indoctrination, 235
Antisocial behavior, 247
Anxiety, 106, 115-116, 120, 121, 140, 255
Apathy, 28
Appearance, 6, 11, 43, 123-124
Aslin, A. L., 215, 230-240, 271, 274, 275,
    280, 290
Aspiration, 142-144
Assertiveness, 24, 169, 202, 203, 224, 263
  anxiety about, 115-116
  training, 106-122, 159, 204, 226, 233,
    257
Attention, 248
Audiotaping, 72
Authority, 138, 243, 244
Autonomy, 100, 101, 177, 200
Awareness, 106
  and motivation, 112-113
  political, 133
  self-, 173, 279

Bandura, A., 112, 121, 140, 149
Behavior:
  aggressive, 108-110
  antisocial, 247
  assertive, 107, 109-111
  change, 245-247
  nonassertive, 107-108, 109, 114
  rehearsal of, 116-120
Behavioral program, 201-203
Behaviorism, 199
Belief system, 113-115
Belson, B. A., 293-306
Bereavement, 237 (*see also* Grief;
  Mourning)
Bernard, J., 26, 31, 294
Berne, E., 200
Bettelheim, B., 162, 170
Biocentric theorizing, 193
Biopsy, 252
Birk, J. M., 208-217, 270, 271, 272, 275,
  277, 286, 288
Birth control, 125, 126, 196
  abortion as, 265
Birth order, 138-140
Birth rate, 15
Black consciousness, 186
Black woman, 286-290
  and career orientation, 84-85
  labor-force participation of, 188-189
  as role model, 169
  self-awareness of, 279
  self-esteem in, 189-191
  strengths of, 186-192
Body:
  build, 147-148
  control, 125-127
  identification with, 96
  posture, 107
Breast cancer, 250-260
Bridwell, M. W., 261-269, 271, 274, 275,
  280, 290
Brodsky, A. M., 277-283
Brooks, L., 218-229, 271, 274, 281, 290

Cancer, breast, 250-260
Career:
  aspiration, 3, 14-15, 20, 26, 50, 52, 77
  choice, 82-88
  commitment, 83
  counseling, 75-93, 235

Career (continued)
  development, 76-82
  and discrimination, 164-165
  and education, 77, 81-87
  -home conflict, 166, 167
  and male attitudes, 87-88
  and marriage, 30, 81, 83, 84
  motivation, 159-172, 274
  pattern, 77
  typology theory, 78-79
Carkhuff Scale, 72
Carpenter, L., 1
Change:
  behavioral, 245-247
  qualitative, 176-177
Child, 3, 12, 53-54, 138-140, 241-249
  care, 165, 166
  custody of, 235, 236
  -parent relationship, 46, 47, 48
  -rearing, 30, 77
  support for, 236
  unborn, 264
Classroom, as social system, 141-146
Cleavage, 140-141
Client:
  Black, 210
  middle-aged, 220
  race of, 212
  self-disclosure, 209, 210
  woman, 208-217
Cognitive-development theory, 12, 173-
  185
Cognitive therapy, 203
Cognitive understanding, 70-71
Communication, 221
  skill, 224, 226
  system, 4
Community:
  action, 19
  mental-health center, 212
Competence, 136, 140, 163
Competition, 23, 24, 25
  in sport, 157-158
Competitiveness, 160
Conceptual systems, 178
Conflict:
  fear of, 201
  and gender role, 14
  home-career, 166, 167
  interpersonal, 106

Conflict (continued)
  reduction, 86
Confrontation, 56, 199
Consciousness raising, 159, 204
  group, 34, 35, 36, 71, 112, 182, 189, 203
  as therapy model, 199
Constructiveness, 137
Continuing Education of Women, 129
Cooperation, 246
Counseling:
  career, 75-93, 235
  and cognitive-development theory,
    180-184
  for education, 235
  group, 233
  interview, 61-66
  of mastectomy patients, 250-260
  material, 66-86
  perceptual task of, 181
  with rape victims, 266-269
  and re-entry, 219, 225
  research, 168-169, 270-276
  sex bias in, 59-74, 213-214, 227
  vocational, 182, 235, 279
Counselor:
  cognitive development of, 272
  education program, 183
  male, 63, 66
  sex of, 182, 209, 273
  woman, 208-217
Countertransference, 289
Courage, 255
Covert manipulation, 24
Crandall Intellectual Responsibility
    Scale, 144
Credit rating, 130
Crisis, 242, 280
Criticism, 199
Custody, 235, 236

Day care, 86
Death, 237, 250, 251, 256, 258
de Beauvoir, S., 10, 296
Decision-making, 219-223
Defensiveness, 39
Deficit model, 186, 191
Democratic social system, 243, 247
Denial, 262, 263, 266
Dependence, 36, 37, 201-202
  and imitation, 140

Dependence (continued)
  vs. independence, 26-27
  need, 66
Depression, 57, 201, 202, 262, 263, 266
  and breast cancer, 253, 254, 255
  postpartum, 261
Despair, 237
Development, as becoming, 241
Developmental self-concept theory, 76-
    77
Developmental theory, 193
Devlin, B., 25
Discontent, 220-221
Discouragement, 57, 245, 246
Discrimination, 130, 189
  in work, 88, 164-165, 235
Disequilibrium, 176, 179
Dissonance, 176, 181
Divorce, 16, **** 30-240, 280, 281, 290
  indoctrination against, 235
  and self-esteem, 20
Doherty, M. A., 94-105
Domestic role, 18
Dominance:
  hierarchy, 141
  male, 23, 35
Double standard:
  of health, 62
  sexual, 197
Doubt, 100
Dreikurs, R., 241, 242, 243, 244, 245, 248,
    249
Dualism, 178, 182

Ectomorph, 147
Education:
  and career, 77, 81-87
  counseling for, 235
  legislation, 166
  life-long, 129
  and work, 15
Egalitarianism, 188, 189
Ego development, 176
Emotion, 10
Emotionality, 103
Empathy, 177, 179, 272, 273
Employment:
  discrimination in, 15, 16, 129
  legislation, 166
  opportunities, 29-30

Empty nest, 219, 281
Encouragement, 245, 247, 248
Endomorph, 148
Environment, 6, 12
  family, 4
Equal Employment Opportunity
    Commission, 128
Equality, 243
Equal opportunity, 159
Equal Pay Act, 15, 128
Equal Rights Amendment, 130, 131, 196
Erikson, E., 96-104, 193, 205
Estrogen, 11, 153, 155, 158
Evans, D. A., 284-292
Expectation, 24, 25, 60, 165
Expert power, 137
Extramarital relationships, 22

Failure, 117, 123-124, 238, 241
  fear of, 55
Familial identification, 142
Family, 197-199
  and achievement motivation, 162-163
  environment, 4
  involvement, 221
  nuclear, 198
  of rape victim, 267
  role, 20, 24
  socialization, 166, 167
  in transition, 243-244
Fantasy, 203, 222
Farmer, H. S., 90, 159-172, 274, 278, 286, 287
Father, 138, 242
Fear, 11, 237, 255, 266, 268
  of conflict, 201
  irrational, 115, 120
  between sexes, 194
  of success, 44, 55, 82, 160, 161-162, 166, 167, 168-169, 203, 204
Femininity, 5, 7, 13, 36, 102, 197
  vs. individuality, 238
  and weakness, 148
Feminism, 159, 227
  counselor and, 27-30
  impact of, 1-33
  and vocational counseling, 279
Feminist therapy, 199-204
Fishbowl technique, 71
Fitzgerald, L. E., 128-134

Ford, D. J., 186-192, 271, 275, 279, 286-287
Freedom, 37, 247
Freiberg, P., 261-269, 271, 274, 275, 280, 290
Freud, S., 9, 35, 95, 96, 101, 104, 183, 195, 200, 201, 261, 262, 269, 291, 292
Friedan, B., 25, 131, 220, 228, 297
Friend, 265, 267, 282
Frigidity, 197
Frustration, 201
Fulfillment, 197
  vs. responsibility, 85

Gender, 135, 136
  behavior, 24-27
  identity, 11-14, 23, 24, 28, 31
  role, 12-24, 28
  and status, 148
  /status effect, 140
Generation, 6
  gap, 188, 244
Genetic variation, 10
Genuineness, 272
Gestalt technique, 199
Goal setting, 223-225
Greer, G., 25, 26, 27, 32, 298
Grief, 237, 261, 268, 290
  and rape, 265-266
  and unwanted pregnancy, 262-264
Group:
  consciousness-raising, 34, 35, 37, 71, 112, 182, 189, 203
  counseling, 233
  encounter, 106
  process in classroom, 144-146
  support, 225
  women in, 34-58
Guilt, 14, 17, 29, 30, 113, 226, 255, 266, 268, 280

Happiness, 114
Harmon, L. W., 123-127, 162, 298
Harris, D. V., 153-158, 274, 280, 287
Hate, 266, 268
  self-, 190, 279
Helping skills, 71-72
Helplessness, 248
  vs. power, 143
Helpless power, 137

Hill, C. E., 270-276
Holiday, 237
Holroyd, J., 193-207, 270, 274, 277, 278, 288
Home-career conflict, 166, 167
Homemaking, 77
Homosexuality, 193, 197, 288
Hormone system, 10, 11 (*see also* Androgen; Estrogen)
Horney, K., 9, 32, 95, 104, 193, 205, 299
Hostility, 194
Housewife, 234
Humanist therapy, 199
Humiliation, 266, 268
Husband, 221, 226, 236, 259

Identity, 29, 96-101, 179
    and body, 96
    and breast cancer, 254
    formation, 178
Ideology:
    and conflict, 7
    and female development, 8-14
    feminist vs. traditional, 13, 17, 26-27
Imitation, 140
Inadequacy, 108, 248
Incest, 268
Independence, 24, 53, 169, 187, 188
    vs. dependence, 26-27
Individual, 4
    differences, 175
    Psychology, 245
    variability, 271, 272
Individuality, 14, 28, 29
    vs. femininity, 238
Inertia, intellectual, 46
Informed consent, 256
Inhibition, 108
Inner-circle/outer-circle technique, 71
Inner space, 97, 101-102
Intelligence, and social power, 145, 146
Interactionism, 175, 176
Intercollegiate Association of Women Students, 130, 131
Interdependence, 177
Internality, 286
Interpersonal conflict, 106
Intimacy, 22, 23, 35, 55, 100
    vs. isolation, 98
It Scale, 139

Jakubowski, P., 106-122
Jefferies, D. (*see* Ford, D. J.)
Job discrimination, 164-165, 235
Johnson, V. E., 21, 22, 122, 193, 194, 196, 206, 301
Judo, 126
Juvenile delinquency, 82-83

Karate, 126
Kinsey, A. C., 21
Kinship role, 198
Knefelkamp, L. L., 173-185, 271, 273, 278, 279, 288, 289
Kohlberg, L., 12, 13, 32, 176, 177, 185
Kreps, J., 18, 32

Law, 9, 130
Lawyer, 233
Learning situation, 248
Legislation, 159, 165, 166
Life-style, 15, 179, 222, 223, 227, 250, 259, 290
Living together, 53-54
Loevinger, J., 175, 176, 177, 185
Loneliness, 237
Loss, 261-262, 280
    of breast, 254, 255, 256, 257, 258, 259
    of wife role, 230, 231, 232
Love, 29

Magic, 137
Male:
    attitudes, 87-88
    contraception, 196
    domination, 23, 35, 135
    as prototype of humanity, 95
Mammography, 252
Mammoplasty, reconstructive, 252, 257
Manipulation, covert, 24
Marital status:
    of client, 209
    of therapist, 209
Marriage, 20, 22, 23, 46
    and achievement motivation, 162
    age at, 15
    and career, 30, 81, 83, 84
    end of, 230, 231, 233
    instability of, 21, 290
Masculine gender role, 28

Mastectomy patient, 250-260, 280, 281, 290
Masters, W.H., 21, 22, 122, 193, 194, 196, 206, 301
Maternal instinct, 280, 282
Maternity leave, 166
Mead, M., 6, 32, 301
Measurement of counseling effectiveness, 275
Mechanistic theory, 8, 9, 10
Media, 2, 7
Melancholia, 262, 290
Menstruation, 155-156
Mental health, 211, 212
Mesomorph, 147
Metastasis, 252
Mink, P., 133
Minnesota Plan for the Continuing Education of Women, 129
Misbehavior, 248
Mobility:
  horizontal, 19
  social, 4
Modeling, 72, 112, 242
  and peer reinforcement, 140-141
  and sex, 140
Morality, 25
Moral reasoning, 176
Mother:
  overprotective, 244
  perfect, 241-249, 281
  power of, 138
  role of, 19. 244-245, 247-249
  status of, 242
  working, 63, 82-83, 163
Motherhood, 20, 102
Mourning, 237, 261, 290
  of child, 235
  loss of breast, 257
  for marriage, 230, 232
  and melancholia, 262
Multiple-job holder, 15
Multiple roles, 220
Mystification, 198
Myth, 165, 166, 167

National Merit Scholarship, 83
National Organization for Women (NOW), 131-132
National Women's Party, 131

National Women's Political Caucus, 133
Nonassertiveness, 107-108, 109, 114
Nontraditional role model, 169
Nuclear family, 198
Nurturance, 24, 26, 103, 187

Object constancy, 287
Observation, 72
Occupation:
  choice of, 83
  conceptual framework for choice of, 79-80
  "masculine," 64, 65
  prediction of, 213-214
  and sex stereotyping, 82
Oedipal complex, 96
Oppression, social, 197
Organismic theory, 8, 10
Orgasm, 193, 196, 197, 258

Parent, 265
Parenthood, 22
Parsons, T., 7, 9, 18, 32, 138, 151
Part-time employment, 86
Part-time study, 86
Passivity, 19, 20, 36, 201-202
Peer reinforcement, 140-141, 149
Perry, W., 176, 177, 185
Personality theory, 35, 78, 94-105, 194
Pervasive androcentrism, 193
Phobia, 201
Physical-fitness program, 127
Physical power, and social power, 146-148
Physical sex differences, 153-158, 274
Physical weakness, 126
Pietrofesa, J. J., 59-74, 173, 185, 214, 217, 302
Plus-one staging, 181
Polarity, 97-100
Politics, 16-17
Postpuberty, 156-158
Power, 29, 43, 137-141, 248, 262, 274
  vs. acceptance, 136
  and birth order, 138-140
  child's perception of, 138-140
  of dependency, 137
  vs. helplessness, 143
  indirect, 138
  informational, 137

Power (continued)
legitimate, 137
vs. physical strength, 278
referent, 137
relations, 136
social, 136
Powerlessness, 143
Preadolescent sex differences, 154
Pregnancy, 281
unwanted, 261-269, 290
Prenatal development, 153-155
Preventive outreach program, 227
Privacy, 282
Psychoanalysis, 194
Psychodrama, 116
Psychotherapy (*see* Therapy)
Puberty, 155-156

Race, and counseling, 210, 271
Rape, 125, 126, 261-269, 280, 289, 290
crisis center, 266
forcible, 267-268
Rational-emotive therapy, 115
Rationality, vs. sensuality, 95
Reality testing, 222
Reasoning:
about knowledge, 176
moral, 176
Reconstructive mammoplasty, 252, 257
Re-entry, 281, 290
counseling, 219-225
woman, 218-229
Regression, 253
Rehabilitation, 252, 254, 255
Relativism, 179, 182
Repression, 253
Research:
on client reaction, 209-210
on counselor reaction, 210-212
suggested, 168, 282-283
Resolution:
and grief, 262, 263-264
and rape, 266
Resources, 165, 166, 167
Responsibility, 177, 187, 247, 248
vs. fulfillment, 85
Revenge, 248
Risk-taking behavior, 166, 167, 168
Role:
change, 227

Role (continued)
compromise model, 224
conflict, 226
division, 9, 14
expectation, 46
integration, 30
kinship, 198
model, 169, 215, 225
of mother, 19, 244-245, 247-249
multiple, 220
playing, 71, 72, 116, 117, 233
questioning, 220
of woman, 178-184
Rootlessness, 19

Sanction, 136
Schain, W. S., 250-260, 271, 274, 280,
281, 290
Schlossberg, N. K., 59-74, 92, 173, 185,
214, 217, 229, 302, 303
School, 7 (*see also* Re-entry)
returning to, 225-226
Security, 29, 287
Self:
-acceptance, 55, 57, 114
-actualization, 97, 106
-awareness, 173, 279
-blame, 241
-concept, 4, 6, 11, 13, 24, 25, 28, 191,
250, 254
-confidence, 28, 116, 160, 166, 167, 168,
189, 218, 219, 225
-control, 100
-devaluation, 143
-development, 21
-disclosure, 209, 210, 270
-esteem, 6, 7, 20, 27, 28, 29, 149, 189-
191, 220
-evaluation, 149
-examination, 106, 184, 190, 230, 279
-expectation, 223
-exploration, 71
-fulfillment, 29
-hate, 190, 279
-image, 257
-knowledge, 190
-perception, 2
-pity, 190, 279
-reliance, 187, 188
-report, 194, 275

Self (continued)
-respect, 55, 248, 261
sense of, 198
-trust, 55
-worth, 250, 256
Sensitivity, 273
Sensuality, vs. rationality, 95
Sex:
bias, 59-74, 94-105, 202, 208, 213-214
chromosomes, 10
of client, 270, 271
of counselor, 182, 209, 273
differences, 153-158, 280
discrimination, 15, 16, 23, 28, 86-88
drive, 21, 22
and modeling, 140
and social power, 144
therapy, 257
-typed behavior, 9
Sexism, 3, 173, 200, 203, 275
Sex role, 106
vs. achievement motivation, 161
ascription, 59, 61-68
division, 14
ideology, 4-5
marital, 231
orientation, 166, 167
stereotyping, 61, 137-138, 169, 203, 208, 227, 284, 287, 288, 290, 291
Sexual attractiveness, 6, 11
Sexual dysfunction, 196, 204
Sexual double standard, 197
Sexual equality, 135
Sexual interaction, 250
Sexual intercourse, early, 252
Sexuality, 195-197, 204
and rape, 280
Sexual life, 251
Sexual relationship, stress in, 20-21, 29
Sexual reproduction, 11
Shame, 14, 29, 30, 100, 101, 266, 268
Sibling power, 138-140
Significant other, 274
Sisterhood, 23, 24
Situational nonassertiveness, 107
Skill training, 111, 112, 116
Skinner, B. F., 120, 122
Slavery, 188, 189
Social acceptance, 146
Social approval, 163

Social change, 194, 197
Social context, and achievement, 165-166
Socialization, 26, 43, 46
of Black woman, 84
family, 162-163, 166, 167
of infant, 154
of status inequality, 135-152
traditional, 231
Social-learning theory, 12
Social mobility, 4
Social myth, 165-166
Social oppression, 197
Social power, 136, 137
and intelligence, 145, 146
and physical power, 146-148
and sex, 144
Social status, and power, 137-141
Sorority, 23
Spock, B., 7
Stage theory, 270, 271
Status:
achieved, 136
ascribed, 136
child's perception of, 138-140
in classroom, 141-142
and gender, 148
social, 137-141
Steinam, G., 23, 32
Stereotype Questionnaire, 61, 62
Strength, 43, 106
Stress, 177
Stroad, B., 173-185, 271, 273, 275, 278, 288, 289
Strong Vocational Interest Blank, 63-64, 86
limitations of, 67-68
Submissiveness, 36
Success, 117, 275
avoidance of, 103
fear of, 44, 55, 82, 160, 161-162, 166, 167, 168-169, 203, 204
Support, 181, 236, 274
Surgery, 255
Survival, 187, 188
mechanism, 10
Swimming, 126

Tanney, M. F., 208-217, 270, 271, 272, 275, 277, 286, 288
Tax benefits, 166

Television, 4, 137, 264
Tennis, 126
Therapist:
  age of, 209
  marital status of, 209
  radical, 198, 199
  sex of, 208-217
Therapy, 36, 66, 112
  bias against, 35
  feminist, 199-204
  humanist, 199
  radical, 197-199, 200, 201
  rational-emotive, 115
Thermography, 252
Time management, 225-226
Training model, 70-72
Transactional analysis, 199
Transference, 291
Transition, 243-244, 290
Trust, 22, 23, 246

Uncleanliness, 268
Underachievement, 201, 203
Unger, R. K., 135-152, 274, 278, 282, 286, 287, 305
Uniform Reciprocal Support Act, 235

Vaginal orgasm, 197
Value clarification, 223
Vetter, L., 75-93, 305
Vicarious achievement, 161-162, 166, 167, 281
Videotaping, 72
Virginity, 262
Vitalistic theory, 8
Vocational counseling, 182, 203, 204, 235, 279
Vocational Development Inventory-Attitude Scale, 77
Vocational maturity, 77

Warmth, 272
Weakness:
  and feminity, 148

Weakness (continued)
  physical, 126
Weekend, 237
Wessler, R., 176, 177, 185
Westervelt, E. M., 1-33, 74, 92, 229, 305
Whiteley, R. M., 34-58
Widick, C. C., 173-185, 271, 273, 275, 278, 288, 289
Widowhood, 230-240, 280, 281, 290
Wilborn, B. L., 241-249, 271, 274, 281, 282, 290
Women:
  caucus of, 132
  center for, 129, 131
  in college, 160
  divorced, 230-240
  economic role of, 197-199
  economic value of, 18
  in graduate work, 164
  in groups, 34-58, 204
  impact of feminism on, 1-33
  in politics, 133
  powerlessness of, 16-17
  religious role of, 132
  revolution of, 1-4
  role of, 178-184, 204
  single-again, 230-240
  studies about, 129, 159
  widowed, 230-240
Women's Equity Action League (WEAL), 131-132
Women's liberation, 193-207
Women's movement, 106, 173, 195 (*see also* Feminism)
Work discrimination, 164-165
Work experience, quality of, 287
Working mother, 63, 163
  and juvenile delinquency, 82-83
Work role, 198
Workshop, for divorced women, 238-239

Xerography, 252

Youth, 6

CRITES

6596059